SEVENTH EDITION

Real Estate Investment

John P. Wiedemer

Joseph E. Goeters
Houston Community College

J. Edward Graham
University of North Carolina Wilmington

United States

Real Estate Investment, Seventh Edition
John P. Wiedemer, Joseph E. Goeters,
and J. Edward Graham

Vice President of Editorial, Business: Jack
W. Calhoun

Vice President/Editor-in-Chief: Dave Shaut

Acquisitions Editor: Sara Glassmeyer

Senior Developmental Editor: Arlin Kauffman,
LEAP

Editorial Assistant: Michelle Melfi

Senior Marketing and Sales Manager:
Mark Linton

Content Project Management:
Pre-PressPMG

Media Editor: Lysa Kosins

Production Technology Analyst: Jeff Weaver

Website Project Manager: Lysa Kosins

Senior Manufacturing Coordinator:
Charlene Taylor

Production Service: Pre-PressPMG

Copyeditor: Lorraine Martindale

Senior Art Director: Pamela Galbreath

Cover Designer: Paul Neff Design

Cover Image: Getty Images, Inc./Photographer's
Choice/Gregor Schuster

For product information and technology assistance, contact us at
OnCourse Learning & Sales Support, 1-855-733-7239.

For permission to use material from this text or product.

Exam*View*® is a registered trademark of eInstruction Corp. Windows is
a registered trademark of the Microsoft Corporation used herein under
license. Macintosh and Power Macintosh are registered trademarks of
Apple Computer, Inc. used herein under license.

Library of Congress Control Number: 2010925681

Student Edition ISBN 13: 978-0-324-78469-5
Student Edition ISBN 10: 0-324-78469-4

Student Edition with CD ISBN 13: 978-0-324-78468-8
Student Edition with CD ISBN 10: 0-324-78468-6

OnCourse Learning
3100 Cumberland Blvd Suite 1450
Atlanta, GA 30339
USA

Printed in the United States of America
5 6 7   19 18 17

BRIEF CONTENTS

CONTENTS

PREFACE

The Greek philosopher Heraclitus said that "The only constant is change." Perhaps he was foreshadowing the real estate market. While the real estate market is not new, its opportunities and regulations have seen many changes in recent decades. It remains cyclical, generating great fortunes during "booms" and great losses during "busts." Investors have made and lost a lot of money during various times of the market but one thing remains the same: knowledge may be the key to wise investments. Luck may also play a role, but luck tends to favor those who prepare.

CHANGING OPPORTUNITIES

Investment opportunities have greatly changed since the 1950s. From investments consisting mainly of government securities, real estate, and individual stocks to the endless menu of offerings today, the world of "investing" is a changed one. However, the fundamentals and history lessons of the market remain the same. Those rules and their lessons were cast in a new light with the onset of the recent Great Recession.

Since the publication of the last edition, many investors worldwide witnessed the evaporation of ten or more years of returns. Questions about the suitability of most investments, for any portfolio, were asked:

- Would an investor in government bonds outperform the average stock investor in the next ten years, as in the last ten?
- Would higher returns be earned by investors for assuming the greater risk of stock and real estate investment in the years ahead?
- Would a new investing method develop that changes the way investors make their investing decisions?

Only time will provide results and answers to these queries, but potential answers can be explored, especially as they relate to real estate.

This 7th Edition addresses continuing misconceptions and misunderstandings about real estate and offers insights into real estate investing, while recognizing the long shadows cast by the economic downturns of the 1980s, 1990s, and 2000s.

As one would expect there is greater transparency with the securities markets, and greater opacity with real estate. A person cannot, as with a common stock, look up the latest analyst's report on the Internet! So in an attempt to master the world of real estate investment, the best one can do is prepare.

That is why the need for this text exists—to provide greater clarity and understanding given the disjointed information available to the real estate investor.

NEW TO THE 7TH EDITION

Global changes to the 7th edition include: updated information and case studies, continued reference to the Great Recession and its implications for real estate investment, expanded sets of discussion questions for each chapter, and an updated glossary. Added throughout the text are new business calculator applications to better portray real estate investment performance.

Other significant changes by chapter include the following:

- *Chapter One*: A new introduction that accounts for the turmoil in the real estate markets between 2006 and 2010, and additional consideration of the inefficient real estate market including the factors contributing to its inefficiency.
- *Chapter Two*: New case histories on evolving real estate laws and consideration of the benchmark case, *Kelo v. City of New London*.
- *Chapter Three*: An expanded consideration of the Green Revolution and its impact on real estate values and environmental enforcement.
- *Chapter Four*: Reference to evolving matters in real estate ownership.
- *Chapter Five*: A review of the legal documents associated with real estate investment.
- *Chapter Six*: A new review of the history since 1980 of federal tax laws affecting real estate, including a consideration of the Bush tax reduction acts of 2001 and 2003, and Obama's tax act of 2009. Expansive new examples illustrate the impact of tax law on the performance of real estate investments, under past and current tax laws. Such factors as depreciation recapture, capital gains details, and installment sales income are portrayed.
- *Chapter Seven*: New and expanded illustrations of tax-deferrals under Section 1031. Installment sales are illustrated by example.
- *Chapter Eight*: A revised discussion of single family homes and condominiums.
- *Chapter Nine*: An expanded discussion of real estate ownership forms and a new table comparing business organizations, with detailed inclusion of the REIT and LLC ownership forms.

- *Chapter Ten*: An updated consideration of real estate financing, with expanded consideration of the risks and rewards of leverage.
- *Chapter Eleven*: A new focus on the omissions of data from real estate prospectuses. New illustrations of computer applications for mortgages, and far less detail on present value tables and mortgage constants.
- *Chapter Twelve*: New tools for comparison screening. Addition of the dividend growth model to describe real estate returns. New examples to contrast the riskiness of real estate cash flows.
- *Chapter Thirteen*: An entirely new chapter on discount analysis that contains seven new examples, with calculator applications illustrated.
- *Chapter Fourteen*: A revised discussion of computer-aided analysis.
- *Chapter Fifteen*: An updated consideration of managing real property risk, with a focus on business and financial risk.
- *Chapter Sixteen*: A revised and updated discussion of the marketing of investment real estate.

The CD-ROM included with the text includes a student version of ARGUS® software to be used with specific exercises providing real-life experience analyzing real estate investment scenarios. ARGUS® software is an industry-leading tool for analyzing commercial transactions, market risks, and leasing strategies to help in calculating investment value and returns.

Case studies throughout the text provide additional real-world application analyzing and building a real estate investment portfolio. Discussion questions at the end of every chapter help clarify and further develop understanding.

INSTRUCTIONAL SUPPORT

Instructors who adopt this book receive access to an online Instructor's Manual written by the authors. Each chapter is supported with chapter rationale, overall focus of classroom discussions, a lecture outline, classroom discussion topics, and supplemental learning activities or quizzes. Plus, there is a 70-question Mid-Term Exam and two 60-question Final Exams.

Online WebTutor™ support for WebCT™ and BlackBoard® is also provided. Designed to accompany this textbook, WebTutor is an eLearning software solution that turns everyone in your classroom into a front-row learner. Whether you want to Web-enhance your class, or offer an entire course online, WebTutor allows you to focus on what you do best—teaching. More than just an interactive study guide, WebTutor is an anytime, anywhere online learning solution providing reinforcement through chapter quizzes, multimedia flashcards, e-mail discussion forums, and other engaging learning tools.

Classroom PowerPoint® presentation slides also support each chapter outlining learning objectives, emphasizing key concepts, and highlighting real-world applications to help further engage learners and generate classroom discussion.

These instructional support materials are available online only to adopters from the text companion site **www.cengage.com/realestate/wiedemer**.

ACKNOWLEDGMENTS

I would like to thank the gentleman who has been my friend, mentor, co-author, and inspiration throughout my 30 years of teaching real estate. Jack Wiedemer has been all of those things to me since the first time I ventured into a classroom in 1980. His passing left a huge void in the real estate education field, but his life has left a huge impact on all who have benefited from his many contributions to real estate education.

I also acknowledge the fantastic support I have received from my spouse, companion, and faithful supporter. My wife, Charlotte, an accomplished real estate practitioner and educator in her own right, has been the "wind beneath my wings" and has been a great help in my work on this book and numerous other publications I have been fortunate enough to be involved .

I would also like to acknowledge Sara Glassmeyer, Mark Linton and all of the truly supportive associates at Cengage Learning; Arlin Kaufman, LEAP Publishing Services; Mary Stone, Pre-PressPMG; fellow author, Chuck Jacobus; and many other educators and real estate practitioners like Jim Wiedemer, Alex Binkley, John Haynie, Dorothy Lewis, and all of the truly wonderful people in the Texas Real Estate Educators Association (TRETA) and the Real Estate Educators Association (REEA). Finally, I thank Edward Graham for his exceptional work on updating this text to current standards.

Joe Goeters

First and most important, I thank my wife Lee for her encouragement and support while working on this book. Also, UNC Wilmington, the Cameron School and the overall department deserve a tip of the hat for the time they allowed me to prepare this new edition of *Real Estate Investment*.

Ed Graham

Both of us express our deep appreciation to the following professionals who carefully reviewed this revision and provided insightful comments and valuable suggestions.

Kevin Smith
West Los Angeles College

Phyllis Lea Goodrich
Academy of Real Estate

Theda C Redwine
North Lake College

ABOUT THE AUTHORS

Joe Goeters has been a commercial real estate broker in Texas since 1970. He has been a teacher at Houston Community College since 1980. Prior to venturing into real estate Joe was in the computer field, working four years as a programmer with Texaco and five years as a marketing rep with IBM. His years in real estate have included ventures as a real estate developer of shopping centers in College Station, Texas; recreational projects in Keystone, Colorado; and Office/Warehouse developments and residential condominiums in Houston, Texas. As a real estate educator, Joe has taught approximately 18 different subjects. He has developed numerous courses for Houston Community College, Galveston College, and the National Association of REALTORS® for both in-class courses and online courses. He has been active in numerous civic associations—past president of the Lions club, past president of the Optimist club, past president of the Briargrove Park Property Owners Association and past president of numerous other church and civic organizations. He has been active in professional organizations including the position of past president of the Texas Real Estate Teachers Association. In 2000 Joe was selected as the recipient of the Don Roose award of excellence. Joe and his wife Charlotte live in Galveston, Texas where they frequently entertain their six children (plus their spouses) and their 13 grandchildren.

J. Edward Graham, Ph.D., is an Associate Professor of Finance in the Department of Economics and Finance at UNC Wilmington. He has been at UNCW since 1998, having earlier received his doctorate in finance at the University of South Carolina. He received his Bachelor of Science in Commerce at Washington and Lee University in 1978 and his MBA at the University of North Florida in 1979. He began investing in residential, commercial, and industrial property in the Jacksonville, Florida area in 1981 and remains active there as an investor, with his home in North Carolina. His academic interests include real estate investment, corporate finance, and the stock market. He has published in a number of finance, economics, and real estate journals. He can be reached at edgraham@uncw.edu.

DEDICATION

This book is dedicated to Jack Wiedemer for his many years of contributions to the real estate education field. He was greatly respected throughout the country as an educator, author, mentor, and dear friend. Jack contributed to the real estate education profession through his long-time involvement in REEA, the Real Estate Educators Association, and especially through his leadership in TRETA, the Texas Real Estate Teachers Association. Jack was one of the founders and loyal supporters of TRETA, where he was past president and recipient of the prestigious Don Roose Award of Excellence. Jack will be greatly missed by all who knew him and all who benefited from his books and teachings.

JOE GOETERS
ED GRAHAM

CHAPTER 1

Real Estate as an Investment

OPPORTUNITIES IN REAL ESTATE

Returns to real estate investors, introduced and discussed at length in the following pages and chapters, have varied greatly over the past few decades. An inflationary environment such as the one that existed in the late 1970s or early 1980s required investors first to deal with a dearth of available financing; what financing that was available was often offered at over 15 percent per year. Coupled with the costly financing, however, for income-producing real estate, were rent escalations that often averaged 1 percent per month. So, while the modest investor in a four-unit apartment building might suffer costly negative cash flows for the first months (or years) of ownership, an expectation was in place that rents would increase, and catch up with the costly financing—a fixed cash outflow—and throw off favorable returns. Then, by the late 1980s, amid changing tax laws pertaining to real estate (covered in detail in Chapters 6 and 7), many real estate investment values collapsed, and a half-decade of "recovery" was required for properties to re-achieve their pre-collapse levels. Buyers that were able to acquire properties in the early to mid-1990s were amply rewarded within a decade with far above average returns for their investments. The willingness of those investors to buy when there was figuratively "blood in the streets" was amply rewarded. Does a similar opportunity exist today? Only time will tell.

A First Look: Real Estate Compared to Other Investments

The losses of the late 1980s have been dwarfed by the losses of 2007–2010. With the exception of some emerging markets, certain specialized investments and those in commodities, such as precious metals, the investment universe completed its worst year in decades in 2008. Losses varied from modest to severe—with the values of some assets losing all of their value. Real estate was no exception. A broad literature will no doubt soon evolve that documents the significant losses borne by the individual and institutional real estate investor in the several years ending in 2010, but anecdotal "evidence" already exists that affirms those losses. From condominium prices that fell from $1 million to a quarter of that in north Florida, to shopping mall values that slipped from close to $100 per square foot in the Midwest to less than $20, any experienced real estate investor can inventory dramatic (and unprecedented) declinations in investment real estate values.

Some of the real estate declines of late were far worse than most traditional investments, like stocks and bonds, but even the security markets were not spared examples of dramatic losses. Much of this may not be recovered for decades, if ever. However, given those losses and assuming only modest recoveries in the next few years, the potential for the out-performance by real estate relative to other investments is underscored.

The general nature of "investing" is described below, with reference to the advantages and pitfalls confronting the investor managing any typical portfolio, whether towards retirement, funding a child's education accounts, or building a rainy-day fund. Following this description of investing, the world of real estate investing is re-introduced, and its idiosyncrasies are described. Those idiosyncrasies can render real estate both more, and less, attractive. Informed on these fronts, one of the primary missions of this text might be achieved. That mission is to provide a foundation with which the prospective real estate investor might make a more informed decision to enter real estate investments, and to select one property or another having made that decision.

INVESTMENTS AND INVESTMENT VALUES

There are many ways for individuals, groups, and companies to invest time and money in the pursuit of a profitable return. No single type of investment is best for everyone. Classical financial theory allows that the size, timing and risk of an investment's cash flows will determine its value today. Such is also the case with real estate; a $100,000 annual rental of a building to the U.S. government is far more valuable than the same building rental to a new restaurant chain. Thus, another of the conundrums confronting the investor: Greater safety of returns and of the principal invested will lead to *lower* returns as investors bid up the price of this safer investment's value. The long-term government lease might have a value of $2 million (dividing the $100,000 annual lease into that $2 million investment yields a 5 percent annual return), and the $100,000 annual restaurant lease has a value of only $1 million (a far riskier 10 percent return); the restaurant is far likelier to go broke and cease paying rent altogether!

Since the purpose of any investment is to achieve some kind of return, investments can best be compared by first defining the measurable returns that are available in our economic system. These sources of returns differ and can best be distinguished as: (1) **income,** (2) **appreciation,** and (3) **value gain.**

1. *Income.* The dollar return on an investment (profit or loss) is its income. Many investments are made largely for the income they

produce. Savings accounts, corporate and municipal bonds, government bonds, and treasury bills all fall into this category. For the holder, these investments generally represent good security for the principal, plus a fixed income. These investments are easily converted into cash (they are highly **liquid**) and provide a cushion for emergency needs. The disadvantage of a fixed-income investment lies in the fact that changing perceptions of the riskiness of the investment or unexpected inflation can reduce its value. For instance, if an investor "demands" a 5 percent return on a $1,000 annual cash flow from some government bonds, he will pay $20,000 for the bonds ($1,000/.05 = $20,000).

The investor earns a 5 percent annual return on the original investment ($1,000/$20,000). However, if the next investor demands a 10 percent return, because of perceptions of a greater likelihood the bonds will not be repaid (**default risk**) or because of higher inflation (**interest rate** *or* **inflation risk**), the bonds previously worth $20,000 are now worth only half that, or $10,000 ($1,000/.10 = $10,000). The financial economist would say that the value of any investment (V) is equal to the income that investment generates (I) divided by some required rate of return (R). If V = I/R, and R doubles, in this context, then V falls by 50 percent. Much more is involved in investment asset valuation, but this generic expression broadly describes the value of any investment; it is particularly handy in quickly describing the exposure of the income investor to default and interest rate or inflation risk.

2. *Appreciation.* Appreciation is an increase in an investment's value resulting from scarcity and price inflation. Some investments are made specifically to profit from an anticipated increase in value caused by appreciation alone. Investments of this type include gold, rare coins, art, and other collectors' items. While investments of this type can provide an intangible return through pride of ownership, an increase in monetary value is not assured; these investments are highly speculative. They require some method of safekeeping, the cost of which can easily outweigh any increase in value. And, except for gold, there are few organized markets for these goods, making a conversion to cash at true value a slow and difficult ask.

3. *Value Gain.* Value gain is the active side of increase in value, as distinguished from the passive type identified as appreciation. Value gain results from the input of expertise by an owner or manager. Examples of investments seeking value gain include such enterprises as building a business operation, developing a tract of land, or purchasing stocks in sufficient quantity to allow the control and redirection of an underperforming publicly-traded firm. This type of investment seeks a profit from growth in real value.

Some investments mix all three types of measurable return. A dividend-paying common stock, for example, could provide a steady dollar income, some degree of appreciation from inflation, and a possible value gain from the profitable growth of the company.

Real estate as an investment covers such a diverse range of properties that the three types of return can be found both separately and in combination as the following examples illustrate:

- *For income only*—mortgage loans
- *For appreciation only*—holding undeveloped land
- *For value gain only*—development of building lots
- *For all three*—income property, such as an apartment building

Because of this diversity, a blanket comparison of real estate investment with other available forms of investment is difficult. Any meaningful comparison must consider how a specific property relates to alternative investment opportunities. Each investor must balance needs and goals, security, and income. And tax requirements affect each taxpayer differently. The selection of an investment is thus a personal matter, requiring the investor to carefully weigh the advantages and disadvantages of each option.

REAL ESTATE AND THE GREAT RECESSION

A famous author once remarked: "It was the best of times, it was the worst of times ..." (*A Tale of Two Cities*, Charles Dickens, 1859). He was considering the plights of varied characters in late 18th century London and Paris; a similar introductory comment might well-introduce an early 21st century text on real estate investment. While the travails of the contemporary real estate professional hardly rise to the level of those suffered by the citizens of France prior to its revolution, there are parallels.

In both environments lay great risk, and the potential for enormous returns. Of uncertain origin, but attributed to the scion of the Rothschild winemaking family, an investor suggested that the time to buy was "when there was blood in the streets" and recent extensions have added: "even (or especially) when the blood is your own." Dickens' opening line, and the investor's admonition (and reminder) to buy when fear is highest and risk seemingly the greatest, both bear recalling in today's uncertain real estate climate. This climate, the **Great Recession**, and the malaise that possesses a great many folk in the real estate business, may well be harbingers of opportunity that occur only a few times in an investor's lifetime.

The origins of the current economic "malaise" can be defensibly attributed to a bubble in residential real estate in the United States. This bubble, in turn, can be traced back to misguided (but well-intentioned) federal tax and banking policy from the time of Jimmy Carter through Bill Clinton and the first term of the second George Bush; Carter promulgated the Community Reinvestment Act (CRA) in 1977, it was endorsed and encouraged by Bill Clinton in the late 1990s and as the first recession of this century unwound early in the 2000s, George W. Bush reaffirmed the intent and the mechanics of the CRA. Each of these U.S. presidents intended merely to open wider the door to home-ownership; those good intentions of the past several presidents, of the Federal Reserve, and of the U.S. Congress all contributed to the economic contraction that followed.

Coupled with these presidential encouragements were a number of factors that added fuel to this economic fire: From congressional mandates to assist the least creditworthy, to Wall Street willingness to subdivide and resell (to willing buyers) the riskiest subprime loans, to credit-rating agency complicity with "AAA" ratings of soon-to-collapse mortgage backed securities (MBS) to the willingness of credit-providers to overlook the most egregious examples of lacks of creditworthiness by prospective borrowers—all of these accelerated the over-buying of residential real estate, the rapid fall in home values when "the music stopped," the snowballing of the real estate correction to the entire economy, and the ushering in for the United States and much of the Western World of the worst recession since the Great Depression.

It is in this changed, and changing, environment that the student of real estate investment finds himself today. In the months and years following this Great Recession—even if it finally ends in 2010 or 2011—greater opportunities will be found in real estate investments than in any period since at least the early 1990s.

So, how might one define "greater opportunities" in real estate and what do the past few decades portend for the real estate investor over the next few decades? How does real estate compare and contrast with other investments, and as the economy as a whole has contracted at the close of the first decade of the 21st century, how has real estate fared?

ADVANTAGES OF REAL ESTATE AS AN INVESTMENT

Itemized below are a number of the advantages of real estate investment, along with some comparisons with other forms of investment.

Returns on Investment

All investors seek a fair return, plus safety for their invested assets. Real estate can provide both, in varying degrees. The three basic types of return on a real estate investment are income, appreciation or capital gains, and tax shelters.

Income

Rental income is among the primary catalysts for real estate investment. Whether rental income from a neighborhood duplex, or annual receipts from a national tenant leasing a string of drug store locations, the attraction to the investor is the same; the periodic dividend from the rental receipts is at the center of most long term real estate investment endeavors.

Expectations of the higher returns often attaching to real estate have a speculative nature; this was especially true as the first decade of the 21st century drew to a close, with real estate investors nursing broad and deep wounds from the under-performance of real estate investments. Income-producing real estate suffered a pair of losses: first, income fell with higher vacancies and reduced rents, and second, property values fell as investors demanded a higher return on whatever rent remained. Both I and R in

V = I/R (from the income discussion above) changed, aversely, for the investor; I fell, and R increased, each change diminishing V.

Appreciation and Capital Gains

A second cash flow pursued by the real estate investor is capital gain(s). This is simply the escalation in a property's underlying value, not merely any attaching income streams. Few forms of investment have appreciated and weathered inflation-caused losses in the purchasing power of a dollar better than real property. Savings accounts and other cash assets lose value as the purchasing power of the dollar is diminished.

Inflation is primarily a monetary phenomenon: When the nation "prints more dollars" to pay for its deficit spending, the value, or purchasing power, of a dollar is reduced. Thus, it takes more dollars than the year before to buy the same commodity, meaning the commodity has increased in price. The consequence is that an increase in price induced by a debased currency does not produce a true gain in value. Such is the case with the Great Recession, as governments across the globe have engaged in enormous deficit spending and increases in the money supply.

Finally, it is a reasonable assumption that few other investments can benefit as much as real property from the input of management expertise. A perceptive owner, or manager, can rehabilitate, upgrade, expand, or even reorient how a property is used. Imaginative and aggressive management can add considerable value to an investment in real property; these value gains augment the appreciation, and supplement the capital gains, that are among the primary motivators of the typical real estate investor.

Tax Shelters

Real estate has always offered certain tax advantages that reached their peak with the Economic Recovery Tax Act of 1981, when depreciation deductions could be taken over a 15-year cost recovery period and accelerated depreciation was allowed. In successive years, Congress reduced depreciation deductions by increasing the length of recovery periods and disallowing accelerated rates of deduction. Since 1993 the nonresidential recovery period has been 39 years while residential property has retained its 27.5 year period. (Tax policy and depreciation are considered at length in Chapters 6 and 7.)

The depreciation deduction is a noncash item, and offers tax savings. But, as will be covered in more detail later in this text, the right to off-set tax losses from real estate investments against *any* other income has been disallowed. This kind of loss can only be off-set against similar kinds of income. Thus, the value of real estate as a tax shelter has been diminished.

Even so, items classed as personal property, such as drapes, appliances, and carpeting, that are necessary for apartment operation, are eligible for greater rates of depreciation than the building, or may be expensed altogether in the current year. In addition, certain improvements, such as sidewalks and parking lots, may qualify for shorter-life (meaning larger) personal property deductions.

Other Advantages

Use as Collateral

Almost all forms of investment assets can serve as **collateral for a loan.** While real property has lost some of its luster for lenders in recent years, it continues to hold good value as collateral. It is tangible, cannot be moved, its ownership is recorded and legally protected, and it can be pledged as loan collateral with its title insured.

If the property has confirmed income from long-term leases, a loan amount may be based on that assured income as valued in an appraiser's income approach. Such a loan could exceed the amount invested in the property, permitting the owner to recoup all the funds invested in the property while still retaining ownership. However, most lenders try to avoid loaning more than the value of a property.

This lending is much restrained following the Great Recession, but if a tenant is of high enough caliber, and the lease terms are long enough, lenders are able even in the post-recession environment to make generous loans on real estate that are unavailable to investors in other arenas. New patterns and practices in commercial real estate might reduce the value of leverage to the real estate investor; a new concept is moving into commercial property loans (but not residential loans as yet), that calls for periodic appraisal and an adjustment of the loan balance if the value has declined.

Land Is Tangible

Land can be seen, and it can be touched. It is **tangible.** It has a specific form and a specific size, and it cannot be lost or misplaced. It gives its owner a sense of security and emotional support.

Ownership Is Recorded

Opinion is divided on whether or not the need to record land ownership is an advantage or disadvantage to the investor. Recording, being a form of public notice, helps to protect an owner's rights against possible third-party claimants. On the other hand, recording also publicizes an asset that may be subject to attachment by the creditor of an owner. Some people protest that the public record discloses ownership of assets that they would prefer to keep private.

Pride of Ownership

The personal satisfaction of any investment is especially important in real property. For many Americans, land ownership retains a mystical quality, with a value that defies measurement.

DISADVANTAGES OF REAL ESTATE AS AN INVESTMENT

Overall Inefficiency of the Real Estate Market

An efficient market is one where prices broadly reflect available and relevant information. Each of the disadvantages below contributes to the inefficiency of the real estate market relative to the exchange-based markets for investments in securities. Those more efficient markets have a much greater flow of information, far lower transaction costs, much greater product **liquidity**, less government interference, far more buyers and sellers, and homogeneous products. All of these factors contribute to the greater likelihood that the prices of the goods traded on the efficient market more accurately reflect available and relevant information. It is almost self-explanatory; one would expect something trading among thousands of traders many times a day to almost immediately reflect changes in relevant information (like a change in the price of oil, or interest rates). This is far less true for real estate that may "trade" every ten years, and then only at a cost of thousands of dollars in commissions and fees, and only after meeting a plethora of government filing and taxation requirements.

Transaction Costs

Among the greatest disadvantages of real estate is the cost of buying and selling. Whether for a buyer or a seller, costs of commissions, lawyers, title insurance, filing fees, and origination costs for financing can reach 10 percent or more of the cost of the underlying real estate. Compare this to the average costs of transacting in stocks of around 1 percent, and the disadvantage suffered by real estate becomes clear. A buyer or seller may feel very strongly about a property's value, but when these costs are added to the "deal," (or taken away from the seller, as with a 6–8 percent commission charged by a typical real estate broker), the attractiveness of the transaction disappears, and no sale takes place; the market, according to economic theory, fails; the market is inefficient as the price, due to the costly imperfections or frictions in the marketplace (in this case, transaction costs), cannot reflect the true value.

Lack of Liquidity

Perhaps the most serious disadvantage of real estate as an investment is the difficulty of converting it into cash. Since the market for a particular piece of property is limited to those people who both desire and can afford it, an immediate need for cash can't always be satisfied through the sale of real property. The record of forced sales is not encouraging—fair value can seldom be obtained. Even if an interested buyer does appear, financing can be time-consuming. Property is often encumbered with existing financing; usually the buyer must either refinance the property or obtain a second mortgage loan. Both actions require considerable time and effort, contributing to the illiquidity of real estate.

Restricted Information Flows

Unlike a widely traded stock, with a dozen or more analysts following the underlying company's every news release, real estate is unique; the quantity and availability of information impacting the value of any given piece of real estate is limited. An investor must expend substantial time and energy gathering the information on a piece of land or other investment property. Even with that expenditure, there is no guarantee that even the most important piece of "news" has been uncovered or secret revealed.

Limited Numbers of Buyers and Sellers

Also unlike broadly traded securities, a piece of real estate may "trade" only a half dozen or so times in an investor's life, unlike a share of Fortune 500 company stock that may trade ten or more million shares a day. This leads to the prices of the underlying real estate less dependably reflecting available and relevant information.

Heterogeneity of the Product

Unlike the commodities or stock markets, each piece of real estate is different, even if it is a condo in a high-rise in Florida; each unit may have a different kitchen, a different view, and a different set of neighbors. When a trader buys a bushel of corn, or a share of IBM stock, little does she care which bushel or which share she receives; they are all the same. With each piece of real estate different, though, each has a different value and each invites a unique perspective, however slight may be the difference between the piece of real estate and another nearby.

Long-Term Investment

A corollary to the lack of liquidity is that one must usually hold on to real estate for a number of years in order to realize the best possible return. It generally takes from three to five years to verify increases in value resulting from inflation and good management. There are, of course, examples of short-term gains in real property, but more often than not, they are speculative investments to begin with.

Management Requirements

Capable business management is fundamental to the success of real estate investments. This necessarily takes the owner's personal time and attention, or else requires the hiring of a professional property manager. The real estate investor may face all of the problems associated with any business operation—sales, customer relations, employee relations, property maintenance and operation, tax and reporting requirements, and many more. Income properties especially benefit from good management, or suffer from the lack of it.

Property Hazards

Any piece of real estate—and particularly the improvements made to it—can be damaged by the elements or by people. Losses from fire, flood, vandalism, or other disasters can usually be recovered through insurance. But such a recovery is rarely a profitable event.

Government Restrictions and Legislation

Unlike many other kinds of investment, real estate is faced with an additional concern. While private property rights have long been subject to state police powers protecting safety and health, there is growing social concern over abuse of the environment. Land-use laws and environmental controls can affect property value by creating certain restrictions on its development (see the next two chapters). Other laws, such as rent controls and development set-asides, also affect where additional investment can be made and its ultimate cost to consumers. Finally, and inasmuch as the investor is just an itinerant owner of something "permanent," civic groups are taking an active role in real estate investment and development, and often present costly "hurdles" that must be addressed by the investor.

Changing Efficiency of the Real Estate Market

The real estate market, though, is becoming more efficient. REITs (real estate stocks traded on the exchanges that are discussed in later chapters), offer greater liquidity and homogeneity of real estate product. Information flows are being enhanced with the Internet alone; there are far more buyers and sellers of real estate, even with the declinations in activity with the Great Recession. Though government restrictions on real estate activity may well be increasing, on average the market is becoming more efficient, with prices more accurately reflecting available and relevant information.

A Second Look: Comparison of Real Estate to Other Investment Opportunities

Please refer to Table 1.1. Some of the more common investment opportunities are listed on the right side of the table. Along the top are listed some of the hopeful outcomes from the investment opportunities.

The investment opportunities are rated using the following scale:

+1 for a positive result

0 for a neutral result

−1 for a negative result

Regardless of the subjective interpretations of the rating scale, real estate ranks very high on the list of investment opportunities. It would seem that the second best investment opportunity is the investment in oneself. This, of course, would include money spent on personal education and career enhancements.

THE VALUE OF LAND

There is strong support for the thesis that land is the basis of all wealth. Historically, landownership distinguished the aristocracy from the rest of the people of a country or state. In early societies, the productivity of land was a major source of wealth along with trading. New ways to produce wealth emerged as economic systems and trade grew, but few of these were completely divorced from land. Today, landownership is a distinction enjoyed by many. While it can prove to be a burden as well as a blessing, it is still commonly associated with power.

The potential productivity of land determines its value. Land's productivity is, in turn, dependent on the addition of labor and capital. Following are

TABLE **1.1**
Investment Opportunities vs. Expected Outcomes

Investment Opportunities	Cash Flow	Appreciation	Value Gain	Pride of Ownership	Leverage	Tax Advantage	Stability	Liquidity	Ease of Management	Tangible	Total Score
						Expected Outcomes					
Real Estate	1	1	1	1	1	1	1	-1	-1	1	6
Precious Metals	0	1	0	1	0	0	0	1	1	1	5
Investment in Self	1	1	1	1	0	0	0	0	0	1	5
Bonds	1	1	0	0	0	0	0	1	1	0	4
Mortgages	1	1	0	0	0	0	0	1	1	0	4
Stocks	1	1	0	0	0	0	-1	1	1	0	3
Commodities	0	1	0	0	0	0	-1	1	1	1	3
Certificates of Deposit	1	0	0	0	0	0	1	0	1	0	3
Collectibles*	0	1	0	1	0	0	-1	0	0	1	2

*Grand Masters, Antique Cars, Etc.

the basic combinations of land, labor, and capital that can produce valuable goods for society—plus wealth for the real estate's owner:

- *Cultivation*—produces grains, vegetables, fruits, timber, flowers, and pasturelands.
- *Mining*—produces coal, fertilizers, clays, oil shale, and metallic ores.
- *Drilling*—produces oil, gas, steam, and water.
- *Development*—produces houses, stores, factories, transportation systems, utility systems, and recreational facilities.

Each type of productivity listed above could be called a form of real estate investment. However, this book confines itself to the development of the land surface with buildings and other facilities used by people.

Raw Land

Raw land is any land lacking the facilities needed to support building construction. It is unproductive land and, if left undeveloped, can create a tax burden for its owner. The value of raw land first depends on its proximity to such features as transportation systems, water, power, mineral resources, and recreational facilities—all of which can attract people. In the final analysis, the value of land for surface development depends on its ability to attract people.

People may be attracted to an area for a variety of reasons. It might be a beautiful recreation area, or it could be able to support a large development project. While even tourist traffic can increase land value, it is the availability of jobs that causes people to settle in an area. An exception to this rule is the growing segment of the population that is now retired and living on incomes independent of current employment.

Where people are present, the major determinant of land value is the land's ultimate potential for use. But, there are no simple formulas—or even complex ones—to guide the land investor. The direction of population growth is the basic clue to rising or falling land values. Population growth follows three main patterns: (1) working patterns, (2) traffic patterns, and (3) **living patterns.**

Working Patterns

Where there are jobs, people will follow. It's that simple. The establishment or growth of any job-producing activity will create demands in the area for supporting services (schools, shops, recreation, etc.), housing, and land that's suitable for development. New jobs provide the primary pressure for land development.

Traffic Patterns

The second influence on growth patterns comes from traffic patterns and the availability of transportation. The growth of large metropolitan areas in the eastern United States was dictated by rail lines radiating from urban centers located along the coast to handle shipping. Some early growth in the West followed wagon trails radiating into and out of settlements to enable river crossings and access to the better mountain passes. Later growth in the West followed rail lines for a time, but later shifted to roadway and freeway patterns.

So far, efforts to integrate automobile transportation with modern rapid transit bus and rail facilities have not yet attracted enough people to create a new pattern. But light rail lines are proving very effective in major cities, relieving some automobile traffic, and are beginning to affect where people live, as with MARTA in Atlanta and BART in the San Francisco Bay area.

Living Patterns

The third (and probably the least important) influence on growth patterns is people's style of living. Most people want better housing, but few are willing or financially able to separate themselves from working and transportation patterns in order to relocate to an improved but possibly remote area.

This universal aspiration for better living conditions inspired Lyndon Johnson's Great Society programs of the 1960s, with the Model Cities program designed to lead the way. Total communities were planned for large tracts of land outlying major urban areas. The federal government provided substantial financial support to private developers for building roads, fire stations, and some schools. Many innovative ideas were implemented, and attractive living patterns were established. However, lacking enough good jobs in the immediate area, these well-planned communities attracted few residents. As a result, most of the 22 Model Cities failed. Only one, The Woodlands, about 25 miles north of Houston, blossomed into a prosperous community.

A few well-planned privately-financed communities, such as Columbia, Maryland, and Reston, Virginia, have been built by private developers. But they developed slowly and took many years to generate profits for the developer. Their eventual success came from the growing availability of jobs as part of the growth. Both have benefitted from the expansion of high-tech companies.

Communities that have prospered primarily from good living patterns are those oriented to retirees. In this category, the resident's income derives from sources outside the local community.

Land Development

As people are attracted to an area, the land becomes more useful and, thus, more valuable. An influx of people may result from manufacturing growth, extraction of natural resources, a recreational area, or a favorable location for commerce. Whatever the cause, the direct result of more people is a demand for more buildings—to live in, to play in, to work in, and to use for storage. Land in a growing area increases in value because of its location, which in turn dictates its use. These uses develop into zoning laws, though one major city—Houston—exists without zoning. Its development is a function of economic agglomeration, with warehousing, port facilities, shopping (as with the Galleria area in Houston) all deriving from the original attractiveness for a specific use of the land in a specific area of town, independent of zoning laws.

CATEGORIES OF LAND USE

Land use may be broadly categorized as (1) single-family residential, (2) multi-family residential, (3) commercial, and (4) industrial. Each category is discussed below.

Single-Family Residential

The largest portion of developed land is used to build single-family houses. When land outlying major growth areas is priced above the use value of single-family housing, it becomes very speculative. But what is the limit of value for land that can be used most profitably for single-family housing? The answer, of course, depends on the local area and the local housing market. Here are some guidelines.

1. A modern subdivision meeting local standards (and, usually Federal Housing Administration [FHA] requirements under the ASP-9 form) will typically have housing density of several building lots per acre. This density allows for curbs and gutters, streets, and utility easements. A small lot in this category would be less than a fifth of an acre; a large lot might be over an acre.

2. The value of a building lot in relation to the value of the building may be expressed as the ratio of the land cost to the total property value. Where land is reasonably plentiful, the value of the land may represent as little as 20 percent of the total value—a $100,000 house, for example, might represent $80,000 in building cost and $20,000 in land cost. Where growth is restricted by natural barriers, the portion attributable to land value increases substantially. In some urban areas, the lot may represent as much as 70 or 80 percent of the total property value.

3. The cost of land development has skyrocketed since the late 1960s. Material and labor costs have escalated, as have the requirements of various governmental authorities. The time lag plus additional work in complying with water standards, sewage disposal requirements, and environmental studies has also increased development costs. At one time, a building lot developer could estimate the development cost at roughly 25 percent of the lot's eventual sale price. Now that estimate has risen to nearly 50 percent, leaving the other 50 percent to cover land costs, the substantial risk factor, and profits. Potential lawsuits by activists who dislike the destruction of most natural environment can be costly and time consuming. The delay in development and the higher costs involved have generally eliminated small land developers, leaving further development to the larger companies.

Return to the earlier question: What is the limit of value for land that's destined for single-family housing lots? Basic percentages don't change as rapidly as costs, which means that the traditional guideline still has some validity: The value of an average-sized finished lot is about equal to the value of an undeveloped acre of land. This guideline is changing, however. As development costs rise, the value of undeveloped land accounts for a diminishing percentage of the finished lot's cost structure.

Increases in the cost of developed lots have encouraged higher-density, single-family units such as townhouses and patio homes. These terms are not clearly defined, and vary somewhat across the country, but both concepts use the zero lot line design. **Zero lot line** means one or more exterior walls abut the property line or are common walls. The townhouse design basically follows the pattern of the historical row house but includes modern variations in exterior design and materials to avoid a monotonous appearance. Patio homes are a cluster type of housing, where three or four units use common or closely-spaced walls; patio or courtyard-style frontal areas; and country lane streets. Density of both types of housing can be increased to six or seven (or more) units per acre, thereby lowering the per-unit land cost.

Multi-Family Residential (Apartment)

Land suitable for an apartment commands a higher price per acre than land suitable only for single-family housing. The density of living units per acre for an apartment varies greatly, starting at approximately 18 to 20 units for a one- or two-story garden apartment. A modern three-story apartment checks in at around 30 to 38 units per acre. High-rise apartment units can have still higher densities. (The FHA prefers to insure multi-family housing with densities of approximately 26 to 28 units per acre.) The apartment builder obviously can offset rising land costs by spreading them over a larger number of housing units.

It would be no more than wild conjecture to set down strict value guidelines for apartment sites, but there are a few clues. One is the relation of housing unit densities. Using ratios as explained above, the one-acre ratio of 28 apartment units compared to 4 single-family units is 7 to 1. Thus, land suitable for apartment development could be worth about seven times as much as land suitable for only single-family housing.

Another clue to land value is the apartment builder's own goal for land-to-building cost ratio. Again the variation is considerable, but the average builder tries to hold land costs per unit to about 20 percent of the cost of each completed unit. For example, for an apartment unit costing $50,000, the land cost per unit should not exceed $10,000. Assuming a density of 25 units per acre, the land cost for this example should not exceed $250,000 per acre.

Commercial Land

Commercial land is that which is suitable for stores, service facilities, office buildings, and warehouses. With the exception of warehouses, the need for accessibility to the general public places a premium on frontage along major thoroughfares and freeways. In fact, commercial land is often valued by the front foot, i.e., a value per lineal foot along the frontage line.

There are few universal guidelines for accurately estimating the value of commercial land. One common measure is the traffic count, or how many cars per hour pass a given point. This is an essential measurement for the location of a service facility such as a gasoline station, and it also carries considerable weight with a shopping center. In downtown areas, a people count can serve a similar purpose. Varied measures of nearby population growth are also popular.

Warehouses have evolved from only a storage facility that does not require thoroughfare frontage land into mini-warehouses and office-warehouses that have more demanding location requirements. Warehouses used for storage need good access to truck traffic and possibly a railroad siding, but not higher cost thoroughfare frontage. Mini-warehouses are best located in areas of higher density residences in need of extra storage space but can be profitable in more visible locations to attract users. Office-warehouses, with thoroughfare frontage, have expanded in numbers because of the variety of uses they can furnish; so called "flex-space," including a modest office of several hundred square feet in front, and several thousand square feet of warehouse or light-industrial space in the rear, has also grown greatly in popularity since the early 1990s.

Industrial Land

Land used for manufacturing, refining, or any other process industry must usually satisfy more specialized needs than the people-oriented residential and commercial categories. Good industrial land must provide access to extensive support facilities, including adequate transportation, power, materials, manpower, service facilities, and suppliers. Of increasing importance is the criterion that industrial land must be so located that industrial operation will not violate the area's environmental or other zoning requirements.

The value of land for industrial use follows no pattern. Many of the most valuable tracts of industrial land were the day before purchase open fields over 20 miles from the nearest city. It depends on how well a particular tract of land fits the purchaser's requirements, and the land's general proximity to large transportation nexuses, whether a seaport or an interstate.

ACQUIRING REAL PROPERTY

Even the simple acts of buying and selling can become complicated if the transaction involves real property. Unlike many other kinds of investment, the price of real property is often negotiable. The true cost can vary enormously with the manner of payment. Some costs of real estate transactions are obvious; others can be buried in the procedures. Neither a standard procedure nor a common form exists to document all the information essential to proper analysis of real estate investment. (The Real Estate Settlement Procedures Act [RESPA], passed by congress in 1974 and later amended, establishes certain standards for information applicable to residential property only.)

The real estate market is too varied to provide the kinds of reference guides and statistical histories that are standard fare for securities investment. The inefficiency of the real estate market, outlined above, contributes to the complexity of any real property analysis.

The Purchase Price

The sum total of a real estate investment includes the purchase price, the cost of acquisition, and all applicable carrying charges. Some acquisition costs may be tax-deductible, and some must be capitalized as a part of the investment. First, let's look at the purchase price, where it soon becomes apparent that the real cost of a property is not simply the acquisition price.

Cost of Search

The idea that there are always good property investments seeking buyers may be true, but finding the right one is not so easy. An experienced investor once expressed the opinion that buying right is just as hard as selling, or even harder. It takes screening and analysis to make a prudent decision and that takes time and money. So the search for a good investment becomes a cost of the acquisition, albeit a difficult one to count in dollars expended.

Cash Price

Like most investments in tangible commodities—and unlike security-type investments—the price of real property is usually negotiable. Cash is almost always the strongest inducement for a seller to accept a lower price than originally asked. As the Great Recession was winding down, in late 2009 and 2010, the very best real estate deals were being captured by cash buyers, often at 20 percent (or more) discounts to offers by other prospective buyers that including financing contingencies. For example, a condominium investor in north Florida during the summer and fall of 2009 was able to purchase investment properties for $48,000 and $38,500, respectively, with cash offers (and a willingness to close his purchases within two weeks) even though offers of $54,000 and $44,000 were "waiting in the wings." Those higher offers were made by purchasers having only 20 percent or 25 percent down payments, with a need to discover financing to fund the balance of the purchase. The desire of the sellers (both properties were foreclosures owned by lenders) to quickly liquidate the properties led to their acceptance of the lower offers. Cash talks.

Extended Payment Terms

Often a seller of real property is willing to assist in the financing of the sale. In these situations, the price is usually somewhat higher than for a cash sale, but the interest rate for future payments may be lower than prevailing market levels. If no other financing is involved, borrowing costs can thus be substantially lower than with a new loan.

Under an extended payment purchase agreement, the seller normally holds a lien, called a vendor's lien, on the property as security for future payments. If the buyer anticipates a partial sale or a building expansion during the term of payments, the sale agreement should provide for it. Most sellers are reluctant to release any portion of their lien rights until full payment has been made or an agreement has been made in advance. Popular in the high-interest period of the late 1970s and early 1980s, **purchase money mortgages** (considered in Chapter 10, and with installment sales in Chapter 7 and Example 7.5) allow the seller to finance the purchase for the buyer, holding a mortgage as if the seller were the mortgage-originating bank.

Carrying Charges

Often overlooked amidst other costs of buying real property are the **carrying charges**. If the acquisition is an income property, carrying charges become a part of the operating expenses. But if the property is being purchased for resale, or for development and resale, the carrying charges become an important addition to the cost. (Tax consequences of either costing or capitalizing expenses for real estate are discussed in Example 6.3 in Chapter 6.) Carrying charges include:

- *Taxes*. No private investment land is fully and forever exempt from taxes, though some commercial properties may be located in tax-favored "zones," to encourage development in a distressed area. When property taxes are assessed, they become a prior lien on the land and must be paid. Otherwise, the owner may forfeit ownership. On unimproved land, property taxes can become a real burden because of the lack of income.
- *Interest*. Property purchased with any form of financing requires the payment of interest, and ultimately principal, on the financing used in its purchase.
- *Maintenance Charges*. Even vacant land will require some maintenance of its outward appearance, or fencing for safety, depending on its proximity to major thoroughfares and city ordinance.
- *Utility Stand-By Charges*. In some cases, utilities may already be installed, but not yet in use. Utility companies may assess a standby fee to cover their investments until they can be put to use.
- *Insurance*. Landowners usually want to be insured against general liabilities and hazards, especially if the property includes buildings.

Preliminary Evaluation Costs

One must usually spend some money to determine if a particular property is a suitable investment. Time and professional advice may be needed to reach a sound decision. The following are among the costs that may be incurred before deciding to buy.

Option Costs

Real property is always a one-of-a-kind investment. No two properties are exactly comparable. Therefore, well-reasoned snap judgments—to buy, or not to buy—are rare, if not impractical. Property owners, on the other hand, aren't always willing to hold property off the market while a prospective buyer studies it and decides whether or not to buy. In a situation of this kind, the prospective buyer may purchase an **option** from the seller. An option agreement assures the prospective buyer that the property will not be sold for a specified period of time. Thus the buyer can spend time and money evaluating the property, secure in the knowledge that it won't be sold to another buyer in the meantime. The prospective buyer pays the owner for temporarily waiving the right to sell. The price of an option is negotiable, depending on the market at the time and the parties involved. The price may range from a token payment of a few dollars to as much as 10 or 20 percent of the purchase price, depending upon the length of the option term, and the price at which the option-holder has the right to purchase the optioned property.

Option agreements can be structured so that the price of the option counts as part of the purchase price if the sale is consummated. Or the option price can be considered an additional charge to the purchase price stated in the option agreement. If the option to buy is not exercised, the option price is normally forfeited to the property owner with no further obligation imposed on either party.

Feasibility Report

A **feasibility report** is a formal study designed to determine the odds for success or failure of an income property. This report contains property evaluation information similar to that found in property appraisals, but it also examines the market in detail. It analyzes the rental structures, rates of occupancy, and expected profitability of competing properties in the same market area. A feasibility report is generally prepared by a qualified appraiser or professional property manager, but can be prepared by the prospective buyer. There are no professional designations in this specialized field. Cost for such a study is comparable to that for a professional appraisal but may be greater because of the in-depth market study.

Property owners and selling brokers commonly present completed feasibility reports to prospective buyers. A report prepared by the owner or owner's agents is always suspect, however, since it is difficult to be objective when one wishes to maximize the selling price, regardless of the property's "true" potential.

Planning Fees

Before an investor can make a sound decision on whether or not to buy a specific piece of real property, it may be necessary to assemble a variety of technical information, each with attaching, and sometimes substantial, costs. This technical information is particularly important if the land in question will be used for development. Architects must be consulted at a very early stage of a project to coordinate all necessary information and determine how that information will affect the cost of the proposed investment. Engineers may be asked to study the property's drainage requirements, including the cost of providing proper drainage. Utility specialists and engineers may be called upon to examine the requirements for, and availability of, electric and water service.

Environmental Study

Any property to be acquired for further development must undergo an environmental study to determine the future effect the development will have on the air, water, and land itself. And the property will need to be examined for the existence or history of environmental irregularities attaching to a current or some prior use of the property. A piece of land once occupied by a battery-processing facility is likely inappropriate for a new day-care center! (Phase I and Phase II environmental assessments are discussed in Chapter 3.)

Impacts of the proposed uses must be reported to the authorities, according to varying, but strict, standards. Such studies first became mandatory for federal projects but later expanded as a requirement for private development by most local authorities. For instance, if the development is a large shopping center, the number of cars anticipated must be calculated, and the effect of their exhaust on the air and damage to the land from parking lot drainage must be submitted, before a permit to build can be released. Many other environmental rules—far too many to list here—generally apply.

Appraisal Costs

A property owner who decides to sell is wise to seek advice from a professional appraiser. The appraiser's objective approach to evaluation can:

1. Provide guidelines in establishing the price.
2. Be useful as a sales tool.
3. Establish the probable limits for a mortgage loan.

Since an appraisal benefits both the buyer and seller, the cost may be negotiable. However, an appraisal made for the purpose of establishing a sales price would be at the seller's expense. If the buyer intends to finance a portion of the purchase price, both the appraiser and the contents of the appraisal must meet the lender's specific requirements. One added reason for this is that after 1992, a loan handled by any federally related institution must have a property appraisal by a federal/state certified appraiser.

In the late 1980s, and again after the Great Recession, real estate appraisals have come under intense regulatory scrutiny. As appraisals are presumed to include objective opinions of a given property's value, and as both the lenders and the buyers often depend upon the appraisals as assurances of the value of an investment or of collateral for a mortgage, the variance of the appraisals from true values is costly. If the lender is a federally insured bank or (as with the nationalization of Fannie Mae and Freddie Mac, considered in Chapter 10) other institution, the taxpayer is ultimately "on the hook" if the loan fails and the property is foreclosed.

In the early and mid-1980s, often to "make a deal work," appraisers were under pressure to suggest a property's value reached some level to assure the availability of financing. Often the appraisers were simply loose with their estimates of value, and other times research showed they were complicit in the over-estimation of value. The reverse may now be true, where appraisers may be overly conservative and underestimate a property's value, protecting their professional reputations, and potentially under-estimating property values. Until a transaction actually takes place, no one can be sure of a parcel of real estate's value, and the appraiser's report is no more than it attests to be—an "opinion" of value.

ORGANIZATION COSTS

It is difficult to draw a sharp line between preliminary evaluation costs and organization expenses. Preliminary evaluation costs are incurred in order to make a sound investment decision. The organization's costs are incurred after the decision to buy has been made and are necessary to properly implement that decision.

Legal Costs

Once an investor has decided to buy a specific property, attention shifts from business decisions to legal decisions. Unless the investor is an attorney (or is represented by an attorney), the investor should draw as clear a line as possible between business negotiations and legal matters. Lawyers are trained to watch for potential problems. As a result, some investors feel that in sensitive preliminary discussions, lawyers may introduce so many obstacles that negotiations can be stifled. Once a buyer and seller have worked out an acceptable deal, however, a knowledgeable attorney is invaluable for reducing the agreement to writing in a way that avoids potential legal pitfalls and provides proper protection.

Also, before any sale of real property is consummated, a qualified attorney should examine the title and assure its proper transfer. Further, counsel can be helpful in creating the proper kind of operating business organization that best meets a buyer's needs. (Issues along these lines are considered at length in Chapter 9.)

Accounting Fees

The need for professional accounting advice varies with the size and complexity of the investment property. If the intended acquisition is income property, an accountant may be needed to examine existing records and verify their accuracy. If financing is involved, financial statements prepared by a professional are better received by lenders than the borrower's own figures. And if a new business venture is established with the property acquisition, a competent accountant is very helpful in establishing new books and records.

Tax laws make it necessary for the taxpayer to determine the correct basis of value for the property and to select a cost recovery method in the year of acquisition. Towards these and other financial "discoveries," a tax-trained accountant may be needed.

Architectural and Engineering Costs

The need for architectural or engineering services depends on the nature of the property being acquired. If the property is an existing building, a preliminary inspection can determine if there are any basic structural defects and if the mechanical and plumbing equipment are adequate. Both an architect and an engineer may be needed to evaluate varying costs of rehabilitation or maintenance of an existing residential or non-residential building. If the investment is for construction of a new building, architectural plans and construction cost estimates are needed (at least to the point of bid drawings) before financing can be obtained.

Financing Charges

A few large investors, such as pension funds, may purchase real property with their own cash. However, most investors borrow a portion of the purchase money needed. (Since the costs of financing can be a major expenditure, a more detailed analysis of the fees involved in loan origination and the interest costs on borrowed money is included later in Chapter 10.)

Closing Costs

There are costs involved when a real estate transaction is closed, or settled. While these costs are generally negotiable—some paid by the buyer, some by the seller—they are part of the cost of acquiring an investment property. These costs include such items as legal fees, commissions, title search and insurance, preparation and filing of deeds, inspection fees, notary fees, and recording fees.

Disposition Costs

The owner of real property may be well-educated and have good contacts with potential buyers and sufficient knowledge to handle a sale without help—and state laws permit a property owner to sell without a license or professional help. (Real estate licensing laws generally apply only to persons offering property belonging to someone else.) However, as this chapter clearly indicates, handling real estate can be a complex matter. Increasingly stringent educational requirements for those working in the industry, along with the complexities outlined above, have made the professional broker's help more valuable than ever.

KEY TERMS

appreciation	feasibility report	liquidity	raw land
carrying charges	Great Recession	living patterns	tangible
collateral	inflation risk	option	value gain
commercial land	interest rate	purchase money	zero lot line
default risk	liquid	mortgages	

DISCUSSION QUESTIONS

1. Define the three forms of investment return: (1) income, (2) appreciation, and (3) value gain.

2. What are the major advantages and disadvantages of a real estate investment?

3. Discuss the value of raw land and how it can be developed into use.

4. List the costs that can be involved in the acquisition of real property.

5. What financing costs may be involved in the acquisition of real property?

6. Define "organization costs" and list several examples.

7. Describe the importance of a feasibility report.

8. List the carrying charges associated with holding real property.

9. What are the differences between commercial and industrial land?

10. What are some of the main features of multi-family residential properties?

11. What is an efficient market?

12. How are real estate markets inefficient?

13. Are real estate markets becoming more efficient? If so, how?

14. Describe, briefly, the Great Recession and how it has impacted investments in general, and real estate investments in particular.

15. In general, what is the history of the collapse in residential and non-residential real estate values between the late 1970s and 2008?

CHAPTER 2

Land Use Controls

Of growing importance to investors is the impact of land use restrictions and environmental control laws. Such laws can enhance value, and they can also reduce value. Enhancement comes when constraints on further development create greater scarcity of the existing usable property. Conversely, if restraints are applied to the use of land, the owner may be unable to use the land as desired, thus diminishing its value.

To better understand the restrictive laws, we will first consider the older land use laws primarily designed to protect the health and safety of citizens and to promote urban growth in an orderly manner. In the next chapter we will examine the more recent development of environmental protection laws that can further restrict how land may be used.

LAND USE CONTROLS

There has been an interesting evolution of government land use regulation, from its beginning during the 19th century's westward migration of settlers, to the police powers exercised by local governments as communities developed, to the present-day concern for adequate safeguards for the living environment.

The concept of private property, as one of the foundations of personal liberty, continues to change as greater emphasis is placed on the needs of society as a whole.

History of the Land Use Laws

As the United States began to grow in its early years, private ownership of land represented only a small portion of available land wealth; most was held by state and federal governments. In these earlier times, public lands were offered free to any settler willing to work the land. The great debates of this 19th-century expansion concerned the proper objectives for the government in the disposition of the vast land areas under its control. Should the purpose be to encourage settlement, as Thomas Jefferson so eloquently argued? Or should the objective be to generate revenue for the federal government, as Alexander Hamilton contended?

As the population moved westward, small towns grew where the need arose—where preparations had to be made to ford a river, where protection could be found from marauding tribes, where mountain passes could cause delays. The small towns grew partly by plan and partly to accommodate existing access trails. Rich farm and ranch land was purchased or homesteaded. By the middle of the 19th century, railroads were creating their own towns—where the tracks stopped, where junctions developed, or where difficult crossings required a support depot. Always it was individuals who found the most expeditious way to overcome the problem at hand.

By the latter part of the 19th century, settlers in the growing western states and territories realized that the unstructured growth of their towns must give way to planned development. By then, there was a different need for urban planning than had been the case in eastern cities.

In the large eastern cities, the focus was on orderly street patterns with some landscaped park areas for beautification. Among the first of these attractive plans was William Penn's design for Philadelphia initiated in 1682, followed by Annapolis, Williamsburg, and Savannah. In 1791, Pierre L'Enfant was chosen to develop a master plan for the nation's new capital city in the District of Columbia.

However, as the nation's growth accelerated, planning for beauty and open spaces within the cities became a less important goal than supporting vibrant economic growth. The new planning centered on the more practical need for water, supplies, sewage systems, and paved streets. It soon became apparent that the layout of streets and location of utility systems could be more efficiently accomplished if the planners also directed the usage of the land to be served.

The initial municipal effort to control the use of private land brought forth **zoning laws**. Zoning designates the use that may be made of each tract of land within a municipal jurisdiction. It obviously results in a major impact on property values. The same police power that allows the city to zone land provides authority to establish and enforce **building codes**, subdivision controls, and overall community planning. With these regulatory powers, the cities were better able to provide the individual landowner with adequate water supplies, sewage disposal systems, streets, schools, and parks.

ZONING

The police power of each state gives it the authority to protect the health, safety, and general welfare of its citizens. It is this authority that gives a state the right to restrict the use of privately owned land. Through zoning laws, a community can (1) designate which tracts of land may be used for residential, commercial, industrial, or agricultural purposes, and (2) enforce these restrictions.

The first zoning law was in New York City, passed in 1916. In 1922, the Advisory Committee on Zoning, set up under Secretary of Commerce Herbert Hoover, released the Zoning Act. And in 1926, the U.S. Department of Commerce published the Standard State Zoning Enabling Act, which set guidelines under which states were allowed to grant existing local governments the police powers needed to regulate the use of privately owned land. Implementation of the Act often resulted in disputes between the cities and the states. Urban groups had become suspicious of legislation enacted by rural-dominated legislatures. In a rather short period of time, nearly all communities adopted zoning plans that essentially confined land use to the status quo. Neighborhoods were simply zoned to their present use, with minimal allowance for any future growth.

Proponents of the zoning concept hoped that these laws could influence growth patterns. However, no procedures were established to influence or control growth in the unincorporated areas surrounding the cities, even though these areas might later be annexed. And no provision was made to cover the relationship of a city to neighboring municipalities. The regional concept of growth did not evolve until later.

Nevertheless, zoning regulations found favor with municipalities. Today, over 98 percent of American cities with populations over 10,000 use zoning to control their development. The major exception, and only large metropolitan area that developed without zoning, is Houston, Texas.

How Zoning Operates

A municipal zoning law is under the control of a regulatory body, usually a zoning commission. This commission develops the plans and establishes the procedures for implementing zoning legislation. A city is divided into districts, with a designation for each district indicating the type of building that may be erected (or how the land may otherwise be used). The rules and designations vary considerably.

Generally, the basic designations are residential, commercial, industrial, and agricultural. Then the breakdown becomes more specific—one area may be zoned for single-family residences, with another for duplex to fourplex residences. Similar sub-designations may be made in all designated areas. The rules may even go further than listing the general type of building that may be constructed. They may set a minimum and/or maximum size, height, living area, setback from the property lines, and size of the lot itself. All communities with zoning laws have plans, available to the public, that identify the zones and the building requirements that apply to each tract of land.

Zoning laws may, of course, be changed. An ordinance may be amended to recognize a changing growth pattern or to accommodate a new development. Or a property owner may seek a **variance** from a zoning requirement that causes undue hardship. Applications for variances usually require substantial evidence of the need for the variance, some proof that it won't change the basic character of the existing zone, and a public notice of the request. While the initial zoning pattern seldom creates any land value that was not already inherent in the property, variance requests are often associated with efforts to increase land value. It is in this area that political pressures can undermine the benefits attributed to zoning laws.

Under zoning laws, a landowner must obtain a building permit from the community government (township, city, or county) before commencing construction of any building. Before the permit can be issued, building plans must be submitted to show that they conform to the zoning regulations. If a building is constructed without a permit, it is subject to demolition. If a building exists before the zoning ordinance becomes effective for that tract of land, it is generally accepted under a grandfather clause as a nonconforming use of the land. However, a grandfathered building often cannot be enlarged or remodeled to extend its life. If the building is demolished, any new building on the site must conform to the law.

BUILDING CODES

Both state and local governments have enacted building codes that are intended to protect the public against low-quality—and possibly dangerous— construction practices. The result has been a hodgepodge of requirements that often perpetuate outmoded and costly construction practices. Metropolitan Chicago, for example, has between 30 and 40 separate codes (depending on what one calls a code). Attempts have been made to standardize requirements and encourage lower-cost modular housing, but these efforts have met with considerable resistance.

In spite of the problems involved, building codes serve a useful purpose in providing minimum standards for structural loads, ventilation, electrical installation, plumbing, and fire protection. Building plans must meet all code requirements before a building permit can be issued. The city building department generally inspects the building during construction to ensure compliance with the laws. Upon the building's completion, the department must issue a certificate of acceptance before the building can be occupied.

Granting a permit to build is not always based on the design of a structure and whether its location meets local health and safety standards. To obtain a building permit in some communities, the authorities negotiate additional requirements, particularly for large development projects. These extras may include reserving certain public areas within the project for parks or community use, and even requiring off-site construction, such as low-income housing, as a condition for granting a building permit.

Building code requirements don't end when construction is complete; they continue during its use. The methods of enforcement vary with the community, but generally the fire and health departments periodically inspect buildings for code compliance and cite any violations.

SUBDIVISION REQUIREMENTS

 In earlier times, a landowner could subdivide land into lots with little concern for government restrictions, particularly if the land lay just outside community limits. Recently, however, local governments have used their police powers to enforce **subdivision** requirements. Flood control districts have been created and given authority to set minimum requirements in land development. The FHA and the Veterans Administration (VA) have set minimum standards for the subdivisions in which they will agree to underwrite homes. New underwriting standards were put in place as the Great Recession ended. And the Office of Interstate Land Sales Registration, part of the Department of Housing and Urban Development (HUD), has certain disclosure requirements (not minimum standards) for larger land developments.

Essentially the requirements for a subdivision concern the design, location, and quality of the streets; the adequacy of water and sewage systems; the location of fire hydrants and street lighting; and the size of the lots themselves. Depending on the size of the subdivision, the developer may be required to commit a portion of the land for schools and public areas. Once all requirements have been met, the community gives its approval for construction. In general, government approval concerns only the physical aspects of the development, not its economic value for the investor.

PLANNING

Although the implementation of zoning laws requires a certain amount of community planning, early zoning's emphasis on the status quo gave little encouragement to the concept of urban or regional planning. As zoning laws began to create a mix of land use districts—some of which were desirable, and some of which were not—communities realized the need for better land use plans to control growth. But these efforts failed largely because communities couldn't control the land outside of their boundaries. Probably the strongest encouragement to overcome this problem came from the federal government, which has authorized planning assistance in each of the National Housing Acts passed since 1954. The key program became known as the "701 Program."

The 701 Program

In Section 701 of the Housing Act of 1954, Congress authorized the first program of Urban Planning Assistance. Its intent was to encourage land use planning—through surveys and land use studies—by providing federal funds to urban communities and to state, metropolitan, and regional planning agencies. As these programs multiplied, the goals were broadened to include human resources planning, fiscal planning, and the preparation of regulatory and administrative measures to implement the plans.

While the initial aim of the 701 Program has been diluted by an expansion of its goals and by increased emphasis on housing requirements, the program has been important to land use planning. One lasting contribution of the program has been its assistance in the training and development of the urban planning profession.

RESTRICTIONS BY PRIVATE AGREEMENT

As will be discussed in Chapter 4, the use of land can be restricted by the wording with which the land is conveyed. When land is conveyed with a restrictive condition (e.g., to grantee so long as the premises are used for a public park), the right of ownership can be forfeited through failure to comply. A more common method of privately limiting the right to use land is the **deed restriction**, which does not carry the potential penalty inherent in the limited conveyance of rights. A lease agreement may also contain clauses that limit the tenant's use of the land.

One purpose of a deed restriction is to protect future property value for both the grantee and the neighborhood. Building lot developers, for example, often set usage standards when a lot is sold. The deed to a lot, for instance, may contain a restrictive covenant that sets a minimum size of 1,500 square feet for the house to be built, requires that it be constructed with a brick or stone facade on the front and sides, and requires a fire resistant roof. The deed restrictions may dictate landscaping and building design, number of stories, setback, and minimum cost.

So long as the requirements are reasonable and generally for the betterment of the neighborhood, deed restrictions can be enforced. (The theory is that if a buyer agrees to restrictions, the buyer is bound by them.) Enforcement is usually accomplished by a damaged party seeking an injunction, which is a court order that forbids a certain act.

CASE STUDY **2.1**

Ski Masters of Texas vs. Heinemeyer, 269 S. W. 3d 662 (Tex. App.-San Antonio, 2008)

Residential subdivision residents sued to enforce a residential-only restrictive covenant against a purchaser planning to operate a business in the general planned area of the community.

The subdivision had been platted in 1956 but the plat was not recorded. The first deed conveyed out was subject to conditions and restrictions for residential use only. The deed further specified that all subsequent conveyances were subject to the same restrictions. Seven of the other deeds referenced and incorporated the restrictions contained in the first deed, containing language to the effect that "this conveyance is subject to the same restrictions set out in the first deed." However, this language was not included in the conveyance of tracts 2 and 4.

Ski Masters bought parts of tract 4 and 5 under a deed referencing the restrictions set out in the first recorded deed. Both the owner and the realtor were aware of the deed restrictions at the time of purchase. The residents of the other tracts sued to enforce the deed restrictions. Ski Masters "sought a declaration that the property was not subject to any valid restrictions enforceable by the residents." The business claimed that the residents did not have the right to sue, as they were not in the chain of title to tract 4 since that deed made no reference to the restrictions.

The court stated that ordinarily a restrictive covenant is only enforceable between the contracting parties to a deed. However, there are circumstances where restrictive covenants may be enforced by someone other than a grantor or grantee, for example, when a subdivision is created under a general plan and affords all property owners the benefits of the same deed restrictions.

In this case, each owner assumes the benefit that is promised to the whole, and each has the right to enforce the restrictions. Such covenants may be enforced, by any one or more of the other owners, against a purchaser who has bought with actual or constructive knowledge of the general plan if the restrictions were part of the subject-matter of the purchase.

Limitations of Private Agreements

Land use cannot be unduly restricted by private agreement. It is not permissible to limit future ownership in a manner that may cause discrimination due to sex, race, national origin, color, creed, marital status, or handicapped status. Furthermore, no private agreement can place an unreasonable restraint upon the disposition of the property that would prohibit any **alienation** (i.e., a sale or other means of disposition) by the grantee. A reasonable restraint on disposition would be to require that the owner offer the property initially to a narrowly defined group for a limited time before offering it to persons outside the group.

Termination of Restrictions

Deed restrictions generally include a time limitation of 25 to 35 years—the character of a neighborhood usually changes during that time, leaving the original restriction irrelevant. There are other methods by which deed restrictions may be terminated. One way is by a failure to enforce the requirements. If a developer has sold all the lots, it is sometimes difficult to find a neighbor willing to sue for enforcement when damages may be ill defined. Other methods of termination include (1) by agreement among the parties involved (which may include a neighborhood association), (2) by a new zoning requirement, which would take precedence, (3) by **condemnation** of the property for a public use, or (4) by other legislative action.

EMINENT DOMAIN

Under the state's right of **eminent domain**, the government can take private property for a public purpose, such as for a roadway. This action can be taken against the owner's wishes through condemnation proceedings. Unlike the exercise of state police powers, the right of eminent domain requires that the landowner receive fair compensation for the land.

Normally, the public authority negotiates with the property owner to determine an acceptable price for the property. If an agreement cannot be reached, the property may be condemned allowing the public project to be built. The price for the land is then determined by court proceedings, with acceptance mandatory upon the landowner. It is through this procedure that the government retains the ultimate right to acquire land for streets, freeways, schools, parks, public parking, public housing, and other purposes that serve the needs of the general public.

Sometimes the government permits the use of eminent domain by private and quasi-public companies that serve a public need. A right-of-way for a power transmission line, pipeline, or railroad may be acquired through the exercise of this governmental right. Sometimes this power of eminent domain is granted to a private property owner for purposes that are questionable as to the "public need." An example of this is allowing the condemnation of private property to expand the parking lot of a shopping center. This may increase the community's tax basis, but is that a public need?

The case of Kelo versus the City of New London illustrates the extent to which the power of eminent domain can be used by local government. The case also reveals the passion felt by property owners when their rights to the possession, use, enjoyment, and disposition (the four basic rights of real estate ownership) of real estate are threatened. In 2005, affirming an earlier decision by the Supreme Court of Connecticut, the U.S. Supreme Court allowed that a city, like New London, can use the powers of eminent domain to condemn and take private property for other uses besides building roads or schools or parks, as is common in most other eminent domain cases. In this case, the drug company, Pfizer, planned to anchor a large-scale commercial development in a downtrodden area of New London. Susette Kelo refused to sell her home to the city, and wished to remain. The Supreme Court held that New London could seize the home through its eminent domain powers if a public use (jobs, expanded tax base, etc.) was served with the taking. The court held this was consistent with the Takings Clause of the Fifth Amendment. Public reaction, across the nation, was noteworthy. A number of states and municipalities soon passed, at the emotional behest of citizen-backed ballot initiatives and regional politicians, a number of laws restricting the ability of many jurisdictions to ever use the Takings Clause in a similar manner—homeowners established new boundaries to preclude the use of eminent domain except for purely public needs. And, recalling the poetry of the universe, Pfizer announced in November of 2009 that it would leave New London altogether, and the impressive new facility that inspired Kelo vs. City of New London was never to be built.

What is fair compensation under eminent domain depends on the rights acquired and the damages that the property owner may suffer. If, for example, the desired right-of-way creates an obstacle to future work on an operating farm, an additional compensation called severance damages may be paid. If land suffers a loss of value due to the construction of a nearby public facility, such as an airport or a sewage plant, the landowner may be entitled to conse-quential damages. Under some conditions, a landowner who feels damaged by a nearby facility can initiate a proceeding to demand that the government pur-chase that property. Such a case is called an inverse condemnation.

DO RESTRICTIVE RULES CLASSIFY AS A TAKING?

After a half century of steady erosion of private property rights, two decisions made in 1987 by the U.S. Supreme Court opened a door to some recognition of a property owner's rights. Over the years, a number of regulations, zoning ordinances, and building permit requirements added restrictions on a land-owner's right to use the land. Until 1987 there had been no clear distinction as to what local authorities could take from a property owner for their usage without fair compensation.

On June 9, 1987, the U.S. Supreme Court ruled that land use officials may be liable for damages if zoning regulations prevent landowners from using their property, even temporarily. The case involved the First English Evangelical Lutheran Church, of Glendale, California, which wanted to reopen its retreat and recreational area for handicapped children after a flood. The County of Los Angeles refused to allow the church to use its land for that purpose since the authorities wanted to use the land as a drainage channel. The church complained that this zoning, even though temporary, amounted to a taking, requiring compensation under the Fifth Amendment to the Constitution.

The U.S. Supreme Court agreed with the church, ruling that even a temporary taking, wherein the owner loses all use of the property, is the same as a permanent taking. There was no question that the government has the authority to take the property for flood control purposes, but it must compensate the owners if it does. The court expressed the opinion that this ruling will undoubtedly lessen to some extent the freedom and flexibility of land-use planners and governing bodies, but, after all, many of the provisions of the Constitution are designed to limit the flexibility and freedom of governmental authorities.

Later in the same month of June 1987, the U.S. Supreme Court ruled in favor of landowners in another California case whereby the state sought to increase access to public beaches by placing conditions on a building permit. The dispute involved a couple with oceanfront property who wanted to tear down an existing house in order to replace it with a larger one. The State Coastal Commission approved the plan on condition that the couples provide increased access for the public along the beach in front of their house. The Supreme Court reversed a California court's decision that favored the state's position. In effect, the Supreme Court said that while the state's idea might be a good one, coastal residents alone should not be compelled to contribute to its realization. If California needs more beach access, it may take the land by eminent domain and must pay fair compensation to the landowners.

Example of a Regulatory "Taking"

In *Lucas v. South Carolina Coastal Council*, the U.S. Supreme Court handed down a decision that gave a rather narrow definition to a landowner's rights in a "regulatory taking." The case concerned a landowner, David Lucas, who owned two waterfront lots and was denied a permit to build houses on them as they were located on a barrier island. Mr. Lucas argued that denial of a permit amounted to a "taking" in violation of the Fifth Amendment, which forbids the government from taking private property without "just compensation" to its owner.

Historically, the "takings clause" of the Constitution was thought to apply only in cases where the government took actual physical possession of the property, as in an eminent domain proceeding. More recently, courts have attempted to define the concept of "regulatory taking," which would require the government to pay compensation when the value of the property is impaired by regulation while still remaining in private hands.

In its decision, the U.S. Supreme Court returned the case to the South Carolina Supreme Court for further findings. In a narrow opinion on the case, the Court said that compensation for a regulatory taking should only be considered if the regulation deprives a property owner of all economic value in the property. This would concern only a small segment of property owners as most government regulations are much more likely to reduce the economic value of land rather than render the property worthless.

GOVERNMENT INFLUENCES ON LAND USE

Completely removed from the categories of rights, laws, and requirements are several government subsidy and assistance programs that effectively direct how land is used. If the landowner expects to receive the benefits offered by the programs, the land use must adhere to the programs' guidelines. Foremost in this category of **government influences** are the FHA and VA loan underwriting programs. Both agencies stipulate land use and building standards that must be met in order to qualify for loan assistance.

A more recent program directed by the federal government subsidizes the purchase of flood insurance in designated areas. The National Flood Insurance Program has established flood plain zones along waterways and in coastal areas. The decision to join this program was, at first, optional for local governments in the affected areas. This left many houses unprotected as homeowners often failed to pay the necessary premiums. After several steps to improve coverage, including requiring the escrow of monthly flood insurance payments, homeowners could still drop payments at their discretion. To make nonpayment more difficult, the 1994 National Flood Insurance Reform Act, effective September 23, 1995, required that property located in a flood-prone area serving as collateral for a loan handled by a federal-related institution or agency must carry flood insurance. The Act places responsibility on lenders and servicers to enforce paying for the insurance if it is required and the borrower fails to buy the coverage.

With Hurricanes Jeanne and Francis in Florida in 2004, Katrina and Rita (and Wilma) in New Orleans and Texas (and Florida) in 2005 and Hurricanes Gustav and Ike in 2008, public outcry about flood and other storm insurance reached a crescendo. Many homeowners in New Orleans, and between Galveston and Houston, purchased no flood insurance coverage prior to the storms. Local and regional and national agencies bore an inordinate share of the otherwise insurable losses. Flood insurance and the development of flood-prone areas came under much greater regulatory scrutiny. Human and material losses such as those following Hurricanes Katrina and Ike illustrated the increasing exposure of growing coastal communities to hurricane damages; these "illustrations" elicited expanded government action to reduce subsequent losses, through stricter building standards and clearer requirements for flood coverage when at flood risk.

LAND RESTRICTIONS DUE TO LACK OF SERVICE

In very recent years, a new form of land use restriction has developed due to (1) shortages of the basic utility services needed to sustain a modern community, and (2) rapid growth that, for some areas, has produced unacceptable problems. "No growth" laws have been enacted, producing an escalation in value for developed property and a sharp drop in value for surrounding land with potential development value.

Restrictions on Sewer and Water Lines

Sewer and drinking water services are usually supplied by a municipality, although in some communities water is furnished by a private utility company. Electricity and natural gas are usually—but not always—furnished by privately owned utility companies. Regardless of who furnishes the services, some areas of the country are encountering difficulties in sustaining the growth rates of recent years. A number of measures have been undertaken to adjust to shortages, particularly in areas where water is in short supply.

Some California and Arizona communities, for example, have enacted building restrictions that virtually forbid new developments. The reasons for these restrictive laws include (1) lack of sufficient water, (2) lack of adequate sewage disposal facilities and the money needed to build suitable plants to meet federal and state pollution control requirements, and (3) the simple desire of many residents to enjoy their community as it is and not to become over-crowded.

Land developers have frequently challenged the right of communities to enact building limitation laws, arguing that these laws are destructive of the landowner's rights to use the land. In the meantime, a potential investor in real estate must be aware of the utility's situation in the area of investment interest.

Water Restrictions

The most important utility-based limitation on land use is shortage of water. Water rights have long been an essential part of landownership in the western states. Indeed, without rights to water for such things as irrigation and use by livestock, ranch land can be worthless.

For land suitable for development in and near cities, the availability of good quality water has only recently become a matter of concern. The location of early settlements was often dictated by the presence of suitable water, and the quantity needed to satisfy community sanitary requirements was not great. But today that situation has changed. Many areas are finding that the cost of cleaning up the water is escalating more rapidly than the tax money available to do the job. As a result, many local governments cannot permit new water taps; in others, delays are increasing. Developers who emphasize growth—and the increase in jobs that growth can produce—are being forced to slow down.

Sewage Disposal

The construction of sewer lines and sewage treatment plants has struggled to keep pace with the surge in housing construction across the country. Many local governments have fallen behind in their efforts to improve sewage treatment facilities in order to meet federal and state environmental standards governing the quality of effluent that may be released into waterways. The techniques for proper treatment of waste material are now available and local shortages of this utility service are being remedied. But time—and, as always, more money—will be needed.

Electricity and Natural Gas

Electricity first became available for limited household use barely 100 years ago. Only since World War II has natural gas been distributed on a national scale. Yet today many homeowners and almost all businesses consider electricity an absolute necessity and natural gas the cleanest and most convenient fuel.

Electric Power

Even in the high-growth areas of the country, developers have traditionally had small cause for concern over the local power company's ability to furnish adequate electric power. This confidence in their ability to meet the increases in demand is now being shaken. The earlier plans of many power companies to supply future demand with nuclear power plants have been substantially curtailed because of the difficulties in construction cost overruns and in obtaining regulatory agency approvals.

Coal-fired plants have been encouraged by various government agencies because coal is the most abundant of the fossil fuels. But coal-fired plants have to meet environmental pollution restrictions that are both uncertain and costly. Plants using natural gas and oil for fuel may be less polluting but are faced with an uncertainty in costs and supplies.

By the late 1990s, California experienced major electricity shortages due to new power plant construction limitations designed to protect the environment, a poorly conceived deregulation law, and a growing economy. The state faced periods of rolling blackouts when production could not meet the higher demand for power.

Such shortages could affect other states with similar growth in demand problems. While new energy sources are developing, such as wind, solar, geothermal, and others, it will be some time before they can be increased sufficiently to help satisfy the growing use of electricity in homes and businesses.

For the investor in real estate, the impact of any future electricity shortage could delay tying new outlets into the local power grid. If this should happen, an alternative source of power would be a privately owned generator added to the building or the development—an increase in the investment cost. Plans for future projects should be cleared with the local power company well in advance of starting construction.

Natural Gas

The use of natural gas as a fuel has increased substantially since World War II. This is partly because it is clean, easy to transport, and has been relatively low in cost compared to alternate fuels. In the late 1950s, the production of natural gas was placed under the regulatory powers of the Federal Power Commission, and price ceilings were set on all gas moving in interstate commerce. For many years the ceilings remained stable while the cost of other fuels increased. A gas shortage developed in the late 1970s, resulting in partial deregulation of prices. Adequate gas has since become available but at substantially higher prices.

Fortunately for the real estate investor, natural gas is rarely a necessity. Most energy needs that have been satisfied by natural gas can be supplied by other means. Some new housing developments are using all-electric heating and cooling (let the power company worry about which fuel is most suitable!).

Both solar heating and heat pumps are being used to augment more conventional systems.

The Green Revolution

Whether global warming or climate change can be convincingly attributed to human activity, the impact upon utility provisions and real estate development will likely be the same. Movements away from the "dirtier" fossil fuels (coal, oil, natural gas) and towards the cleaner, but dramatically more costly, "green" power sources will be encouraged by governments around the world. Initiatives to expand the provision of nuclear power, more efficient power consumption, higher mileage cars, living and working closer to urban cores, bike paths, green space, and the like will be at the center of environmental discussions for decades to come.

The real estate investor is well-advised to remain abreast of these topics, as harbingers of certain types of real estate falling out of favor (suburban "McMansions"), and other types becoming more attractive (urban lofts).

ENVIRONMENTAL IMPACT STATEMENT

An early step in recognizing the importance of protecting the environment through land use control was the requirement of a special predevelopment study of the effects that a new project would have on the surrounding land, air, and water. To achieve this goal, Congress passed the National Environmental Policy Act of 1969. The Act requires the preparation of an environmental impact study for any major federal project that will affect the environment. The idea appealed to state legislatures, almost all of which have adopted similar requirements. Many local governments have construed state requirements to include them or have added environmental statements to their local zoning or planning ordinances. The courts have generally supported the requirements as a prerequisite to land development.

The thrust of the National Environmental Policy Act is to require an **environmental impact statement** (EIS) for government projects. But in the idea's adoption at lower levels of government, the burden of preparing such statements has also been placed on the private developer. If a new project is proposed, or a change is requested in a zoning classification, the local government authority generally requires a report on the expected impact the proposal will have on many hard-to-define areas such as noise, air quality, public health and safety, wildlife, and vegetation. The report must also estimate the impact on more easily measurable aspects of community life such as population density, automobile traffic, energy consumption, the need for sewer and water facilities, employment, and school enrollment. Not every project must first be studied—the laws generally specify how large a project must be to require an environmental statement. (This threshold varies with the locality.)

The information contained in an EIS is helpful to many agencies of the government. Copies of the statement are commonly submitted to the affected school district, water department, sewage control district, flood control district, and highway department. The EIS is also made available to the public, with open hearings held on the application. If federal or state money is involved in the project, additional federal or state hearings must be held.

Statement Preparation

Preparation of a statement is generally not subject to any qualification or competency standards. For a government project, the EIS is prepared by the agency involved with the project (sometimes with the help of a private consultant). If the development is privately owned, the statement may be prepared by the developer or by a private firm specializing in environmental studies. The cost of preparing an EIS is usually the least of the new environment-based costs of a project. The need to study the statement and process the application through prolonged public hearings has added many months to the preparatory time required before construction can commence. With inflation continuing, delay means cost escalation. An additional problem is that an EIS sometimes provides a major weapon to opponents of a project—even a mere handful of opponents—who wish to stop growth rather than control it.

SOME CLOSING REMARKS ON LAND USE CONTROLS

Among the comments shared in Chapter 1 are statements concerning the relative increasing efficiency of the real estate market. While this market has long suffered from costly frictions, such as large transaction costs, government regulations and the overall illiquidity of real estate, the market is becoming more efficient: there are more buyers and sellers sharing more information about properties, transaction costs are coming down and real estate is becoming more liquid with real estate investment trusts and the Internet (in spite of the Great Recession). However, increasing community and government land use controls are adding a costly additional hurdle that developers, builders, and homeowners must cross with even the most mundane real estate decision (like the size of water pipes allowed to service an outside faucet). A community's beautification or security, citywide plans to enhance an area's attractiveness to one favored group or another, government and civic concerns with endless environmental issues—these are just a few of the matters that have become the catalysts for expanding government restrictions on the options available to property owners as they consider the most productive manner with which their property may be used. Right or wrong, these expanding initiatives restrict the efficiency of the real estate market, and should be used by the real estate investor in identifying special risks and opportunities.

KEY TERMS

alienation

building codes

condemnation

deed restriction

eminent domain

environmental
   impact statement

government
   influences

sewer and drinking
   water services

subdivision

variance

zoning laws

DISCUSSION QUESTIONS

1. How do governments control land use?

2. What is meant by "eminent domain"?

3. Discuss the current status of interpretation of the "takings clause" in the U.S. Constitution.

4. How may land use be restricted by lack of services?

5. What is the purpose and use of an environmental impact statement?

6. What are some examples of government influences on land use?

7. Explain how land use restrictions could be considered compensable takings.

8. Define the term "variance" and describe how one would be obtained.

9. List the zoning designations that exist in your area.

CHAPTER 3

Environmental Constraints

Investors in real property need to be aware of the various environmental protection laws now in effect that can restrict how land may be used. The concern is not only for restricted land usage, but the severe monetary and criminal penalties that can ensue from noncompliance. Thus, environmental risk has become an added factor in the evaluation of a real estate investment.

This chapter will review the major legislation and discuss the special areas of land use that now require permits and regulatory approvals for any change in the present status of the land. The laws, and how they are being implemented, are not new but are still being further clarified by court decisions. However, there are key requirements that can be explained. With knowledge of potential problem areas, an investor will be better able to make informed decisions on property evaluation, and a landowner will learn how to best protect the property's value and to control future usage so as to minimize potential liability.

The underlying issue of private property rights vs. the public right to a safe environment has confrontational aspects that must be resolved. Property owners have a vested interest in both sides of the problem and are in a key position to help resolve the issues. It is important that those involved in any aspect of real estate be aware of the problems and stay abreast of the changes in laws and regulations as they occur.

A major concern in assessing environmental problems is that they are not always visible on the surface, nor are they subject to clear definitions. For instance, toxic waste damage may be deep underground and could be seeping in from neighboring property. The habitats of endangered species are not always known, inasmuch as the list of endangered life forms is still being expanded. Whether or not an area is classed as a "wetland" is difficult to determine since the definition includes many gray areas.

To reduce the risk that may be involved in acquiring environmentally damaged land, prudent investors are now asking that professional investigations be undertaken prior to closing a property transaction. A growing group of environmental specialists is available for this purpose but, thus far, there are few controls in place to assure the consumer of expertise. Some licensed engineers are entering this field, offering professional benefits. Some appraisers are taking additional courses on the environment so as to add this expertise to their examination of properties. However, careful selection of the investigator is necessary to assure a comprehensive and accurate environmental evaluation.

HOW THE ENVIRONMENT AFFECTS HUMANS

For the past three decades, most studies and research about the environment have focused on the detrimental effect that humans have had on it. Indeed, in the 1970s federal and state laws were directed at protection of the environment from such acts as dumping waste that inflicted long-term damage to the land, water, and air that we depend on for healthy lives. Little study was given to the damaging effects certain elements of the environment could have on individuals. That pattern changed in the last quarter of the 20th century, as endless studies affirmed the adverse health impacts of a number of compounds present in the land, water and air.

Evidence of declinations in childhood development adjacent to environmental damage has generated grave concerns. Enough examples of chemical damage affecting a child's brain development have surfaced to warrant much further study. As land areas have been discovered that may be the cause of such brain damage, the economic effect on the land's value has been substantial.

Contaminated land, ignoring the liabilities for prior owners and of parties responsible for its contamination, is often not suitable for any use and is blocked off from human access completely. Other land may be permitted for only "hard" commercial uses, such as for parking or warehousing, *after* substantial portions of the dirt has been removed and the surface has been sealed with asphalt or concrete. Dirt removed from such sites must be transported to permitted sites, typically comprised of clay or other "waterproof" materials.

Work examining the impacts on infants of the presence of **polychlorinated biphenyls or PCBs** has been damning; mental acuity and motor skills are compromised by high levels of PCBs. Adverse findings attach also to the presence of tetrachloroethylene (**polychloroethylene or PCE**), a dry cleaning fluid, in the soil or ground water; liver and kidney damage result from exposure to PCE. Ubiquitous findings with lead, discussed below, also reveal the negative impact decades of chemical use and disposal have had on the environment, on land values, and on human health.

ENVIRONMENTAL ISSUES EXAMINED

Both the federal and state governments are involved with legislation, regulatory agencies, rules, and court decisions that affect environmental issues. This means that many troublesome areas have problems that overlap and come under the jurisdiction of multiple agencies. This text will limit its discussion to information on federal law and federal agencies, primarily because federal courts have consistently ruled that federal law preempts state law due to the overwhelming need for a consistent national policy on these important concerns.

Environmental constraints extend to many areas that only indirectly affect an investor's evaluation of land. Examples of such concerns are restraints on automobile exhaust and industrial emissions, the transportation of hazardous substances, the handling of effluent, and others. We will, therefore, examine the major kinds of pollution that most affect private land ownership. These will be reviewed under the following 11 categories:

1. Toxic waste sites.
2. **Lead** poisoning.
3. Indoor air pollution.
4. Clean water measures.
5. **Wetlands protection.**
6. Storm water runoff regulations.
7. Endangered species protection.
8. Underground storage tanks.
9. **Electromagnetic forces.**
10. Mold
11. **Carbon monoxide.**

TOXIC WASTE SITES

The first national notice that toxic waste sites could endanger people's lives made the news on August 3, 1978, datelined Love Canal, New York. For years the Hooker Chemical Company, and to a much lesser degree the City of Niagara Falls and the United States, had dumped nearly 22,000 tons of chemical waste in what had been Love Canal. The wastes included PCBs, dioxin, and long-lasting pesticides.

In 1953 Hooker filled in the dump and sold it to the city for $1. Later a road was built on top of the fill, making way for houses and a public school. Complaints of foul odors, the surfacing of a black sludge, and minor burn marks appearing on children in the area were not heeded until the late 1970s, when New York state began an investigation.

The public shock created by the discovery of massive health problems found near Love Canal brought Congressional action in the passage of the Comprehensive Environmental Response, Compensation and Liability Act of 1980 (**CERCLA**). The Act set up a $1.6 billion Hazardous Waste Fund that became known as "Superfund." The money was to be used to clean up the worst existing sites and to respond to emergency situations. In 1985, the Environmental Protection Agency (EPA) developed the Chemical Emergency Preparedness Program to help states and local communities prepare for, and respond to, chemical accidents. In 1986, Congress passed the Superfund Amendments and Reauthorization Act, which increased the Superfund to $8.5 billion. Additional funding has followed, under this and other acts.

CERCLA and subsequent legislation provide a federal regulatory mechanism to identify, investigate, evaluate, and clean up inactive and abandoned waste sites throughout the United States. It further authorizes states and private parties to take appropriate action to clean up contaminated sites and to seek reimbursement from the responsible parties.

Determination of Violations

The liability for hazardous waste cleanup created by CERCLA is broadly stated to cover the release, or threatened release, of hazardous substances from a facility into the environment that causes the incurrence of response costs. Following are some useful definitions.

Release

Any spilling, leaking, pumping, pouring, emitting, emptying, discharging, injection, escaping, leaching, dumping, or disposing into the environment.

Hazardous Substance

The EPA currently lists 717 different poisonous materials as hazardous. How the hazardous nature of the material is determined is defined under CERCLA legislation and subsequent laws. In general, if any law designates a substance as toxic or hazardous, it falls under the Superfund designation as such. The Resource Conservation and Recovery Act gives some definition to a "hazardous characteristic" as ignitability, reactivity, corrosivity, or toxicity (meaning poisonous).

Facility

The term "facility" is broadly defined to include any location where a hazardous substance has been disposed of or stored. The area is not limited to, or coextensive with, an owner's boundary lines.

Environment

As defined by the Superfund Act, the environment includes the air, land, surface water, and ground water, but not the interior of buildings or other manmade structures.

Potentially Responsible Parties

Responsibility for cleanup costs places strict, joint and several liability on all who may have been involved in creating the waste site. On a practical basis, this means whoever can be located and has the "deepest pockets." The 1986 Superfund Amendment identifies four categories of persons or companies specifically liable for cleanup costs as follows:

1. The party who arranged for the disposal or treatment of the hazardous material.
2. The party who transported the hazardous substance to the facility.
3. The prior owner or operator of the facility.
4. The current owner or operator of the facility.

Owner or Operator

An owner or operator means the person who owned, operated, or otherwise controlled the facility. If the site has been conveyed to a unit of state or local government in connection with bankruptcy, foreclosure, or abandonment, the owner or operator is the person who controlled the facility immediately prior to such conveyance. A lender holding a lien or conditional title to protect a security interest is not classed as an owner so long as there is no participation in management of the facility.

While the Superfund Act refers to the term "owner and operator" rather than "owner or operator," courts have consistently interpreted the phrase to mean that either the owner or operator may be liable parties.

There is no limitation on the amount of response costs for which a responsible party may be held liable. However, liability for damages to natural resources is limited to $50 million.

Strict, Joint and Several Liability of Responsible Parties

In a typical Superfund case, there are usually several different companies disposing of different types of waste and many transporters of same. In addition, both the toxicity and the volume of wastes varies substantially among the parties involved. Courts have held that there is no minimum to create liability. A key issue is whether or not liability is based on the kind and amount of waste disposed of and how it can then be apportioned among the responsible parties.

The general rule is that unless a statutory or equitable defense applies to a responsible party, all parties are "strictly" liable for response costs. This means liable regardless of individual fault. In addition, liability is "joint and several." This means each party is both singularly and jointly liable for all costs. Any one party, regardless of the degree of fault, can be 100 percent liable for the response costs. There is a defense to such an all-inclusive liability if the defendant can prove the environmental damage is divisible and that there is a reasonable basis for apportioning said damage.

However, the Superfund act provides that ultimate liability of a **potentially responsible party** to the government cannot be transferred to a third party. The act does permit responsible parties to allocate liability among themselves through an indemnification agreement.

Defenses to Cost Recovery Actions

Only a few defenses can be asserted in a Superfund cost recovery action. These include a challenge to the quality of the government's evidence, statutory defenses based on unforeseen circumstances or acts by third parties, and the statute of limitations. Another important defense is available if certain steps are undertaken prior to acquisition of a property. Inspection for environmental problems before title is conveyed has become a more common practice. The Superfund act allows an environmental assessment that meets certain requirements to qualify an owner for what is referred to as the "**innocent landowner defense.**"

Innocent Landowner Defense

A defense against liability for response costs, if caused by other than the landowner, may be sustained provided the defendant did not know, and had no reason to know, that the facility had been used for the disposal of hazardous substances prior to its acquisition by the present owner. To maintain this defense, an innocent landowner must have made an appropriate inquiry into the previous ownership and uses of the property. Such a pre-purchase assessment, or **phase assessment**, is defined as part of the Superfund act and is called an "environmental due diligence assessment."

The purpose of such an assessment is to analyze, evaluate, and manage a potential environmental risk. The scope of the assessment will vary, depending on its purpose and the circumstances involved, such as the type of transaction, timing and financial pressures involved, the uses that are or have been conducted on the site, the extent of contamination, and the resulting legal issues involved.

The assessment should be conducted in two phases as presently identified: (1) Phase I Assessment is designed to qualify the owner for the innocent landowner defense, and (2) Phase II Assessment is to confirm the presence or absence of contamination and its extent when found. If both assessments are necessary, they must be conducted prior to acquiring title.

Phase I Assessment

This is a limited inquiry focusing on readily available sources of data and culminating in an inspection of the site, including an environmental consultant when needed. If no contamination is revealed, further study would not be necessary. Following is a list of the various matters that should be included in a Phase I study:

1. Current and previous users of the site.
2. Legal description, survey, and site map.
3. List of current and previous owners and operators of the site.
4. Status of title to the site.
5. Interviews with persons knowledgeable about the site.
6. Zoning status of the site.
7. Aerial photographs.
8. Topographic maps.

9. Information and documents from governmental agencies:
   a. U.S. Environmental Protection Agency (EPA).
   b. Securities and Exchange Commission (SEC).
   c. State Water and/or Health Commissions.
10. Information and documents from current owner or operator.
11. Storage tanks on site:
    a. Internal lining of tanks.
    b. Cathodic protection.
    c. Spill and overfill prevention equipment.
    d. Release detection systems.
12. Asbestos-containing materials on site.
13. Polychlorinated biphenyls (PCBs) and PCB items on site.
14. Site inspection.

Phase II Assessment

If information obtained in the Phase I Assessment indicates actual or potential contamination, a Phase II Assessment is required. Unlike the Phase I Assessment, there is no specific format for Phase II. The purpose is to target those areas believed to be contaminated and includes the collection and chemical analysis of soil samples and other relevant investigations. Any sampling must be made in accordance with EPA or state regulatory agency procedures or both.

Phase III Assessment

While a Phase II assessment determines the type and extent of contamination, Phase III defines the steps needed to clean up the contaminated areas.

EPA Policy on Homeowner Liability for Cleanup

In July 1991, the EPA issued a statement called "Policy Toward Owners of Residential Property at Superfund Sites." It states that the EPA will not hold homeowners liable for Superfund cleanup costs unless the owner knowingly contaminates a property or fails to cooperate with the EPA in its cleanup efforts (such as failing to allow the EPA access to the Superfund site). The protection applies only to property used for residential purposes and includes lenders who might acquire residential property through foreclosure.

It should be noted that the EPA's policy statement is not a statutory exemption. Rather, it is intended as guidance for EPA enforcement employees. This means the EPA is stating that it will not exercise its right to pursue homeowners, but the EPA also remains free to rescind the policy or take actions at variance with it.

Brownfields

Urban land that has become contaminated over the years often lies idle because of the cost, and possible liability, involved with its cleanup and restoration to good economic use. The site may have been previously used for a service station, dry cleaning operation, or other contaminating facility. Federal agencies, including the EPA, the Federal Housing Finance Board, and HUD, have been working with the private sector to aid in redeveloping these **brownfield** sites.

An example of what has been done is an Alabama shopping center that had become an environmentalist's nightmare by 1989. The center was filled with asbestos and tainted with a leaky underground waste oil tank from an auto repair shop. Now all cleaned up and sporting a brand new facade with thriving retail stores, the center is generating income of almost four times what it was generating before cleanup.

The transformation can be traced to the easing of rules that required contaminated sites to meet residential standards, even if they were never to be used for such purposes. Under new, more relaxed federal guidelines, a cleaned-up site can receive clearance if it meets a standard of offering less than a 1-in-10,000 chance of contracting cancer, compared to the stricter 1-in-1,000,000 requirement for a residential site.

The EPA is working with states and localities to develop and issue guidelines that will clarify the liability of prospective purchasers, lenders, property owners, and others regarding their association with and activities at a contaminated site. These guidelines will state the EPA's decision to use its enforcement discretion in pursuing such parties for cleanup costs. It is anticipated that these cleanup statements will alleviate concerns these parties may have and will facilitate more cleanup and redevelopment.

Since 1995, the EPA has provided funding for 250 Brownfields Assessment Demonstration Pilots. These pilots, funded at over $200,000 each, test redevelopment models, direct special efforts toward removing regulatory barriers without sacrificing protectiveness, and facilitate coordinated site assessment, environmental cleanup, and redevelopment efforts at the federal, state, and local level.

Brownfields redevelopment can also be ecologically, economically, and socially sustainable. By integrating the concepts of sustainable development, community involvement, risk management, and collaborative project teams with brownfield redevelopment, brownfield redevelopers can avoid re-creating brownfields and continuing their legacy.

While it is possible to receive "comfort letters" from the EPA, some developers are finding that they are not relieved from liability to third parties. A future owner may still bring action for cleanup costs, so continued "due diligence" is always advisable.

Because this is an ever-changing effort, it is recommended that current research be conducted to determine the latest status in each different state or locality. The following website can serve as a starting point for this research into EPA actions towards the management of brownfields, and the recent history of judicial responses to EPA guidelines:

www.epa.gov/www.lawsite.com/BROWNFIELDS/

LEAD POISONING

Lead is a heavy, relatively soft, malleable, bluish-gray metal. It cannot be broken down or destroyed. Because of the ease with which it can be shaped, it has been used for centuries in the form of pipe and other building materials.

More recently it has been alloyed for use as solder that can secure pipe joints, and as a component of paint. Paint containing high levels of lead was found to be more durable and looked fresher for a greater length of time.

Although lead seemed to have some advantages for buildings, its ingestion into the human body can only do harm. Lead can be more damaging to children up to seven years of age than adults because of their higher rates of respiration and metabolism. Lead can be most damaging to the brain. Testing found that children with the lowest IQs were often the children with the highest levels of lead in their blood.

With the implementation of new restrictions on lead in gasoline, paint, plumbing, and other household items, there has been a dramatic drop in the number of children under six who have high levels of lead in their blood. The reasons for this decline are attributed to federal initiatives to end the use of lead in gasoline, of lead solder in piping and the seams of cans, and of lead-based paint in homes.

Sources of Lead Poisoning

There are two ways that lead can be absorbed into the body: inhalation and ingestion.

Inhalation

Airborne lead is caused by emissions from certain industrial plants, internal combustion engines (primarily cars still using gasoline containing lead), and dust that can be found in the household deriving from lead-based paint and other lead-containing items.

Ingestion

Household dust and the soil around a house can contain lead that may be ingested. Water passing through lead pipes, or copper pipes with lead solder joints, can contain lead. And lead-containing nonfood items such as toys, cosmetics, and jewelry can end up in children's mouths as can hands covered with dirt.

1996 Lead-Based Paint Rules

In March 1996, HUD and the EPA issued a joint rule that requires sellers and renters of houses built prior to 1978 to disclose to potential buyers or tenants the presence of lead-based paint hazards in the housing. To comply, the seller or renter of such property must disclose in writing to the buyer or tenant any known lead hazard condition, allow an inspection prior to conveyance, and present the buyer or tenant with a HUD Pamphlet entitled "Protect Your Family from Lead in Your Home."

INDOOR AIR POLLUTION

A definition of acceptable air quality is "Air in which there are no known contaminants at harmful concentrations." The measure is not as simple as it sounds. As public awareness of the potential hazards associated with air

Two Real Estate Corporations Charged with Failing to Warn Purchasers and Tenants about Lead Paint in New England

EPA inspections and review of submitted information revealed that several real estate offices together committed 102 violations of the Lead Disclosure Rule during 34 real estate transactions between 2005 and 2007. The corporations that own and operate the offices face penalties of up to $11,000 for each violation cited in the complaint.

This case is one of the largest cases brought against a real estate company and is among dozens of lead-related civil and criminal cases the EPA has taken in New England to make sure property owners, property managers, and real estate agents are complying with federal lead disclosure laws.

This action contributes to the EPA's record-shattering enforcement results for the 2008 fiscal year. Nationwide, the EPA has concluded enforcement actions requiring polluters to spend an estimated $11 billion on pollution controls, cleanup, and environmental projects, an all time record for EPA. After these activities are completed, the EPA expects annual pollution reductions of more than three billion *pounds*.

---

pollution increases, the problem becomes a growing concern for anyone seeking to sell, or invest in, any kind of real property structure. What steps can be taken to minimize potential risks?

First, a prudent investor must become acquainted with the several hazards that have been identified and especially those that are common to the local area. With this knowledge, a visual inspection of the subject property can be more effective in detecting anything unusual or hazardous. Consultations with the property owner/seller should disclose known environmental hazards. If doubts persist, the advice of a reputable professional environmental engineer can be most helpful. The purpose of such an investigation is to determine the future usability of the building.

Not surprisingly, studies by the EPA have indicated that indoor air can be several times more polluted than outdoor air. The EPA has estimated that half of all illnesses are directly attributable to seven types of indoor air pollution. These are:

1. Formaldehyde gas.
2. Asbestos as used in building materials.
3. Tobacco smoke.
4. Biological pollutants such as bacteria, viruses, and fungi.
5. Volatile organic compounds found in cleaning and repair work.
6. Radon gas.
7. Combustion by-products from wood, coal, or oil.

Of the seven types of indoor pollution, formaldehyde gas, asbestos, and radon are among the most dangerous and the most difficult to assess. Further consideration will be given to these three types of pollution.

Formaldehyde Gas

Formaldehyde gas is a colorless, toxic, water-soluble gas with a strong pungent, pickle-like smell. It can be emitted by a number of household materials such as urea-formaldehyde foam insulation, adhesives used in pressed wood, particle board, and plywood, as well as draperies and carpeting. This gas can cause health problems ranging from minor eye, nose, and throat irritation to serious effects such as nasal cancer.

Such problems are not normally found in the average building but may pose problems in manufactured or mobile homes, high energy efficient houses, tightly constructed newer office buildings, and schools. Wall paneling, floors, shelves, cabinets, and office furniture are all possible sources for the emission of formaldehyde.

Urea-Formaldehyde Foam Insulation (UFFI) was a popular building material in the late 1970s and early 1980s. While it has since been banned from usage, it can still be found in some houses. While the greatest danger of gas escaping occurs when UFFI begins to dry, gas can also be released later if the material is dampened or exposed to high temperatures. What is of greater concern, however, is the action of urea-formaldehyde when used as an adhesive in wood products such as wall paneling, cabinets, and shelves. The gas can, and does, escape from such materials depending on temperature, humidity, and ventilation.

Only manufactured homes are required to carry warning labels stating they contain products made with formaldehyde and buyers must sign statements acknowledging the presence of any such materials. Other buildings have no such requirements. Thus, in other buildings, an investor may find it necessary to use a commercial testing device or a professional consultant to determine the possible presence of formaldehyde gas.

Remedies

If the presence of formaldehyde gas is found, the best remedy is removal of the gas-emitting material. However, this may be a complex and expensive process. Increasing the ventilation or lowering the temperature and humidity in an office building can easily reduce the concentration of gas. Another effective procedure is to seal particle board and other wood products with paints or veneers.

Asbestos as Used in Building Materials

Asbestos is a group of naturally occurring mineral fibers found in rocks. It has been used in such products as patching compounds, wood-burning stoves, siding, roofing shingles, and vinyl floors. Asbestos has a number of advantages since it can strengthen a material, provide thermal insulation and acoustical insulation on exposed surfaces, and fireproof a product or material. But it has at least one disadvantage: It can kill you. And that has been known since 1924 when a young woman who worked with asbestos died with extensively scarred lungs.

This kind of illness is called asbestoses, a noncancerous disease that scars the lung tissues. And it can cause several different kinds of cancer in the lungs, esophagus, stomach, and intestines. Yet it is a difficult type of pollution to accurately assess. Media attention has focused on the problems of asbestos as a health hazard in schools and office buildings. While less attention has been given to it, the same problems can exist in homes. Nevertheless, recent studies have indicated that the real danger lies with "loose" asbestos, rather than with that occurring in "hard" form.

Construction materials have contained asbestos for hundreds of years. When bonded into another hard material, asbestos can be relatively harmless. This "nonfriable" condition, common in asbestos siding, usually poses no threat unless drilled or sanded, thus releasing fibers. It is the effort to remove hard asbestos materials that can cause health hazards as the material is disturbed.

The soft, or crumbling, forms of **asbestos**, called "friable," pose greater risks. Damaged asbestos insulation around pipes or ceiling tiles may release airborne microscopic fibers. These fibers may cause respiratory diseases that are not detected until years later. However, to date, there have been no conclusive studies that a health hazard is caused from ingesting food or water containing asbestos or that the fibers can penetrate the skin. Asbestos becomes dangerous only when it breaks down and fibers are released into the air.

Friable asbestos is defined as any material containing more than 1 percent asbestos by weight that hand pressure can crumble, pulverize, or reduce to powder when dry. The threshold level for reporting to the EPA's National Emission Standards for Hazardous Air Pollution (NESHAP) any demolition or renovation of commercial buildings is when at least 260 linear feet of friable asbestos-containing materials found on pipes or at least 160 square feet of asbestos-containing material is being stripped or removed.

For an investor to determine if asbestos poses a problem in a property under consideration, a review of other buildings in the neighborhood could be helpful. If there is an indication of problems, an EPA-certified asbestos inspector can determine if asbestos is present in the building.

Asbestos Management Plan

Building owners and managers have had to make critical decisions either to remove asbestos or to implement in-place management programs. Many owners have removed asbestos out of fear of potential liability even when there is no evidence of significant health risk.

To help guide an owner's decision, the EPA released (in 1990) a document entitled "Managing Asbestos in Place: A Building Owner's Guide to Operations and Maintenance Programs." Its objective is to reinforce the EPA position, held since 1985, that removal of asbestos is not always the most prudent option and that in-place management is often a better, and far less costly, alternative for building owners. According to the EPA, an effective management program includes the training of maintenance personnel, proper cleaning practices, monitoring the air for pollution, and informing tenants and others of the presence of asbestos in the building.

Radon Gas

In 1989, the Administrator of the EPA pronounced radon as "the second leading cause of cancer in this country." The EPA estimates that radon causes as many as 20,000 deaths each year. The hazard was not discovered until

1984 when an engineer working on the construction of the Limerick Nuclear Plant in Pennsylvania was found to be bringing radiation into the plant from his home!

Radon is an invisible radioactive gas. It cannot be felt, seen, or smelled. Outside, it is virtually harmless as it dissipates. In fact, it only becomes a significant problem inside a building where it can accumulate into dangerous concentrations. Radon comes from decaying uranium which can be found in many places. It is in the earth's soil, black shale, phosphatic rocks, and even granite. It can be found in areas that have been contaminated with industrial wastes such as by-products of uranium and phosphate mining.

The danger arises when such materials are located directly underneath an inhabited building and the gas seeps inside. Entry into the building can be through cracks in the slab or openings found around pipes. The gas can enter through well water. In building areas that may lack adequate ventilation, such as a basement, the gas can become concentrated and dangerous.

While the materials that cause radon gas are widely dispersed, they are not found everywhere. Clues about its possible presence can be obtained from local, state, and federal environmental and health officials or from information gathered in the local neighborhood about other buildings. While any building can contain radon gas, well-insulated and energy-efficient homes may actually experience higher levels of contamination.

If the presence of radon is suspected, air tests should be made. A simple test involves placing an activated charcoal filter canister (available at hardware stores) in the basement or ground level of the building for seven days, then returning it to a laboratory for analysis. If professional testing is preferred, the EPA has a list of proficient radon testing contractors.

Remedies

There are several remedies that reduce the problem of radon gas pollution. Basement floor cracks and pipe openings can be sealed to prevent further seepage. Ventilation devices alone may be sufficient to reduce radon concentration to a minimum level.

CLEAN WATER MEASURES

There is no such thing as "pure water." Concern over contaminated water can be traced back as far as 2,000 B.C. In this country, it was in the mid-1800s that two cholera epidemics were traced to contaminated water. At about the same time, typhoid fever, then one of the ten leading causes of death, was also related to contaminated water. In 1908 chlorination was added to water to kill both typhoid and cholera germs. Later, it was discovered that chlorine could interact with other elements in the water and form carcinogenic compounds.

One of the earliest pieces of legislation to improve water supplies was the Public Health Service Act passed by Congress in 1912. Several more attempts were made in subsequent years to address the problem of impure water. The Safe Drinking Water Act passed in the early 1970s expanded federal responsibility for the safety of drinking water to all community systems with 15 or more outlets or 25 or more customers. Even so, a survey in 1988 by the United States Geological Survey found contamination in groundwater increasing in every state.

In June 1989 the EPA published rules aimed at eliminating microbes from public drinking water. Under these rules, many water systems relying on surface water will have to operate pollution control equipment that destroys disease-causing bacteria.

Clean Water Act

In 1972, Congress passed the initial Clean Water Act as an amendment to the Water Pollution Act of 1948. Then, in 1987, Congress passed the Water Pollution and Control Act, which expanded the earlier legislation, and this has become known as the Clean Water Act (CWA). The CWA introduced a permit system to control the discharge of any pollutant into waters of the United States and it also includes the protection of wetlands. The CWA defines "pollutant" as any dredged spoil, rock, or sand but it does not define the term "waters of the United States."

Authority under the CWA to issue permits is divided between the Environmental Protection Agency and the Army Corps of Engineers (Corps). The EPA issues discharge permits while the Corps issues permits for dredged and fill materials. However, the EPA retains a veto power over issuance of a Corps permit. Further, the EPA may approve state proposals to administer permit programs for dredge-and-fill discharges into intrastate waters.

WETLANDS PROTECTION

The 1987 Clean Water Act placed the protection of wetlands under regulation. While the law does not define "waters of the United States," the 33 Code of Federal Regulations, Section 328.3, does define the term as including wetlands and adjacent wetlands. Essentially, the effect of the law and regulation is that a wetland cannot be disturbed without a proper permit.

In the past, swampy, marshy, or water-saturated soils were considered a source of sickness, a breeding place for disease-bearing mosquitoes. Farmers were encouraged to drain or fill such areas. In addition, large areas of wetlands were eliminated due to the development of federal flood control projects, canal building, and mosquito control projects. Then, too late in many cases, scientists learned that wetlands have positive values and can help control flooding, filter out pollution, clean drinking water, and provide habitat for fish and other wildlife. Environmentalists were quick to expand the new intelligence with rather far-reaching and perhaps over-intended results.

Wetlands laws and regulations have a very extensive reach and many landowners can discover to their dismay that they are unable to use their land as they desire because the land falls under the definition of a "protected wetland." This can include land that is dry for all but seven days a year.

Wetlands may be natural or man-made. Decorative lakes or water hazards on golf courses, for example, may become protected wetlands. If an area that involves a wetland is disturbed before discovering that it is so defined, the result can be enforcement action including the assessment of administrative, civil, or criminal penalties.

Wetlands Definition

There are, of course, special criteria that identify a wetland but they are difficult to put into practical usage. As defined by the Corps, wetlands are "areas inundated or saturated by surface or ground water at a frequency and duration sufficient to support, and that under normal circumstances do support, a prevalence of vegetation typically adapted for life in saturated soil conditions." The definition is broad and leaves many landowners with less than a clear understanding of its consequences.

If cattails are growing in a landowner's swampland, that is most likely a wetlands area. But many areas may, or may not, qualify depending on how one interprets such words as "normal circumstance" and "prevalence of vegetation." Since both the Corps and the EPA exercise authority over wetlands, the two agencies have combined to produce the Federal Wetlands Determination Manual, which explains the technical criteria in greater detail. However, the manual does not distinguish between natural and man-made wetlands. Thus, a wet area in a corn field created by a farmer's irrigation ditch would be classified in the same way as an ancient cypress swamp in the Florida Everglades.

Further complications can result from the fact that two other federal agencies continue to play a supporting regulatory role in the handling of wetlands. These are the U.S. Fish and Wildlife Service and the U.S. Soil Conservation Service.

Obviously, the judgment criteria can cover a great number of isolated situations, far removed from the traditional concept of coastal bays and estuaries. While there is no question that the purpose of the law is to provide greater protection to the nation's wetlands, the broad brush definitions can bring land within the jurisdiction of the Corps that has only a marginal relationship to the true concept of a wetland. As a result, it is quite possible for landowners to unintentionally violate the law if they disturb such land in an effort to bring it to a different use.

In an important decision, the U.S. Supreme Court narrowed the scope of wetlands law. On January 9, 2001, the Court ruled in Solid Waste Agency of Northern Cook County v. U.S. Army Corps of Engineers that the Corps had overstepped its authority when it tried to regulate land use on isolated sites including ponds used by migratory birds. The case involved a consortium of Chicago area municipalities that purchased a 523 acre property to use as a landfill. The site had been mined for sand and gravel for about 30 years, ending in the 1960s, after which the trenches became ponds visited by migratory birds. The Corps had refused to issue the necessary Clean Water Act permit to allow the landfill.

As a result of the technical problems, the only way to be certain whether or not an area comes under the wetlands definition is to request the Corps to make an inspection and issue its own determination. Each of the 26 Corps District

---

CASE STUDY **3.2**

Supreme Court Toughens Standing Requirements for Environmental Plaintiffs

On March 3, 2009, the U.S. Supreme Court held in *Summers v. Earth Island Institute* that five conservation groups lacked standing to challenge U.S. Forest Service ("USFS") regulations that exempt small timber sales from the notice, comment, and appeal process used in more significant land management decisions.

The majority's opinion reinforces the Court's jurisprudence limiting standing to sue for generalized grievances, and makes clear that claims based on a deprivation of procedural rights require "a concrete interest" that is affected by the deprivation in order to meet the minimum threshold for constitutional standing. *Summers* provides potent precedent to challenge the standing of environmental plaintiffs in citizen suits, Administrative Procedure Act cases, and other federal litigation, requiring them to provide sworn evidence particularizing harm from the precise action challenged.

The case arose out of the September 2003 USFS approval of the Burnt Ridge Project, a salvage sale of timber on 238 acres of fire-damaged federal land. The project was approved consistent with USFS regulations that exempted small sales from formal notice-and-comment procedures and an appeals process. Earth Island Institute, Sierra Club, and other conservation organizations brought a facial challenge to the regulations and to the Burnt Ridge project itself, arguing the exemption violated the 1992 Appeals Reform Act, which requires the USFS to provide a notice, comment, and appeals process for all land and resource management plans. The District Court granted a preliminary injunction as to the sale, and the parties then settled over the Burnt Ridge dispute. However, despite the settlement, the District Court proceeded to hear the merits of the plaintiffs' challenges and invalidated the USFS regulations, issuing a nationwide injunction. The Ninth Circuit, predictably, affirmed this portion of the District Court ruling.

In the 5–4 decision, Justice Scalia wrote for the majority that the plaintiffs lacked standing because, "after voluntarily settling their portion of their lawsuit relevant to Burnt Ridge, respondents and their members are no longer under threat of injury from that project." The Court emphasized that "[w]e know of no precedent for the proposition that when a plaintiff has sued to challenge the lawfulness of certain action ... but has settled that suit, he retains standing to challenge the basis for that action ... apart from any concrete application that threatens imminent harm to his interests. Such a holding would fly in the face of Article III's injury-in-fact requirement."

The majority also rejected plaintiffs' affidavits claiming planned future visits to National Forests as too vague to show the threat of imminent harm. Specifically, the Court wrote that "we are asked to assume that not only will [affiant] stumble across a project tract unlawfully subject to the regulations, but also that the tract is about to be developed by the Forest Service in a way that harms his recreational interests, and that he would have commented on the project but for the regulation."

Offices throughout the country is authorized to make these determinations, which are final unless the landowner brings suit in federal court to overturn the ruling. In this case, there is no right to administrative appeal.

Wetland Permit Requirements

If a landowner's projected plans for a development would change the nature of land in a way that could cause disturbance to a wetlands area, a permit is needed prior to commencement of the work. This means that if a project is not exempt, or a general permit does not apply, the landowner must apply to the Corps for a Section 404 permit that approves changing the nature of the wetlands area. These regulations create a presumption against permits unless the district engineer finds the benefits outweigh the damage to the wetlands. The guidelines used to make this determination follow four major considerations:

1. Whether or not the proposed project is the only practical and feasible method and that there are no alternatives.
2. Whether or not the proposed activity will avoid causing or contributing to significant degradation of the wetlands area.
3. Whether or not the applicant can minimize adverse impacts from unavoidable filling of wetlands areas by restoration or creation of new wetlands in other areas.
4. Whether or not the applicant may obtain state certification that the proposed discharge will comply with effluent limits and water quality standards.

If these four criteria cannot be met, the application for a permit will be denied.

There is yet another requirement for project approval. The Corps must also grant an approval based on its "Public Interest Review." This review considers such items as economics, wetlands, fish and wildlife values, water quality, energy needs, public and private need for the project, historic value, and state and local use decisions. However, this review is different from the preceding one in that the presumption is in favor of the project and the permit will be granted unless it is contrary to the public interest.

For an investor considering the acquisition of land, if development is involved that might require disposition of materials into lakes, streams, or rivers, a permit to do so is most likely required. A question ensues as to which agency issues the proper permit and that could necessitate dealing with at least three of them: the EPA, the Corps, and a state agency.

Wetlands Mitigation Banking

Another possibility that might aid a land developer if a wetlands area must be filled to complete a development project is to offer a substitute wetlands area. It is possible to obtain the necessary Corps permit by restoring, or creating, another wetlands area—usually on a ratio of one and one-half acres of new wetland for every acre of developed wetland—on or near the project site. To obtain a permit for such work, the developer must agree to flood the area, plant trees and other vegetation, and guarantee to maintain the new wetland in perpetuity. This is a big obstacle and another method may be available.

Entrepreneurs are developing large reserves, or banks, comprising 500 acres or more, of functioning wetlands at a cost of $10,000 or more per acre. Developers may buy rights to such acreage as may be needed to use as a credit to fulfill the Corps' requirements. The developer does not take title to the land, which the entrepreneur continues to maintain. The method is known as **"mitigation banking."**

Exemptions from Permit Requirements

There are some exemptions from permit requirements under Section 404(f)(1) of the CWA. The discharge of dredged or fill material is allowed without a special permit if it is associated with any of the following activities:

1. Ongoing farming, silva-culture (timber or forestry), and ranching activities including plowing, seeding, cultivating, and minor drainage.
2. Maintenance of structures such as dikes, dams, levees, and bridge abutments.
3. Construction or maintenance of farm or stock ponds, irrigation ditches, or the maintenance of existing drainage ditches.
4. Construction of temporary sedimentation basins as might be used at a construction site.
5. Construction or maintenance of farm or forest roads for moving mining equipment, if the roads are constructed so as not to impact the flow, circulation patterns, or reach of the waters and so as to minimize any adverse effects.

Nevertheless, if any of these activities are intended to change the land so that it can be put to a different use, such as a conversion from swamp to farmland, then a permit to do so is required.

Nationwide Permits

There is a process through which a landowner can sometimes avoid the lengthy process of obtaining a discharge permit from the Corps. If the proposed activity or the affected land falls in the category of a similar nature, such as bank stabilization activities or discharges incidental to bridge construction, it is possible to apply to the Corps for a nationwide permit. With such a permit, the landowner is not required to inform the Corps of activity so long as the required conditions are met.

Enforcement

The Corps and the EPA share enforcement powers for violations of the wetlands program. Under a Memorandum Agreement between the two agencies, the Corps handles enforcement actions involving violations of Corps-issued permits and instances of unpermitted discharges. The EPA is the lead agency solely in unpermitted discharge cases that involve repeat violators and flagrant violations.

Enforcement action may also be instigated by citizen groups who may sue the regulatory agencies for improper issuance of a permit or illegal actions by the alleged violator. However, these groups are not entitled to compensation for damages they may have suffered, but they can seek compliance and the imposition of civil penalties. Citizen groups may also recover litigation costs if the court feels the award is appropriate.

STORM WATER RUNOFF REGULATIONS

For several years past, the EPA has proposed regulations covering storm water runoffs that affect municipal storm sewer systems, industrial storm water runoffs, and construction activities that disturb more than five acres of ground. A strong negative response from both industrial and real estate interests caused Congress to statutorily bar the EPA from promulgating these regulations. The time allowed has now expired, meaning that any significant real estate development is now subject to the regulations.

In the language of the EPA, a "point source" of liquid waste occurs when, say, an industrial plant discharges waste through a pipe. A "nonpoint source discharge" is when rain falls on land or a parking lot and runs off into a creek without being diverted into a retention pond.

The main target of the EPA regulations initially is directed to municipalities and their handling of storm water runoff. The rules prohibit a discharge of sanitary sewer effluent into storm sewer systems. In addition, municipalities are expected to regulate the discharge of pollutants such as pesticides, herbicides, and fertilizers into storm sewer systems. A phase-in period is allowed for implementation of these rules.

Directly affecting the real estate developer, local governments must establish regulations as required under the Clean Water Act to control the quality of storm water runoff. The rules apply to industrial activity, construction of new developments, and significant redevelopments. Parking lot owners are now required to minimize trash and other pollutants flowing into the storm water runoff.

ENDANGERED SPECIES PROTECTION

The **Endangered Species Act** was passed in 1973 and is becoming a more significant factor in determining real property values. Under this Act, the federal government, through its U.S. Fish and Wildlife Service, has the authority under certain conditions to deny a landowner the use of his property.

The Act prohibits the "taking" of endangered species as listed by the federal government—a list that is still growing. For this purpose, taking means the killing of a particular plant, animal, fish, or insect, and is expanded to include the destruction of its habitat. The regulations state that a taking includes habitat modifications that significantly impair essential behavioral patterns of the species. In this sense, the clearing of nesting areas may be construed as a taking and thus prohibited under the law.

The very broad definition is further complicated by the fact that there is little regulatory or case law guidance as to what activities constitute a "taking." The U.S. Fish and Wildlife Service is authorized under the law to issue permits for "incidental takings," defined as "... unrelated directly to the species or its habitat...." However, since a violation of the statute carries both civil and criminal penalties, many developers have hesitated to proceed with development plans until the matter is resolved.

A case in point is the shutdown of a substantial development on the outskirts of Austin, Texas. In this case, the developer had commenced land clearing and construction when an unusual beetle and several birds of a limited species were discovered inhabiting the same area. A court then ordered a five-year halt in further development so that a determination could be made as to whether or not the wildlife comprised an endangered species subject to this Act. Later, the court modified the order permitting limited construction to resume.

Because the difficulties of this law have encouraged some landowners to "shoot, shovel, and shut up," in recent years the U.S. Fish and Wildlife Service began making deals that relaxed sections of the law. For example, golf course developers in the Carolinas agreed to provide a habitat for the red-cockaded woodpecker, which likes the openness of golf courses, as long as the government promised to do nothing legally to impair the future use of their land. Such "safe harbor" deals, and a similar law softening policy called "no surprises," have been encouraged by the Department of Interior under its then Secretary, Bruce Babbitt.

A difficult provision of this Act is that it provides a legal procedure for environmental and "no-growth" activists to challenge any new development. The Endangered Species Act authorizes citizen suits to enjoin a violation of the Act or to compel the Secretary of the Interior to enforce its provisions. It allows recovery of awards and attorney's fees in connection with private actions. The effect, of course, is a substantial increase in the risk for any new development with an added increase in the cost that must eventually be borne by the consumer.

The question arises as to whether or not a prohibition against modification, or denial of certain usages of private property, in order to protect an endangered species or the non-disturbance of a wetland area, is tantamount to condemnation. A few court cases have indicated that a regulatory authority's denial of a permit to use one's land in a certain way is a "taking" and must provide compensation for the landowner. The reasoning is that, while the right to deny a permit may be fully justified, the cost burden should not be borne solely by the landowner. However, the weight of legal opinion remains in support of a regulator's power to enforce the law regardless of a landowner's fault.

UNDERGROUND STORAGE TANKS

The Resources Conservation and Recovery Act of 1976 (RCRA) has been amended so as to require the EPA to develop a comprehensive program to prevent, detect, and correct releases from underground storage tanks (USTs). Under the EPA definition, a UST is any tank that has 10 percent or more of its volume below ground and contains either petroleum or hazardous substances. The EPA estimates that 2 million USTs are covered by the regulations and that 95 percent of those are used to store petroleum and its products.

Certain tanks are excluded from the definition, including farm or residential tanks of 1,100 gallons or less storing fuel for noncommercial purposes, heating oil tanks for consumption on premises, septic tanks, wastewater collection systems, and storage tanks located in an enclosed underground area (basement). Even though excluded by the EPA, state or local laws may cover these types of tanks.

UST owners must provide certain safety precautions, including corrosion protection, leak detection by monthly monitoring or inventory control and tank tightness testing, and spill and overflow devices. Compliance was a phased-in requirement.

USTs installed after December 1988 must have all of the requirements in place upon installation. Qualified contractors must install new tanks according to code and owners must provide the EPA with certification of proper installation. The same is true for tank removal.

There are reporting requirements for containment of leaks and spills, plus various records that must be kept to evidence a tank owner's ongoing compliance with the regulations. Since October 1990, owners and operators of USTs must demonstrate responsibility for corrective actions and be able to compensate for injury or property damage from $500,000 to $4 million, depending on the number of tanks owned.

If a landowner discovers an underground tank on the property, the first question is to find out what it contains and in what condition it may be. Some abandoned tanks have been filled with sand, gravel, or other inert material. If the tank contains a liquid, the landowner needs to find out what it is so it can be disposed of properly. Also a determination must be made as to whether or not the tank has leaked or is leaking. A professional may be needed to perform a tank tightness test. If a hazardous substance is involved, a report to the EPA may be necessary.

Landlords whose tenants have tanks, mortgagees whose borrowers have tanks, and purchasers of property on which tanks are located must make sure they are in compliance with regulations. Familiarity with these regulations, which may also include state and local laws and rules, will enable a real estate agent to provide competent, professional suggestions in transactions involving USTs.

ELECTROMAGNETIC FORCES

Most environmental concerns are real and should always be considered when dealing with land and what may be built on it. Yet, there is no doubt that some people profit from environmental scares. Whether or not electromagnetic force is mostly a scare tactic or a real concern has yet to be fully determined. But because it could be a consideration in buying or evaluating property, it is a subject that an investor must consider.

Electromagnetic fields fit nicely into scare tactics. They are silent, invisible, and few nonscientists know what they are or where they come from. Yet they exist anywhere electrons zip through transmission lines, or the innards of appliances, or electric blankets, so they are nearly impossible to avoid.

Over the years, various studies have linked electromagnetic fields (EMFs) to cancer. In 1979, epidemiologists found that children living near high-current power lines in Denver got leukemia at 1.5 times the expected rate. But those studies are hobbled because it is nearly impossible to continuously monitor actual EMFs inside thousands of houses. So a stand-in for EMF exposure is used. The stand-in is called a "wire code rating" and reflects a home's distance from a power line and the size of wires close by. But when researchers actually measure EMFs, they find that fields are no higher in homes with leukemia cases than homes without.

Thus far no clear relationship has been found between the strength of an electromagnetic field and the incidence of leukemia. In November 1996, the National Research Council, after three years of examining more than

500 studies, issued its report, which states: "The current body of evidence does not show that exposure to these fields presents a human-health hazard." There is one possible exception—everyday levels of EMF do suppress a cell's production of melatonin, a hormone that slows the growth of breast cells on their way to becoming cancerous.

The federal government has researched problems with EMFs but, so far, has issued no rules or regulations. States vary somewhat in their approach to the problem and have regulated power line construction and its improvement in several different ways, but the science suggests EMF's are far less a concern than once suggested.

MOLD

Mold has likewise received endless condemnation in the press and in the tort law, but except for persons already immune-compromised or with mold-specific allergies, mold represents no grave health risks. It may smell, and be unpleasant, and as the result of susceptible juries lead to negative impacts on real estate values. However, "no studies have shown that inhalation of mold spores, and possibly mycotoxins (the most toxic molds), at levels expected in mold-contaminated indoor environments are responsible for causing measurable health effects." (Harbison, et al, "Toxicology and Risk Assessment of Mycotoxins, *Journal of Land Use*, Vol. 19, No. 2, Spring 2004). Extensive research affirms this finding. In fact, a mycotoxin specialist remarked upon viewing the hazmat suits worn by laborers cleaning homes after Hurricane Katrina in New Orleans; he said the gravest health risk being taken by the laborers was *not* the mold they were guarding against with their body-covering white suits and breathing filters, but the risk of heat-stroke from wearing the suits in the oppressive heat and humidity of the late-summer Gulf Coast!

But, as a result of continuing legal action, and the ability of tort lawyers to sway otherwise well-intentioned but misinformed juries, real estate practitioners and inspectors need to understand the mold issue. The presence of mold or mold-causing conditions, such as previous water damage, should be disclosed by sellers—especially when a homeowner knows about an ongoing mold problem that may not be apparent from a basic inspection. When to disclose is a fact-specific legal issue, but mold disclosure will probably not be uncommon in the near future. Bleach and primer, along with ample mildecide in fresh paint, can typically abate mold problems indefinitely, provided the homeowner or property manager is vigilant in preventing moisture accumulations later on or within a building.

CARBON MONOXIDE

Carbon monoxide (CO) is an odorless, colorless gas produced by the combustion of fuels such as natural gas, oil, and propane in devices such as furnaces, water heaters, and stoves. These items are normally designed to vent the CO to the outside, but harmful interior levels of CO can result from incomplete combustion of fuel, improper installation, or blockages, leaks, or cracks in the venting systems. Homeowners can take action against potential CO poisoning by following the steps given below:

- Have all fuel-burning appliances professionally inspected yearly, preferably before the start of the cold-weather season when heaters and furnaces are first used.
- These appliances include gas stoves and ovens, furnaces and heaters, water heaters, generators, and clothes dryers.
- All such devices should be properly installed and vented to the outside whenever possible.
- If repairs are necessary, be sure they are performed by a qualified technician.
- Always use the proper fuel specified for the device.
- Have flues and chimneys for fuel-burning fireplaces or wood stoves inspected regularly for cracks, leaks, and blockages that may allow a buildup of CO to occur.
- Never use gas stoves or ovens to heat the home, even temporarily.
- Do not start or idle a vehicle in a garage, even with the outer garage door open. For additional protection, purchase a CO detector (either battery operated or plug-in) and follow the manufacturer's instructions for proper location and installation.
- Learn what to do should the CO alarm activate.

If anyone in the home experiences symptoms such as fatigue, dizziness, blurred vision, nausea, or confusion, everyone should leave immediately and seek medical attention. If no symptoms are felt, shut off all fuel-burning devices that may be potential sources of CO. Professionals differ on whether windows and doors are to be opened or left closed. It would be well-advised for landowners to check with professionals in their area.

FINANCING SOLAR POWER

The sun's energy is clean, cheap, and plentiful, but the upfront costs of installing solar panels once presented a daunting barrier to entry for many companies. Fortunately a financing tool, known as **Power Purchase Agreements (PPAs)**, is clearing the path. Though the details vary from state to state and from company to company, PPAs are based on the same general framework:

- A third-party solar company funds, installs, and maintains a solar energy system for the participating business.
- The solar company then sells electricity to the business, usually on a 15- to 20-year, fixed-rate contract, often at prices lower than those typically offered for electricity by the local utility.

In California, Macy's used a mix of PPAs and traditional solar panel purchases to put solar arrays on the rooftops of 26 stores—while upgrading its lighting, heating and cooling, and energy-management systems to boost efficiency. The result is an estimated 40 percent reduction on its utility bills and an estimated 88,450 metric tons annual reduction in CO_2 emissions.

Other major companies, including Wal-Mart, Whole Foods, Kohl's, Staples, Target, Kinkos, Google, and Microsoft, have also entered into PPAs with various providers. The benefits, for both business and the environment, are multiple:

- Eliminate the financial barrier to entry normally associated with **solar power**.
- Reduce demand for conventional energy sources.
- Cut CO_2 emissions.
- Add renewable power to the grid.

At a time of volatile energy prices, PPAs also give companies predictable electricity bills and the opportunity to save money on operating costs. Industry analysts predict PPAs will gain 65–75 percent market share for commercial solar installation in 2008 alone. However, continued growth is dependent upon the expansion of state and federal solar incentives. PPAs are currently most prevalent in states with favorable government programs, like California and Hawaii.

WIND ENERGY

Environmental Concerns

Even though wind energy is renewable and apparently environmentally beneficial, it seems as though there are some who oppose the wholesale conversion of wind energy into electricity. Perhaps the most vocal opposition to wind energy comes from a minority of environmentalists, who object to the destruction caused when birds and bats collide with the spinning wind turbine blades. Wind power, however, is perhaps the most favored renewable energy option among most environmentalists and environmental groups. Migratory and indigenous avian mortality is, however, associated with wind power generation—just as deer mortality from cars increased with the construction of the interstate highway system—and greater mortality will result as wind power generation expands; this is a topic for continued discussion, no doubt, as the "green" movement grows.

Construction Time for Wind Farms and Transmission Lines

Construction time for wind farms is out of sync with construction time for transmission lines needed to transport the electricity. It takes about a year to build a wind farm, but about five years to construct transmission lines to send power to cities. Presently, the capacity to generate electricity in the favorable wind regions exceeds the capacity to move it, resulting in "stranded" electricity.

Tax Implications of Expanding Wind and Solar Energy

Federal encouragements for the production, transmission, and consumption of wind- and solar-generated electricity will likely expand in the coming years. These encouragements, along with the likely relaxation of any standard that stands in the way of these renewable energy sources, will favor them for

CASE STUDY **3.3**

The Coastal Habitat Alliance Sues to Halt Construction of Wind Farms

The Coastal Habitat Alliance Inc., formed to protect the Texas Gulf Coast, filed federal and state lawsuits in December 2007 seeking to halt construction of two wind farms. The suit alleges that state officials and developers violated the Federal Coastal Zone Management Act by building the farms without an environmental review or permit. Loss of scenic beauty and possible harm to the bat population resulted in a moratorium on wind development in Gillespie County, Texas.

Several other lawsuits were filed against landowners and wind farms alleging they constituted an unreasonable interference with the use and enjoyment of nearby property. Loss of view and noise were two of the primary complaints. At the trial level, the lawsuits proved unsuccessful. Texas case law supports the free use of property in a legal, non-nuisance manner.

The Texas courts have repeatedly ruled that the owner of real estate may, in the absence of restrictions or other regulations, erect a building, wall, fence or other structure on the premises, even if it obstructs a neighbor's vision, light, or air and even if it depreciates the value of a neighbor's land. The court dismissed the issue of the wind farm's visual degradation by granting the defendants summary judgment. This was appealed.

The trial basically ended when a landowner near the wind farm testified that noise from jet engines at Dyess Air Force Base about 20 miles away drowned out any noise from nearby wind turbines. The 11th Court of Civil Appeals upheld the trial court's decision to grant the defendants summary judgment regarding wind farms' visual impact. Ruling on case precedents, the court said, "Matters that annoy by being disagreeable, unsightly, and undesirable are not nuisances simply because they may to some extent affect the value of property."

---

at least the intermediate future, independent of their actual economic disincentives. Fossil fuels are very cost-effective sources of energy production, and "competing" with them (coal and natural gas power plants enjoy a three- or four-fold cost savings advantage over solar and wind power) with wind or solar power will require continuing tax and regulatory incentives. Absent those tax incentives or regulatory requirements, the wind and solar facilities will not be built on any sort of meaningful scale.

ENVIRONMENTAL CONSTRAINTS AND GLOBAL WARMING: SOME CONCLUDING REMARKS

In late 2009, most of the countries of the world met in Copenhagen to discuss world-wide environmental degradation, atmospheric carbon dioxide levels, and the purported warming of the planet due to human activities. While no meaningful contractual obligation of the participating nations derived from the conference, it nonetheless underscored the intensity of the feelings of a great many peoples about the damage done to the earth by human activity.

The extension of these feelings to potential impacts upon real estate investment value is fairly straightforward. Lenders and prospective buyers or tenants often reject involvement with a property simply because of the prospect of *potential* environmental degradation (as with a nearby dry cleaner or gas station) later on. Thus, the environment should be favored in as many of the real estate investor's activities as possible, if only as a marketing ploy (solar panels on the roof) and to curry favor among neighbors (xeriscaping to minimize irrigation water consumption) and prospective tenants, lenders, or buyers.

Lead content in household items, asbestos, the presence of PCB's and PCE's in ground water, and public aversion to ubiquitous molds and mildews because they *might* engender some health risk are all emblematic—whether good or bad and largely independent of their basis in fact—of a move towards environmental *sensitivity* by the citizenry. This movement should be kept in mind as the investor anticipates regulatory change, and as the property owner sells or leases her real estate investment.

KEY TERMS

asbestos	Endangered Species Act	phase assessment	potentially responsible party
brownfield	innocent landowner defense	polychlorinated biphenyls or PCBs	Power Purchase Agreements (PPAs)
carbon monoxide			
CERCLA	lead	polychloroethylene or PCE	wetlands protection
electromagnetic forces	mitigation banking		

DISCUSSION QUESTIONS

1. Discuss the nature of and restrictions applicable to toxic waste sites.

2. Define the rules applicable to the handling of asbestos located in a public building.

3. What criteria are used to judge a wetlands area?

4. If a wetlands area is located on an owner's property, what obligations are involved?

5. What rules control the use of land containing an endangered species or its habitat?

6. What are the chief indoor air contaminants that impact real estate?

7. What recent case laws affect current decision making regarding real estate investments? This discussion item will require accessing the Internet for research purposes.

8. What are some of the problems precluding the unlimited use of wind energy?

9. In what three main products has the federal government mandated the reduction or complete elimination of lead content? Why was this action taken?

10. What are some of the ways that a real estate investor might show her environmental awareness with a new strip shopping center?

CHAPTER 4

Ownership of Real Property

Land is everlasting, and that makes it different from everything else that can be owned. Land can be used for many purposes. The laws concerning landownership have developed in ways that recognize the many uses of land and the changing needs of the population. Landownership consists of legal rights, which can be limited in nature and duration. When a person owns all of the rights to a tract of land with no time limitation, the ownership is termed "fee simple." As the number of ownership rights diminishes, so does the quality of ownership. Following are the major rights to land:

- *Possession.* The actual holding or occupancy of land.
- *Use.* The employment of the property.
- *Enjoyment.* The right to use without interference or harassment.
- *Disposition.* The right to sell, lease, mortgage, give away, or otherwise dispose of the land.

How these rights are held differentiates the various land interests, or **estates**, that can be owned.

In modern law, the right of **disposition**, which includes the right to sell or mortgage the property, necessarily includes the right to determine the duration of the ownership term. It is this crucial right of disposition—more than mere possession or use, both of which can be obtained under a lease—that provides the best test of ownership.

Land rights and ownership methods are embodied in the laws of each state, and there are differences that stem from the origin of the region. The eastern and midwestern states normally follow English common law. The southwestern states incorporate Spanish law, with its emphasis on community property rights. Louisiana is unique, with property rights based on French civil law.

This chapter focuses on real property law and is intended to provide the real estate investor with an overview of the law and its terminology. By understanding the major rights that are involved in landownership and the complex nature of the law, the investor can readily recognize the need for competent legal counsel. The conveyance of land is a legal matter best handled by a qualified attorney. However, an investor can better understand legal advice if he or she holds a basic knowledge of the subject and its terminology.

CLASSIFICATION OF ESTATES

The laws of real property concern the many aspects of landownership, its use, and its conveyance. Its subjects include estates, ownership, leaseholds, contracts, mortgages, deeds, land titles, recording, and more. This chapter concentrates on two of these subjects—estates and landownership. It outlines property rights as they relate to (1) the interest in land and (2) how the land is owned.

Definition of Estate

In real property law, an estate is an interest in land. It is the sum of property rights and/or things affixed to the land, which have a given duration of time (including infinity). An estate is concerned with the land; an ownership is concerned with people. But obviously the two concepts are not truly separable.

Historical Background

Today, every person in most free societies has the right to acquire an interest in land. We tend to overlook the fact that this was not always true. Going back to Roman times, ownership of land by individuals was absolute. This is called the allodial concept of ownership. But then ownership of land was restricted to an elite group of wealthy and powerful landowners. Later, another form of landownership known as the feudal system came into existence.

In the early Middle Ages as the Roman army withdrew from Europe, marauding tribes began to threaten many farmers. For protection, groups gathered under a leader pledging control of their land in return for protection from marauders. This became the feudal system and caused the rise of lords and kings with large amounts of land under their control. Under the feudal system at that time, landownership represented far more power than it does today. Landholding provided a basis for government, as well as for military protection. It was used to determine both the social and economic status of the landowner. Land was parceled out by the king to various lords, who might pass on a portion of their land to lesser lords in exchange for some form of service. Actual possession or use of the land was usually left to the lower classes, who worked the land for a share of its produce.

This right to work the land was essentially a lease and did not grant any continuing interest in the land or the right to dispose of it. Upon the death of a tenant, all rights returned to the landlord. Thus landownership was primarily an ownership of **present interest**. English land law developed as a modified feudal system dating from about the Norman conquest of England in 1066. About this same time, certain other rights to land began to crystallize which we now identify as **future interests** as well as the terminology distinguishing **freehold estates** from **nonfreehold estates**. Freehold came to mean the more extensive rights of ownership, while nonfreehold was considered to be the lease for years. Medieval law was essentially the law of freehold estates (since the rights of tenants in nonfreehold estates were not a matter of great concern). Future interests, which are principally the **reversions** and remainders stemming from life estates, began when the varieties of freehold estates came to be differentiated.

While both systems shaped the ownership of land in the United States, the allodial concept dominates because ownership of real property is free and absolute, subject only to government and voluntary restrictions.

The law—and subsequent court rulings—has identified a number of qualifications to the precise nature of land interests, which makes understanding difficult for the person who is not a student of the law. Further confusion results from the fact that the word *estate* has other real estate meanings, being both a large property with an elaborate house and the property of a deceased person. For the purpose of this text, the word *estate* means the degree or quantity of interest that a person has in land, the nature of the right, its duration, and its relation to the rights of others.

There is also a distinction in the law between an heir and anyone else to whom a grantor conveys property upon his death. An **heir** is the legally designated person who would be entitled to receive the deceased person's property in the absence of a will. If a grantor conveys property by will to someone other than an heir, that person is known as a **devisee**.

MAJOR CLASSES OF ESTATES

Following is an outline of the major classes of estates, which are explained in the following sections.

1. Present Possessory Freehold Estates of Potentially Infinite Duration.
   a. Fee Simple Absolute.
   b. Fee Simple Conditional.
   c. Fee Simple Estates of Potentially Limited Duration.

    (1)   Fee Simple Determinable.

    (2)   Fee Simple Subject to Condition Subsequent.

    (3)   Fee Simple Subject to Executory Limitation.

2.   Present Possessory Freehold Estates of Limited Duration (Life Estates).

   a. Conventional Life Estates.

    (1)   Life Estate for Grantee's Life.

    (2)   Life Estate Limited by Life of Someone Other than Grantee.

   b. Legal Life Estates.

    (1)   Dower.

    (2)   Curtesy.

    (3)   Homestead Protection.

3.   Future Interests.

   a. Reversion.

   b. Remainder.

   c. Executory Interests.

    (1)   Springing Executory Interests.

    (2)   Shifting Executory Interests.

4.   Nonfreehold Estates (Leaseholds).

   a. Tenancy for Years.

   b. Tenancy from Period to Period.

   c. Tenancy at Will.

   d. Tenancy at Sufferance.

5.   Land Interests Not Deemed Estates.

   a. Easements.

   b. Licenses.

   c. Profit.

   d. Covenants.

Present Possessory Freehold Estates of Potentially Infinite Duration

The legal expression "present possessory" can be defined as "to own now." "Possessory" is to possess, or to own. "Present" means "now," not after someone has passed away or made a gift of the property. The modern definition of "freehold" is almost the same as the medieval definition, i.e., ownership of land. "Infinite duration" means that the property is inheritable by the heirs and devisees of the owner. It is not subject to "defeasance," meaning that inheritance cannot be defeated by any limiting condition in the *title* to the property.

Fee Simple Absolute

The highest and most extensive estate in common law is called **fee simple absolute.** It is inheritable and not limited to a particular class of heirs. Termination of the estate can be accomplished only if the owner dies without a will (intestate) *and* without heirs. If these two circumstances occur, the property passes to the state "by escheat."

    The origin of the term "fee simple absolute" has a historical background. The word fee derives from an old Anglo-Saxon word that meant cattle or property. In that time, cattle were used as a medium of exchange or payment; then property consisted chiefly of cattle. Today, fee means property, an estate, of potentially infinite duration. This means that nothing in the conveyance of title can cause its loss, such as not using the property as may be required by its grant of title. The word simple passes to us from English law and means there are no limits on the inheritability of the property. Title can thus be passed to anyone, regardless of who the person is. Absolute means the estate is indefeasible and cannot be divested. This means that the property is under the full control of its owner who has the right to possess, use, dispose of, or pledge the property without triggering any clause in the conveyance instrument that might divest the owner of title. Thus, fee simple, or fee as it is sometimes called, is an estate in land without limitation, which is inheritable without restrictions by the heirs of the owner. A fee simple may be absolute, as described above, or it may be qualified. Qualified means there are some conditions in the conveyance of title that may restrict future use or transfer of the property. This is more fully explained in the next section.

Fee Simple Conditional

If the owner places a limit on which heirs are entitled to inherit the property, a conditional estate may be created. In early common law, the grantor might convey land "to grantee and the heirs of his body." This wording was interpreted to mean that the conveyance was conditional on the grantee's having a child, i.e., if no children came to the grantee, then the estate became a life estate for the grantee. Such an estate would terminate with the death of the grantee, and the estate would then revert to the original grantor and/or his other heirs. This interpretation of the conditions of inheritance was modified in England in 1285 to provide a life estate for the grantee and a *fee* for his heirs. Later judicial rulings limited the fee so conveyed to a life estate. If the lineal, directly descended heirs failed to produce children, the estate, as before, reverted to the original grantor and his heirs. The result of these rulings is the **fee tail**, which is a form of estate controlled by the grantor after his death through restrictions on the class of potential transferees. This kind of restriction on who might inherit land stems from medieval English law designed to protect the landowning families. If you were not a family member, it was very difficult to gain title to the land. This concept of restricting land conveyance has not been accepted in the United States.

Fee Simple Estates of Potentially Limited Duration

When the owner, or grantor, wants to control the *use* of land after his death, the wording used to convey the property expresses the intended limitation. How the conveyance is worded determines the type of estate that is granted. This method of limitation was not available under early common law, but came into existence in England after passage of the Statute of Uses in 1536. Under modern law, there are three forms of controlling land use by words of conveyance.

1. *Fee Simple Determinable.* The words of conveyance to the grantee can read, for example, "so long as the premises are used for a public park," or "until premises are no longer used for a public park," or "while

premises are used for a public park." The conveyance may be silent as to disposition of the property if the limiting conditions are no longer met. The law holds that, in such a case, the possibility exists that the property would revert to the grantor or grantor's heirs.

2. *Fee Simple Subject to Condition Subsequent.* The words of conveyance to grantee contain a disposition clause in the event the limiting conditions are not met. These words could be "but if the property is not used for a public park, grantor may reenter." Modern law requires court action as a pre-requisite to enforcement of the grantor's right to reenter the property.

3. *Fee Simple Subject to Executory Limitation.* This form of estate is similar to "fee simple subject to condition subsequent." The distinguishing feature is that the executory limitation causes a transfer of the interest to a third party named in the instrument of conveyance, rather than a return of the interest to the grantor. The conveyance wording might be "to grantee, but if not used for a public park, then to a third party (not the grantor)."

It should be noted that all three of these forms of conveyance—fee simple determinable, fee simple subject to condition subsequent, and fee simple subject to executory limitation—create a present possessory interest in the grantee, plus a future interest for the grantor in the event that the expressed condition causes a termination of the limited fee simple estate.

Present Possessory Freehold Estates of Limited Duration (Life Estates)

A **life estate** is limited to the lifetime(s) of one or more persons. Because of its limited duration, some legal definitions class this form as a "less than freehold" interest. There are two forms of life estates: (1) the conventional form, created by an express act of the parties, and (2) legal life estates, created by operation of the law.

Conventional Life Estates

The purpose of granting a life estate is to provide for the financial well-being of the grantee during his or her life but to deny him or her the right to pass on the property to heirs or others. The limitation can be based either on the life of the grantee or on the life of someone else.

1. *Life Estate for Grantee's Life.* When the intention of the grantor is to limit the benefit from an estate to the grantee's life, the conveyance might be "to grantee for his life." The recipient might be, for example, an uncle faced with heavy family medical expenses. Upon his death, the property would revert to the grantor.

2. *Life Estate Limited by Life of Someone Other than Grantee.* In this form of estate, the conveyance would read "to grantee for the life of (a third party)." The purpose might be to provide the benefit of an income property to a brother needing assistance until the death of a parent whose estate would pass in part to the brother.

Legal Life Estates

This form of estate is created by statute (not common law). The thrust of these state laws is to protect the interests of parties to a marriage. English common law considered property acquired during marriage as belonging to the husband only. As a measure of balance, these statutes grant the wife ownership of one-third (one-half in some states) of the family's property *upon the death of the husband*. This estate owned by the wife is termed **dower right**.

1. *Dower.* To be eligible for dower rights, a wife must meet three legal requirements. These are (1) a valid marriage, (2) possession of property by the husband during marriage, and (3) the death of the husband. In those states that still recognize a wife's dower rights, a purchaser of property must obtain the wife's written consent to the sale, either through signing the deed with her husband or through a separate **quit claim deed**. Failure to obtain the wife's consent to the sale of property leaves her dower rights intact, and they may be asserted upon the husband's death at a much later date. This is one more reason for a purchaser of real property both to require a title search by a qualified attorney and to insure the title.

2. *Curtesy.* In some states a husband holds benefits in his deceased wife's property—called **curtesy**—that are similar to dower rights. These rights are not so clear as dower and may be defeated by the wife in her will. In some states the law requires that a child be born of the marriage before a husband may qualify for curtesy.

   Both the dower and curtesy rights developed from a concept of male dominance in marriage that is contrary to the modern concept of equal rights for men and women. The current trend favors a more equitable system of husband-wife property ownership, as under community property laws.

3. *Homestead Protection.* The third form of legal life estate—**homestead protection**—is associated with marriage and provides almost equal protection for husband and wife. All but seven states[1] have some form of homestead protection that amounts to a life estate in the family residence. These laws are directed toward providing legal protection for a husband and wife against the forced sale of the family home as a result of debts or judgments. The laws further restrict the rights of a husband or wife to act without the other when conveying their homestead or offering it as collateral for a loan. Depending on the state, the law may require that the homestead right be indicated by a written declaration recorded in the public records. This is unlike dower and curtesy rights, which are **automatic**—not recorded—in the states that recognize them.

---

[1] Connecticut, Delaware, Hawaii, Maryland, New Jersey, Pennsylvania, and Rhode Island (plus the District of Columbia).

Future Interests

A future interest is a right to real property that allows possession at some future time. The term itself is somewhat imprecise since the interest must also have a present existence. There are three general classes of future interests: reversion, remainder, and executory interest.

Reversion

If a grantor conveys an interest in property to someone for that person's life (a life estate) and makes no disposition of the property upon the death of the grantee, the law presumes that the grantor intended that the interest would come back to himself (revert) or to his estate. The grantor can, of course, be more specific, stipulating in the conveyance that the property reverts to him upon the death of the grantee.

Remainder

Remainder is like reversion, except that it favors a third party, rather than the grantor. The **remainder** is created when a grantor conveys a life estate to someone, specifying that upon that person's death the interest passes to a third party. For example, a man might convey an interest in real property to his wife for the rest of her life, and specify that upon her death the interest is to be divided equally among the surviving children. The children own a future interest in the property and are called **remaindermen**. Since remaindermen do hold an interest in the property, they have a right to require both maintenance of the premises and payment of taxes, property assessments, and any interest on debt secured by the property.

Executory Interests

Executory interests are future interests very similar to a remainder, except that possession is not taken immediately upon the death of the person holding the life estate. These future interests follow limited interests held by others. There are two types:

1. *Springing Executory Interests.* The interest comes after a reversion of limited duration. A typical conveyance would read "to life tenant for life tenant's life; then, one year after life tenant's death, to (a third party) and his heirs." For the year following the death of the life tenant, the interest would revert to the grantor (or his estate). At the end of that year, the fee simple interest would automatically pass to the third party named in the conveyance.

2. *Shifting Executory Interests.* The future interest comes after a limited interest in persons other than the grantor. An example of the conveyance that might be used is "to life tenant for life tenant's life; but if life tenant marries outside the faith, then to (a third party) and his heirs." A marriage "outside the faith" would automatically divest the life

tenant of the life estate, and simultaneously vest a fee simple estate in the third party.

Nonfreehold Estates (Leaseholds)

As developed under common law, the type of estate that conveys possession and use to the grantee—but retains ownership (with the right of disposition) in the grantor—is called a **leasehold estate**. It is not a freehold estate because it is not ownership of the land. The types of lease are not always clearly defined, and state laws provide some variations in interpretation. However, the following classification explains the basic kinds of tenancy under a lease-hold estate.

Tenancy for Years

This estate is defined as any leasehold with a term that must end on or before a specified date. Most states limit the number of years for which a leasehold may be created. In California, for example, the maximum term is 15 years for farm property and 99 years for urban property.

Tenancy from Period to Period

Also called a "periodic tenancy," the duration of the lease is expressed as "from (time period) to (time period)." The permissible periods may be from a day to a year in length. A term longer than one year would fall under the "for years" classification. The periodic tenancy is the leasehold found in a month-to-month apartment lease. Terminating a period-to-period lease requires some form of notification. The rule varies from state to state. Generally the notification requirement is the length of the period, but no more than six months.

Tenancy at Will

This type of leasehold estate lasts as long as both landlord and tenant wish it to last. Either party may terminate this lease at any time. Usually, however, the terminating party must satisfy a notification requirement.

Tenancy at Sufferance

When a tenant fails to vacate the premises at the expiration of a lease, continued occupancy is termed "tenancy at sufferance." This tenancy is without right, and without the landlord's consent. However, if the landlord fails to take the necessary steps to evict the tenant, continued occupancy can be interpreted as a periodic estate. Even under tenancy at sufferance, some states require a termination notice.

Land Interests Not Deemed Estates

Some *relationships* regarding land can be created between a landowner and others which fall short of being *interests* in the land. Prime examples include easements, licenses, profit, and covenants as described next.

Easements

An easement is a right to *use* a piece of land, but carries no other rights of ownership. Under the law, the right of "use" is not the same as the right of "possession."

Licenses

A license is similar to an easement, in that it grants the right to use a portion of the land. But it differs from an easement in that it is revocable. For example, the license of a guest to use an owner's home may be revoked at any time by the owner.

Profit

The right to sever and remove certain things attached to the land, such as ore or live timber, is called in the law a "profit."

Covenants

Steps an owner takes to restrict the use of land under his control are called "covenants." A covenant can benefit the noncovenanting party, but does not entitle him or her to personal use.

CLASSIFICATION OF PROPERTY OWNERSHIP

Ownership of land may be held by individuals in a number of ways. When two or more individuals hold a property, the manner in which they hold it determines whether or not each individual owner may dispose of his or her interest separately, and whether or not there is a right of survivorship. Following are the categories of ownership.

Sole Ownership

Property held by one person is called an **estate in severalty**. Don't let the legal terminology confuse you; think of severalty as *severed* ownership. Both single and married persons can be sole owners of property. However, state requirements concerning community property, dower, and curtesy rights must be considered when a married person is a sole owner.

Tenants in Common

When two or more persons hold undivided shares in a single property, they may do so as **tenants in common.**[2] No owner can claim a specific portion of the property, as each has a right to possession of the entire property. Interests need not all be the same size. Each owner can sell, mortgage, or otherwise dispose of his or her individual interest. There is no right of survivorship in this form of ownership, which means that each individual's share passes to the heirs or devisees as part of his or her estate. The share does not pass automatically to any of the other owners holding shares as tenants in common.

---

[2] Recognized by all states except Louisiana.

Ownership Example—Tenancy in Common

In most states, if two or more persons are named in the deed, and if there is no specific mention regarding how they are taking title, they are presumed to be tenants in common. When Joe Don Bailey and Billy Don Baker take title to a property, the law would consider them to be tenants in common. They would be considered to hold equal interests in the property. An important exception to this presumption is if the owners are married to each other. The assumption, in this case, is that they may be automatically considered to be taking ownership as community property.

Joint Tenancy

A **joint tenancy**[3] of two or more persons is distinguished by the following features.

1. Each owner has an **undivided interest,** with the right of possession to the entire property.
2. All joint tenants' ownerships must be acquired simultaneously. New joint tenants cannot be added later without creating a new joint tenancy.
3. There is only one title to the property, and each owner has a share in it. If a share is sold, the new owner must join with the remaining joint tenants to create a new joint tenancy, or else the new share owner becomes a tenant in common.
4. The interest of each joint tenant is considered equal, regardless of how much each has contributed. If there are two joint tenants, each would own one-half; if three, each would own one-third. If shares are claimed disproportionately, the law considers the owners to be tenants in common.
5. The major distinction between joint tenants and tenants in common is that joint tenancy includes **the right of survivorship,** i.e., when a joint tenant dies, his or her interest passes automatically and immediately to the remaining joint tenants. The deceased person's interest never becomes a part of the probate estate.

Ownership Example—Joint Tenancy

Joint tenancy, sometimes called a "Poor Man's Will," contains a right of survivorship feature. However, it really differs from a will in that a will can be changed as the principal's circumstances change and it involves only the one specific property held by the joint tenancy. A will can be changed but once a joint tenancy is formed, the title is permanently conveyed and no

---

[3] Recognized by all states except Alaska, Georgia, Louisiana, Ohio, and Oregon.

further opportunity for change exists, unless the joint tenancy is terminated. Another important aspect of joint tenancy is that it can be used to defeat dower or curtesy rights. For example, if a married woman forms a joint tenancy with someone other than her spouse and then dies, the spouse has no rights in that property.

Tenancy by the Entirety

This form of ownership is available *only* for property owned by a husband and wife. It is similar to a joint tenancy in that it carries the right of survivorship. (The surviving spouse becomes the sole owner.) It is different from a joint tenancy in that while they both live neither husband nor wife can dispose of any interest in the property without the consent of the other. Many states do not recognize this form of ownership, while others restrict its use.

Community Property

In the southwestern United States, Spanish law provided a basis for **community property**[4] ownership, which is limited to married persons. There is some variation among the several state laws, but they are all based on the concept that a husband and wife contribute equally to a marriage and should therefore share equally any property acquired during the marriage. In contrast, English law is based on the concept that a husband and wife merge upon marriage.

Under community property ownership, both spouses must sign any conveyance or mortgage on the property. Each spouse has the right to devise his or her one-half interest to whomever he or she pleases. An interest need not go to the surviving spouse. If there is no will, however, the surviving spouse retains certain rights, which vary among the community property states.

Under community property law, both husband and wife may own **separate property**, i.e., property that is excluded from the community property estate. Separate property includes:

1. Property owned by either husband or wife *before* marriage, the separate nature of which is retained after marriage.
2. Property acquired by either husband or wife after marriage through gift, devise, or inheritance.
3. Property purchased with funds that have been maintained as separate funds after marriage.

Separate property *can* be conveyed or mortgaged without the signature of the owner's spouse. Nevertheless, in a community property state, it is not unusual for a lender to require both spouse's signatures even though separate

---

[4] Recognized in Arizona, California, Idaho, Louisiana, Nevada, New Mexico, Texas, and Washington. Replaces tenancy by the entirety.

property is pledged as collateral for a loan. In doing so, the lender is simply avoiding possible future questions as to the legal distinction of separate property.

Because both parties to a marriage retain equal ownership rights to property accumulated during the marriage, community property states recognize neither dower nor curtesy rights.

TRUSTS

One method of holding real estate is in the form of a trust. The belief that trusts are only for the wealthy overlooks the advantages that they offer everyone. A **trust** places assets under the absolute control of a **trustee** for the benefit of a designated beneficiary. It protects the assets held in trust while allowing income to be distributed to its beneficiaries. While trusts must pay income tax like other taxpayers, by separating a person's income, the tax brackets for each could be lower. Beneficiaries of a trust do not participate in its management, else they risk becoming liable for the trust's operations. If the beneficial interests are transferable, a trust can be treated as a corporation for tax purposes.

A real property investment is not like other **assets**, such as cash or securities, inasmuch as it is difficult to divide into parts. For example, for property owned within a family, separate interests can be conveyed to each. This works fine so long as there is no dissension. But if one insists on withdrawing his or her interest, it could mean a forced sale of the entire property. A trust would limit this kind of action as the trustee is responsible for considering the best interests of all beneficiaries. Thus, a trust allows a person to exercise some control over how personal assets are distributed.

The creation of a trust is a complex matter and the use of this procedure should not be undertaken without professional counsel. Since there are many variations in kinds of trusts, only a few key points and some basic terminology are considered next.

Trust Estates

Assets may be assigned to a trustee for the benefit of a recipient by agreement or by will. The trustee has discretion over the operation and disposition of the trust assets, but must always act for the best interest of the beneficiary.

An example of a simple trust procedure is the transfer of property from A to B as trustee, with instructions to pay the income to C at periodic intervals. A is the grantor, creator, or trustor in this action; B is the trustee, or fiduciary; and C is the beneficiary. The property transferred is the corpus, or principal, of the trust. A new taxable entity is thus created for which returns must be filed and taxes paid.[5]

The estate or trust—unlike a partnership—may be required to pay a federal income tax, as may the beneficiary of a share of the estate's income.

---

[5] For further information, see IRS Publication Number 448, "Estate and Gift Taxes, Federal."

There is no double tax, however, as with a corporation. Some trusts require the distribution of all current income, which must be reported by the beneficiary whether or not it is actually received. Other trusts grant the trustee discretion to distribute all or part of the current income. The beneficiary must then report only the income that is required to be distributed plus any optional distribution actually made during the tax year. Any losses incurred by the estate or trust are generally not deductible by a beneficiary.

Inter Vivos Trust

An inter vivos trust is one that takes effect during the life of the trustor or creator of the trust. One can transfer property to a trustee with instructions that income from the trust be paid to one's children, a spouse, relatives, or a charity.

Testamentary Trust

A testamentary trust takes effect after the death of the creator. An individual can leave instructions in a will that upon death certain assets are to be placed in a trust. A bank, a trust company, or even a friend can be designated as trustee. Instructions are left to the trustee as to who the beneficiaries will be, how and when the trust income should be disbursed to them, and how the assets are to be managed. Because trusts offer property management and financial control as well as a number of tax and estate planning advantages, this form of property ownership is growing in popularity.

Land Trust

The **land trust** is a form of ownership permitted in Illinois, Indiana, Florida, North Dakota, and Virginia. Under the land trust procedure, a landowner conveys title to a trustee under a trust agreement that designates the beneficiary and gives the trustee full power to manage the property according to written instructions from the beneficiary. The beneficial interest is not transferable and is considered personal property (even though the asset is real estate), which simplifies the succession of ownership.

One advantage of the land trust is that it allows privacy of ownership—only the trustee's name appears on the record of title. Because this procedure can also be used to conceal conflicts of interest or withhold material information from a potential purchaser, its use has been restricted in most states.

Real Estate Investment Trust (REIT)

In passing the **Real Estate Investment Trust** Act in 1960, Congress intended to provide a means for the smaller investor to participate in real estate projects, as well as to increase the amount of money available for real estate financing. As an incentive, the Act permits a trust that qualifies under its requirements to pay no tax at the corporate level. Thus income is taxed only once—when it is distributed to the shareholders. REITs are further examined in Chapter 9, where evolving regulations are discussed.

The pooling of funds from smaller investors—thereby creating a substantial investment capacity—is the same general concept used by mutual funds (for investment in stocks and bonds), drilling funds (for oil and gas drilling prospects), and money market funds (for the purchase of Treasury bills or other short-term paper). REITs have been sponsored by banks, insurance companies, and a few mortgage companies, with management of the investments contracted to a specialized management team. The REIT investor has little voice in management and generally selects among funds by comparing their investment policies and records of accomplishment. Beneficial interests usually sell for $100 or less per unit.

To qualify as an investment trust under the Act, each year a trust must:

1. Be beneficially owned by at least 100 persons holding transferable shares or certificates, with not more than 50 percent of its shares held by five or fewer individuals.
2. Earn 95 percent or more of its gross income from passive sources including dividends, interest, real property rents, or gains from sale of stock, securities, and real property.
3. Earn 75 percent or more of its gross income from real property rents, interest on real property, or gain from its sale.
4. Generally have 75 percent of its assets represented by real estate assets, cash, or government securities.
5. Distribute a percentage of income to its shareholders subject to certain rules and penalties.

The 1986 Tax Act granted some relief to prior rules regarding distribution of an REIT's income. The required distribution, loosened in 2009, was: 85 percent of ordinary income, 95 percent of capital gain net income, and any shortfall of distribution from the prior year.

There is a 4 percent excise tax on any excess of that amount required to be distributed over the amount actually distributed in any one calendar year. More recently, the REIT concept has been utilized in the disposition of large properties. By conveying an asset, such as Rockefeller Center, to an REIT, the former owners are able to convert their asset into cash through the sale of interests in the asset-holding REIT.

Ownership Example—REIT

All American Realty has property holdings around the country. They want to raise a significant amount of equity dollars. They want to do this by creating an equity REIT. They choose the following holdings to include in the public offering:

Three apartment projects in Texas

A downtown office building in Atlanta

A four-building office park in San Diego

Regional shopping centers in Colorado, Nevada, New York, Connecticut, Massachusetts, Florida, and Illinois

Choice raw land tracts in seven different states.

The participants in the REIT will have the equivalent of a stockholder's interest in all of these properties and will benefit from profits, much like dividends. As an alternative, All American Realty could form a debt REIT where the investors would be providing financing for various properties. In this case, the investors would be in a similar situation to bond holders and would receive a fixed return much like mortgage payments.

KEY TERMS

assets	fee simple absolute	life estate	remaindermen
automatic	fee tail	nonfreehold estates	reversions
community property	freehold estates	present interest	right of survivorship
curtesy	future interests	quit claim deed	separate property
devisee	heir	Real Estate Investment Trust	tenants in common
disposition	homestead protection		trust
dower right	joint tenancy	remainder	trustee
estate in severalty	land trust		undivided interest
estates	leasehold estate		

DISCUSSION QUESTIONS

1. Discuss the meaning of an "estate" and its historical background.
2. What is meant by "homestead protection" as a legal life estate?
3. Describe a lease as a nonfreehold estate.
4. What is the purpose and use of an "easement"?
5. Discuss the use and meaning of "community property."
6. What are the major rights in land?
7. Name the different forms of legal life estates.
8. What is meant by the term "inter vivos trust"?
9. Give an example of who would be considered a remainderman.
10. What circumstances would exist to create a tenancy at sufferance?

CHAPTER 5

Legal Documents

The documents involved in income-producing investment properties can be exceedingly complex because of the many considerations involved. Unlike documents involving residential properties, which are frequently "fill-in-the-blank" promulgated forms, commercial documents are almost always prepared by attorneys specifically for the property involved in the transaction.

When a major company was negotiating a lease for a large space in New York City, it took two years just to prepare the letter of intent! Leases for much smaller spaces can be just as complicated because there are so many items to be dealt with. Even though attorneys draw up these documents, it is important that real estate professionals, real estate investors, lenders, appraisers, developers, and other real estate practitioners be knowledgeable about the architecture and contents of the major legal documents.

Three of the important documents that will be discussed here are (1) the deed, (2) the earnest money contract, and (3) the commercial lease. While these documents may differ widely from transaction to transaction, many standard features will be common to most commercial legal documents.

THE DEED

A **deed** is a written instrument by which a property owner as "grantor" conveys to a "grantee" an ownership interest in real property. There are many types of deeds, including warranty deeds, bargain and sale deeds, quit claim deeds, gift deeds, executor's deeds, sheriff's deeds, and deeds in trust. The major difference among them is the type of covenant made by the grantor. Probably the most commonly used deed is the general warranty deed.

Title to leasehold property is transferred by an "assignment of lease" document rather than a deed.

To be valid, a deed must contain the following elements.

Grantor

The deed must name a grantor who is of legal age and sound mind. A mistake in spelling of the grantor's name or signature does not invalidate the deed if the identity is otherwise clear. If there are multiple property owners, each must be named as a grantor in the deed to convey his or her interest, or each may convey separately in separate deeds.

Grantee

There must be an actual grantee. Thus, a deed delivered to a corporation before its coming into legal existence (by filing its articles of incorporation) is void for lack of a grantee. A deed delivered to the estate of a dead person is void, although a deed delivered to a minor or incompetent is valid. Whereas a deed to a fictitious person is void, a deed to a person using a fictitious name is valid. It is a good idea to include the status of the parties—such as married, minor, trustee, or personal representative. A grantor cannot be the sole grantee, but the grantor could convey the property by deed jointly to the grantor and another person, or to the grantor's corporation.

A deed is not operative as a valid conveyance until the grantee's name is inserted in it by the grantor personally, by someone at the grantor's request and in his or her presence, or by the grantor's agent duly authorized in writing.

Consideration

A deed should recite some consideration, although in most cases it need not be actual consideration. Most deeds recite a nominal consideration, such as "for $10 and other good and valuable consideration." Deeds granted by fiduciaries, however, must state the actual consideration, and in all cases the contract of sale states the actual consideration.

Words of Conveyance

Words such as "I hereby grant and convey" distinguish the deed from a mortgage instrument.

Legal Description

There must be a legal description of the land conveyed, either by metes and bounds, by lot block and subdivision, or by a government survey description. In a condominium deed, however, the apartment designation and post office address are generally sufficient because the full legal description is already recited in the recorded declaration. Note that if the deed conveys more property than the seller actually owns (through an incorrect legal description), the deed is not void but is usually valid for that portion of the description actually owned by the grantor.

Signature

The grantor must sign the deed. If the grantee is assuming an existing mortgage or is agreeing to abide by a restrictive provision in the deed, then the grantee is also required to sign. In some states, the signature must be witnessed and/or notarized. A date of execution is not essential but is customary and tends to establish the date of delivery.

Delivery

A deed must be delivered to be valid. Delivery is the final act of the grantor, signifying an intention that the deed shall currently take effect. However, when transferring property registered under the Torrens system, it is the registration of the deed and not the act of delivery that conveys title.

Upon valid delivery of the deed by the grantor and acceptance by the grantee, title passes and the deed ceases to be an operative instrument. Thereafter in law, it is merely evidence of conveyance of title, not the title itself, and thus its loss or destruction does not adversely affect the grantee's title.

The delivered deed must be accepted by the grantee. This requirement is often presumed by the courts where beneficial to the grantee (called **constructive acceptance**), as in cases of a beneficial conveyance to a person incapable of consenting, such as a deed to a minor or an incompetent person. The acceptance can be presumed by the grantee's retaining the deed, recording the deed, encumbering the title, or any other act of ownership.

Though not essential for validity, a deed is normally recorded to protect the grantee against claims of a third party. For valid recordation, a deed must be properly recorded in the chain of title.

THE EARNEST MONEY CONTRACT

Any successful investment in real estate depends on the terms and conditions of the acquisition of the property. A property must be purchased under the right conditions or even the best real estate may not yield the desired results. The proper terms and conditions must be spelled out in the purchase contract. While each purchase agreement is unique, there are numerous features that will most likely appear in most contracts.

In most cases, the actual document will be prepared by an attorney. However, it is important that the principles and their agents be familiar with the basic contents of the contract. The following items should be considered when structuring the earnest money contract.

The Parties

The sellers should be identified exactly as they are named in the deed records. If more than one entity owns the property, all must agree to the sales contract. Also, the purchaser should be accurately identified to facilitate future assignments or transfers. In many cases the parties are other than individuals. Corporations, partnerships, trustees, and joint ventures are frequently utilized as purchasing entities. It is quite important that the entity be described accurately in the contract.

Consideration

The consideration, or purchase price, should be described in the proper detail. There may be items other than cash that need to be clarified. For instance, there could be assumptions of existing financing as part of the consideration. Also, owner financing in the form of wraparound mortgages, second liens, or earn-out financing could be part of the consideration.

Survey and Metes and Bounds Description

Most transactions will require a new on-the-ground metes and bounds survey. This paragraph should indicate who pays for the survey since this is typically negotiable.

Financing Conditions

Large investment properties are typically financed by institutions requiring extensive documentation. As a result, arranging financing can be very time consuming so ample time should be requested in the contract. If financing cannot be arranged to the purchaser's satisfaction, then the contract should allow cancellation. The contract should stipulate that the sellers will assist in the loan application process in any way possible since it will be mutually beneficial to buyer and seller.

Earnest Money

This is a difficult item to negotiate since the sales of most large investment properties take many months to consummate. The seller will want as much money as possible to compensate for taking the property off the market for an extended period. On the other hand, the purchaser will not want the money tied up while he or she is expending considerable funds in doing the due diligence. Sometimes the seller may be willing to accept a promissory note with the expectation of receiving all of the materials and documentation that the purchaser has generated in performing due diligence.

Property Inspections

An essential feature of any purchase agreement is the provision for the inspection of the property. This typically is an extensive, expensive, and time consuming process. As a result of the inspections, the purchaser may want to cancel the contract or negotiate remediation of any problems that are discovered.

Environmental Assessments

To maintain the innocent landowner defense, the purchaser must have performed certain environmental assessments prior to accepting title. There are many environmental considerations that could dramatically affect the soundness of the purchase. Chapter 3 discusses these issues. The discovery of contamination or other environmental problems may dissuade the purchaser from consummating the transaction.

Title Exceptions

Title exceptions need to be researched and dealt with. Many title matters are endemic to the property and cannot be removed. There may be certain encumbrances that cannot be cured and therefore the contract will be canceled. However, some issues, such as tax liens and other encumbrances, may have to be cleared up before the purchaser will be willing to proceed to close. Since investment properties are frequently very large, the purchaser may want to delete the standard exception as to area and boundary discrepancies in the title policy. Typically, an additional premium must be paid for this kind of title insurance. This paragraph should stipulate who pays the extra premium.

Case Law

Strictly Construing an Ambiguous Contract Against the Maker

A real estate broker sued its client for an alleged breach of a residential buyer/tenant representation agreement. The broker was granted the exclusive right to act as the real estate agent for the purpose of buying or leasing property during a six-month period.

The commission terms of the agreement included the provision that the broker was to receive 6 percent of the gross sales price if the client agreed to purchase property in the agreed-upon market area. The disputed term of the agreement arose over the specific form of the lease commission agreement, which stated: "if client agrees to lease property in the market a fee equal to (*check only one box*) _____% of one month's rent or 6% of all rents to be paid over the term of the lease." Neither box was checked on the executed exclusive agency agreement.

It was agreed by all parties, and found by the court, that the broker was to represent the client in the purchase or lease of real estate. The court found that the lease commission provision was ambiguous, and could be read in "one of two ways: (1) as providing for a lease commission because the number "6" is typed, or (2) as making no provision for a lease commission because no box is checked."

This ambiguity was the result of the broker not closely following the instructions on the form, and the omission of the check was considered a scrivener's error. Since an ambiguity exists as to what the contract means, the court strictly construed the contract against the maker of the document, the broker, and held "the agreement made no provision for a commission when the client leased the property because no commission calculation was selected."

Compliance with Regulations

Compliance with all governmental regulations, such as zoning ordinances, building codes, sanitation laws, county flood controls, Fair Housing laws, Americans with Disabilities Act requirements, deed restrictions, etc., should be verified. The purchaser will not want to inherit any existing problems with a property that is not in compliance with all appropriate regulations, codes, ordinances, and restrictions. As with inspections and title matters, any problems either need to be solved or dealt with in some manner, or they may cause a cancellation of the contract.

Assessments

The contract should contain a provision allowing the purchaser to research any assessments or pending condemnations—paving assessments or the like. Commercial properties are frequently encumbered with a paving assessment that requires annual payments for several years into the future. The assessments pass with the property so they could become a liability for the purchaser. Therefore, the purchaser will want to stipulate options for dealing with any assessments that may be discovered. There may also be a pending condemnation of all or part of the property. This may affect the purchaser's intended use of the property and therefore his or her decision to proceed with the purchase.

Crossover Easements and Curb Cuts

Frequently a shopping center will involve multiple ownership of stand-alone retail pads. It is important for the owners of the separate tracts to have crossover agreements with the other owners so that there will be unencumbered access to all of the retail buildings. This needs to be verified prior to closing the transaction. Additionally, the existence of curb cuts, or the possibility of obtaining new curb cuts for future expansion or modification of the property, needs to be ascertained.

Estoppel Letters from Tenants

There may be problems with the tenants that may not be obvious to a potential purchaser. Therefore, it is essential to get estoppel letters from each of the tenants stating they are in agreement and compliance with all terms of the existing leases and are not contemplating any action against the landlord.

Review of All Leases

As with the other contingencies, the integrity of the leases may be a deciding factor on whether to continue with the acquisition. Typically, when a prospective purchaser has indicated an interest in a property, the owner will provide a rent roll and tenant profile. However, it is important to review the actual leases to determine if there are any contingencies that may have a deleterious effect on the soundness of the investment. One might discover that concessions have been given to a tenant that could affect future cash flows. When reviewing rent rolls it may be discovered that there are patterns of vacancy that may affect future cash flows.

Review of All Income and Expense Statements

When a prospective purchaser indicates an interest in a property, the seller will provide basic information on income and expenses but typically will not provide actual figures until a firm purchase agreement has been negotiated. So it is important to review actual income and expenses for a reasonable period prior to acquisition. Anywhere from two to five years would be a reasonable period for review. Frequently purchasers will evaluate properties based on what they think the properties will do in the future rather than what the properties have done in the past. All investors assume that they are going to do a better job of managing their properties than the previous owners. However, it is important to consider past performance to discover anomalies that may raise red flags about the property. For example, if the water bills are exceedingly high there may be problems with the plumbing. Likewise, high electric bills may indicate problems with the HVAC or the swimming pool equipment.

Insurance Coverage

Evaluate the amount of fire and hazard insurance, payment of premiums, and rights and obligations of parties in case of fire or damage to the premises from other causes during the contract period. It is important to know what obligations may be endemic to the property with regard to insurance coverage. This is one of the major expense items that an income property may sustain. Since the time between contract execution and closing may be many months, there is a reasonable chance that something could happen to the property during the contract period. The contract needs to address the rights and obligations of the parties in the event of fire or casualty damage to the property.

Review of Maintenance Contracts

Another financial obligation that encumbers a property concerns maintenance contracts and other contractual obligations. Frequently, contracts regarding properties are cancelable if the current owner sells the property. However, if that is not the case, the purchaser needs to understand the obligations that inure to subsequent owners.

Contract Situations

SCI, a successful national shopping center developer, is desirous of acquiring a well-located track of land for development of a 400,000 square foot shopping center. The location is perfect for their favorite anchor tenant, Shopper's Delight. When they draw up the contract for the purchase of the tract, they will be insistent on including a provision that "this contract is subject to purchaser, within 120 days of the effective date of this contract, having successfully executed a lease for 80,000 square feet of space to Shopper's Delight."

Of course, they will also make the offer subject to being able to obtain suitable financing. Other "subject to" provisions will include the ability to obtain municipal approval for curb cuts, zoning variances, fire and building code approvals, utility capacity approvals, flood control approvals, and many other necessary approvals.

When SCI negotiates the sale of pad sites for small strip centers or small retailers, one important provision that they will require in their sales contracts will be a provision for cross-over easements. It is important that the center have complete vehicle circulation. The center should give the public perception that it is an integral development under one ownership, when in reality there may be multiple owners.

Understanding the Issues

While the attorney who draws up the contract will be familiar with all of the necessary contingencies, it is important that the principles and their agents understand these issues. The contingencies involve business as well as legal issues and are essential to making the purchase a sound investment. Individual contracts will include many more issues, but the ones listed above apply to almost all contracts involving income properties.

THE COMMERCIAL LEASE

These elements of a commercial lease are common in almost every type of income property, which includes retail, office, office/warehouse, and most other leases in which building space is being rented.

Outline

Since commercial leases are typically quite lengthy, it is important to begin with an outline or table of contents.

The Parties

As with any lease, the parties must be legally qualified to contract (a lease is a contract) and must be properly identified. The parties to a lease are referred to as the *landlord* and *tenant* or the **lessor** and **lessee** or simply as the *parties*.

The Demised Premises

If the space being leased is in a multi-tenant building, the demised premises are typically described as a specified number of square feet in a specified location in the building. If a tenant is leasing the entire building, then the demised premises would be described by the legal description of the property.

Consideration—Rent

The rent is typically stated as a monthly charge to be paid at the beginning of each month. However, additional charges and considerations are frequently involved. The following are some of the most common considerations:

1. *Rent Increases—CPI, etc.* Because leases are frequently for extended periods (20 years with four five-year options for large retail stores), the landlord attempts to offset the burden of inflation by structuring rental increases at prescribed intervals.

2. *Pass-Through Provisions.* Office leases typically will contain a provision whereby the landlord will pay all expenses up to an agreed upon amount and then pass on all expenses above that amount to the tenants. The tenants would be obligated to pay their prorated share of all over-age expenses as additional rent. The expense level is typically calculated on a "base year" basis. If the expenses for the year the tenant signed the lease are running $10 per square foot, then the tenant would pay for all expenses above $10 in subsequent years.

3. *Base Rents—Net Usable Area/Net Rentable Area.* Because multitenant buildings have a significant amount of common areas—lobby, elevators, corridors, wash rooms, maintenance and utility closets, etc.—the tenant will typically pay for more space than exists within their demised pre-mises. As an example, if a tenant leases 10,000 square feet of "usable" space, they may be paying rent on 11,500 square feet of "rentable" space. The additional 15 percent is referred to as an "add-on factor" and may vary by the floor in the building depending on the building design. For instance, in a 12-story multitenant building, the add-on factor could be 15 percent on floors 2 through 11 and 20 percent on floors 1 and 12.

4. *Percentage Rents.* In most retail facilities, it is common practice to include, as additional rent, a percentage of the tenant's gross revenue. The amount of revenue considered would typically be the tenant's gross sales less any sales tax.

5. *Common Area Maintenance (CAM).* In most retail leases a separate share is imposed for common area maintenance. This is in addition to the base rent. In a standard strip center the base rent may be $20 per square foot and the CAM charge could be an additional $2 per square foot. This would cover such items as parking lot sweeping, exterior lighting, parking lot striping, security personnel, trash removal, and other such items that benefit all of the tenants.

6. *Expenses Paid by:*
   a. *Gross.* In most office leases the landlord pays all of the expenses, even within the tenant's demised premises. This would include vacuuming, emptying waste baskets, emptying ash trays (in those buildings that still allow smoking), and other routine maintenance. This would be limited to the "base year" pass-through provision discussed above.
   b. *Net.* The term "net lease" is frequently used for what is truly a "triple net" lease. The usage and definition of these terms—"net,"

"net/net," and "net/net/net"—vary around the country so local custom should be ascertained. The order of who pays what is generally based on the importance of payment to the landlord's ownership. "Net lease" frequently means that the tenant pays maintenance expenses while the landlord pays insurance and property taxes.

    c. *Net/Net*. This can mean that the tenant pays for maintenance and insurance while the landlord pays property taxes.

    d. *Net/Net/Net (Triple Net)*. This is the most common type of retail lease and means that the tenant pays all maintenance, insurance, and taxes. For example, if a tenant occupies ten percent of the square footage of a building for which the owner/landlord is paying $100,000 per year in CAM costs (from number 5 above), property taxes, and insurance, the tenant would be responsible for $10,000.

7. *Maintenance*. This portion of the lease describes the responsibilities for each party as regards maintenance.

8. *Taxes*. This portion of the lease describes the responsibilities for each party as regards payment of property taxes.

9. *Insurance*. This portion of the lease describes the responsibilities for each party as regards payment of property and casualty insurance. It also addresses the responsibility for and the amount of public liability insurance.

10. *Provisions for Auditing Landlord's Books*. Where the tenant is responsible for payment of expenses beyond a base year amount, the tenant will be given the opportunity to review the landlord's expense records to determine the suitability of the charges being passed on to the tenant.

Ownership Example—Joint Venture

Thomas, an experienced real estate developer, has contracted to purchase a well-located tract in the downtown area. He meets with his financial partner in many of his other ventures, a safeway insurance company. They agree to finance his proposed 15 storey office building with the provision that they share in the cash flows and ultimate profits when the building sells. Another provision in Thomas's agreement with the insurance company is that there be at least 30 percent equity in the project.

Thomas contacts a number of his former investors for the purpose of raising the equity dollars. Since the proposed development involves a great deal of risk, the investors do not want any liability beyond the initial investment. Therefore they will be forming a limited liability partnership (LP) which will be registered with the state in much the same way as a corporation.

Thomas, providing the expertise, the insurance company providing the long term financing, and the LP providing the equity dollars, will form a joint venture (JV). This entity will be very similar to a general partnership as far as the legal documents are concerned. The term JV typically describes the banding together of participants in a development venture as described above.

Because of the complexities of the negotiations with all of the potential JV partners, Thomas will make his contract to purchase the downtown tract subject to him being able to reach agreements with all parties involved. He will ask for 12 months to negotiate with his potential partners. He will state in the purchase contract that if after a year he has been unable to arrange with all of the key entities his earnest money will be returned to him and the contract will be null and void.

Term and Renewal Options

This portion of the lease establishes the term or length of the lease and any options that the tenant may have for extending the lease. For multi-tenant office space, a three- or five-year lease is typical. For larger, more extensive office space, ten years would not be excessive. Options to renew the base lease would typically involve a higher base rent. A typical box store lease could have a term of 20 years with four five-year options. Because 20 years is a long period and it is difficult to predict an appropriate base rent increase, it is frequently tied to an indicator such as the consumer price index.

Assignment and Subletting

The tenant would like the option to assign or sublet his or her space should the space requirements change during the term of the lease. However, the landlord would like to retain control of the occupants of the building and will most likely require that they approve any sublease or assignment. In a market of increasing rents, the landlord may prohibit such action to prevent the tenant from leasing their space for more money, hence competing with the landlord.

Signage

The landlord will want to control the quality and quantity of any signage on the premises. This usually applies to retail space; however, there would likely be signage in a medical or professional building.

Hold Harmless

Typically, the landlord will insist on being held harmless for things that may happen to the tenants and their visitors. Frequently the tenant will want to be held harmless for happenings caused by the landlord.

Insurance

1. *Landlord Carries*—fire and extended coverage on the building. If landlord owns multiple buildings, he or she will most likely have blanket policies that will also cover liability that is not covered by the tenant's

insurance. The tenant wants to know that the building is insured so that the space will be rebuilt in the event of a disaster.

2. *Tenant Carries*—insurance on contents and also public liability to cover visitors, guests, and customers, or clients.

Use Clause—How Will Tenant Use the Premises?

The landlord will want to specify exactly what the premises will be used for. Any variation in the usage will constitute a default in the terms of the lease.

Merchant Association

Most multitenant retail facilities will have a merchant association and will stipulate that the landlord be actively involved. The tenants may wish to schedule promotional events to attract shoppers to the property. Both landlord and tenant will want these events to be handled in an acceptable manner.

Alterations and Additions

If alterations are permitted, they must be done in conformity to the style and quality of the building. The landlord may insist that the alterations be done through or by the landlord to ensure proper control.

Landlord Obligations

This is sometimes considered as boilerplate in the lease but it is important to stipulate that the landlord will ensure quiet enjoyment for the tenant. And also, to the best of his or her ability, the landlord is to provide uninterrupted services to the tenant.

Landlord Remedies

This portion simply outlines the landlord's remedies in the event of default by the tenant of any of the terms of the lease.

Landlord Default

This segment outlines the activities or occurrences that could constitute default by the landlord of the terms of the lease.

Tenant Obligations

Among other obligations, the tenant is responsible for paying his or her rent in a timely fashion, using the premises for only the stipulated purposes, maintaining the premises in a proper fashion, and performing all of the duties incumbent in the lease.

Tenant Remedies

This portion simply outlines the tenant's remedies in the event of default by the landlord of any of the terms of the lease.

Tenant Default

This segment outlines the activities or occurrences that could constitute default by the tenant of the terms of the lease.

Parking

This section deals with any assigned parking spaces, charges for parking (if applicable), assuring compliance with handicap laws, and any other matter having to do with parking.

Common Areas

This portion describes and defines common areas and the responsible parties for maintenance of such areas.

Office Building Lease Negotiations

Hye and Wyde have a very successful agency representing many of the top professional baseball players. Their firm has just signed a contract to represent Lefty Leftowitch, the hottest prospect to come out of the college ranks in several years. In order to properly showcase their company's successes, Hye and Wyde want to move into prestigious office space in the downtown area.

The building standard for tenant finish is $12 per square foot. In order to have all of the amenities that the tenant requires—sauna, workout room, wet bar, and velveteen wall treatments—the construction cost estimate was $20 per square foot. As a concession, the landlord has agreed to pay up to $15 per square foot. Hye and Wyde had asked for a lower rent but the landlord would not budge on the rent amount. The value of the building is specifically based on the rental income so the landlord wants to keep the building value as high as possible. The landlord also reasoned that the additional amenities would make the space easier to lease out at the end of their ten year lease.

In their anxiety to have Hye and Wyde as tenants, the owners were willing to give several months free rent and to pay their moving expenses from their present location in the suburbs. However, they were adamant about not reducing the base rent. They were also adamant about the pass-through provision. The lease required that the tenant pay for any of the owner's expenses that were over $12 per square foot per year. Because the original lease term was ten years, the landlord did not want to be exposed to rising expenses.

Condemnation

What happens if all or part of the property is condemned becomes a major consideration for landlord and tenant.

Hazardous Materials Provisions

Environmental issues are exceedingly important to property owners as evidenced by the discussions in Chapter 3 of this book. Many courts have held landowners liable for damage from tenant's use of hazardous materials. This clause attempts to limit, control, or even eliminate the tenant's use of such materials.

Holding Over

This clause describes the conditions that will arise as a result of the tenant's holding over after the lease has expired. Generally, the rent escalates to an inordinately high rate to discourage the tenant from holding over. The landlord has the option of treating this as a tenancy at sufferance or a renewal of the original lease.

Landlord's Right of Entry

Because of the inherent liability to the landlord for activities of tenants on their property, the landlord will want to retain the right to enter the demised premises to determine conformity to the terms of the lease.

Noncompete Clause—Retail

It is not uncommon for tenants in a shopping center to restrict the landlord from leasing nearby space to certain of the tenant's direct competitors. This restriction does not seem as prevalent as it once was. Now it is not uncommon to see several major competitors contiguous to each other or directly across the street from each other.

Notice

This clause simply establishes the manner in which legal notice must be served to meet the requirements for having been served. It spells out the permanent addresses for each of the parties.

Destruction of Premises

In the event of partial or total damage or destruction of the subject property by fire, storm, explosion, removal, or other method, this clause stipulates the options open to the parties.

Right of Landlord to Sell Property

Because most landlords are holding the properties as investments, they will want the right to sell the property if an opportunity arises. Therefore this clause will recite the landlord's right to do so and the resulting situation for the tenant.

Broker's Commission

The broker's compensation will be stated as part of the lease rather than in a separate document. One of the reasons for this is the fact that the broker frequently will be entitled to additional compensation for each renewal option exercised by the tenant. The compensation may not be at the same rate as the initial base commission so it should be spelled out at the time the lease is negotiated. There are many ways that commissions for leases can be paid. The commissions could be cashed out up front at a slightly lower percentage, or paid on a monthly or annual basis over the term of the lease. It is not uncommon to have the rent calculated for the term of the lease and give a percent of that total rent to the broker as commission. A popular way to pay that amount is one-third when the lease is signed, one-third when construction on the space is begun, and one-third when the tenant moves in.

Trade Fixtures

A fixture is considered to be part of the real estate and therefore the property of the landlord. However, an exception to this occurs in certain instances where a tenant "attaches" trade fixtures to the real estate with the understanding that at the end of the lease the fixtures are the property of the tenant and therefore can be removed by the tenant. An example of this would be a barber's chair that is securely attached to the real estate and looks as though it is part of the real estate. However, by agreement in the lease, the barber may remove the chair at the termination of the lease. Even though the barber may legally remove the fixture, he is obligated to leave the premises in the condition it was in prior to installation of the chair.

Letter of Intent

Because a lease document is a very complex and extensive document it may take many months to prepare. For this reason, many landlords and tenants enter into a letter of intent agreement prior to the formal preparation of the lease agreement.

Work Letter

A major consideration in leasing space is the layout of the space to fit the tenant's needs. Almost all lease space must be altered for a new tenant. In many cases this alteration may be extensive and costly. Generally, a landlord will pay for a certain amount of the alteration. The quality of improvement that the landlord provides is referred to as "building standard." More than likely the tenant will want some upgrades from "building standard." These upgrades typically will be at the expense of the tenant. A work letter sets out the work to be done and at which party's expense.

SUMMARY

As indicated earlier, no two commercial leases are identical. It is critical to the viability of the lease to have a good understanding of the needs and desires of the parties. Landlords and tenants alike should be aware of the current statutes. For landlords, the awareness is critical; knowledge helps avoid liability. Tenants, on the other hand, need to know the law so they can preserve, protect, and claim their rights and remedies.

KEY TERMS

constructive acceptance	deed	lessee	lessor

DISCUSSION QUESTIONS

1. What are the principal elements of a deed?

2. Discuss the financing requirements usually found in an Earnest Money Contract.

3. What are the principal documents that should be reviewed before negotiating an Earnest Money Contract?

4. Discuss the various kinds of rent that may be found in commercial leases.

5. How are property and liability insurance handled in a commercial lease?

6. Name at least ten items that would be important to include in an office building lease.

7. Name at least ten items that would be important in negotiating a retail lease in a regional shopping center.

8. If you are purchasing a tract of land to build a 600-unit apartment project, what would be the key clauses you would want in the purchase contract?

9. What is the purpose of a "work letter"?

10. Under what conditions would you request a review of all income and expense statements in your purchase offer?

CHAPTER 6

Property Taxes and Income Taxes

Two particular kinds of taxes are of special importance to the real estate investor:

- *Property taxes*—sometimes called **ad valorem** taxes, which are levied on the value of taxable property.
- *Income taxes*—taxes on individuals and corporations based on the amount of taxable income.

The three major tax authorities—federal, state, and local—have in practice assigned the assessment of property taxes almost exclusively to local authorities; one exception is the effective property tax assessed against the value of real estate included in a taxable estate at the time of an investor's death. The taxation of income, however, is dominated by the federal government, although most states and some municipalities levy income taxes, as well.

This chapter begins with a review of property taxes, followed by an introduction to the complex world of federal income taxation. The federal income tax discussion is especially meaningful, given the changing impact of income taxes upon real estate investment over the past few decades and given also the economic distress prevalent across the globe as the first decade of the 21st century draws to a close. While varied interests assign blame for the worst recession in several decades to sundry players in the financial realm, little doubt exists that the origin of the crisis lay in real estate and real estate lending; the history of the impact of changes in the income tax treatment of real estate on the economy may offer lessons to policymakers.

PROPERTY TAXES

As a major source of revenue, property taxes support many local government programs and services. The range of these services includes governmental administration, fire and police departments, street construction and maintenance, airport improvements, public schools and libraries, parks, hospitals, flood control, and drainage. The state grants taxing authority to local districts and may participate in a portion of the revenues.

Determination of Property Taxes

Each recognized tax authority initiates three basic steps to determine the amount of taxes levied. First, the authority estimates its budget requirements for the year. Second, the taxable property within the district is appraised. And third, the tax authority's needs are measured against the total value of property subject to tax, then allocated in such a manner that each parcel pays an equitable share. Following is a discussion of the three steps.

Budget Requirements

Each taxing authority prepares its own budget for the tax year. These authorities include counties, cities, towns, school boards, sanitation districts, hospital districts, flood control units, county road departments, and in some cases, the state. To determine the authority's needs, other revenue sources, including sales taxes, federal revenue sharing, and business licenses and fees, are calculated and then deducted from the budget requirements. The balance needed must come from property taxes.

In practice, the majority of property taxes paid will go into some sort of general revenue fund of the local taxing authority, to be distributed to such interests—police, fire, parks and recreation, etc.—the local political interests choose to fund. However, in many taxing districts, local public school needs will be a separate line item on the property tax bill, and as those bills are paid, the funds move immediately into accounts supporting public schools. As well, and with many regions across the country, other "special" local funding requirements (typically capital needs for such things as highways, parks, or entertainment or convention facilities whose funding requirements are excluded from participation in other general property tax revenues) may be delineated with line items on a property tax bill, which charges when paid also move into a fund dedicated to the specific needs met with the charges. This last item may exist for a fixed period of time, and typically arises by voter approval at the ballot box.

Appraisal

Not all land within an authority's district is subject to tax, but whatever is must be appraised to determine its value. This work may be done by the county or state appraiser, or in some cases, by private appraisal companies under contract to the taxing authority. While appraisal methods vary among different authorities, the purpose is to establish a fair value for each parcel. To develop more equitable values, some states have taken steps to establish uniform procedures for their taxing authorities. These rules set appraisal standards and determine how assessments can be calculated. If property owners are not satisfied with their valuations, they have the right to challenge them and may find relief through special tax assessor hearings or through the courts.

Assessment

It is a common belief that property taxes derive directly from property value, but this is only partly true; real estate property taxes derive more specifically from the financial needs of the local taxing authority. Once those budget requirements are known, and the total value of taxable property determined, it is a simple matter to determine the **tax assessment** for a given piece of property. Practice varies as to how the assessment is determined—some districts use the appraised value as the assessed value; others use a percentage of the appraised value as the tax basis, and as outlined below many parcels of real estate are granted varying exceptions, which exceptions typically reduce the assessment and the arising property tax bill.

EXAMPLE 6.1

If, for example, the total property-tax-funded budgetary requirements of a community are $20 million—with $8 million for the town's three schools and $12 million for general needs—and the assessed value of taxable property within the community's boundaries (whether a city or a county) is $1 billion, a total tax rate of 2 percent of the $1 billion is implied. Property taxes are generally expressed as a **millage** rate, where a **mill** is one-one thousandth, and 20 mills is 2 percent. A tax bill for a residence in this community with an assessed value of $200,000 would be 2 percent (20 mills) of $200,000 or $4,000. This is often called an ad valorem (from the Latin: *to or against the value*) tax. The bill would be comprised of an 8-mill portion or $1,600 for schools, and the balance of 12 mills or 1.2 percent ($2,400) for the area's other property-tax-funded needs.

Property tax rates are generally between .5 percent (5 mills) and 3 percent (30 mills) of assessed property values across the United States, and property tax rates vary depending upon an area's dependence upon property taxes to meet budgetary needs. Property tax rates are higher in Florida, for example, with no state income tax, than in North Carolina, which assesses an income tax. This pattern is broken, though, in states like California, New York, and New Jersey, which have some of the country's highest property tax rates while also assessing among the highest state income taxes. Millage rates are readily available online and at county records offices.

Collection of Property Taxes

Property taxes carry a unique distinction in regard to priority of claim on the land since they automatically become a specific lien at the time a tax bill or ordinance is enacted. A specific lien is a claim against a designated parcel of land as contrasted to a general lien, which is a claim against all assets owned by the target of the lien. Payment of the tax releases the lien. Counties maintain separate files for property taxes as a matter of public record. This ensures recognition of any property tax liabilities whenever title is examined prior to a conveyance.

Failure to pay property taxes can result in a foreclosure and sale of the property at public auction. State laws control foreclosure procedures, but generally a property tax claim carries a very high priority, even exceeding that of a first mortgage claim that may have been recorded many years earlier. In some states, the maintenance assessments made by neighborhood associations may carry lien rights equivalent to a tax claim. These issues are of special importance in the midst of the record foreclosures taking place across the country, as lenders address the millions of non-performing mortgages through work-outs and property sales.

Property Tax Exemptions

In all tax districts, some land is exempt from property taxes. This includes government-owned property (states do not tax federal land and vice versa), parks, schools, churches, public roads, public hospitals, charitable organizations, military bases, and cemeteries. As well, some areas in the United States offer exemptions for such things as a homeowner's primary residence, handicap status or age; a homestead exemption reduction of $25,000 in a 20 mills district, for instance, equates to a reduction in the property taxes of 2 percent of $25,000 or $500. A similar exemption is offered to the disabled in Florida. Many exemptions exist across the country.

Some communities offer a limited exemption from property taxes as an inducement to attract industry. The expectation is that jobs provided by the new business will be of greater benefit to the community than the limited loss of tax revenues. Other uses of tax exemptions include special exclusions extended to encourage needed development, such as low-cost housing. Senior citizens are sometimes granted benefits that limit their property tax increases. Another interesting example of tax limitation is found in California and Texas, where qualified elderly homeowners are not required to pay property taxes when due, allowing them instead to accrue against the homestead (with interest added) for collection whenever it is sold.

Special Assessments

The revenue from property taxes need not necessarily be used for the general welfare of all taxpayers. When the need arises for an improvement, such as pavement of a street in front of a home or business, which is of special benefit to a limited area, it is possible to set up a special improvement district or a special assessment district. In such a case, all or part of the cost of the improvement is borne by the taxpayers who directly benefit. This kind of assessment may be payable in full in one tax period, or possibly in a limited number of installments. Or the cost may be covered from the sale of a special bond issue secured by an assignment of the tax assessment revenues.

Tax Revenue Bonds

The state, and its locally-authorized taxing districts, may raise money through the sale of bonds as long as they comply with state regulations and federal tax requirements. The purpose of such bond money is generally to build large facilities needed by communities, which cost more than can be paid using a single year's tax revenues. By means of borrowing money through the sale of a bond issue, the tax authority can build a hospital or a sewage treatment plant and spread its cost over the years needed to repay the bond-holders. Repayment on the bonds is made through a pledge of anticipated revenue from the new facility, or from a tax assessment. This is similar to the use of some special sales taxes, in many states, to provide new infrastructure or school funding.

Bonds issued under state or municipal authority pay interest that is exempt from federal income taxes. This means investors can accept lower interest rates on "municipals" (or "muni's," in the security brokerage lexicon) than other corporate-type bonds because the after-tax return is better; an 8 percent taxable bond for an investor in the 40 percent bracket yields an after-tax return of 4.8 percent ((1 − tax rate) × 8 percent), giving a tax-free municipal bond yielding 5 percent a better after-tax return than the 8 percent taxable bond. It is this tax advantage that encourages the use of bond money as a way to make lower-cost money available to home buyers. Recent federal tax law has placed limitations on the use of this kind of money by making a distinction between that used for private purposes (such as financing home mortgages) and that for public purposes (such as financing a water treatment plant). The use of tax-exempt bond money, such as industrial revenue bonds to pay for the purchase or improvement of privately owned commercial real estate, must undergo scrutiny by the IRS and is limited in amount.

Deductibility of Property Taxes

Generally, property taxes are deductible for federal income tax purposes. Deductions are subject to the limits of the Alternative Minimum Tax (AMT). While Congress has passed varying "patches" for the AMT, taxpayers are still subject to limitations on the deductibility of property taxes and other itemized deductions. Taxpayers from states with high state income tax rates and/or property tax rates are inordinately susceptible to having deductions such as the one for property taxes excluded, as those taxpayers are more likely to cross the IRS threshold that begins to limit deductions for individual taxpayers whose deductions reach a certain percent of income. Following are rules applicable in special situations:

1. *Homeowner*—Taxes are fully deductible (not limited to first and second home).
2. *Business*—Property taxes are fully deductible.

3. *Mortgagee*—A lender cannot deduct property taxes paid for periods prior to acquiring title to the property as such payment is considered an additional loan. If paid after foreclosure, the payment represents an additional cost of the property.

4. *Back Taxes Paid by the Buyer*—A buyer is allowed no deduction for back taxes paid to close a transaction. The sum paid is added to the purchase price.

FEDERAL INCOME TAXES

The enormous section of federal law covering income taxes is called the Internal Revenue Code. It consists of an accumulation of many years of laws and regulations, so the information contained in this section may change as a result of new tax legislation, Treasury Department regulations, IRS interpretations, or judicial interpretations of existing tax law. A review of the recent background of changing IRS treatment of real estate income is telling, both for its historical perspective and as a guide to the 21st century real estate investor and policymaker. The most meaningful changes in federal tax rules over the past thirty years follow:

Economic Recovery Tax Act of 1981 (ERTA)

Prior to the election of Ronald Reagan in 1980, real estate investors were guided in their tax planning by the Internal Revenue Code of 1954. In August of 1981, congress passed and the president signed ERTA. While offering a number of provisions intended to encourage investment and job-creation—resulting in the so-called "trickle down" effect of economic prosperity deriving first from the enhancement of capital formation—the 1981 Act created a whole new set of **depreciation** schedules and tax allowances that spurred real estate investment. Much of that investment was undertaken not because of the economic attractiveness of the investment itself, but because of the tax benefits afforded investors, independent of the "deal's" success.

ERTA replaced the 1954 depreciation allowances for commercial investment real estate with a new straight line 15-year rule. Coupled with an emergence of generous lending terms, the entry of the thrift sector into traditionally commercial banking sectors like investment real estate lending, limited partnerships and other joint ventures, the impact of the 1981 Act was striking. An example illustrates:

EXAMPLE 6.2

A $5.625 million office building is syndicated and sold to unrelated investors in early 1982, under the auspices of the 1981 Act. The building is only a third occupied, but the rental from that third is adequate to cover all operating expenses—property taxes, insurance, common area maintenance, etc. Eighty percent of the building's cost is depreciable (80 percent of $5.625 million equals $4.5 million), so the first and second year's depreciation is $4.5 million divided by 15 or $300,000. If 90 percent financing is acquired, investors borrowed (.9 × $5.625 million) $5,062,500. Also borrowed was the interest for the first two years of the loan, resulting in no out-of-pocket financing charges for the investors for the first two years. Only 10 percent equity is required on this deal, or $562,500. If ten investors each invest $56,250, and the income and expenses of the investment pass through to the investors, as with a limited liability corporation or a limited partnership (considered in greater detail in Chapter 9), the after tax cash flows for each investor seem to be impressive. Ignoring costs of financing (covered with the loan for the first two years), each investor gets one-tenth of the $300,000 depreciation allowance in each of the first two years, with no additional investment. If the investor is in the 50 percent marginal tax bracket, the highest bracket of the 1981 Act, that $30,000 non-cash depreciation deduction represents a $15,000 annual cash flow (50 percent of the $30,000 deduction), each of the first two years (with a reduction of that amount in the investor's tax bill), against an investment of "only" $56,250. To a prospective investor, not considering the consequences of having to service the mortgage beginning in the third year, this seems an extraordinary annual return of over 26 percent ($15,000 divided by the initial $56,250 investment). But the accumulation of indebtedness with the loan over the first two years, the non-rental of the vacant units in many of these investments in the early 1980s, and the later disallowance of the deductions by the IRS, revealed the folly of these sorts of investments by the late 1980s.

The 1981 Act encouraged these deals just for the tax benefits without consideration of the non-economic nature of many of the investments. Whether an office building in Houston, TX or an apartment complex in Utica, NY, most investors later regretted choosing to invest in these syndicates; the sole beneficiaries of most of the investments were the general partners and companies that packaged the deals in the first place. There were no reasons to pursue the deals except to reduce investor tax bills, and absent cash flows sufficient to fund the investments, most of the deals collapsed. The passage of the 1986 **Tax Reform Act** addressed this deficiency and the misallocation of capital resources encouraged by the 1981 Act, but the consequences of the 1986 Act for lenders, and the thrift industry in particular, were egregious.

Tax Reform Act of 1986

Seeking to simplify the tax code, and to eliminate the tax loopholes outlined above with the 1981 Act, congress passed the Tax Reform Act in October of 1986. Depreciation schedules were changed, with new allowances for a 27.5 year schedule for residential real estate, and a 39-year schedule for non-residential real estate. Depreciation of individual components, largely forgone with the 1981 Act, was re-introduced (for such things as a building's HVAC system, parking lot, or roof, which require replacement more frequently than each 27.5 years) and the 15 year allowances of the 1981 Act were eliminated. By that time, as well, the IRS and the Department of Justice had begun an ambitious investigation of the abuses of the 1981 Act, and many of the tax shelters and abuses of the 1981 Act were uncovered.

Investment property values, with greatly reduced after-tax cash flows available to investors, fell significantly after the passage of the 1986 Act. Absent the tax shelters and their adjacent attractiveness to well-heeled investors, new investments had to stand on their own merits, and not simply be conduits for deductions against the returns of taxpayers. The reduced attractiveness of the investment properties was amplified by the reduction in the top marginal federal tax rate from 50 percent to 28 percent with the 1986 Act. Interest on consumer debt and state and local taxes were no longer deductible, and the capital gains tax rate was the same as the ordinary tax rate. Pass-through losses had greater value with the 1981 Act and its higher tax rates. Losses after the 1986 Act had far less value. With falling property values, and leverage levels in the early 1980s often exceeding 90 percent, a great many properties failed and became the property of the lenders. The lenders, many savings and loans and other thrifts, burdened with non-productive assets, often failed as well. Fallout from the failure of the investments, and later of the foreclosing thrifts, led to a nationwide scandal as promoters, appraisers, lenders, and politicians shared in the blame not just for the 1981 Act itself, but for the excesses in the private sector that were encouraged by the 1981 Act. New standards for real estate lending and appraisal were adopted, and a great many of the shortfalls revealed by the 1981 Act were addressed. The sort of over-development of commercial properties that took place as a result of the 1981 Act has not recurred in the United States, though the commercial property sector came under great duress with the Great Recession.

As commercial investment real estate values fell, close to $400 billion in assets—real estate and non-performing mortgages—were seized and the Office of Thrift Supervision was created to oversee the disposition of the seized assets. The Financial Institutions Reform, Recovery, and Enforcement Act (**FIRREA**) of 1989 was passed to address the broad failure of the thrift industry in the environment that developed following the passage of the 1986 Act. The Resolution Trust Corporation (**RTC**) was established by FIRREA, its mission to close the failed thrifts, dispose of the seized assets (primarily real estate) and return the funds to the new insurers of the thrift industry, under supervision by the FDIC. It was an unprecedented endeavor, but the RTC completed its mission by 1995, disposing of the assets of hundreds of failed thrifts. The success of the RTC is a model for new legislation dealing with the millions of foreclosed homes across the US as of early 2010. Lenders have become much more prudent with commercial real estate lending. It will likely be many years before much of the dust settles and a clearer vision of the causes of the current recession—whose roots are certainly embedded in residential real estate—are known.

Economic Growth and Tax Reconciliation Act of 2001 and the Jobs and Growth Tax Relief Reconciliation Act of 2003

Both of the Bush tax cuts reduced the potential taxes, especially in absolute terms for the highest income earners, of investors. As such, after-tax cash flows from such investments as real estate were enhanced. Federal income taxes on dividends and long term capital gains were reduced to 15 percent with the 2003 Act. Investment real estate values were augmented, and with the exception of investments in residential development, the use of leverage in commercial real estate investment was largely restrained, and the sorts of excesses resolved by the RTC in the early 1990s have not recurred. Such has not been the case with residential real estate, whose collapse is at the core of the financial crisis that began to develop in 2006 and that is a certain contributor to the recession that began in 2007.

American Recovery and Reinvestment Act (ARRA) of 2009

ARRA broadly reduces taxes for most taxpayers, but increases them for many of the higher income earners who most frequently invest in real estate. This 2009 Act provides an $8,000 tax credit for first-time homeowners (or 10 percent of the purchase price, if the home cost less than $80,000), it makes special provision for selected "green" initiatives, such as providing tax credits (direct reductions in a taxpayer's federal income tax bill) of up to $1,500 to homeowners for enhancing the energy efficiency of their homes, and it makes allowances for the taxation and distribution of Real Estate Investment Trust (REIT) dividends (discussed in detail in Chapter 9). The overall impact of ARRA, and its other real estate provisions, cannot be easily determined. The recession that began in late 2007 has reduced almost all investment real estate values (except some of those in the Washington, D.C. area), and the recovery of those values to pre-recession values will likely follow an arduous path.

For the real estate investor, a general knowledge of this history and these general tax rules is important, together with an understanding of the basic language used in the tax world. The brief exposure to tax procedures in this text will not make anyone an expert, but it should serve to give the reader enough understanding to more effectively discuss questions with a tax counselor.

How the IRS interprets and implements the tax law is crucial in determining a taxpayer's liability. Tax law does not always clearly indicate how a particular tax provision should be applied, granting the IRS some leeway in its interpretations. So it becomes a combination of laws, IRS regulations, and court decisions that ultimately determines tax liability.

To better explain income taxation, the text first examines business income and some problems a taxpayer has in determining proper expense deductions. This is followed by an explanation of the four kinds of income identified in the tax code and how each is treated for tax purposes.

BUSINESS INCOME

Real estate investors are often sole owners, or participants in the ownership, of an operating business organization. While the tax laws treat each type of organization differently as to reporting requirements and even levels of taxation (see Chapter 9), the determination of income that is subject to tax is similar.

Income

Business income has many sources, and the IRS identifies a few in the following general categories for reporting purposes:

1. Gross receipts less cost of goods sold and/or cost of operations, which includes labor costs.
2. Interest and dividends.

3. Rental and royalty income.
4. Net capital gain or loss.

Deductions from Income

Most operating businesses handling income property deal with gross receipts and deductible costs of operations rather than the costs of goods sold. For this purpose, deductible expenses—as with those attaching to real estate investments—are defined by the IRS as all ordinary and necessary business expenses, including the following:

- Salaries and wages
- Management expenses
- Property taxes
- Repairs and maintenance
- Insurance
- Utility costs
- Depreciation
- Interest

It is important to make a distinction between operating and non-operating expenses; it is operating expenses that offset real estate income toward calculating Net Operating Income or NOI. And it is with NOI that the real estate investor, in later examinations in this text, estimates real estate investment value. Of the items above, everything listed is an operating expense incurred in normal day-to-day operations, except interest (a financing cost, not the burden of the property itself but a choice of the investor later *imposed* upon the property). Costs of financing, including interest, are not an operating expense, and are accounted for separately, as is depreciation, though depreciation *is* an operating expense.

Capitalizing an Expense

Under certain conditions, such as during a construction period, the taxpayer may elect, or be required, to *capitalize* an item that could otherwise be deducted as an expense. What this means is that the expense, such as construction interest cost, must be added to the property value rather than deducted in the year the cost is incurred. The IRS identifies this procedure as an increase in the *basis of value*. Then the deduction for *cost recovery* is allowed to be taken over a period of years. There is a distinction between such deductions in their terminology:

- If the capitalized item is non-tangible, like interest, the recovery of the cost is *amortized* over a period of years.
- If the capitalized item consists of tangible property, such as a specific improvement, its recovery is taken as *depreciation* over a cost-recovery time period, discussed below.

Problem Areas of Deductions

Most of the expense items listed above are easily identified and present no real problems for taxpayers. Such expenses as salaries, wages, taxes, and insurance costs are clearly defined. The more difficult expense deductions requiring definition are found in just three categories: (1) repairs and maintenance, (2) interest, and (3) depreciation, or cost recovery, deductions.

Repairs and Maintenance

The big question for the taxpayer is whether a cost item can be deducted from income or must be capitalized (added to the property's basis of value and depreciated over a period of years). Is it an expense or is it an investment of capital? Repairs and maintenance costs represent many difficult areas for decisions.

Repairs vs. Improvements

Tax law draws an important distinction as to what kind of work classifies as a repair and what is an improvement. The repair is deductible in the year it is made, while an improvement must be capitalized and its cost recovered over a period of years. The IRS rule that makes this distinction defines a repair as "something that maintains a property but does not increase its useful life," while an improvement is either an addition to the property (with a useful life of more than one year) or something that prolongs the property's useful life. It is a difficult rule to apply in practice. Faced with such a decision, the taxpayer is most likely to choose the classification that allows the greatest deduction. Unless a taxpayer has some certainty that his tax rate will increase significantly in the near term—rendering a later deduction more valuable as it offsets income taxed at a higher rate—taking the deduction now, as with a repair, makes more sense. This example illustrates:

EXAMPLE 6.3	An investor is currently in the 20 percent tax bracket, and has just completed $100,000 in repairs to the stucco exterior of a strip shopping center. The improvement does not extend the life or increase the size of the property, but it is an improvement with an expected life of at least five years. Should the investor expense or capitalize the improvement? The improvement may effectively reduce the investor's income, under the provisions of the 2009 Tax Act, to zero, saving him something around $15,000 or $20,000 this year. If he expects his income to increase in the coming years to over $200,000 per year, he will find himself in the 35 percent or higher bracket, and the $100,000 in deductions could have a longer term value of $35,000 ($100,000 stucco investment depreciated over five years at $20,000 per year); each of five years of deductions valued at $20,000 × .35 or $7,000. Depending on the investor's consideration of the time value of money and the actual likelihood of his income increasing dramatically in the short term, he may decide to either expense the stucco this year, or deduct it over several years. Given the option, it is common for such investments as the stucco to be deducted as an expense in the year incurred.

Capitalizing an expense and effectively "saving" the deduction for later years generally makes little sense for tax-planning purposes, but is often required by the IRS. If an expense increases the size or useful life of a property, it must be capitalized. If a gray area exists, for example with the provision to a strip shopping center of new stucco or a special insulating roof sealer, it may be up to the investor's own discretion to expense or capitalize the activity. Capitalizing the expense will rarely attract IRS attention. The IRS position is that they will examine the deduction on a case-by-case basis to determine whether or not it is justified.

Replacement vs. Maintenance

A decision to capitalize or expense an item is also confronted where a distinction needs to made between designating a cost as a replacement item or as an ordinary maintenance expense. A replacement must be capitalized and depreciation taken over its proper recovery period, while maintenance is the same as a repair and thus deductible immediately. There is no difference, for practical tax reasons, between a repair and maintenance. If the replacement item is a complete unit, such as a refrigerator, rather than simply a maintenance part, it is more likely to be a capital expenditure and its cost should be recovered over a period of years. However, in most instances, the IRS considers the "prolonging of useful life" to be that of the entire property, not its various components; this said, the implied practice of the IRS, though one would fail if ever he or she tried to get the IRS to commit to this, is to allow any reasonable expenditure—such as the replacement of an AC compressor or the plumbing in an office—to be expensed, as either a repair or maintenance. This allows the more favorable tax outcome—the immediate deduction of a property's cash outflow versus a series of annual depreciation deductions—provided the expense does not increase a building's size or extend its useful life.

Interest Expense

The tax deductibility of interest must be in accordance with the following rules:

- Business interest is fully deductible.
- An individual's **investment interest** is deductible up to the amount of net investment income.
- Personal interest (homeowner's mortgage interest) is deductible for mortgages on a first and second home up to the acquisition cost of the homes plus the costs of improvements, subject to a set of limitations. (See Chapter 8 for limitation details.)

Prepaid Interest

The interest deduction is only allowed for interest both due and paid within the tax year. Any prepayment of interest is not deductible.

Investment Interest

Investment interest is that paid on money borrowed to purchase or carry assets held for investment. This does not include interest paid on a personal residence or passive activity interest. (Passive activity is discussed later in this chapter.) Property "held for investment" includes that producing income defined as interest, dividends, annuities, or royalties, and any trade or business in which the taxpayer does not materially participate, so long as that activity is not treated as a passive activity. Also, property subject to a net lease is not treated as investment property because it is subject to the passive loss rules. Investment interest expense is limited to net investment income for the tax year. Amounts disallowed can be carried forward indefinitely and are allowable against future net investment income.

Interest on Rollover Loans

If an old loan, including interest cost, is settled with the proceeds of a new loan, what is the tax treatment for that portion representing interest? The IRS has the support of several court decisions in its contention that interest on the old loan, replaced by a new one, is not deductible because the previous loan interest has not been paid in cash or its equivalent. That is, the purported payment of interest is nothing more than a postponement of the taxpayer's interest obligation.

Accrued Interest

Interest that is not paid but added to the principal balance of a loan is not deductible for a cash basis taxpayer. Most real estate investors are cash basis taxpayers. In order to offer the borrower a lower initial payment amount, a portion of the interest cost may not be paid with each monthly payment, allowing it to "accrue." Periodically, the lender adds the unpaid interest to the principal balance. This is also referred to as **negative amortization**. New mortgage terms of this sort are virtually unknown in the real estate lending environment of 2008 and beyond, but were popular in the early 2000s. These negative amortization terms were attached to a great many of the mortgages on "investment" homes between 2003 and 2007, and are common among the detritus that populates the foreclosed home landscape in 2009 and 2010.

Loan Discount

To increase the yield on a loan, a lender will sometimes require the borrower to pay a discount in addition to whatever interest rate is agreed to. The discount is normally paid when a loan is closed, in cash or as a deduction from the loan proceeds. Since it is a cost of borrowed money, the same as interest, it is deemed deductible by the rules that apply to interest.

If the discount applies to a home loan, it must be clearly identified on the HUD-1 form used in closing, it must be computed as a percentage of the loan amount, and the amount must conform to standard business practice in the local area. The taxpayer must have paid an amount in cash at least equal to the discount. The cash can be for a down payment, escrow deposits, or other funds actually paid at closing. (Details on loan discounts and their impacts on the effective costs of borrowing, for homes or investment property, are covered in Chapter 10.)

TYPES OF INCOME FOR TAX PURPOSES

In the discussion of taxable income that follows, mention is made of "tax credits," as with the tax credits attaching to Obama's American Recovery and Reinvestment Act of 2009 described above. Specific tax credits that apply to real estate investments are examined in Chapter 7. For now, a distinction should be made between a tax credit and a tax deduction. The prior section on Business Income refers to "deductions" that may be taken from a taxpayer's income. A deduction reduces the income subject to tax. A "tax credit" is a much greater benefit for the taxpayer. A credit reduces the tax itself. In effect, when a tax credit is allowed, it is the same as the government accepting that credit in lieu of a tax payment. Call it a payment by Uncle Sam!

The tax code now identifies four kinds of income: (1) **active income**, (2) **passive activity income**, (3) **portfolio income**, and (4) **capital gain income**.

Active Income

Also known as earned income, active income is that earned by one's labor compensated for in salary, wages, commissions, fees, or bonuses. Active income is subject to tax at whatever graduated rates apply for that tax year.

Passive Activity Income

Passive activity income refers to earnings derived from any activity involving a trade or business in which the taxpayer does not materially participate, or any engagement in rental activity. IRS rules define "material participation" as spending more than 500 hours in the activity during the tax year. Or, if the taxpayer participates more than 100 hours, and not less than any other individual, it is considered material participation. Further, it is material participation if one has done so for any five of the previous ten years. If the activity is personal service, such as law or consulting, in which the taxpayer has materially participated any three years preceding the year in question, the taxpayer is considered to be a material participant, and thus not engaged in a passive activity.

The purpose of this classification is to limit the deduction of losses in this category against any other income. Giving separate definition to this kind of income, or loss, directly affects those who invest in property primarily for tax benefits rather than for earnings from the property.

To prevent such accounting transfers, passive activity rules disallow the deduction of passive activity losses and passive activity credits against other active sources of income. Passive losses may, however, be used to offset other passive income. For example, if an investor owns several income-producing properties, and one or two of them lose substantial sums in a given year, those losses may offset the positive income of the other properties, up to a limit on the total losses of $25,000. (Specific rules and loss limits vary with changes in the tax code.) That limit is non-binding for real estate professionals, considered briefly below; the tax code provides a description of who is, and is not, a real estate professional. Losses may be carried forward indefinitely and applied against future passive income. However, carry-backs are not permitted. Any unrealized losses are allowed in full upon a taxable disposition of the activity.

Limited Partners and Limited Liability Corporations

A blanket classification is given to any interest held by a taxpayer as a limited partner or limited liability corporation (LLC) member; annual income (or losses) from these interests are listed on a form K-1 by the managing partner which is given to the limited partners or LLC shareholders each year. Income on the K-1s is automatically treated as passive income. The limited partnership is an ownership form used far less frequently now than in the 1980s—it was very popular within the confines of Reagan's 1981 Tax Act. The LLC, considered in Chapter 9, has displaced the limited partnership as the most popular ownership vehicle in syndicated real estate investing.

Real Estate Rental Activity Exception for Real Estate Professionals

A special rule applies to real estate rental activity for qualified professionals making the activity not a passive activity. To qualify, the real estate professional must perform more than half of the personal services during the year in real property trades or businesses in which the person materially participated. Further, the services performed in real property businesses must exceed 750 hours during the tax year. An example would be owning and operating a motel or an apartment building.

The rule that disallows a passive activity loss to be offset against other income has been modified to allow such an offset for the real estate professional against other active real estate generated income.

Portfolio Income

Portfolio income is essentially passive income, with some exceptions and exclusions to prevent taxpayers from reducing taxable unearned income with passive income losses. It includes interest, dividends, rents, royalties, and investment income that is not otherwise classified as passive activity income. It also includes the gain or loss from the disposition of any property producing such income. Expenses (other than interest) that are clearly and directly allocable to this kind of property must be applied to portfolio income.

Any portfolio income of a taxpayer engaged in a passive activity must be separated from the passive income or losses of the taxpayer. The purpose is to prevent a taxpayer from using passive losses to offset portfolio income. Allowing otherwise would permit those taxpayers with portfolio income an advantage not permitted those whose principal income is wages and salaries. An example illustrates:

EXAMPLE 6.4   An investor owns several small apartment buildings that generate total losses in the difficult real estate environment of 2009 of $50,000. Passive loss limits of $25,000 apply. The taxpayer also receives portfolio income (dividends and interest in a stock brokerage account) of $30,000. The unused $25,000 real estate passive loss cannot offset or reduce the portfolio income, the taxpayer being required to carry the passive loss forward and pay the taxes on the $30,000 of portfolio income.

Capital Gain Income

Profit realized in the sale, exchange, or other disposition of a capital asset (a capital asset is any asset whose useful life is greater than one year, and for which the owner is taking or has previously taken depreciation) is considered income to the taxpayer, and is subject to income taxes. Capital gains holding periods vary with changing tax codes, but for real estate held for investment under the 2001, 2003, and 2009 Acts, a long term capital gain is taken for ownership lasting more than one year, and a short term capital gain for ownership periods of less than one year. Short term gains are taxed at the federal level as ordinary income; long term gains are taxed at the long term capital gains rate, which at the end of 2009 was 15 percent for most real estate investors (excluding capital gains taxes at the state level), with lower rates available to lower income earners. The tax applies to gains on both real and personal property. And the tax applies to gains whether or not the property was used for business purposes or for personal purposes. However, a loss in the disposition of any capital asset is deductible only if the property was used for business purposes, or to offset a gain in the sale of another non-business asset. Thus, a loss in the sale of rental property is deductible, but a loss in the sale of a personal residence is not. And, if the taxpayer has overall capital losses, after adding up all of her capital gains and losses for that tax year, there are limits to the amount of the loss that can be used to offset ordinary income. With larger amounts, unused capital losses must be carried forward to offset later gains; these losses cannot be carried back at the federal level for the individual. Effective with the 2001 Act, the tax rate on capital gains for assets held more than five years depends on the tax bracket of the taxpayer.

What needs further explanation is the method used to determine capital gain. The applicable rules follow.

DETERMINING CAPITAL GAIN

The capital gain is the difference between the net sales price (the selling price less the costs of sale—like commissions, fees, county recording costs, etc.) and the **adjusted basis** of the investment real estate. Thus, to determine the amount of a gain, the taxpayer must know and make use of just two figures: (1) the adjusted basis of value for the property and (2) the amount realized or net sales price. The gain or loss is simply the difference between the two figures. Exactly how the IRS defines these two items is the key to a correct result. The example below illustrates:

EXAMPLE 6.5	Suppose an investor purchased a small 5,000 square foot commercial building in 1996 for $50 per square foot or $250,000. He sold it for cash in 2006 for a net sales price of $500,000 or $100 per square foot. Applying straight line depreciation to the *depreciable basis* (that portion of a property's cost representing the building and other physical improvements, not the land, as land is not depreciable) of the property resulted in the owner taking ten years of depreciation (out of 39 years required by the Tax Reform Act of 1986). Eighty percent of the property's price was available for depreciation, or $200,000; $50,000 was non-depreciable land. Ten years depreciation equals 10/39 of $200,000, or .2564 × $200,000, equals $51,282. The adjusted basis of the property becomes the original purchase price reduced by the depreciation taken plus any capital improvements. Keeping this example simple, no capital improvements were made, but were they made, they would simply have been added to the basis, with additional depreciation taken upon them

depending upon their useful lives. (For example, parking lot resurfacing or a new roof might be depreciated separately, as components, over a period of 15 years.) In this case, the adjusted basis is simply $250,000 – $51,282 or $198,718. The capital gain then becomes $500,000 reduced by $198,718 or $301,282. The capital gain may also be calculated as the net sales price minus the original purchase price plus the depreciation taken, or $500,000 minus $250,000 plus $51,282 or $301,282. As well, and this likewise varies with the tax code in effect at the time of sale, the recapture of the depreciation (earlier expensed against the investor's taxable income) may be taxed at a higher rate than the long-term capital gains rate. For example, at the federal level, the gain on this property's sale in 2006 would be taxed at 15 percent for the ordinary portion of the gain ($250,000 or just the sale price minus the purchase price) and at 25 percent for that portion of the gain representing the recapture of depreciation. Total federal taxes on this transaction in 2006? (.15 × $250,000) + (.25 × $51,282) or $50,320.

Basis of Value

Extending the remarks above in computing the investment property's adjusted basis, for tax purposes, the basis of value is also determined by the method of acquisition. While most properties are purchased with the purchase amount simply becoming the initial basis, not all properties are so acquired. The IRS recognizes many ways of acquiring property, several of which are identified here to illustrate some of the differences.

Purchased Property

The basis of value for purchased property is the amount paid including cash, plus any acquired debt, and any other consideration given to purchase the property. When a homeowner pays $200,000 for a new condo, and shows up at the closing with $50,000 and assumes a loan for $150,000, the buyer has paid $200,000 for the home, and not $50,000. Whether a loan is assumed, or a new loan obtained, makes no difference in regard to basis of value—so long as it is a part of the total consideration given for the property.

Property Purchased with Other Property

If a purchase consideration includes payment other than cash or a mortgage, such as a car, a diamond, or securities, the *fair market value* of the property used to make the purchase is the value of the consideration. Fair market value is the price at which property changes hands between a willing seller and a willing and capable buyer, when neither is forced to buy or sell, and both have a reasonable knowledge of the relevant facts. For example, a diamond acquired for $1,000, now worth $3,000, would represent a purchase value of $3,000; no prudent buyer would exchange the diamond for property whose current value is equal only to the acquisition value of the diamond some years ago.

Using other property as purchase consideration creates another tax situation. If the adjusted basis of value of the property offered as purchase consideration is less than its fair market value, the difference between its adjusted basis and fair market value becomes capital gain and subject to tax for the buyer. The reason is that conveyance of property as consideration is classed as disposition of that property. An example would be a buyer purchasing a $150,000 property with Apple Computer stock that had a market value of $150,000. Say the buyer had acquired the stock earlier at a cost of $120,000. Then the difference between the $120,000 basis of value and the $150,000 market value when conveyed as consideration, or $30,000, amounts to a capital gain for the buyer subject to tax. The taxable basis of the Apple stock for the seller that took the stock in trade will be $150,000.

Property Exchanges

The tax code has a special section, Section 1031, that offers certain tax benefits if like-kind property is exchanged, rather than sold. For real estate, *like-kind property* is broadly interpreted as any investment property. An example would be exchanging an office building for an apartment property. If the exchange is completed according to the requirements of Section 1031, the basis of value is also exchanged. Thus, the basis of value of the property given up becomes the basis for the property acquired. If, for example, the owner of the property in Example 6.5 above had instead of selling his property exchanged it for another property worth $500,000, then the adjusted basis of the property acquired would become the basis of the old property, or $198,718. So the basis of the previously owned property becomes the basis for the newly acquired property. Section 1031 has a great many rules attaching to it, and these are discussed in Chapter 7.

Inherited Property

If property is inherited, the basis of value generally becomes the market value as of the date of the decedent's death. If a Federal Estate Tax Return must be filed, the heir may elect to use a market value as of six months after the date of death.

Gift Property

The recipient of gift property assumes the donor's adjusted basis of value at the time of the gift. If the donor pays a gift tax on the property, the amount of tax is added to the donor's basis and thus to the recipient's. The gift tax is simply a tax on the transfer of property for which the donor receives nothing, or a tax on the difference between the value of property given up and cash or property received. The recipient's basis cannot be increased above the fair market value of the property at the time of the gift. As of 2009, donors are limited to gifts of $13,000 per recipient per year with the donor's lifetime limit of non-taxed gifts to all non-charitable beneficiaries being $3.5 million; a husband and wife could give away $7 million. However, though the basis of the donor becomes the recipient's basis, gift tax restrictions apply to the market value of the property.

| **EXAMPLE 6.6** | For example, a husband and wife seeking to gift a vacation condo on the beach in Florida to their four children would be restricted to gifts totaling 4 × $13,000 (the annual exclusion available as of January 1, 2009) or |

$52,000 per year. Even though the condo might have cost them only $30,000 in the 1970's, its current market value of $250,000 suggests it will take five years to complete a gift-tax-free transfer to their children. Four years gifts totaling $208,000 (4 × $13,000 × 4 years) and a fifth year gift for the final portion, $42,000, are required to avoid gift taxes: a total of $208,000 plus $42,000 or $250,000. Then, if the children choose to later sell the condo, their basis for capital gains tax purposes will be their parent's original purchase cost of $30,000 plus the value of any capital improvements the children make to the property.

Other special rules on the transfer of primary and secondary residences, through the use of sometimes complex trusts portrayed in the Internal Revenue Code, exist, but are frankly beyond the practical scope of this text.

Property Purchased for Services Rendered

For property acquired in exchange for services rendered, the basis of value is the fair market value of the acquired property. Further, the fair market value of the acquired property becomes the value of the services rendered and is considered as ordinary income taxable to the recipient of the property.

Foreclosed Property

If a seller of real property holds a purchase money mortgage—as with the case where the seller receives a down payment and a fully executed mortgage in lieu of cash at closing—as a part of the consideration and is later forced to repossess the property, the basis of value is the sum of (1) the original value of the property, plus (2) any recognized gain, plus (3) the cost of repossession.

EXAMPLE 6.7

Suppose an owner sells a piece of land that earlier cost her $100,000 for $200,000. Terms of sale are for the buyer to bring $50,000 cash to closing, and a mortgage to give the seller (the purchase money mortgage, considered in greater detail in Chapter 10) that has a face value of $150,000. Total selling price is the down payment plus the mortgage, or $200,000. Half the selling price, $100,000/$200,000, is the capital gain divided by the selling price, and represents the portion of funds received by the seller that are capital gains. For the down payment, half becomes a return of the seller's initial invested capital in the land, and the other half is capital gain. The seller recognizes half of the $50,000 down payment as a capital gain, or $25,000. The buyer never makes a payment on the purchase money mortgage, and the seller of the land forecloses on the land, paying an attorney and the courthouse $10,000 in costs to arrange the foreclosure sale on the county courthouse steps. The seller gets the property back at the sale, and there are no other bidders at the sale. The seller bids $160,000 at the foreclosure auction, the sum of the costs of executing the foreclosure plus the unpaid mortgage balance ($10,000 plus $150,000). The seller's new basis for later capital gains tax computation purposes? $75,000 (the original cost reduced by half the down payment) plus $25,000 (the capital gain recognized in the down payment at the earlier sale) plus $10,000 (attorney's fees and other costs of repossession) or $110,000.

If the property to be repossessed is personal property, the market value becomes the basis of value because the seller's gain or loss occurs at the time of the repossession.

Adjustments to the Basis of Value

The basis of value as explained above is called the "unadjusted basis," the "original basis," or sometimes the "initial basis" of value. For land upon with there have been no capital improvements, the original basis becomes the adjusted basis, as there are no adjustments. However, with improved real estate occupied by depreciable assets, and commonly with capital improvements undertaken during a given period of ownership, there are adjustments to that original or initial basis. Property may be improved or added to, or it may be subject to depreciation or other reductions in value. These adjustments are not the same as the changes that may occur in the market value of a property. Example 6.5 highlighted the adjustments to a property's basis during an ownership period of ten years. Those adjustments are permitted, or required, by the tax laws. Each successive year a property is held, the basis of value for tax purposes may change and the newly established basis is called simply an *adjusted basis of value*.

Additions to the Basis of Value

When a property is acquired, certain additions are allowable to the basis including any purchaser-paid commissions, legal fees to perfect or defend the title, and any title insurance costs paid by the buyer. Since additions to the basis ultimately reduce the amount of a capital gain upon disposition, it is important to include these permissible costs in the basis amount. It should be noted that a sales commission paid by a seller reduces the realized selling price, but not the basis of value for the buyer. And any costs the seller is able to expense, and not capitalize into the value of a property, ought typically be expensed in the current period, if such expensing is allowed by IRS guidelines. For active real estate investors, and real estate professionals, such expensing is typically easier than for the "passive" real estate investor.

During the holding period, any improvements to the property or replacements that are capitalized become additions to the basis of value, such additions of course reduced by depreciation taken upon them. While additions or expansions may be increases to the initial basis, certain additions may be treated as separate property with a new basis of value, depending on the nature of the change. If, for example, the addition is a parcel of land acquired at a different time, then it must be given a separate basis even though it may be contiguous to the existing property. IRS rules exist to compute the capital gain and tax consequences for partial sales of land acquired at different times.

Reductions to the Basis of Value

If a portion of the property is disposed of, whatever is realized from the disposition reduces the basis of value by that amount. Likewise, if the disposition is the granting of an easement, the basis must be reduced by the amount of any payment received.

If a property owner sustains a casualty, the loss is the difference between the property value immediately before and immediately after the casualty. If the property loss is insured, the basis must be reduced by the sum of the insurance proceeds received plus the amount of casualty loss deducted. However, the loss cannot exceed the adjusted basis at the time of the loss.

Insurance proceeds are taxable income and their receipt is treated as an effective sale of a piece of real estate if the insurance proceeds received by the owner are not used to rebuild the damaged property or re-invested in another income property within the prescribed period (typically a period greater than one year—reference to current tax code is required). Sections 1245 and 1250 of the Internal Revenue Code describe the taxation of insurance proceeds that cover previously depreciated non-real estate assets, like furniture or fixtures destroyed in a fire. Balances received on the depreciated property from the insurer are taxed as a recapture of depreciation, and then for capital gains purposes as an effective sale of the property, if the property is not repaired or replaced. Involuntary conversions, as with the state buying land or buildings to construct a highway, are treated similarly, with the proceeds ultimately taxed as with the insurance proceeds. The owner of a damaged and insured piece of real estate (or property seized by eminent domain in an involuntary conversion) has the right to invest the proceeds in another property, to repair the afflicted property, or to pay the taxes on the proceeds. Tax counsel can provide details on this topic, as real estate investors maintain an awareness of the special duties and factors attaching to the income tax obligations of the real estate investor.

Depreciation The major reduction in the basis of value is depreciation. Depreciation must be taken as a reduction in the basis of value (which increases any capital gain) whether or not the deduction is taken by the taxpayer on the annual tax return. Depreciation is permitted for real and personal property used for business purposes only. If property is used partly for business and partly for personal purposes, depreciation deductions are permitted, but must be allocated to that portion used for business purposes. Also, if depreciable property is owned for a portion of the tax year, recovery is permitted for only that part of the year it is owned and in service. No personal property, such as a personal residence, is eligible for this deduction.

Depreciation may not be taken in excess of the basis of value even though the property's market value may be much higher. The kind of depreciation taken depends on the prevailing rules at the time the property was placed in service by the taxpayer.

Method of Calculating Depreciation The taxpayer must use a **cost recovery period** with a straight-line methodology from one of two classes of real property. There are six classes that apply to "Other Tangible Property," such as when an investor chooses component depreciation on a given real estate investment; these are more fully described later in this chapter. A straight-line amount is calculated by dividing the depreciable basis of value of a property by the number of years in its recovery period, as shown in Examples 6.2, 6.3 and 6.5. The straight-line depreciation may be claimed as a deduction each year.

Cost Recovery Period

Real property assets are assigned to two cost recovery periods as follows:

1. Residential rental property is eligible for recovery over 27.5 years. If a duplex investment costing $150,000 has an assigned land value of $50,000, leaving $100,000 available for depreciation, the annual depreciation deduction is $100,000 divided by 27.5 or $3,636.
2. Nonresidential property is eligible for recovery over 39 years. As with one of the properties above, if 80 percent of a $250,000 commercial property is depreciable, the annual depreciation is $200,000 divided by 39 or $5,128.

Residential Property Defined

The IRS defines residential property as that wherein at least 80 percent of the property's gross rental income is derived from dwelling units. This does not include property rented to transients, such as hotels or motels, which are classed as nonresidential. The determination must be made for each tax year and may alter the amount of depreciation allowable for that year.

Midmonth Convention

This rule considers the property as placed in service at the middle of the month regardless of the actual date of the month it is placed in service. The midmonth convention also applies to the year of disposition.

Excluded Real Estate

Not all real estate is included in the 27.5-year residential class or the 39-year nonresidential class. This includes many important land improvements such as sidewalks, roads, parking lots, fences, landscaping, and others. Even though property may be considered real by state law, it may not be so classified for federal tax purposes. Such improvements are accounted for in other tangible property classes and may be depreciated over shorter time periods. As well, such structures as mobile homes, while serving as residences for the inhabitants, are not considered real estate for federal tax purposes and are depreciated over much shorter periods.

Realized Selling Price

The other key figure in the equation to determine capital gain is the realized selling price. *Realized selling price* is best defined as the total consideration received less certain permissible deductions. Factors influencing the net sales price or realized selling price include the following:

Consideration Received

The total consideration for the disposition of a capital asset is the sum of all the following items that may be received:

1. All cash received.
2. The fair market value of any property used as consideration or services rendered in payment.

3. Any liabilities of the seller assumed by the buyer:
   a. Liabilities that the property may be subject to such as property taxes.
   b. Liability on a mortgage loan assumed by a buyer.
   c. Any liability of the seller assumed by the buyer as a part of the transaction, even though not related to the property, whether or not the seller remains personally liable for the debt. For example, if the buyer agrees to pay a roofing bill on *another* property belonging to the seller, even though the roofer is going to hold the seller responsible until the bill is paid, then the amount of that commitment is added to the consideration and the purchase/selling price of the property.

Permitted Selling Costs

The realized selling price is the total consideration less certain permissible deductions. These are essentially those costs incurred in the disposition of the property. Such costs include the sales commission, advertising, legal fees, any loan discount, and closing costs, as long as the item is paid by the seller.

Example of a Capital Gain Calculation

Example 6.8 illustrates a hypothetical disposition of an asset for a sales price of $600,000, showing some typical changes in the basis of value over a four-year holding period. The capital gain is the difference between the realized selling price and the adjusted basis of value. Because of the frequent changes in tax law, counseling is advised.

EXAMPLE 6.8			
Sale price of asset		$600,000	
Less: Sales commission, fees, other selling charges		($30,000)	
Realized selling price			$570,000
Initial basis of value		$400,000	
Plus: Addition of storeroom	$20,000		
Replacement of fixture	$5,000		
Additions to basis		$25,000	
Less: Depreciation deductions, 4 years averaging $12,000/yr.	($48,000)		
Sale of an easement	($60,000)		
Reductions to basis		($108,000)	
Adjusted basis of value (400 + 25 − 108) × $1,000 =			$317,000
Capital gain ($570,000 − $317,000) =			$253,000

ALLOCATION OF LAND COSTS AND BUILDING COSTS

With the purchase of income-producing investment properties, as with shopping centers and office or apartment buildings, an **allocation** must be made between the building and land costs of the properties being acquired. The IRS provides no hard and fast rules for this allocation, but as land is not depreciable, and the tax shelter of depreciation is one of the most attractive features of real estate investment, the investor is motivated to maximize the allocations to the building. However, inordinate or indefensible building allocations will be disallowed by the IRS, resulting in later penalties and interest due from the investor. There are four methods that help support a land-building cost allocation.

1. The purchase contract may specify the prices for major components of the property. If the allocation is reasonable, is negotiated without undue pressure, and is not an inside family transaction, a solid justification is provided for later component and/or building depreciation schedule formulations.
2. An appraisal by a professional (but not the taxpayer) gives good evidence of a proper allocation.
3. The taxpayer may use a property tax (ad valorem tax) assessment of the property. The tax appraisal usually distinguishes between the value of land and the value of its improvements. From these values, a ratio between them can be obtained and applied to the acquisition cost of the property.

EXAMPLE 6.9

If a property tax bill includes an assessment on a $1 million property of $250,000 for the land, and $750,000 for the building, and the new buyer is paying $2 million for the property, then the new buyer can defensibly conclude that one-fourth (250,000/1 million) of the $2 million purchase price can reasonably be assigned to the land, and the balance—$1.5 million—to the depreciable building. The tax consequences bear mention: If the investor in the property is in an overall income tax bracket of 40 percent (the sum of federal and state marginal income tax rates), each additional thousand dollars of depreciation saves the investor $400 in taxes, enhancing the value of depreciation and the motivation to maximize this deduction.

4. The greater relative allocation of the property's cost to the depreciable building occurs with the investment property fully developed. This seems obvious, but bears mention; if a $1 million property is a 5,000 square foot building sitting on a fully paved parcel of land that is just under one acre, or around 40,000 square feet, with 30 parking spaces and no "room" for expansion, the property is fully developed and a 75 percent (or even 80 percent) allocation to the building is likely easily defensible. If, however, the property is a five-acre parcel with ample room for later building expansion or parcel sales, a much smaller portion of the value can be allocated to the building, as the land has a much greater relative value than in the case of a one-acre purchase.

COST RECOVERY FOR OTHER TANGIBLE PROPERTY

Other tangible property has been assigned to a number of recovery classes identified by the number of years allowed for calculating depreciation amounts for each class. Depreciation allowances and special tax credits and tax treatments of non-real assets (depreciable assets other than buildings or other physical improvements to real estate) vary with each successive tax bill, and while allowances for accelerated cost recoveries and the classification of such assets as computers, cars, trucks, planes, farm equipment, and such generally fall into the same 3, 5, 7, 10, 15, or 20 year ranges, a business person is strongly advised to seek information from IRS publications and tax counsel before assigning an asset to one class or another. Depreciation schedules and annual allowances derive from the depreciation "families" into which an asset is assigned by IRS dictum.

PROPERTY TAX AND INCOME TAX SUMMARY

Property taxes and income taxes are typically the largest cash expenses of a successful real estate investor (debt service and mortgage payments are not an expense, though they are a substantial cash outflow). An unsuccessful real estate investor pays no income taxes! As such, these expenses deserve extensive study by the student of real estate investment.

The remarks in this chapter are only introductory concerning the calculation and allocation of property taxes. These charges are a primary source of funding for local governments, and a growing expense for the real estate investor. As well, in the economic climate at the close of 2009, property taxes have been cast in ever more stark relief, as other funding sources such as state income and sales taxes have fallen.

There have been continuing changes in the methods and degrees of income taxation at the federal level over the past 25 or 30 years, each impacting the real estate investor to a different degree. Given the challenged status of the economy as a whole, and real estate investments in particular in 2009 and 2010, the potential impact of a changing federal tax environment is underscored. These federal taxes, and special considerations for the real estate investor relative to these costs, are considered much more extensively in the following pages.

KEY TERMS

active income	capital gain income	mill	portfolio income
ad valorem	cost recovery period	millage	RTC
adjusted basis	depreciation	negative amortization	tax assessment
allocation	FIRREA	passive activity income	Tax Reform Act
ARRA	investment interest		

DISCUSSION QUESTIONS

1. What was the impact of the Economic Recovery Tax Act of 1981 on real estate investment?

2. What are the lessons of the Resolution Trust Corporation and FIRREA 1989 for policy makers in 2009 and beyond?

3. How are property taxes assessed? What is the primary driver of the level of property taxes?

4. What is the difference between residential and non-residential property?

5. What type(s) of property is(are) eligible for depreciation deductions?

6. What is a real estate "professional" and what are some of the special tax allowances afforded the real estate professional?

7. What are the factors influencing the classification of real estate expenses as repairs vs. maintenance and improvements vs. maintenance?

8. Given the choice, why might an investor choose to capitalize over a period of years a property expense, rather than expensing it in the year incurred?

9. Define active, passive, portfolio, and capital gain income.

10. How does a real estate investor accomplish the allocation of an investment property's basis to its depreciable and non-depreciable (land) portions after purchase?

CHAPTER 7

Special Income Tax Rules Applicable to Real Estate

Chapter 6 examined basic tax procedures including tax code definitions of income, the calculation of a capital gain, and how depreciation is figured. That chapter also alluded to several special circumstances within which real estate curries favor in the tax code; this chapter extends that topic and considers the special treatment afforded certain types of real estate and specified categories of real property transactions.

TAX-DEFERRED EXCHANGES OF PROPERTY

In a typical transaction involving the sale of an asset and the purchase of another, the IRS taxes any realized capital gain on the initial sale. Section 1031 (the section) of the Internal Revenue Code (the code), however, allows for holders of any "property held for productive use or investment" to sell the property at a price greater than its adjusted basis and **defer** part or all of the taxes on the capital gain. The section does not apply to the sale or trading of stocks, bonds, or other securities. After executing the "exchange," the cost basis of the newly acquired asset is decreased by the amount of the capital gain. Thus, the payment of tax is deferred until the sale of the new asset, provided that sale is not itself part of a new tax-deferred exchange. The widest use of this section is in the sale and subsequent purchase of investment real estate. The section grew enormously in popularity among real estate traders in the 1990s and early 2000s.

Capital gains tax deferment is allowed provided that the sale proceeds are reinvested in **like-kind property** according to the terms of the section.

The terms of the section are somewhat involved and the IRS has yet to provide specific guidelines on its implementation in every circumstance. Nonetheless, the code allows that an appreciated capital asset can be sold and its capital gains tax deferred if several basic criteria are met. Any real estate held for business or investment qualifies as "like-kind."

First, the property sold must be "investment" real estate (not inventory real estate of the sort held by developers for long periods and not homesteaded residential real estate, which enjoys special tax treatment in other sections of the code) and the funds derived from its sale must never be in the direct control of the seller; the property is either directly exchanged for the new property or the funds are held by an approved **escrow agent**—such as a title company or an attorney—until the new property is purchased. The property may also be any capital or depreciable asset used in a taxpayer's business, but the focus here is upon investment real estate. From a legal perspective, the titles given and received, such as fee simple, in the sale and purchase must be the same.

Second, the new property must be purchased within 45 days of the closing of the sale of the old property or, if such purchase does not take place within 45 days, the new property must be identified by the seller of the old property within 45 days. The code provides that if the seller does not complete the exchange within 45 days, he may register with the escrow agent a list of three properties that are under consideration for purchase. Up to six properties may be listed, contemplating the purchase of more than one property to take full advantage of the section, provided the total market value of the six properties is less than 200 percent of the sale price of the old property.

Third, and assuming the new property purchase does not take place within 45 days of the original sale, a property listed with the escrow agent must be bought within 180 days of the sale of the old property or by the time of the taxpayer's next income tax filing, whichever comes first. For example, a late-December sale must be followed by a new property purchase before April 15. To take full advantage of the section and the full 180-day grace period, the taxpayer could, of course, simply use Form 4868 to apply for an extension and would have until June to consummate the Section 1031 exchange.

Fourth, the basis of the newly acquired property, for later depreciation and capital gains tax computation purposes, will be the purchase price of the new property reduced by the untaxed capital gain. The investor uses Form 8824 to report the exchange. For example, if a $1,000,000 property is acquired in a 1031 exchange and a $200,000 capital gain is deferred in the transaction, the basis of the new property will be $800,000. Case Study 7.1 illustrates the use of this section of the code.

Unlike Property

If a like-kind exchange includes unlike property to complete the transaction, a capital gain tax is due from the recipient of the unlike items. There are three kinds of unlike property identified in these transactions: cash, other property, and net loan relief. The gain subject to tax as a result of the receipt of cash, other property, or net loan relief is identified as "recognized gain" in this section of the code.

CASE STUDY **7.1**

Walgreen's purchased a property in Jacksonville, Florida from Graham Properties in late 1997 for $405,000. Graham Properties had purchased the property in October of 1983 for $84,000, had used the generous 15-year depreciation rules available in 1983, and after improvements and operations for 14 years had depreciated the property down to an **adjusted basis** of $21,659 at year's end 1997.

The property sold was a 5,000 square-foot strip shopping center built in the late 1950s and early 1960s. The developer's intent to demolish the aging structure, and the gas station next to it, and construct a new building, was well received by the community and the property owners. Net sales proceeds, after commissions and other costs of sale, were $376,705. A capital gain of $355,046 (the net sales proceeds reduced by the adjusted basis of $21,659) was earned with the sale. The sole proprietorship was confronted with the option of either paying approximately 20 percent of this gain (the capital gains tax rate at the time) in taxes, or $71,009, or of reinvesting the sales proceeds of $376,705 in a new "like-kind" property, thus deferring the capital gains tax. The alterative to reinvesting all the sales proceeds was to pay the tax and be left with $305,696 ($376,705 minus the taxes of $71,009) after the sale.

The owner of Graham Properties ended up buying Venetia Plaza; it was a 24,000 square foot strip shopping center located about five miles east of the property that was sold. It was available for $1,060,000, and with additional costs of sale of $34,382, could be purchased for a gross price of $1,094,382. The basis of Venetia Plaza after the purchase became $1,094,382 minus the deferral of $355,046 or $739,336. Depreciation allowances on the property purchased in this exchange were also reduced, as depreciation is calculated against the reduced Section 1031 basis, and not the actual purchase price.

In completing the purchase of Venetia Plaza, the monies from the sale of the older property were escrowed with a title company in California, Graham Properties never having control of the funds. The formal closing of the sale of the older property took place on December 31 of 1997; the purchase of Venetia Plaza was completed on January 18th of 1998, meeting all the requirements of the code for a tax-free exchange. Graham properties simply instructed the escrow agent to deliver the $376,705 in escrowed sales proceeds to the seller of Venetia Plaza, making up the difference of $717,677 with additional cash and a new loan from a commercial lender in north Florida.

If Venetia Plaza is later sold (and it had not been sold as of September 1, 2009), the sale will recapture the previously deferred capital gain, and the capital gain tax will be due, calculated at the capital gains tax rate in effect at the time of the later sale.

Cash

If any cash is received in the transaction and not reinvested, it is taxable as unlike property. Instead of cash, the money might first be used by the buyer to purchase another piece of like-kind property for use in the transaction. If the buyer of the appreciated asset being sold first purchases another piece of real estate as part of the consideration desired by the seller of that asset, the integrity of the tax deferral could be retained; that would not be the case if the seller received cash instead of real estate at the time of closing. Example 7.1 highlights the impact of the receipt of cash in a 1031 transaction.

EXAMPLE 7.1 Suppose an investor sells a property which cost him $100,000 for $500,000. He reinvests only $400,000 in a property purchase that meets the other terms of the section. A gain of $300,000 would be deferred. The basis of the replacement property would become the $400,000 purchase price, reduced by the deferred gain of $300,000, or $100,000. The remaining uninvested $100,000 received would be taxed as a capital gain.

Other Property

"Unlike property," other than cash, is called boot. The expression derives from an old German word *bute*, meaning exchange or to obtain as booty. An example of boot would be a car or a mobile home as a part of the consideration in a real estate exchange. The gain attributable to boot is taxable to the recipient. However, the grantor may also face a tax consequence in that the conveyance amounts to a disposition and may therefore be subject to a capital gain tax. This would be true if the market value of the boot at the time of the trade is greater than its adjusted basis of value. Such a difference amounts to a gain and is subject to tax. For example, say a mobile home used as boot in a real estate trade had been acquired for $7,000 and had a market value of $9,000 at the time of the trade. The difference of $2,000 would be treated as capital gain to the grantor of the mobile home.

Net Loan Relief

Another kind of unlike property in an exchange is the **relief of debt**. Relief of debt in this section of the tax code means the debt given up on the property exchanged. Say Owner Smith owes $50,000 on property conveyed to another in a property exchange. The conveyance itself is deemed to include relief of the debt for Smith. Such relief is subject to a capital gain tax whether or not liability for the debt is assumed by the recipient of the property subject to the debt.

A special rule applies to debt relief in exchanges where both properties have mortgage debts. The rule is that the two mortgages are netted out, and the amount of unlike property received is the amount that the mortgage debt on the property given up exceeds the amount of the mortgage on the property received. The following two brief examples illustrate these situations:

EXAMPLE 7.2

An investor sells a property with a basis of $100,000 for $500,000; he has a mortgage on the property of $200,000. He receives $300,000 at closing, and passes liability for the mortgage onto the new owner of the property sold. He adheres to the terms of Section 1031 and soon buys a replacement property for at least $500,000, reinvesting the entire sales price of the appreciated property. But, he will defer a capital gain and its adjacent taxes for only $200,000 of the $400,000 gain, owing taxes on that portion of the capital gain represented by the debt assumed by the buyer of the appreciated property. A simple strategy for the investor would have been to pay off the mortgage prior to the sale, with a short term loan not secured by the property or other available cash, and then borrow against the replacement property after the sale, restoring the investor's balance sheet to its condition prior to the sale, and yet maintaining the deferral of the entire $400,000 gain. The evacuated liability of $200,000 on the old mortgage is treated as net loan relief and a capital gain, if it is transferred at the sale of the old property.

EXAMPLE 7.3

Suppose the investor from Example 7.2 completes the same sale of the property with a basis of $100,000, exchanging it for a new property worth $500,000, transferring liability on the $200,000 mortgage, but instead receives in exchange the ownership of the new $500,000 property with an

attaching $200,000 mortgage? In this case, the investor will be able to defer the taxation on the capital gain, his gain effectively being $200,000; he traded his $300,000 of equity in the old property (its $500,000 value reduced by the $200,000 mortgage) for the effective $300,000 in equity in the new property (its value of $500,000 reduced by its attaching mortgage of $200,000). If the new property has a mortage of less than $200,000, he will be liable on the capital gains taxes on the difference. If the new mortgage has a balance of more than $200,000, that amount will reduce the gain, and the gain deferred, but will not affect the taxes due.

Transaction Costs

When unlike property is a part of the exchange, the recipient of such property is liable for capital gain taxes. However, the amount subject to tax is reduced by the amount of any transaction costs. Such expenses as brokerage commissions, taxes, filing fees, and escrow costs, if paid by the recipient of the unlike property, can reduce the amount of gain recognized by the amount of expenses paid. If a property owner receives a $10,000 car as part of a real estate exchange (not like-kind property), and suffers $500 in title transfer and sales tax costs, the $10,000 "gain" would be reduced by $500.

Congress Plugs a 1031 "Loop-hole"

With the passage of the **American Jobs Creation Act of 2004 (AJCA)**, the U.S. Congress addressed an interesting deficiency of Section 1031 of the Internal Revenue Code. With the original section, in what the industry refers to as a Starker exchange (referencing a court decision that basically allowed a property seller to defer recognition of capital gains provided a replacement property is purchased within 180 days according to the terms of the section), an investor could sell an appreciated investment property with a gain of $500,000, buy an investment home in a favored community, rent it out for a year, and then move into the rental home. As is described in Chapter 8, the investor could then treat the new investment property as his primary residence, and after two years in the home could sell it and (filing his tax return jointly with his wife) forever avoid taxes on the first $500,000 in gains. (This ignores depreciation and the taxation of its recapture.) AJCA now precludes the investor from taking advantage of the $500,000 permanent exclusion for at least five years after the home's purchase in the 1031 exchange; the 1031 exchange itself requires the home to be treated as investment property and rented out for at least one year after it is acquired in the exchange. AJCA is not clear on the minimum period the property must be owned in total (is it the one year rental period *plus* the five year holding period or just five years in total?), but it has at least reduced the attractiveness of this particular loophole.

TAX CREDITS

A **tax credit** reduces a tax payment dollar-for-dollar. A 10 percent tax credit against a $100,000 expenditure reduces a taxpayer's (or group of taxpayers') taxes payable by $10,000. It is a concept borrowed from several European countries and was first added to our tax law as an "investment tax credit" in

1962. Since then, the investment tax credit has been added to and then rescinded from the tax law several times. But, the concept of tax credits has been used for a number of other purposes, such as encouraging political contributions, supporting energy conservation, and attracting investment into low-income housing.

Two kinds of currently available tax credits are of particular interest to the real estate investor: an investment tax credit for rehabilitation and low-income housing tax credits. The rehabilitation tax credit has been revised from prior law, while the low-income housing credit was first offered in 1987.

Investment Tax Credit for Rehabilitation

To encourage restoration of certain existing buildings, the investment tax credit for **rehabilitation** is allowed for older nonresidential buildings (placed in service before 1936) and certified historic structures (residential or nonresidential). The rehabilitation credit applies to costs of renovation, restoration, and reconstruction, but not to the enlargement of a building or new construction. Credits are generally for 10 percent of qualifying expenditures on buildings placed in service before 1936 (the non-historic tax credit) and 20 percent against costs of restoring, renovating, or reconstructing certified historic structures (the historic tax credit). These historic structures are those listed in the *National Register of Historic Places* by the Department of the Interior. Enhanced credits were allowed for hurricane-damaged buildings (after Katrina, Rita, and Wilma in 2005) along the Gulf Coast for repairs up to January 1 of 2009.

Rehabilitation Defined

To qualify for the tax credit, there must be *substantial rehabilitation* of the building. For this purpose, "substantial" is defined as an amount of expenditures during the current tax year, plus those made in the preceding year, exceeding the greater of the adjusted basis of value of the property, or $5,000. Rehabilitation expenditures do not include the costs of acquiring or enlarging a building. The rehabilitation tax credit is disallowed for both historic and non-historic buildings given certain mixes of tax-exempt tenants (the government seemingly desiring that the credit encourage occupancy by tax-paying entities!), or if the building is sold or encumbered by a lease with fixed terms of over 20 years.

Rehabilitation costs must be treated as new property with a separate tax basis of value, for later depreciation and capital gains tax computations. Rehab costs must be recovered using straight-line depreciation allowances and the overall basis of the rehabilitated property must be reduced by the full amount of the credit taken. A further requirement for qualification of the rehabilitation credit refers to walls and internal structure requiring at least the following:

- Fifty percent of external walls (measured by area) must be retained in place as external walls.
- Seventy-five percent of the external walls retained in place as either internal or external walls.
- Seventy-five percent of the building's internal structural framework retained in place.

EXAMPLE 7.4   A group of investors purchases an historic structure in downtown Wilmington, NC. It cost them $100,000 and they completed $300,000 in qualifying repairs. Half the building is leased to a local tax-exempt charity, under a fixed ten-year lease with two ten-year options, at fixed lease rates. Fifty percent of the available tax credit is lost because over 35 percent of the building is leased to a tax-exempt organization; as well, the 30-year fixed price lease is an effective sale and an additional disqualifier. Were less than 35 percent of the building to have been leased to the local charity, and the lease terms were specified to be "at market" at the time of lease renewal, the entire credit of 20 percent of the $300,000 or $60,000 would be available to the investors in the building.

The rehabilitation tax credit is taken in full in the year the property is placed in service. Unused credits may be carried back three years or forward for 15 years.

Low-Income Housing Tax Credits (LIHTC)

The LIHTC program is an indirect manner with which the federal government increases the availability of housing for the poor. Section 42 of the code provides the foundation for this program. Tax credits are given to developers of low-income property, which credits can then be distributed among investors in the property; provided the property remains in compliance with the terms of the code, the credits are available each year for ten years as a dollar-for-dollar offset against federal income tax liabilities. Previous tax incentives to encourage construction of low-income housing included preferential depreciation rates, five-year amortization of rehabilitation expenses, and special treatment for construction period interest and taxes. These have been replaced by tax credits. And since 1990 investors are required to keep the building in low-income use for 30 years rather than the former 15.

To qualify for low-income housing tax credits, the project must meet certain set-aside requirements (explained below) and is subject to the 30-year compliance period. The tax credit is allowed for each of ten taxable years beginning with the year the building is placed in service. The credit is available on a per-dwelling unit basis since a single building may have both units that qualify and those that do not.

Qualification of Building

To qualify for a low-income housing credit, the building may be part of a multiple building project that serves the function of providing residential rental units to the general public on a nontransient basis. **General public** means that tenants are not limited to members of a social organization or to employees of an employer who is providing the housing. **Nontransient** means, generally, that the basis of the initial lease term extends to six months or more.

The building must meet the minimum set-aside requirements during the time that it is subject to the 30-year compliance rule.

Set-Aside Requirements

The total annual housing tax credit is limited to an inflation-adjusted $1.75 (using 2003 as a base year) per resident for each state. A state with a population of ten million in 2003 would have been allowed a federal credit to allocate among accepted projects of $17.5 million. The state has two years to "use up" its available tax credits or return them to a "national pool for re-allocation." Tax credits are allocated in each state depending on the likelihood that a given proposed low-income housing project will serve low-income residents for the longest possible period. Only the first year of the expected ten years of tax credits count against the allocation; the tax credits taken by investors in a given state in the second and later years of a LIHTC investment do not count against this earlier allocation. The credit amount for a given project is based on the cost of the project and the number of units within the project that qualify for low-come housing. As well, many states augment the federal allocation with a separate state allocation.

Residential rental projects providing low-income housing qualify for the credits only if they meet the following tests:

- Twenty percent or more of the aggregate residential rental units in a project are occupied by individuals with incomes of 50 percent or less of area's HUD-determined median income, as adjusted for family size (the 20-50 rule), or
- Forty percent or more of the aggregate residential rental units in a project are occupied by individuals with income of 60 percent or less of area's HUD-determined median income, as adjusted for family size (the 40-60 rule).

The minimum **set-aside requirements** must be met within 12 months of the date the project is placed in service. Additionally, 10 percent of each state's housing tax credit allocation must be set aside for projects owned by non-profit entities.

Calculating the LIHTC Rate and Total Credits Allowed

Interestingly, and depending upon the allocation made in a given year to a given state, the total of state and federal credits awarded a given low-income project could well exceed the costs of constructing that community, excluding the costs of land or financing. A number of other rules and restrictions apply to the LIHTC programs, but these are the general manners with which the credits are calculated.

If 100 percent of the units qualify as low-income housing, the property is not otherwise subsidized by the federal government, and the units remain rented to **qualifying tenants**, 9 percent of the cost or **eligible basis** (typically very close to the depreciable basis of a "normal" real estate investment) is available as a federal credit each year for ten years; state credits may push this 90 percent total beyond the total costs of a project's construction or substantial rehabilitation. If less than 100 percent of the low-income housing project is leased to qualifying tenants, the eligible basis is the lesser of the percentage of the square feet of the whole project leased to low-income tenants or the percentage of the units in the project leased to low-income tenants, times the qualifying costs of construction or rehabilitation. The basis of the building for depreciation and later capital gains computation purposes is not reduced by the credits taken. If all units are not used for low-income housing, or some of the tenants don't meet the low-income requirements, the credit is prorated. Special provisions deal with tax-exempt bonds and state volume limitations. A similar approach is used to calculate credits available to investors in the rehabilitation of residential units for low-income housing; minimum expenditures of the greater of $3,000 per unit or 10 percent of the initial adjusted basis of the building are required in the first 24 months of ownership. Lesser credits are given to owners of buildings that operate or are developed with federal subsidies. Such subsidies include HUD Section 8, Section 221(d)3, and Section 236 programs.

Rent Restriction

The gross rent charged to a tenant cannot exceed 30 percent of the qualifying income level for the tenant's family size. Properties must adhere to rent and income restrictions for 30 years or longer to maintain LIHTC compliance and avoid termination of remaining credits or claw-backs of prior ones. Gross rent includes utilities paid by the tenant (other than telephone), but does not include payments under Section 8 or similar rental assistance payments received by the tenant. (For those persons eligible for Section 8 assistance, HUD pays the difference between the tenant's contribution and the contract rent.)

INVOLUNTARY EXCHANGE

An **involuntary exchange** is also called an **involuntary conversion**, and occurs when property is converted into cash or other consideration through (1) condemnation by a governmental authority, (2) a natural disaster such as a fire where an insurance company may pay the loss, or (3) any other conversion contrary to the wishes of the owner, such as when a foreign government "seizes or nationalizes a property." If the proceeds from the conversion exceed the basis of value of the property lost, a gain results. Under these circumstances, the taxpayer can postpone liability for the capital gain tax by acquiring a replacement property before the end of the second year after the year in which the gain was realized. If the taxpayer elects to postpone the tax on the gain, then the basis of value for the replacement property must be reduced by the amount of the untaxed gain, similar to the basis adjustments with Section 1031 deferrals. If all the proceeds from an involuntary conversion are not used to acquire a replacement property—that is, if the replacement property costs less than the proceeds—then the unspent portion of the gain is subject to the capital gains tax.

In order to qualify for a tax deferment under this section of the tax code, a replacement property must offer approximately the same function as the property it replaces. However, there is a helpful exception to this rule for real estate investors. When real property is held for the production of income or for investment, replacement property need only be expected to do the same. It is immaterial that the properties are unrelated in use or service. Thus, unimproved property would be an acceptable replacement for improved property since both are held for investment purposes.

INSTALLMENT SALES

Section 453 of the Internal Revenue Code allows for the special tax treatments available to a real estate investor receiving the sales proceeds for a real estate sale over a period of time. The IRS defines an **installment sale** as one in which the taxpayer receives at least one payment after the year of sale. The tax treatment for the installment method applies only when the transaction results in a gain, whether or not the property sold was used for personal purposes or for business purposes. As well, use of the installment method is typically not allowed for certain kinds of sales, such as those of securities or those by dealers holding property in inventory and related party transfers.

Loss incurred on an installment sale of business assets cannot be spread over future years but must be deducted in the year of sale. A capital loss on the sale of property held for personal use is not deductible under any rule.

Under current tax rules, the taxpayer pays a capital gain tax only on the amount actually received during the tax year, regardless of the amount of payment received. The 1986 Tax Act retained this general concept but added certain limitations if money is borrowed by pledging an installment note.

Reporting Gain on the Installment Method

When property is sold on the installment basis, the amount of gain subject to tax must be determined. This is done by figuring what percentage of the sales price is capital gain. Remember, capital gain is the difference between realized selling price and the adjusted basis of value. For example, if the seller realizes $100,000 in the sale of an asset with an adjusted basis of $60,000, the difference amounts to $40,000 of capital gain. The $40,000 gain represents 40 percent of the $100,000 sale. So for each principal payment received by the seller, 40 percent must be reported as capital gain. If the down payment amounts to $20,000, 40 percent, or $8,000, is capital gain. If the next installment is $10,000, 40 percent, or $4,000, is capital gain. Whatever is received each year is subject to a similar calculation of taxable gain. It becomes a bit more complex in the "real world" as precise applications are necessary to accurately determine capital gain and ordinary income receipts from the installment sale, and the resultant tax liabilities.

The example below portrays the calculations completed by a real estate investor using Form 6252 to determine **selling price, gross profit, gross profit percentage,** and **installment sale income.** Capital gain income and interest income are reported separately, with interest income being taxed as ordinary income. Capital gain income is likewise taxed as ordinary income at the state level by some states. The example below portrays the tax implications for the installment sale at the federal level only.

EXAMPLE 7.5

Suppose a property with a basis of $225,000 is sold for a selling price of $525,000. (This example ignores depreciation recapture.) Our gross profit or capital gain (CG) is $300,000 or 57.14% (300,000/525,000) of the selling price. This dollar gain is referred to as installment sale income and the 57.14% as the gross profit percentage on Form 6252. It is a tough lending market, so to assist the sale, the sellers take back financing on 75% of the price with a purchase money mortgage or PMM. The 25% down payment is .25 × $525,000 or $131,250; the balance of $393,750 is the PMM. The PMM is at 6% for 20 years with monthly payments.

What are the tax consequences of this transaction at sale, and in the first year after the sale, assuming the PMM payments are made in a timely fashion?

The tax on the down payment at sale, given a capital gains tax rate of 25% becomes:

$$\text{Down Payment} \times \text{gross profit percentage} \times .25 = \$131,250 \times .5714 \times .25$$
$$= \$18,749$$

57.14% of the down payment (or 300,000 divided by 525,000), and 57.14% of subsequent principal received, are capital gains and 42.86% is the return of the original capital invested.

The ordinary tax rate, at which interest is taxed, is 50%; these ordinary and capital gain tax rates allow for escalating federal income taxes in the years ahead.

Using a business calculator, and portraying the key strokes with a Texas Instruments BA II Plus:

393,750 PV
20 × 12 = N
6/12 = I/Y
CPT PMT = 2,820.94, 2nd, Amort:
P1 = 1 (the first month of the first year)
P2 = 12 (the last month of the first year)
BAL = $383,238
PRN = $10,512
INT = $23,339
(Affirming the calculations, the sum of PRN and INT the first year is $33,851. Dividing this by 12 months, and the payment of $2,821 is confirmed!)

What are the taxes on the mortgage? CG tax is .25 × (CG/sale price) × PRN received the first year,

$$= .25 \times .5714 \times \$10,512 = \$1,502$$

Ordinary tax is the ordinary tax rate of .5 × INT received or .5 × $23,339 = $11,670

Total taxes on this PMM in the first year on this mortgage is $1,502 plus $11,670 or approximately $13,172.

Exceptions to Treatment as an Installment Sale

In general, the installment method of tax treatment is not available to dealers who sell from an inventory, such as building lots, as a normal method of transacting business. Also, a taxpayer does have the option of electing out of the installment method, which would mean payment of the entire capital gain tax in the year of sale.

Borrowing Money on an Installment Note

If an installment obligation is pledged as collateral for a loan, the proceeds of that loan are treated the same as a payment received. For example, if an installment note was pledged by the holder as collateral to obtain a $50,000 loan, the entire $50,000 would be treated as a payment received for calculation of tax; the same procedure as that employed in Example 7.5 would be employed to determine the portions of the $50,000 attributable to capital gain, and to the return of capital. In that case, the $50,000 would effectively be treated as a prepayment on the PPM, with 57.14% subject to taxation, and the balance as a return of capital or a tax-free return of the adjusted basis. The intention is to tax cash as it is received.

Additional Rules for Installment Sales

There are special rules for the tax treatment of installment sales to related parties. For instance, a sale to a spouse, child, grandchild, parent, and certain related business organizations may be disallowed as an installment sale if the related party sells or otherwise disposes of the property before all payments have been made on the first sale. Special tax rules apply in these circumstances.

Prior law for installment sales treatment permitted no sales contingencies. Current law allows greater flexibility since it is possible to leave such questions as total sale price and terms of sale open, dependent upon later developments. Parties to the transaction may negotiate a deal utilizing such contingencies as future profits, cost of living escalators, and others. The key element is that whatever amount is received in payment on principal, the capital gain on that amount must be reported and paid in that tax year. Adequate records must be maintained on the entire transaction when reporting an installment sale.

Imputed Interest and Applicable Federal Rates

Special rules apply to investors using installment sales terms to finance appreciated (or non-appreciated) property sales. Installment terms could otherwise be used to shelter a person from higher ordinary tax rates, or to effectively gift appreciated assets to related parties, granting such parties below-market terms. The example below illustrates this first concept.

EXAMPLE 7.6	Extend Example 7.5 above. To avoid taxes, the seller offers to sell to the buyer the same property, with the same down payment of $131,250 and more favorable loan terms, with a twist. Now, the interest rate will be only 3%, for 20 years, with monthly payments reduced to only $2,500 per month. Backing out the value of the mortgage using the same BA II Plus calculator reveals:

−$2,500 PMT
240 N
3/12 = I/Y
CPT PV = $450,777
P1 = 1 (the first month of the first year)
P2 = 12 (the last month of the first year)

BAL = $434,072
PRN = $16,705
INT = $13,295

Here, the total implied purchase price becomes the down payment of $131,250 plus the new mortgage value of $450,777 or $582,027. Even with the lower payment, it seems the seller is getting a higher price (and greater capital gain) even while receiving smaller monthly payments. Our *gross profit* or *capital gain* (CG) is now $582,027−$225,000 = $357,027 or 61.34% (382,027/582,027) of the *selling price*. This dollar gain becomes the new *installment sale income* and the 61.34% is the new *gross profit percentage*.

What are the tax consequences of this transaction at sale, and in the first year after the sale, assuming the PMM payments are made in a timely fashion?

The tax on the down payment at sale, given a capital gains tax rate of 25% becomes:

$$\text{down payment} \times \text{gross profit percentage} \times .25 = \$131,250 \times .6134 \times .25$$
$$= \$20,127$$

61.34% of the down payment or 357,027/582,027, and 61.34% of subsequent principal received, are capital gains and 38.36% is the return of the original capital invested or the adjusted basis. The ordinary tax rate is 50% as in Example 7.5.

What are the taxes on the mortgage? CG tax is .25 × (CG/sale price) × PRN received the first year, =.25 × .6134 × $16,705 = $2,562

Ordinary tax is the ordinary tax rate of .5 × INT received or .5 × $13,295 = $6,648

Total taxes on this PMM in the first year on this mortgage are $2,562 plus $6,648 or approximately $9,210. Contrasting this with the first year's total PMM tax bill of $13,172 in Example 7.5, and the "loss" to the mortgage holder at the new lower rate of 3% is largely covered. Benefits to the borrower under these new terms are both the lower mortgage payment and potentially more generous depreciation allowances with the higher purchase price. Those would offset the reduced interest deductions on this new, lower-cost, mortgage.

The PMM holder now accepts a payment $320 lower, which reduction is offset with the lower tax bill, *thus the exclusion of this sort of arrangement by the code.*

Related parties could likewise effectively gift property with overly generous PMMs. The outcome should be transparent: if the market rate on a loan to purchase a given investment property would otherwise be 8 percent, and a parent or grandparent grants terms of 3 or 4 percent, then a gifting has effectively taken place. Transactions of this sort, and the one in Example 7.6, must apply interest rates known as **Applicable Federal Rates (AFR)** as determined and published monthly by the IRS. From the tax-payer's perspective, the rates appear generous: 2009 rates were less than 1 percent for maturities of less than three years, around 3 percent for loans with maturities of three to nine years, and just over 4 percent for maturities of greater than nine years.

Related party transactions at well below these rates might effectively frame a gift when contrasted with the AFRs. For the lender, such rates may trigger additional income tax obligations, as well as gift tax consequences. The enforcement of these tax rules suggests that the forgone interest is a gift to the borrower, who is then presumed to pay the interest to the "lender" as the tax bill is assessed. For a sale-leaseback transaction involving seller financing, the rate must be 110 percent of the AFR. Published rates are determined for various compounding periods and loan terms. Loans of $10,000 or less are not subject to these rules, provided the funds were not used to control or acquire income-producing property.

SALE-AND-LEASEBACK OF REAL PROPERTY

A sales transaction that can produce immediate benefits for both buyer and seller involves a property owner selling to an investor. The selling owner then leases the property back from the investor for continued occupancy. The sale-and-leaseback transaction offers an investor acquisition of an income-producing property while the former owner receives cash or other consideration, and the continued use of the premises. National tenants, such as some hamburger franchises or drug store chains, often control the development of store-sites, assuring the design and quality of their facilities, and then sell the properties to investors. This allows the store to attach their imprimatur to the lease, elevating the sale price, and to allow themselves the option at multiyear intervals (initial lease terms are typically for at least five, but often ten, years) to vacate to newer facilities. The drug store or hamburger chain gets out of the real estate business, and the investor gets a high-quality **credit-tenant** whose lease can easily be used with a bank (even in the distressed late 2000s) to secure a loan to purchase the property.

AT-RISK RULES

Deductible losses generated by a taxpayer's business activities are generally limited and cannot exceed the amount the taxpayer has at risk in that particular activity. The amount at risk is determined at the close of the tax year. *At risk* is defined as the sum of three contributions by the taxpayer to the activity: (1) cash, (2) the adjusted basis of other property contributed, and (3) any amounts borrowed for use in the activity for which the taxpayer is personally liable. In other words, the amount at risk for which a deduction may be allowed is simply limited to the total amount of money an investor could actually lose.

If an investor contributes $100,000 in cash and other property to the purchase of a warehouse, but the property is financed with nonrecourse debt, then the rules limit the losses deductible by the taxpayer to $100,000, this amount perhaps further reduced depending on the depreciation taken by the investor during the period of ownership. Once losses taken on a given investment sum up to the total amount invested in the deal by the investor, no more losses may be taken, until additional sums are invested, either directly or through full-recourse debt (money for which the investor is liable, which money went to the improvement or enhancement of the warehouse, for example). If someone invests $100,000 in this warehouse, and takes $10,000 losses on his tax return each year for ten years, no more losses can be taken until additional monies are invested, unless the warehouse was purchased with debt for which he is personally liable. If losses in the activity exceed the amount at risk, the excess losses are disallowed.

SPECIAL INCOME TAX RULES SUMMARY

The three types of cash flows pursued by real estate investors are rental income, appreciation income, and tax shelter benefits. The tax flows deriving from this third area, tax shelters, derive from the myriad provisions in the tax code which favor real estate in some form or fashion.

While many of the tax benefits outlined in this and the preceding chapter are not exclusive to real estate, several are tailored specifically for the real estate investor. The Section 1031 tax-free exchange has grown enormously in popularity during the late 1990s and early 2000s, and has been a feature of a multitude of appreciated-property transactions. Beginning with encouragements in President Johnson's Great Society of the mid-1960s, a series of tax credits has been designed to motivate the rehabilitation of older urban areas and to augment the provision of housing to the poor. Finally, involuntary conversions of real estate due to disaster or the use of eminent domain and the sale of real estate via seller financing have also garnered special tax consideration. Sale-leaseback provisions and at-risk rules need to be assessed by the real estate investor, as well.

These are some of the main features of the tax code beyond simple depreciation allowances that either frame real estate in a particularly favorable light or which recognize the special costs confronted by the real estate investor. Each should be kept in mind in the management and acquisition of real estate investments.

KEY TERMS

adjusted basis	defer	installment sale	qualifying tenants
American Jobs Creation Act of 2004 (AJCA)	eligible basis	installment sale income	rehabilitation
	escrow agent	involuntary conversion	relief of debt
	general public	involuntary exchange	selling price
Applicable Federal Rates (AFR)	gross profit	like-kind property	set-aside requirements
	gross profit percentage	nontransient	tax credit
credit-tenant			

DISCUSSION QUESTIONS

1. What is the difference between a tax credit and a tax deduction?

2. Why is an apartment building exchanged for an office building eligible for a tax-deferred exchange under the "like-kind" rule?

3. Give an example of an involuntary exchange of property.

4. Describe how the capital gain tax is determined on a qualified installment sale.

5. What does a property owner gain from a sale and leaseback transaction?

6. What are the main requirements for a Section 1031 exchange?

7. Describe the Section 1031 "loophole" closed by the American Jobs Creation Act of 2004.

8. What are the two main types of real estate investment tax credits. Briefly describe them.

9. How could available tax credits exceed the "hard" development costs of a low-income housing project?

CHAPTER 8

Single-Family Dwellings and Condominiums

One of the largest and most important investments that the average person makes is a personal residence. Long ago, it was considered an acquisition of living accommodations and was expected to decline in value as it grew older and more outdated. However, by the late 1950s, a house was often purchased with a view to capitalizing on the growth in value. Indeed, the solid increase in value brought considerable speculation into home buying. This reached a crescendo in the early 2000s, as speculative home purchases contributed significantly to the Great Recession. Many homeowners purchased homes farther and farther out of financial reach, depending upon those homes' appreciation to fund otherwise unaffordable lifestyles and even more expensive home purchases; when the "music stopped," millions of homeowners faced foreclosure and a return to more prosaic lifestyles.

However, economic cycles ought not influence most home purchases as family housing needs arise independent of whether we are in a recession or an expansion! Thus, a distinction needs to be made between property purchased as an investment and property purchased for the personal purpose of living accommodations. The home, for most people, is a far more important piece of real estate than other real property investments.

The purchaser of a home wants a property that will meet the living requirements of an individual or a family. The size of the home, the number and arrangement of the rooms, and its proximity to schools, churches, shopping centers, and recreational facilities are all important. On the other hand, a purchaser of rental property is seeking an investment that will attract tenants and produce a profit. Far different motivations influence the home and investment property purchases.

Those physical characteristics of a residential property that are so important to the prospective homeowner are of less concern to the investment purchaser. A home buyer might see some value in a high-cost amenity, for example, a beautiful swimming pool; the investment buyer would look only to the amenity's contribution to the property's income.

This chapter considers the special tax treatment accorded a home-owner, which is quite different from the rules applying to rental houses. Certain deductions are permitted to the homeowner while living in the house. And if the personal residence is sold for a profit, there is a tax exclusion available. Also, some special tax rules apply to personal dwelling units that are rented for part of the year. Another major area of concern for homeowners is the distinctive nature of condominium ownership with its joint use and responsibility for common areas separated from the dwelling unit itself. These curious aspects of residential property are examined in this chapter.

THE PRINCIPAL RESIDENCE

A taxpayer is permitted only one principal residence, that place where she actually lives most of the time and calls "home." That home may be a condominium, a single-family house, or a vacant lot upon which is placed the tent or mobile home in which her family lives. Retirement units and any other multi-unit residential facility may also qualify as the principal residence depending upon the type of title received when the resident occupies the home. Rental units never qualify. And she hasn't the power to "assign" principal residence status to one home or another; there are many families in New York City who have a second "home" in Florida (or Texas), where there are no income taxes, spend only a day or two there per year, and would love to claim it as their principal residence. A Manhattan household with "only" $1 million in annual income could avoid $100,000 in New York state and local income taxes with such an assignment, and pay all the expenses of the second home with the tax savings! Loosely defined, the principal residence is where a family spends most of its time; for a family with more than two homes, it becomes tedious in assigning the "principal" designation, but suffice it to say that a homeowner in a heavily-taxed jurisdiction will be scrutinized as he works in one state, and claims residency in another. The federal tax rules for the homeowner are more straightforward and are considered below—some of those rules apply to both first and second homes. These rules should be considered in concert with those special tax rules for real estate investors described in Chapters 6 and 7.

Allowable Tax Deductions

A homeowner can deduct certain costs of the principal residence from ordinary taxable income. These are:

1. *Interest.* Interest paid on mortgage debt during the taxable year. (Subject to limitations.)
2. *Taxes.* All property taxes applicable to the residence.
3. *Casualty Losses.* Limited to the lesser of (1) the decrease in fair market value of the property resulting from the casualty, or (2) the adjusted basis in property. The first $100 of loss is *not* deductible, and any insurance proceeds that are received must be used to reduce the amount of the loss. Further, personal casualty losses must be reduced by 10 percent of the taxpayer's adjusted gross income.

Limits on Interest Deductions

While the 1986 Tax Act retained almost all the benefits available to homeownership, limitations were placed on the deductibility of mortgage interest. The rules for deductibility apply to a first or second residence. And such debt must be collateralized by a security interest in the taxpayer's principal or second residence. Two kinds of debt are identified and limited: (1) home acquisition debt and (2) home equity debt.

Home Acquisition Debt

Acquisition debt is defined as that incurred in acquiring, constructing, or substantially improving any qualified residence (principal residence plus one other) and which is secured by that residence. For such mortgages originated after October 13, 1987, interest is deductible on debt that does not exceed $1 million (includes any grandfathered debt and first and second residences). Mortgages originated prior to October 14th of 1987 were exempt from the interest limit, but interest rates have fallen significantly since then, in several cycles, and that "grandfather" clause is no longer meaningful, as the "old" mortgages have all been repaid or refinanced. The debt is limited to $500,000 for each married taxpayer filing separately or a single person. Acquisition debt is no longer limited by the fair market value of the property. This is particularly important in cases where the fair market value of a home is not increased by as much as the cost of substantial improvements.

Home Equity Debt

In addition to the acquisition debt, interest is deductible on loans up to $100,000 ($50,000 for each married taxpayer filing separately) on the equity in the residence regardless of how the proceeds are used (unless it is used to receive tax free income). Such debt must have originated after October 13, 1987. **Home equity debt** is defined as debt other than acquisition indebtedness secured by the home, to the extent that the aggregate amount of debt does not exceed the fair market value of the home reduced by the acquisition indebtedness. Thus, a home with a fair market value of $120,000 and acquisition debt of $70,000 could justify a home equity loan up to $50,000 ($120,000 minus $70,000 = $50,000) on which the interest is deductible.

Additional Qualified Residential Property

Interest on mortgages for mobile homes, boats, or vacation cabins used as second homes still qualify for the interest deduction within the overall $1 million debt limit. To qualify a living unit for this purpose, it must have sleeping accommodations, kitchen facilities, and an indoor toilet.

Discount as a Deduction

A discount paid by the borrower for a mortgage loan in the acquisition of a personal residence is deductible the same as interest. If the loan is for the *purchase* of the residence, it is deductible in full in the year it is paid. However, if the discount is for *refinancing* an existing loan, the discount is deductible over the life of the loan, not in the year paid. For example, if the cost of discount for refinancing is $2,400, and the term of the loan is 20 years, the taxpayer may deduct only $120 each year. (See Chapter 10 for further information.)

Property Tax Deduction

Property taxes are deductible for taxpayer-owned residences without limitations. While mortgage interest deductions are limited to only two qualified residences, there is no such limitation for state and local property taxes. The Alternative Minimum Tax, however, mentioned in chapter 6, may limit overall deductions of interest, property taxes, and non-federal income taxes.

Tax Treatment on Gain from Sale

If the principal residence is sold or exchanged during the tax year, it need not be reported on the tax return unless the gain exceeds the **exclusion** or either of the two eligibility requirements are not met. If the taxpayer is eligible for the exclusion, it amounts to $250,000 if single or $500,000 if married and filing jointly. There are exceptions, but the exclusion is limited to once every two years.

Eligibility for Exclusion

Two requirements must be met:

1. The house must be owned and used as the taxpayer's main home for two or more years during the five-year period ending on the date the house was sold or exchanged. If married, only one spouse needs to meet this requirement.
2. The taxpayer must not have sold or exchanged another main home during the two-year period ending on the date the house was sold or exchanged.

If the above two requirements are not met, or if the taxpayer used any part of the house for business or rental purposes, or the gain exceeds the exclusion amount, then the sale must be reported on the tax return and a capital gain tax may be due.

Temporary Absences

Short temporary absences for vacation or other seasonal absences, even if the property is rented out during the absences, are counted as periods of use. For example, Homer Homeowner, who is single, bought and moved into his home on February 1, 2006. Each year during 2006 and 2007, Homer left his home for a two month summer vacation. Homer sold his house on March 1, 2008. Although the total time Homer used his home is less than two years (21 months) he may exclude any gain up to $250,000. The two month vacations are short temporary absences and are counted as periods of use in determining whether Homer used the home for the required two years; the home's basis for computing taxable gain will be reduced, though, by any depreciation taken for the rental periods.

Consider another example. Holly Homeseller, who is single, bought and moved into a house on August 28, 2005. She lived in it as her main home continuously until January 5, 2007, when she went abroad for a one-year sabbatical from her teaching job. On February 6, 2008, one month after returning from her leave, Holly sold the house at a gain. Because her leave was not a short temporary absence, she cannot include the period of leave to meet the two-year use test. She cannot exclude any part of her gain, because she did not use the residence for the required two years.

Calculation of Capital Gain on Sale of Personal Residence

The calculation of a gain upon the sale or exchange of a personal residence follows the same pattern as investment property, with two major exceptions: (1) a homeowner may *not* deduct depreciation which reduces the basis of value (except for that period during which the home was rented out or for that area of the home used for business purposes) and (2) the tax code does *not* permit a homeowner to deduct any *loss* on the sale of a personal residence.

The **capital gain** from the sale of a personal residence is the difference between the **adjusted basis of the home** and the **realized selling price**. The important point to consider is how the tax code defines these two figures.

Is Land Considered a Residence?

If the land on which a main residence is located is sold, but not the house itself, the gain from the sale of the land cannot be excluded. However, if the taxpayer sells vacant land used as part of their main home and that is adjacent to it, the taxpayer may be able to exclude the gain from the sale under certain circumstances. Reference "Vacant land" under "Main Home" in IRS Publication 523 for more specific information.

Example: You buy a piece of land and move your main home to it. Then you sell the land on which your main home was located. This sale is not considered a sale of your main home, and you cannot exclude any gain on the sale of the land.

Basis of Property Value

The basis of value for a personal residence is determined no differently from any other property investment. It is the *method of acquisition* that determines the basis. While most residences are acquired by purchase, there are tax rules that apply to acquisitions by gift, by inheritance, and for services rendered.

Adjusted Basis

The original basis can be increased or decreased during the property holding period.

Increases to the basis include:

1. Improvements (does not include maintenance).
2. Additions.
3. Other capital expenses.
4. Special assessments for local improvements.
5. Amounts spent to restore damaged property.

Decreases to the basis include:

1. Insurance reimbursements for casualty losses.
2. Deductible casualty losses not covered by insurance.
3. Payments received for easement or right-of-way granted.
4. Depreciation allowed, but only if the home is used for business or rental purposes.

Even though the tax exclusion on the sale of a personal residence is high enough to eliminate a capital gain tax for most homeowners, it is a prudent step to keep records of all applicable transactions. When necessary, the IRS requires reasonable proof that the adjusted basis has been adequately calculated. Remember that any increase in the adjusted basis reduces the amount of taxable capital gain when the property is sold.

Sample Calculation of Property Basis

A duplex was acquired a number of years ago for $450,000, with $350,000 being allocated to the building. Since the purchase, there have been fire damage, a partial sale, improvements added, and depreciation taken. The adjusted basis is calculated as follows:

Original cost of duplex		$450,000
Addition to duplex		20,000
Total cost of duplex		470,000
Minus: Depreciation		70,000
Adjusted basis before casualty		400,000
Minus: Insurance proceeds	$29,700	
Deducted casualty loss	6,000	
Salvage proceeds	5,300	
	$41,000	41,000
Adjusted basis after casualty		359,000
Add: Cost of restoring duplex		15,000
Adjusted basis after restoration		$374,000

Realized Selling Price

Since capital gain is the difference between the adjusted basis of the property and the amount realized from the sale of that property, the next step is to determine how to calculate the realized selling price. The calculation starts with the total consideration received from the sale.

Total Consideration Received

This includes cash, notes, mortgages, and the fair market value of any real or personal property received in the transaction. If the taxpayer is moved by an employer, any payment from the employer as reimbursement for a decline in property value, or as payment in excess of fair market value, is *not* included in the selling price in the calculation of capital gain. Any such money received from an employer must be reported as *ordinary* income for services rendered. The sales price for any personal property is not included in total consideration received.

Deduct Selling Expenses

The expenses that the homeowner can deduct from the sales price in calculating the realized selling price are:

1. Sales commission.
2. Advertising paid for by the seller.
3. Legal fees incurred in the sale.
4. Loan placement fees or discount points paid by the seller.

Deduct Fixing-Up Expenses

Fixing-up expenses are not deductible from ordinary income. Fixing-up expenses are only deductible in determining the gain on which taxes are payable. They cannot be deducted in figuring actual profit or the reduction in basis for the replacement home.

For tax purposes, fixing-up expenses include decorating and repair costs incurred solely to assist in the sale of the property. These expenses must have been incurred for work performed within 90 days before the sales contract is signed and must have been paid no more than 30 days after the sale. Capital expenditures or improvements cannot be included in fixing-up expenses.

Record Keeping

The records that should be kept include:

- Proof of the home's purchase price and purchase expenses.
- Receipts and other records for all improvements, additions, and other items that affect the home's adjusted basis.
- Any worksheets or other computations that were used to figure the adjusted basis of the home that was sold, the gain or loss on the sale, the exclusion, and the taxable gain.
- Any Form 982 that was filed to report any discharge of qualified principal residence indebtedness.
- Any Form 2119, "Sale of Your Home," that was filed to postpone gain from the sale of a previous home before May 7, 1997.
- Any worksheets that were used to prepare Form 2119, such as the "Adjusted Basis of Home Sold Worksheet" or the "**Capital Improvement Worksheet**" from the Form 2119 instructions, or other source of computations.

Sale of a Principal Residence Married Couple Filing Jointly Example # 1

Purchase Price	$180,000
Purchase Costs	$10,000
Acquisition Basis	$190,000
Capital Improvements	$30,000
Adjusted Basis	$220,000
Sales Price	$700,000
Less Adjusted Basis	$220,000
Gain on the Sale	$480,000
Less Exclusion	$500,000
Taxable Gain	-0-
Capital Gains Tax Rate*	20%
Tax Due	-0-

*Subject to change—depends on the tax year, and excludes taxes at the state level.

Sale of a Principal Residence Married Couple Filing Jointly Example # 2

Purchase Price	$180,000
Purchase Costs	$10,000
Acquisition Basis	$190,000
Capital Improvements	$30,000
Adjusted Basis	$220,000
Sales Price	$800,000
Less Adjusted Basis	$220,000
Gain on the Sale	$580,000
Less Exclusion	$500,000
Taxable Gain	$80,000
Capital Gains Tax Rate*	20%
Tax Due	$16,000

*Subject to change—depends on the tax year, and excludes taxes at the state level.

RESIDENCE CONVERTED TO RENTAL USE

If a taxpayer's personal residence is converted (in whole or in part) for use in the taxpayer's business or for the production of rental income, it is necessary to determine the basis from which the property may be depreciated. This basis is the *lesser* of:

1. The fair market value of the property on the date of conversion.
2. The adjusted basis of the property (as explained earlier in this chapter).

The income and expenses of rental property are subject to IRS rules, which are examined next.

Rental Income

Regular Payments

The money received for the normal use of the rental property is income when it is received.

Advance Rent

Advance rentals must be included as regular income in the year they are received, regardless of the time period covered and the accounting method used by the taxpayer.

Payment for Lease Cancellation

Such a payment must be treated as rental income in the year it is received, regardless of the taxpayer's accounting method.

Expenses Paid by Tenant

If a tenant pays any of the landlord's expenses, these payments are rental income to the landlord and must be reported. However, the landlord may deduct those expenses that are normally deductible.

Rental Expenses

Cost Recovery (Depreciation)

After determining the basis of the building and of any personal property included as rental property, it is necessary to determine the cost recovery period for each class of property.

Repairs and Maintenance

Any repairs to maintain the buildings and equipment or other rental property in an efficient condition are considered operating expenses and are deductible. Anything that adds to the value of the property or prolongs its useful life is considered an improvement, which is capitalized and then recovered over the appropriate recovery period.

Handicap Exception

The taxpayer may elect to deduct up to $25,000 each year for an improvement or alteration (such as a ramp) that assists a handicapped or elderly person's access to the building. This rule applies to all kinds of rental properties, not just to residential units.

Other Expenses

All normal operating expenses for the property are deductible. These include advertising, trash collection, maintenance services, employee's wages, utilities, fire and liability insurance, taxes, interest, and commissions paid to rent the property or to collect the rents.

Rental of a Room

A room may be rented in a personal residence and is eligible for the same deductions available for renting an entire house. However, the deductions must be allocated only to that portion of the house that is rented. The taxpayer may use any reasonable method of dividing the expenses. The most commonly used methods are: (1) based on number of rooms in the house and (2) based on the square foot area in the house.

The percentage of the property rented is applied to the deduction amounts. For example, if a room comprises 15 percent of the total living area, only 15 percent of the eligible business deductions, such as depreciation, repairs, maintenance, utilities, and insurance, can be taken. Taxes and mortgage loan interest are deductible for both a personal residence and a business property, so are taken in full for this calculation. Note: Any depreciation taken reduces the basis of value in the personal residence.

If rental expenses exceed the gross rental income, the excess is not deductible in the tax year but may be carried forward and may be deductible in future years.

Business Use of the Home

If a portion of the personal residence is used by the owner for business purposes, the taxpayer may be able to deduct operating and depreciation expenses. To qualify, a specific part of the residence must be set aside (it need not be a separate room) and used exclusively and on a regular basis as (1) the principal place of any business that the taxpayer engages in, or (2) a place where the taxpayer meets with patients, clients, or customers. Also, an employee is allowed a home-office deduction if its use is for the convenience of the employer. Managing a personal investment portfolio does not qualify as a separate business for this purpose.

Permissible deductions include depreciation, maintenance, insurance, and utility expenses as allocated to the portion of the house used for business purposes. The tax code does not specify, but the allocation can most likely be made on a basis of square feet or on number of rooms in the house. Any deduction taken for depreciation reduces the basis of value for the principal residence.

The limit on deductions that can be taken for the **business use of a home** is the gross income from that business minus the sum of:

1. The business percentage of the otherwise deductible real estate taxes and casualty and theft losses.
2. The business expenses not attributable to the use of the home, such as salaries and supplies.

Taxpayers may no longer lease a portion of a home to an employer and claim deductions as a business usage.

If the taxpayer occupies rental housing, it may qualify for office-in-home deductions. There are some rather stringent guidelines, but eligible renters may deduct a proportionate share of their rent and utilities.

PART-TIME RENTAL UNITS

If the same dwelling unit is used **part-time for rental purposes** and part-time as a personal residence, it is necessary to allocate expenses between the rental use and the personal use. Special tax rules apply to this allocation. The rules apply to any type of dwelling unit so used, but they are most commonly used for vacation homes. If the taxpayer owns a partial interest in such property, the deduction is only the proportionate share of ownership expenses, even if more than a proportionate share was paid.

Tax Definition of Dwelling Unit

For tax purposes, a dwelling unit may be a house, apartment, condominium, mobile home, boat, or other similar property. The term does not include hotels, motels, and inns that are operated as businesses.

Tax Definition of Personal Use

Personal use occurs any day or part of a day when a dwelling unit is used by:

1. The taxpayer, a member of the family, or any other person with an interest in the property, unless a fair market rental is paid.
2. Anyone under a reciprocal arrangement that enables the taxpayer to use some other dwelling unit.
3. Anyone at less than a fair rental.

Allocation of Expenses

Expenses must be allocated between personal use and rental use. However, the allocation method and the deductible expenses vary with the number of days of personal use during the year. There are three categories of use, each of which is governed by its own tax rules:

1. Used primarily as a personal residence, and rented for less than 15 days during the year.
2. Used as a personal residence for more than the greater of (a) 14 days, or (b) 10 percent of the number of days during the tax year when the property was rented for a fair price.
3. Used as a personal residence, but for not more than the greater of (a) 14 days, or (b) 10 percent of the number of days it was rented at a fair price.

Category 1—Rented Less Than 15 Days

A personal residence rented for less than 15 days during the year is excluded from the rule permitting deduction of expenses (other than interest, taxes, and casualty losses). Any rent received under this category is not included in personal gross income. The normal deductions permitted for a personal residence—interest, taxes, and casualty losses—are deductible only if the taxpayer itemizes deductions (Schedule A, Form 1040).

Category 2—Part Rental, Part Personal Use

If the dwelling unit is substantially used both as a residence and for rental purposes, expenses must be allocated between the two. The allocation is based on the number of days that the property is used during the year, not on the 365-day year. The number of days used includes those for both rental and personal purposes but not those days on which the unit was held out for rent. To count as a rental day, the unit must be rented at a fair price. For example, if the taxpayer owns a beach cabin that has been rented for 120 days during the tax year and used for personal purposes for 30 days, the total days used would be 150. To allocate:

$$\text{For rental}: \frac{120}{150} = 0.80 \text{ or } 80\% \text{ of expenses}$$

$$\text{For personal use}: \frac{30}{150} = 0.20 \text{ or } 20\% \text{ of expenses}$$

Limitations on Allocation of Expenses

Under this category, the amount of deducted expenses may not exceed the unit's gross rental income. However, the income from rental property is classed as passive: If a profit is made, it may be used as an offset for other passive activity losses. If a loss is incurred, it may be carried forward indefinitely for write-off against future income from the property, or claimed as a deduction when the property is disposed of.

For tax reporting purposes, the taxpayer must first deduct from gross rental income that portion of total expense for interest, taxes, and casualty losses that is allocated to rental use. Next, the taxpayer deducts the portion of operating expenses allocated to rental use. Finally, the allocation for depreciation is deducted. The following example will illustrate the steps in allocating deductions.

Start with the following expenses for the beach cabin for a year:

Interest	$1,400
Taxes	$1,000
Utilities	$750
Maintenance	$300
Cost recovery (depreciation)	$1,200

As calculated above, the cabin was used for rental purposes 80 percent of the time it was in use and 20 percent for personal purposes. Assuming that gross rental income is $3,300 the results are as follows:

Gross rental income		$3,300
Interest (80% of $1,400)	1,120	
Taxes (80% of $1,000)	800	
Less: Interest and taxes		$1,920
Rental income exceeding interest and taxes		$1,380
Utilities (80% of $750)	600	
Maintenance (80% of $300)	240	
Less: Utilities and maintenance		$ 840
Rental income exceeding interest, taxes and operating expenses		$ 540
Less: Cost recovery (depreciation). Limited in this example to the lesser of 80% of $1,200 [$960] or the remainder of the gross rental income not already deducted ($540)		$ 540
Net rental income		0

Rental income and expenses should be reported on Schedule E (Form 1040). Interest and taxes allocated to personal use (20% of each, in the example above) are deductible on Schedule A (Form 1040), *provided* that the taxpayer itemizes deductions (rather than taking the standard deduction).

Category 3—Personal Use, Less Than 15 Days

If a dwelling unit is used primarily for rental with the expectation of making a profit, it is not considered the taxpayer's personal residence. To qualify in this category, use as a personal residence during the year must not exceed the greater of (a) 14 days, or (b) 10 percent of the number of days it was rented at a fair price. As rental property, this class is considered a passive activity, but losses are not limited to the unit's income as with Category 2. However, any losses sustained can only be offset by other passive activity income.

Even so, as personal use property for only a portion of the time, it is still necessary to calculate total days of use and to allocate expenses between rental use and personal use, as in Category 2.

TIME-SHARING OWNERSHIP

While the concept of time-sharing lacks the quality of ownership embodied in the other forms of ownership discussed in this text, it is growing in importance and needs to be understood.

Time-sharing ownership means the holding of rights to exclusive use of real estate for a designated length of time (such as two weeks or a month) each year. Because ownership rights are not always clearly defined, the sale of time-share interests has encountered some abuse. A few sales agents have used intensive, and sometimes misleading, promotional campaigns. The time available has been oversold and management has been lax in some cases. A number of states have enacted restrictive legislation designed to provide consumers with better protection when dealing with the purchase of a time-share interest.

There are two basic methods used to create time-sharing arrangements: one is through a **long-term lease**, and the other is through condominium-type ownership.

Long-Term Lease

Under the long-term lease arrangement, the developer or promoter acquires a hotel, motel, or an apartment building in a suitable resort area. For each unit in the building, the developer sells, say, 25 two-week leases out of each year for 30 years. That leaves a two-week period unallocated each year that can be used for general maintenance work. The sale of the leases is calculated to pay for the building, and the lessee pays a proportionate share of the cost for management, maintenance, and any services that are commonly provided. A specific unit may be assigned to the lessee, or the lessee may be allowed to use any unit available on a first-come, first-served basis. In an arrangement of this kind, the leasehold interest should have the right to sell; 30 years is a long time for one vacation spot.

Condominium Time-Sharing

The purpose of a condominium plan is to grant an owner the right to use a unit for a specified period each year. An example might be the sale of a unit to 24 buyers as tenants in common. Each holds the right to use the unit for two weeks out of each year. Or the arrangement could be a sale to 12 owners, each of whom has the right to use the unit for two weeks in the summer and two weeks in the winter.

Management and maintenance problems are somewhat more difficult with time-sharing as compared with full-time occupancy of a condominium. An ownership agreement is necessary to define user priorities, assign responsibilities for maintenance (probably a professional management company), and detail the procedures to be used if an owner wants to sell his interest. Another matter of concern is the allocation of expenses and debt service if one or more of the owners fail to pay their share.

CONDOMINIUMS

The ownership of a condominium as a dwelling or as a business property is of fairly recent origin. It has taken enabling legislation in each of the 50 states to properly define a condominium as a piece of real estate. Through this type of legislation, an owner holds title to a particular apartment or unit in a larger building or building complex (an improved cube of airspace). He also holds title to an undivided interest—usually as a tenant in common with other unit owners—in the land on which the building stands and in the other common elements of the property that are used by the owners as a group. Condominiums may be residential or commercial (shopping centers or office buildings, for example).

Condominiums did not appear in large numbers on the housing market until the early 1960s. It was not until 1967 that all 50 states had enacted the necessary legislation to permit condominium ownership as it is known today. While the ownership of a condominium has similarities to that of a free-standing house, there are some differences to be considered. A condominium owner typically holds a fee simple estate (see Chapter 4) in a specific unit, while owning the community property (elevators and stairwells, hallways, recreational facilities, common areas, etc.) as a tenant in common.

The Unit Owner

In general, the owner of a condominium unit holds the same tax status as any other real property owner. That is, if the property is occupied as a personal residence, the same rules apply to the condo owner as to a single-family residence owner in regard to deductibility of interest and taxes and the non-deductibility of maintenance costs and depreciation. If the condominium is used for business purposes—either all or a part of it—the same rules apply as with other forms of business property. Several aspects of condominium ownership are unique and should be considered.

Mortgage Interest

The owner of a condominium may mortgage the unit, and the interest paid on such a mortgage is deductible. Since the unit owner's undivided interest in common areas is inseparable from the unit, this, too, would be included in the mortgage.

In most instances, the lender furnishing financing for the construction of a condominium project provides for the release of a portion of the construction mortgage as the individual units are sold. The construction mortgage is repaid from the proceeds of the sales. Thus, there is no overall mortgage to concern the unit owner. However, there are situations—especially when an existing building is converted to a condominium—when the unit purchaser assumes a specified dollar amount of an existing overall mortgage on the premises. Under these circumstances, the share of interest paid on such a mortgage is deductible.

If the condominium is used as a business property, the interest is fully deductible. There is a slight possibility that a portion of interest costs could be reallocated to the unit owner's association, if any part of the common area is used for the production of income.

Real Estate Taxes

A condominium owner may deduct real estate taxes paid, or accrued, for the property the same as for any other real estate.

However, assessment procedures do vary from state to state. In some states, each unit owner is assessed separately along with her corresponding percentage of ownership in the common elements. That is, a single assessment is made against each owner. In other states, the assessment is made only against the unit with no mention of the common elements. In such a case, a single assessment could be made against the common elements as a whole to be paid for by the unit owner's association. The association then assesses each unit owner her proportionate share of the taxes, which would be deductible when paid by the owner. If some of the unit owners should default in paying their share, the other owners, as tenants in common, could deduct the share of the deficit that they paid.

In states that permit condominiums to be created on long-term lease-holds, there is often a provision for the tax assessment to be made against individual units, which creates no problem for deductibility. In states that have no such provision and where the tax assessment is made against the landowner (the owner of the leased land), it is doubtful that unit owners can deduct any share of the taxes. The theory is that a lessee may not deduct taxes imposed on the lessor because this should be treated as a part of the rental payments. Such rental payments are deductible only if the property is used in business and not as a personal residence.

Maintenance, Repairs, Insurance

If a condominium is occupied as a personal residence, expenses for repairs, maintenance, or insurance are not deductible whether or not the payment is made individually or as an assessment levied by the unit owner's association.

These are considered personal expenditures of a homeowner. If the unit is used, all or part, for business purposes, the same rules of prorated deductibility for expenses apply as to other real estate.

An overassessment for common expenses by a unit owner's association is generally not deductible, particularly if the association has agreed to refund such overpayment or apply it to the following year's assessment. There are administrative complications in properly informing the unit members of the time when each expenditure was paid. Thus, an overassessment can be a normal result of prudent management.

Depreciation or Cost Recovery

The unit owner may not deduct depreciation if the unit is occupied as a personal residence. It is deductible if the unit is used as rental property. While the IRS distinguishes between residential and commercial rental property in determining qualification for cost-recovery class, the rule was not clearly designed with condominiums in mind. The IRS identifies residential rental property as a building with at least 80 percent of its gross rental income derived from dwelling units. The most logical interpretation for a condominium is that the unit itself comprises the building and, therefore, should qualify under its own usage category.

There is one small problem in condominium depreciation. If the unit owner's association is considered to be a taxable entity, like a corporation, and it is considered to be the owner of the common areas, there could be a question if any part of the common area is used to produce income. The IRS might attempt to allocate a portion of any depreciation claimed by a unit owner to the corporation.

Capital Improvements

An assessment for capital improvements would normally be capitalized and depreciated over its useful life, if the unit is rental property. This is not permitted if the unit is used as a personal residence. For owners of rental condominiums, care should be taken that a capital improvement assessment is not handled as a contribution to the capital of the owners' association corporation. As such, it would be neither deductible nor depreciable for the unit owners because the corporation would hold the depreciable interest in the improvements.

Sale or Exchange of a Unit

The owner of a condominium unit used as a personal residence qualifies for all of the normal tax benefits available in the sale of this type of property. The unit is a capital asset and, if sold at a gain, the gain is taxable if it exceeds the personal residence exclusion. A loss is not deductible.

If the unit is used for the production of rental income (or used in the owner's business), it is eligible for the same tax deductions that apply to other commercial real estate. Capital gain taxes can be deferred through a property exchange (as with a Section 1031 exchange discussed in Chapter 7), and losses in a sale may be deducted as a Section 1231 asset.

KEY TERMS

acquisition debt

adjusted basis of the home

advance rentals

business use of a home

capital gain

capital improvement exclusion

home equity debt

long-term lease

part-time for rental purposes

realized selling price

time-sharing ownership

DISCUSSION QUESTIONS

1. Describe the three costs that are tax-deductible for a homeowner.

2. Discuss the current exemption from capital gain tax available to a homeowner.

3. What are the two basic methods of creating a timesharing arrangement?

4. What is the basis for declaring a condominium with no direct attachment to the land a piece of real estate?

5. Describe complications that may arise in the assessment of real estate taxes on a condominium.

6. List the items that increase the basis of a residential property.

7. List the items that decrease the basis of a residential property.

8. What is the formula for calculating the capital gain on the sale of a residential property?

9. What are the terms for a homeowner to take advantage of the capital gains tax exclusion on a principal residence?

10. What is the amount of the capital gains tax exclusion for a single taxpayer? What is the exclusion for a married couple filing jointly?

11. What are the limits on interest deductions on a residential property?

CHAPTER 9

Business Organizations

An investor in real estate can choose one of several methods for holding and operating the property. The investor may select a sole proprietorship, partnership, some sort of trust or syndication, or one of several corporate forms. Each method carries its own advantages, disadvantages, and income tax reporting requirements. State laws govern both business organizations and landownership. Income tax laws are set by the federal government and are generally followed in those states that have their own income tax requirements.

This chapter considers the major forms of business organization, the responsibilities and benefits that can accrue from each, and the various federal tax reporting requirements.

SOLE PROPRIETORSHIP

The simplest form of business organization is the **sole proprietorship.** It has the lowest costs of formation and the lowest costs of record-keeping and tax filing. An individual can own land and/or operate a business in his own name, under a trade name, or under an assumed name. Most states require that a trade name or an assumed name be publicly registered or recorded if it differs from the individual's name, reducing the possibility of misrepresentation to creditors or others. Another advantage of the sole proprietorship is that the owner has absolute control over management decisions and an absolute right to dispose of profits or assets.

The sole proprietorship offers an owner no protection against financial losses or claims that may arise from the operation of the business; the veil of protection offered by corporate and some partnership forms of business ownership is absent. The proprietor is potentially liable for the satisfaction of a judgment or lien, depending on the state in which the proprietor is operating. However, insurance is available to limit these sorts of losses, and as the same sort of insurance (against property losses and personal liability claims, for example) is typically purchased with the other forms of ownership, the simplicity of the sole proprietorship form often leads to its selection by the individual investor purchasing investment real estate.

Income Tax Reports for a Sole Proprietorship

All taxable income of a sole proprietorship must be reported as part of the individual owner's income or loss. It must be reported for the same calendar year used for the personal income tax return. The business report is submitted on Schedule C, Form 1040, "Profit (or Loss) from Business or Profession" of the federal tax forms. Individual tax returns normally cover a calendar year, that is, the 12-month period from January 1 through December 31.[1] For sole proprietorships, selections of other than the calendar year for tax reporting is uncommon, entails additional reporting requirements, and often requires IRS consent.

Accounting Method Used for a Sole Proprietorship

The sole proprietor may select any accounting system, but is required by law to keep all records needed, such as receipts and bank statements, to prepare a complete and accurate income tax return. The most common accounting methods are the *cash method* and the *accrual method* (see Chapter 11). The taxpayer must select one method for each business when it begins to operate. (The same accounting method need not be used for all of a taxpayer's businesses.) Once a method has been selected, any change requires IRS consent. For income-producing real estate investments typically chosen by the sole proprietor, such as single-family housing or small commercial buildings, the cash method is widely favored. With that method, rental income and expenses are recognized as they are received or paid, and depreciation, a non-cash tax deduction, is allowed.

EXAMPLE 9.1	John Headley is investing in small commercial properties in Jacksonville, Florida. He will own each property by himself, and he is able to insure against fire, flood, and personal liability with area insurers. He would be required to provide personal guarantees on the mortgages to buy the properties regardless of the ownership form chosen. He chooses the sole proprietorship form, as he will own each property in his own name, expects to pay off the mortgages in a timely fashion, and wishes to save the time, money, and effort entailed in owning the properties in any other form.

---

[1] Further information may be obtained from IRS Publication 538, "Tax Information on Accounting Periods and Methods."

Disposition of a Sole Proprietorship

If the assets of a sole proprietorship are disposed of, they must be classified into four separate categories.[2] The gain or loss and tax consequences for each category must be computed separately. Guidelines are as follows:

1. *Capital assets.* Sale results in a capital gain or loss, with tax consequences a function of the net capital gain and depreciation recaptured (see Example 6.5).
2. *Depreciable property used in the business.* Sale results in a gain or loss against the adjusted basis as a Section 1231 transaction, and there will be tax consequences for recaptured depreciation.
3. *Real property used in the business.* Sale must be reported separately, but the tax treatment is the same as for depreciable property.
4. *Property held as inventory or stock in trade.* Sale results in ordinary income or loss.

PARTNERSHIP

The laws of partnerships stem from civil law, common law, equity, and law merchant. In 1914, the Commissioners on Uniform State Laws drafted the Uniform Partnership Act, which codified the general rules prevailing at the time. The Partnership Act is the basis for all state laws regarding partnerships.

The Partnership Act defines a **partnership** as an association of two or more persons, who carry on a business as co-owners for profit. Partnerships can be classified as trading and non-trading. Non-trading partnerships are those formed by professionals, such as lawyers, accountants, and physicians. However, this text discusses the trading partnership. These trading partnerships can be further classified as general or limited, though the limited partnership form of real estate ownership has been largely displaced by the **limited liability company** (LLC). (Limited partnerships and LLCs are discussed in a separate section of this chapter.)

Formation of a Partnership

A general partnership can be formed by either oral agreement or a written contract between (or among) the partners.

By Oral Agreement

A valid partnership can be formed with an oral agreement, although some states limit the life of such a partnership to one year. Courts have held that a partnership formed by oral agreement may hold title to land even though state laws require land transfer agreements to be in written form. Many states, however, do not allow the ownership of and by a partnership formed orally; those states, such as Louisiana, require the partnership to be written

---

[2] Further information may be obtained from IRS Publication 544, "Sales and Other Dispositions of Assets."

for it to own real estate. For states allowing oral partnerships to own land, courts have interpreted the law to govern the form of the land transaction, not the form of the partnership. A group of childhood friends might purchase a beach home or fishing lodge by oral agreement, in equal shares; such a partnership would be valid in many jurisdictions, especially if that validity were ratified, for example, by partners later sharing equally in insurance and property tax payments.

By Written Agreement

Even though oral partnerships are valid in some states, a written understanding is preferable. A written agreement should obviously contain the name of the partnership, the names of the partners, the duration of the agreement, and the partnership's place of business. Not so obviously, it should also clearly indicate the capital contributions of each partner, their duties, a method for settling disputes, a procedure for cash withdrawals required by the partners, the way in which profits or losses will be divided, and a method by which the partnership may be dissolved. Some states have statutory requirements regarding the names that can be used for a partnership, and most require that any fictitious or assumed name be published or filed with a designated authority. The Partnership Act does not prevent a corporation from becoming a partner. On the contrary, the Act defines the word *persons* as individuals, partnerships, corporations, and other associations.

Partnership Operations

In a general partnership, the partners determine the responsibility for management. Each partner might have a specific area of management responsibility, with major policy decisions made by a majority vote of the partners. The partnership agreement should define the duties of each partner, as well as any shared responsibilities.

Liabilities

In a general partnership, each partner is liable for all obligations incurred on behalf of the partnership by any of the partners. The partnership agreement can limit liabilities among the partners themselves, making partners responsible for their own commitments. But, the responsibility of each partner to the general public and to the partnership's creditors cannot be limited by internal agreement among the general partners.

Disadvantages of a Partnership

The most obvious disadvantage of the general partnership is each partner's unlimited liability for the partnership's losses. Insurance coverage is rarely available to protect the partners against bad management or poor judgment. Another disadvantage of a partnership is the limited life of the partnership agreement. Unlike a corporation, a partnership may be terminated by the death of any one partner, or by the withdrawal of a partner. Termination can also result from mutual agreement among the partners, an act in default of the partnership agreement by one or more of the partners, or through bankruptcy. The partnership form does not provide an investment interest that is easily liquidated or readily sold. Each partner has, in effect, both an undivided interest in the partnership's property and an equal right of possession. The close relationship among the partners, which is all-important for successful operation, is not readily replaced. Generally, partnership agreements contain restrictions on each partner's right to sell an interest to outsiders.

Advantages of a Partnership

T12

A partnership is formed primarily to combine the capital and expertise of two or more people, and it does so effectively. All partners have a voice in the management; all participate directly in the success of the partnership's operation. Partnerships are not required to file reports or pay franchise taxes to the state, while corporations must. And, the partnership is not a taxable entity for income tax purposes.

Partnership Income Tax Reports

Although a partnership pays no income tax, it must file an information return— Form 1065—each year. This return shows the results of the partnership's operations for the tax year, separating the items of income, gain, loss, deduction, or credit that affect each partner's individual income tax return. (These items are the partner's distributive share.) Since 1987, a partnership is required to conform its tax year to the same as the tax year of either its majority partners (owning more than 50 percent), its principal partners (holding 5 percent or more interest), or a calendar year, in that order, unless it can establish a business purpose acceptable to the IRS for using a different tax year. The deferral of income to partners is not considered a business purpose.

Partnership income is treated by the partners as having been distributed on the last day of the partnership year. Each partner must include the distributive share of partnership items on her individual return for the tax year in which the last day of the partnership year falls. A partner reports her share of the partnership's ordinary income or loss on Schedule E, Form 1040.

The manner in which profits and losses are distributed is usually set out in the partnership agreement. If there is no agreement on sharing a specific item of gain or loss, each partner's share is determined in accordance with that partner's proportional interest in the partnership.

Partnership income and gains are taxable to each partner—to the extent of the individual's share—whether or not they are distributed. This is an important point to consider when selecting a form of business operation, particularly if cash flows must be retained in the business for a number of years while operations are getting off the ground. The distributive share of partnership losses is limited to the adjusted basis of each partner's interest at the end of the partnership year in which the losses occurred. Partnership income or losses may be allocated to each partner only for that portion of the year that the taxpayer is a member of the partnership. The IRS claims the right to reallocate the distributive shares of partnership income, losses, or other items to the proper parties if the allocation lacks substantial economic justification.

When a taxpayer-partner has the right to exercise an election, the partnership—not the taxpayer-partner—makes the decision. These decisions include the method of accounting, the method of computing depreciation, the use of installment sales provisions, and others. The elections apply to all partners collectively. There are exceptions to this procedure, however, notably when foreign taxes are involved or certain oil or mineral exploration expenditures are incurred.

Guaranteed Payments

If a partner is paid a salary for services rendered or interest for the use of capital, these guaranteed payments are generally deductible as business expenses to the partnership. But guaranteed payments for a partner's services in forming the partnership, selling interests in the partnership, or acquiring property for the partnership are not deductible as a business expense to the partnership. Any guaranteed payments to a partner must be reported on that individual's return as salary or interest income.

Distributive Items

When the IRS uses the term "distributive item," it means the various forms of income and loss that may be taxed in different fashions for the individual partners. Schedule K of Form 1065 contains a list of a partnership's distributive share items. A copy of this list (Schedule K-1) shows each partner's share of the distributive items. Items commonly reported on Schedule K include:

1. Ordinary income or loss.
2. Partner's salary and interest.
3. Gains and losses from property used in trade or business, and from involuntary conversions.
4. Qualifying dividends.
5. Contributions.
6. Net self-employment income.
7. First-year asset expense option.
8. Expense account allowance.
9. Tax preference items.

Each partner's distributive share of the partnership's income, gain, loss, deduction, or credit must be shown separately on his or her own Form 1040. These items are treated generally as if each partner had realized or incurred them personally. If a partner itemizes deductions on Form 1040, the distributive share of items such as "partnership's contributions" may be included. These are not deductible in computing partnership income.[3]

JOINT STOCK COMPANIES

Some states permit the **joint-stock company** as a form of business ownership. It has some features of a corporation but is actually a general partnership. Management is placed in the hands of trustees or directors, but the partners

---

[3] Further information may be obtained from IRS Publication 541, "Tax Information on Partnership Income and Losses."

retain unlimited financial liability for company operations. Under the organization's constitution and bylaws, certificates are issued that represent ownership shares. Transferring shares does not cause dissolution of a joint-stock arrangement. So the death of a shareholder does not dissolve the organization, as it does in the case of a partnership. In many states, suit may be brought against a joint-stock company as a separate entity, just as with a corporation. More and more often, LLCs—discussed at length below—displace the joint-stock company as an ownership method.

LIMITED PARTNERSHIP

The **limited partnership** puts a ceiling on the financial liability of each person designated as a limited partner. And as with the joint stock companies above, the limited partnership as an ownership form has been displaced by the LLC in recent years. Limited partnerships were quite popular in the several years following the passage of the Economic Recovery Tax Act in 1981 (see Chapter 6), as they provided an attractive vehicle for a single or group of "dealmakers" (the general or managing partners in a limited partnership) to offer desirable terms to investors, while limiting the risk and economic upside of those investors at the same time. (Example 6.2 is the sort of investment that lent itself to syndication as a limited partnership.) Though now typically employed in only limited circumstances, as with the development of a grocery store-anchored shopping center, the limited partnership can be formed only by written agreement, and is subject to the terms of the state in which it is formed.

The origin of the limited partnership is the Uniform Limited Partnership Act, which has been adopted by every state except Louisiana (which has its own Act covering limited partnerships). The essence of a limited partnership is that it consists of one or more persons, known as limited partners, who do not participate in the management of the business and are personally liable to creditors only for the amount of their capital investment in the partnership. The limited partnership also has one or more persons, known as general partners, who are responsible for the management of the business and are personally liable for financial obligations of the partnership without regard to their investment.

The Limited Partnership Act states that a general partner possesses all the rights—and is subject to all the restrictions and liabilities—of a partner, in a general partnership. However, the Act provides additional restrictions on the general partner; for example, he cannot act contrary to the partnership certificate, and cannot admit someone as a general or limited partner. The death or retirement of a general partner generally terminates the limited partnership, but this can be overcome through a specific provision in the partnership agreement.

According to the provisions of the Act, a limited partner does not become financially liable as a general partner unless the limited partner participates in the management and control of the business. The limited partner is authorized to inspect the books of the partnership and to receive, on demand, full information on all matters affecting the partnership. The limited partner may lend money to the partnership and can transact other business with the partnership. The limited partner may make a capital contribution of cash or property to the partnership, but cannot contribute services.

Courts have held that a limited partnership may be dissolved if it is operating at a loss. The Limited Partnership Act establishes priorities for distributing assets upon dissolution of a partnership, giving general creditors first rights over limited partners, and limited partners generally having priority over general partners.

Disadvantages of a Limited Partnership

Problems that can arise in a limited partnership are like those found in a general partnership, including the difficulty of selling a partnership interest and the possibility of early termination of the business through death or withdrawal of a general partner. The general partner takes the same risks as in a general partnership, plus the possibility of challenge by the limited partners if management decisions are less than prudent. Limited partners, who generally contribute most or all of the capital, have very little voice in the management of the partnership.

All limited partnerships create passive activity income or losses. This means that any losses from a limited partnership interest may only be offset against passive activity income. It prevents the transfer of losses against other active income and substantially reduces the tax-shelter attraction of this form of business organization, which attraction had been among the motivations for limited partnerships in the early 1980s.

Finally, and perhaps the gravest disadvantage of a limited partnership, a ceiling is placed on the returns available to limited partners, though they typically put up most or all of the capital required to fund a given real estate investment. Though the general partners may be skilled managers of real assets, and deserve credit for having discovered or refined a selected real estate project, returns to many general partners are often not easily defended. Many of the limited partnership deals in the mid 1980s, for example, offered limited partners substantial tax write-offs, with the projects' most meaningful cash flows and management fees flowing disproportionately to the general partners. Those deals almost uniformly failed, with the loss of prior tax write-offs after IRS scrutiny and adverse rulings in the mid and late 1980s, and all partners much worse off financially; this legacy contributed to the failure of the thrift industry in the late 1980s and an aversion by investors to limited partnerships for years to come.

Advantages of a Limited Partnership

For both general and limited partners, the limited partnership offers the same direct pass-through of profits and losses for taxation purposes that is found in a general partnership. The limited partnership is not a taxable entity and files only an information return.

For the limited partner, there is the added advantage of limited liability. The limited partner has minimal management responsibility, which may release his time for other endeavors. The general partners can also provide expertise in a specialized form of business activity that might otherwise be beyond the reach of the limited partner.

Limited Partnership Income Tax Reports

The limited partnership—like the general partnership—files the Form 1065 information return. Each partner, general or limited, must report a distributive share of the partnership's ordinary income or net loss on her personal return (Schedule E, Form 1040), regardless of whether or not the income is disbursed.

JOINT VENTURE

A **joint venture** is distinguished by how the property is owned. Normally, each party in the venture holds an undivided share in the property. The business organization that operates the property, which may be a partnership or a corporation, usually holds a management agreement, but not the ownership of the property. The management company may be owned by the joint venturers, or it could be a separate company under contract.

The joint venture is often used to divide the ownership between a large developer and an institutional investor to build a complex development. Strip shopping centers, apartment complexes, hotels, and industrial developments are often structured as joint ventures by the initial investors. Many joint ventures are composed of individuals, corporations, and partnerships that together can better accomplish a common purpose. Large real estate ventures can involve landowners, builders, a real estate sales or leasing firm, and several institutional lenders, each with an equity interest in the project and a strong incentive to make it succeed.

LIMITED LIABILITY COMPANIES

The limited liability company (LLC) is an ownership form that has come into enormous popularity over the past ten years or so, both with small privately funded startups and with real estate investments. Combining some of the tax-favored features of the Sub-S corporation (discussed later in this chapter) without the ownership restrictions of the Sub-S, the LLC has grown in interest to professional groups such as real estate brokers and lawyers, as well as with real estate investments.

The LLC is a hybrid form of business ownership that incorporates the pass-through provisions of a partnership or Sub-S with the protections against liability of a corporation, though as with any corporation or indirect ownership form, this corporate "veil" is not a guarantee against liability. And it is a mistake to refer to the LLC as a limited liability "corporation;" it is a limited liability company with certain distinct characteristics.

Interests in the LLC are held by members, similar in most respects to shareholders, with those members' relative power dictated by the bylaws of the LLC—subject to the dictum of the jurisdiction or state where the LLC is formed—and their percentage ownership in the LLC. Unlike a limited partnership where the limited partners might be largely excluded from firing or changing management, except in the most extreme circumstances, LLC members often have the ability to change management simply by gathering the votes of a majority ownership interest among the members. Unlike the limited partnerships popular in the 1980s with real estate investment, the managing members of an LLC (often the same people who "put together" the LLC "deal") typically receive some modest additional membership interest in exchange for originating the investment.

EXAMPLE 9.2

A group of investors buys a 150,000 square foot warehouse on U.S. 1 in North Florida. The two originating investors had control of the purchase contract, but inadequate capital to complete the purchase for $2.5 million in 2003. To attract other investors, the two investors agree to purchase only 49 percent of the "deal," giving control of the other 51 percent to an area manager active in the industrial market. He quickly finds investors attracted to the terms of the investment. The incentive for this area manager? He received an additional 1 percent interest in the warehouse for assembling the other investors, and he collected 3 percent or $10,000 from the annual rents (around $325,000). He and one of the originating investors shared in a 5 percent sales commission, as well. The ownership form chosen? An LLC. Why? Given a total of between eight and ten investors of unequal amounts in the warehouse, and given also that several of the investors did not even know one-another and that the non-recourse purchase mortgage would include no personal guarantees after one year, the LLC was ideal: it protects each investor from the foibles of the other investors outside the warehouse deal; it provides a clear avenue for the sale or exchange of ownership interests (simply selling the interest), as each investor was provided shares in the company owning the warehouse based upon his initial investment; it provides for continuity in the investment even in the case of the death of an investor, with the ownership simply passing to an heir; the LLC protects against personal liability and shields several of the quite-wealthy investors from legal recourse; it allows at least one shareholder to be a trust, or another corporation, not allowed by Sub-S forms or partnerships in many jurisdictions; and, finally, the later sale of the warehouse might be simplified, the buyer simply buying the interests of the existing members, in a manner far simpler than a direct real estate sale (though many jurisdictions would still require the payment of customary documentary and recording fees). The bylaws of the LLC also provided guidelines for the sale or exchange of shares within and outside the shareholder group—members being required to first offer the shares to other LLC members. And, in the event the originating investors become dissatisfied with the organizing manager, they need only buy anything over 1 percent of the other outstanding shares to carry their 49 percent interest past 50 percent, giving them control and the right to select new management.

Disadvantages of an LLC

The limited liability company may not automatically provide the protections of the corporate ownership form in a given state, and the company's bylaws need to address governance and liability issues, as well as such topics as the sale of member interests, as with the warehouse in Example 9.2. Formation and annual filing fees differ from state to state; LLCs are ill-advised for the District of Columbia, it taxing the LLC's income at the local level. Many states have not formalized or fully developed the state-level provisions of an LLC, though at the federal level the LLC is currently recognized in basically the same manner as a Sub-S or partnership. The LLC is generally more complex than a partnership.

The LLC provides no special protection for the members from the debt of the LLC, as the lender, especially with real estate investment–based LLCs, may require the personal guarantee of the LLC investors for the acquisition debt of an LLC formed to acquire investment real estate. This corporate shield from the liability for debt repayments can be foregone with any ownership form, including REITs and C-Corporations, if the lender requires personal guarantees on the corporate debt. Many REIT and C-Corp investors, discussed below, rediscovered this issue in 2009 and 2010, as large real estate development debt came up for renewal, or as the underlying corporations failed; commonly, terms of the debt were not met, and the lender went to the investors to enforce the earlier-provided guarantees.

Income Taxation and Other Advantages of an LLC

The greatest advantages of the LLC relate to its tax status, simple administration, and ability to have members that are other corporations, trusts, or partnerships; all the shareholders of a Sub-S must be people. All 50 states allow the formation of an LLC. The IRS actually refers to an LLC as a passthough entity, not paying income taxes at the federal level. The LLC typically chooses to be treated by the IRS in a manner similar to the Sub-S or partnership, but at the federal level, it can elect to be taxed as a corporation, partnership or sole proprietorship; it provides the same protections against liabilities as a corporation, subject to the personal guarantees and misuse of the corporate veil mentioned above. Passthroughs of income and expenses, reported with Form 1065 and a K-1, are provided; these may offset or augment other K-1 income reported on Schedule E. The income of the LLC "retains its character" at the personal level, being taxed as ordinary income (loss) or capital gain, depending on the nature of the income at the organization level.

REAL ESTATE INVESTMENT TRUSTS

The Real Estate Investment Trust (REIT), introduced in Chapter 4, was originated by the U.S. Congress in 1960 to allow the agglomeration of capital for ever-larger real estate investments. As U.S. suburban residential sprawl and downtown developments were gathering steam and scale, there was a recognized need for some sort of tax-favored entity to serve as a foundation for the accumulation and expenditure of the large sums of capital being directed towards real estate; the REIT was congress' answer.

Types of REITs

Many REITs are of substantial enough size that they are traded like other common stock on the exchanges. There are three general types of REITs: the equity REIT, the mortgage REIT, and the hybrid REIT. The equity REIT involves investing strictly in real estate, often concentrating on a given property type—such as apartments or shopping centers—or a given geographic region, such as the southeast or southwest. The mortgage REIT focuses on the investment in and ownership of real estate debt. The hybrid invests in a mix of real estate and mortgages.

Taxation and Regulation of REITs

Provided the REITs meet certain requirements, they are afforded special tax treatment. A REIT is formed as a corporation, in a given state, and unlike the LLC has a board of directors (or trustees). Like the LLC, they are not taxed at the corporate level, but unlike the LLC they have scale and payout requirements that must be strictly adhered to lest the REIT lose its REIT status and be treated as a C-Corporation—taxed at the corporate level. These requirements broadly include minimum payouts to shareholders of funds from operations (basically a net operating income measure reduced by debt service), a minimum number of shareholders and a minimum portion of the firm's income that is generated by passive real estate investment. There is also a requirement that any ownership group holding 50 percent or more of the firm's stock be comprised of at least five people. Seventy-five percent of the REIT's assets and gross revenues must derive from real estate or real estate debt. The percentages of the firm's income that must be paid out each year have varied; at one point, 95 percent of a REIT's funds from operations needed to be paid out in dividends; this was reduced to 90 percent in the early 2000s, and as a result of the recession beginning in 2007 and based on an IRS ruling in December of 2008, REITs were temporarily allowed to pay out up to 90 percent of the required cash dividends with a stock dividend instead. REIT investors were taxed, though, as if they received a cash payout from the REIT, even though a large portion of the "dividend" may have been paid with stock.

EXAMPLE 9.3

A REIT is not taxed at the corporate level provided it pays out a minimum cash dividend; this requirement was amended in late 2008. The ruling required that at least 10 percent of the dividend be paid in cash, and the rest in stock. Two REITs, Simon Property Group and Vornado Realty Trust, took advantage of this December 2008 IRS ruling, allowing REITs to forgo the required cash dividend of 90 percent of funds from operations. For Simon in the first quarter of 2009, the dividend would have been 90 cents a share in cash, the firm instead paying only nine cents in cash, and the balance in a stock dividend. Vornado was less aggressive with the ruling, paying out 40 percent of its quarterly dividend in cash, and 60 percent in stock. The change was designed to allow REITs to hold onto cash in a period of dramatic reductions in existing and prospective capital for real estate investments. REITs such as Kimco Realty and Duke Realty paid all-cash dividends in the same quarter.

As a result of the tax-favored status of REITs, a majority of REIT shareholders are either institutional or tax-favored. REIT shares are often held by untaxed shareholders such as universities or foundations or in accounts such as retirement accounts that are tax-deferred. The dividends paid by a REIT to its shareholders are counted as ordinary income, and are not "qualifying" dividends which receive special treatment under the Bush tax cuts of 2001 and 2003, and which received favored treatment under prior tax regimes as well. REIT dividends are taxed at the marginal tax rate for the recipient. This contrasts with the LLC and Sub-S, considered below, where *all* of the taxable income or losses of the LLC or Sub-S passes through to the owners based upon their fractional interest in the real estate; an owner with a 10 percent interest in an apartment complex would receive a K-1 revealing the overall income of the complex, the cash distributions to the member or shareholder in the LLC or Sub-S, and the taxable 10 percent portion that the owner would include in Schedule E, Form 1040.

REAL ESTATE SYNDICATE

A **syndicate** is a consortium of people or institutions that come together to share funding and/or expertise in a particular business endeavor; that endeavor is often real estate investment or development. It is not in itself a form of business or ownership. A syndicate can be a general partnership, a limited partnership, a corporation, or even a landholder. In practice, the syndicate provides a way for individuals or firms to combine their investment capital to undertake a larger project than might be possible for any one of them alone. It is used as a means to raise equity cash or to sell investment property. This section considers the syndicate as a method of investment, rather than as a form of ownership.

Regulations of a Real Estate Syndicate

Depending on the number of persons involved, the wording of the syndication agreement, and the manner in which it is sold, the sale of a participating interest in real property can be considered a sale of securities. Both federal and state laws control the sale of securities to the general public. These laws are designed to protect the public from fraud and misrepresentation and to require full disclosure of the facts by sellers of securities.

Insofar as real estate is concerned, regulatory authorities are concerned whenever a certificate that is sold to the public represents some future interest in land. It can be called an earnest money agreement, a security deposit, an advance payment, or a preconstruction sale of a right to some unit of property. The name doesn't matter. What matters is that if the sales document grants some right or interest in land without a specific assignment of title, the document of sale may be held to be a security and is, therefore, subject to registration requirements. Violations of the securities laws can bring fines and prosecution. Charges can be brought against any or all of the parties involved in the sale of an unauthorized issue, including the original promoter, the sales personnel (who may not even be aware of the noncompliance), and the mortgage lender.

The state statutes in this area vary considerably, but registration of syndicated offerings is required by most states. And, if the offering is made to potential buyers across state lines, or to more than 35 persons within a state, then registration is also required with the federal regulator, the Securities and Exchange Commission (SEC). These features have contributed to the declination in the number of syndicated real estate investments, with the LLC form not limiting the number or type of investors (except in the District of Columbia and Massachusetts) or being subject to stringent SEC requirements; the LLC form is still evolving, however, and investors should always seek counsel on the regulations of a particular jurisdiction.

CORPORATIONS

The **corporation**, a form of business created by state chartering laws, is an artificial "person" with rights and powers to transact business of a limited and designated nature.

The Corporate Entity

In their earliest U.S. forms, corporations were chartered by special acts of the state legislatures. As this procedure became increasingly cumbersome, the states enacted corporation statutes to provide a more expeditious method of forming a corporation. Although several model procedures have been developed, including a Model Business Corporations Act, by the American Bar Association, there is still no uniform statute to guide state lawmakers.

The courts have played a considerable role in developing the law of corporations. While there are diverse opinions on the true nature of a corporation, the dominant theory conceives of it as a legal entity separate and distinct from its shareholders. A corporation may enter into contracts with its shareholders, and sue and be sued by them as a separate legal entity.

A corporation is held to be a "person" under some provisions of the U.S. Constitution, but a corporation does not have the status of a citizen for all legal purposes. For example, a corporation cannot move freely into any state to conduct business, while a citizen may. On the other hand, a corporation cannot be deprived of its property without due process, which is the same protection accorded citizens. Regular corporations are now referred to as C corporations by the IRS to distinguish them from S corporations, described later. An LLC is not a corporation; a REIT is a corporation restricted to investment in real estate and real estate lending, whose ownership and dividend policies allow it to avoid taxation at the corporate level.

The Corporate Structure

The ownership of a corporation lies with its shareholders and is evidenced by shares of stock. Stock is issued and sold by the corporation, as regulated by state laws and by the SEC if stock is sold publicly. A corporation may issue several classes of stock, including **common stock** and **preferred stock**, with each class giving the holder different rights.

The shareholders elect directors who, as a group, are responsible for the corporation's finances and operating policies. Corporate directors can be held personally liable for negligence in corporate matters and for any illegal actions by the corporation.

The board of directors selects the officers of the corporation, who are charged with managing the corporation's day-to-day operations. Officers may or may not be directors or shareholders of the company.

Corporations may borrow money from banks, insurance companies, or other lenders. The loans may be unsecured, or secured by a pledge of certain corporate assets. Corporations also have borrowing methods that are not generally available to others. For example, corporations can sell unsecured promissory notes (more commonly known as commercial paper) in the open market. And they can issue and sell bonds as a method of borrowing money. These bonds vary, depending on their purpose, collateral, and repayment commitment. One common type is a mortgage bond, which is secured by a pledge of specified real property owned by the corporation. These are not the same as *mortgage-backed securities*, drawn from pools of mortgages and traded on the secondary markets; these mortgage-backed securities, with variants including collateralized mortgage-backed securities and commercial mortgage-backed securities and other collateralized debt obligations, were at the center of the credit crisis during the Great Recession.

Corporations for Profit

The corporation most commonly used for real estate investment is operated for the purpose of making a profit. It may be a closed corporation or a publicly traded corporation. Closed corporations have only a single or a few closely knit shareholders, such as a family. Public corporations are authorized to sell stock and bonds to the general public and are subject to a number of state and federal regulations on such sales. States also have special rules for incorporating particular classes of business such as banks, insurance companies, and savings associations.

Nonprofit Corporations

Certain state statutes provide for the formation of corporations that are not established for profit. These include charitable, educational, recreational, religious, and social organizations, all of which are convenient methods of holding and operating property. Nonprofit corporations do not distribute dividends to members on their invested capital. Government and quasi-government corporations, such as Amtrak, operate not-for-profit but serve a public need left unaddressed in the private sector.

Disadvantages of the Corporation

For the real estate investor, the major disadvantage of the corporate form lies in the method of its taxation. There are two problems:

1. Double taxation. Corporate income is subject to corporate income taxes, after which the remaining income may be distributed to shareholders as dividends. Ordinary dividends received by shareholders are subject to a second taxation at the individual level.
2. No pass-through of tax deductions. The corporation—not the shareholder—is entitled to the normal deductions for depreciation and other losses. Corporate losses—unlike partnership losses—cannot be deducted from the shareholder's taxable income.

Another disadvantage of the corporate form is the investor's lack of a voice in management; there is a separation of ownership and control. From a practical standpoint, the investor will have little control over management unless he is a major shareholder. This is known as the agency issue, leading to *agency costs*, and receives extensive attention in the traditional financial literature.

Advantages of the Corporation

The advantages of the corporate form are that (1) the shareholder has limited liability, and (2) shares of stock are generally more liquid than an interest in any other form of business organization. One of the primary *inefficiencies* of the real estate market is the illiquidity of the real estate investment; with both the exchange-traded REIT and the public corporation, this is largely bypassed as the firms' stock is highly liquid, typically traded throughout the trading day on the respective exchanges. Stockbrokers and stock exchanges promote the buying and selling of publicly held corporate stock. As well, there is an over-the-counter market for stock that is not listed on the major stock exchanges. Many shares in smaller companies are traded daily in these specialized markets.

Corporate Income Tax Reports

Corporations must file an annual income tax return with the IRS—Form 1120—and pay the taxes due. It is beyond the scope of this text to consider the substantial body of corporate tax law, but suffice it to say that individual shareholders must report dividends received from the corporation as their own dividend income, with the corporation responsible for taxes at the corporate level.

S CORPORATIONS

A limited partnership is a hybrid between a corporation and a partnership in terms of *liability*; an **S corporation** is a similar hybrid, this time in terms of income taxes. The S corporation, formerly identified by the IRS as a "Subchapter S Corporation," allows the income of a corporation to be treated in a similar manner to that of a partnership. That is, the corporation as such pays no income taxes; its income is passed through to its stockholders who become liable for the tax. Essentially, an S corporation is any normally chartered corporation with no more than 35 shareholders (husband and wife are treated as one shareholder) that has elected to be taxed as a partnership. The S corporation files an annual information return allocating its income among the shareholders, who must then report the income (or loss) on their personal tax returns whether or not the distribution has been received.

The IRS regulations covering the S corporation recognize that corporate taxes can unfairly penalize the corporate form of business ownership. This is particularly true for smaller, closely held corporations whose shareholders are expected to distribute profits. The S corporation offers an alternative procedure that may better suit certain business activities. The Sub-S form of business organization was popular for selected real estate investments prior to the adoption of LLC standards, the LLC having often displaced the Sub-S in the late 1990s and early 2000s.

Advantages and Disadvantages of the Sub-S

The S corporation has the tax advantages of the partnership form and the limited liability advantage of the corporate form. If the business operates at a loss, the S corporation allows a pass through of the loss as a possible offset to the taxpayer's other income. However, any passive activity loss may only be offset against the taxpayer's other passive activity income. As noted above in the LLC discussion, the Sub-S allows only individuals as shareholders, and not trusts or other corporations. If the business is operating at a profit and is not able to distribute that profit because of internal cash demands, a disadvantage arises in that the shareholder must still pay income taxes on that profit. Another disadvantage with the S corporation is that it must meet the qualifying standards each year. Failure to do so disallows the special tax treatment for that year.

There has been some relaxation in rules that formerly made any violation of the fairly complex regulations for a Sub-S a cause for large, retroactive tax bills. This was true even though the violation may have been unintentional.

EXAMPLE 9.4

John Headley and his life-long friend, Jeffrey Harris, purchased a 20,000 square foot light manufacturing warehouse in north Florida in 1997 strictly as a real estate investment. Mr. Harris had been in the industrial real estate business for some time, Mr. Headley no longer lived in the town where Mr. Harris worked and where the warehouse was located, and the two needed to select an ownership form suitable for their investment. They chose the Sub-S, as it provided a pass-through of the losses expected in the first couple of years, it guarded them against personal liability—though both were required to provide personal guarantees on the mortgage financing—and it allowed a simple, but separate, set of records for the one property in their new corporation. The corporation was dissolved soon after the property was sold in 2007.

S Corporation Tax Reports

The Sub-S corporation must file a tax return on Form 1120S for each year that the election under S corporation is effective. Shareholders must include their prorated shares of the corporation's taxable income and gains in their returns, whether or not the amount is actually distributed; this is similar to the income and loss reporting requirements for the LLC, where gains and losses pass through independent of cash distributions. However, a shareholder must report income differently from a partner. If the shareholder's tax year is different from that of the corporation, any distribution of current taxable income must be reported in the tax year it is actually received. (For a partnership, any distributive share of partnership items is reported in the tax year in which the last day of the partnership year falls, regardless of the date actually received.) The S corporation reports any undistributed income in the personal tax year in which the tax year of the corporation ends.

COMPARISON OF BUSINESS ORGANIZATIONS

Table 9.1 provides a quick reference for comparing the general characteristics of the major forms of business organizations. An investor's selection of the best business form depends on many additional facts—individual goals, personal income and tax obligations, and the other people involved.

TABLE **9.1**
Comparison of Business Organizations

Advantages and Disadvantages

1. **Sole Proprietorships:** The sole proprietorship is the simplest business organization, and can quite literally be formed by declaration at the moment an investment piece of real estate is acquired by an investor. It has the additional advantage of all income and expenses flowing directly through to the taxpayer/ proprietor. A major disadvantage is the exposure of the proprietor to individual liability for all the debts or obligations of the "business." The proprietorship terminates upon the death of the founder, and capital access is limited to the wherewithal of this founder. Ownership transfer, cash distribution, and asset sales are at the discretion of the founder, subject to credit and mortgage requirements.

2. **General and Limited Partnerships:** The general partnership is a stepped-up version of the sole proprietorship in most states, and involves additional tax and administrative duties beyond those required of a sole proprietorship. Income and expenses flow through to partners, according to partnership agreement, based typically upon the relative investment in the partnership by the partners. Partners are subject to taxes and liabilities deriving from the partnership, independent of any cash distributions. Capital access is limited to the partners, and the partnership may terminate upon the death of a partner. Partnership interests are not easily bought or sold. A limited partnership, used commonly in real estate investments in the early to mid 1980s, limits the liability of the limited partners to the capital invested, but limits their income potential, as well. Limited partnerships were often employed to allow passive investment by high-income investors in real estate deals whose primary appeal were the pass-throughs of substantial tax write-offs against marginal tax rates at the time of 50 percent (or more, including state taxes). Many limited partnerships were disallowed by the IRS in the late 1980s. The limited partnership has been largely displaced by the LLC in obtaining the same or superior objectives in the late 1990s and 2000s.

3. **Limited Liability Company (LLC):** The LLC is a hybrid between the corporate and partnership forms of business organization. It is allowed in all 50 states, though modest administrative differences exist. An LLC investor is a member, not a shareholder. The largest advantages include the flow through of income and losses; the allowance of members that are not individuals; the separation of the owners from direct liability; and the easier transferability of ownership interests than in a partnership, typically according to the by-laws of the LLC. Gains and losses flow through to investors based upon their percentage investment in the property acquired by the LLC. It is governed by a managing member, typically elected by a majority vote of membership interests. Its disadvantages include capital access limited to the owners' wealth; the frequent requirement for personal guarantees of LLC mortgage funding; the potential ease of "piercing the corporate veil" of the LLC; and the misallocation of LLC resources by the managing member.

4. **Real Estate Investment Trust (REIT):** The REIT was created with federal legislation passed in 1960 to allow the accumulation of capital to fund large-scale real estate investment. Founded and managed largely like a typical public corporation, the REIT is afforded special tax treatment if 75 percent of the assets and income of the REIT are derived from real estate or mortgages; no less than five shareholders control 50 percent of the REIT; and a specified portion of the REIT's income or funds from operations is paid out in a non-qualifying dividend each year. The greatest advantages of the REIT are the non-payment of taxes at the corporate level, the liquidity of the REIT shares traded on the stock exchanges, and the substantial availability of capital. The clearest disadvantages are the agency costs suffered with any large company.

5. **General or C-class Corporation:** Large corporations, like those traded on the organized exchanges, are generally not the most ideal business form for real estate investment. The primary advantage of the general corporation is the liquidity of the ownership interests, as the shares can be bought and sold with some ease, and the access of the firm to substantial capital through stock or bond sales. Real estate assets are not highly liquid, but publicly traded common stock is. The major disadvantages include the double-taxation of income, at the corporate and personal level as dividends are distributed, and the agency costs arising with the separation of owners from management.

6. **Subchapter S Corporation:** Like the LLC, the Sub-S is a hybrid exhibiting features of both partnerships and corporations. The Sub-S has the primary advantages of a pass-through of income or losses, and modest (though penetrable) protections against the liabilities of the business for the shareholders. Disadvantages include restrictions on ownership to individuals, the limited ease of ownership transfers, and shareholder tax obligations independent of cash distributions by the Sub-S. This form has been largely supplanted by the LLC for most real estate investments that might previously have been pursued using the Sub-S form of business organization.

KEY TERMS

common stock	joint venture	limited partnership	S corporation
corporation	limited liability	partnership	sole proprietorship
joint-stock company	company	preferred stock	syndicate

DISCUSSION QUESTIONS

1. How does a partnership handle payment of income taxes?

2. Discuss the organization of a limited partnership.

3. What are the advantages of the LLC form of real estate ownership over the Sub-S form?

4. What are the advantages and disadvantages of a corporation?

5. What is meant by the pass-through provisions of an LLC and a Sub-S?

6. What is the agency issue and how does it impact the real estate investor in a large corporation or Real Estate Investment Trust?

7. The text mentions several prospective business organizations available to the real estate investor. List these, and briefly describe how each might be attractive in one particular investment setting or another.

CHAPTER 10

Financing Real Estate Investments

Traditional financial theory sometimes holds that investing and financing decisions exist separately and are independent; the corporate financial manager will determine the firm's cost of capital and if a given investment meets or exceeds this cost, or minimum percentage return on investment, then the firm will "do the deal." This implied separation of investing (asset purchase) and financing (loans or stock sales to fund the purchase) decisions does not, however, apply to real estate investments. The performance and attractiveness of most real estate investments is directly related to the borrowing used to fund the investment.

RISK AND THE IMPACT OF LEVERAGE

The attractiveness and importance of financing for the real estate investor can be easily, and prosaically, illustrated: Suppose Jane Smith is considering an office building purchase. It is a 20,000 square foot building generating net operating income (NOI) of $200,000 per year or $10 a foot. It is for sale for $2 million. If she pays cash, she receives a 10 percent return or $200,000/$2 million. (As discussed in Chapter 13, this property is being sold at a 10 percent "cap rate.") If, however, she borrows $1 million, paying the other $1 million or 50 percent down, and the loan has a total cost (ignoring taxes and principal pay down) of $80,000 per year, her return is improved. How is it enhanced? She now has a cash flow before taxes of the $200,000 NOI reduced by the

$80,000 debt cost or $120,000. Against her down payment of $1 million, this represents a return on her invested capital of 12 percent (($200,000 − $80,000)/ $1 million), versus the 10 percent return without the use of debt. (Additional examples later in this chapter illustrate this relationship.) The greatest risk of debt arises if, for example, the building generates an NOI of less than $80,000; then, though she still paid $1 million down on the building, it provides cash flows of less than the debt service. She must invest additional capital each year to avoid defaulting on the debt, and potentially losing the building through foreclosure.

Ms. Smith's circumstances with her office building are noteworthy. As the Great Recession developed near the end of the 2000s, and the 2010s began, many real estate investments confronted just the sorts of cash flow issues she encountered. Even investments with equity portions of 50 percent or more (as with her $1 million investment in a $2 million property) were faced with escalating vacancies and falling rents, that in concert with existing financing led to property failures and foreclosures. Only the fortunate few with little or no mortgage debt, with no need to refinance existing debt, and in markets less impacted by the economy, were not experiencing sleepless nights due to the struggling real estate investment markets.

Among the most desirable features of real estate investment, for the lender and investor/borrower alike, is the ability of real estate, in normal markets, to shoulder significant debt financing. The ability of investors to use leverage is one of the most significant features of real estate investment. For the investor, the returns—as with Jane Smith above—are straightforward: She is able, with a mostly-leased building, to turn a modest return into a far more favorable return with two added features: First, she is able to deploy her invested capital in such a manner that she earns a higher return. That advantage is readily transparent. But the second feature is often overlooked; if she does not invest all of her available funds in the first property, she is left with monies for additional investments, or for much larger investments. Think about it: If she is allocating $2 million to various real estate investments, and requires "only" $1 million to buy that first $2 million property, she is left with the other million dollars to invest elsewhere. She could, given the same low-risk parameter of 50 percent leverage, buy another $2 million property. Or, at the outset, she would have been able to buy a $4 million property, using her $2 million as a down payment, and exposing herself to only $2 million in debt.

Real estate investments have traditionally been made with loan-to-value or debt ratios of far more than 50 percent. Jane's far-less-risky use of only 50 percent leverage echoes both the more binding constraints that lenders adopted in recent years, and the ability of debt financing, even at relatively low levels, to augment returns to investors. But even the most modest "augmentation" comes with risk, as Jane Smith might have discovered in early 2005 were she the owner of a neighborhood strip shopping center anchored by Winn Dixie. Winn Dixie filed for bankruptcy in early 2005, and later judicial decrees released the firm from a number of leases, prior to its exit from bankruptcy. Strip centers across many neighborhoods in the south were crushed, not only with the exit of the anchor, but with the failure of the same strip's other tenants with the grocer's exit. With leverage comes risk, even at the lowest levels. That was a lesson learned across the US in the late 1980s and early 1990s, and again with the Great Recession.

The use of mortgage financing will remain an important feature of any real estate investment analysis, but the terms of the debt and the conditions in which it will be offered have likely changed for years to come. Whereas investors in the past might routinely have secured financing for 75 percent or more of a planned office building or apartment complex, such financing is no longer available. Unless a deep-pocketed investor is willing to offer his personal guarantee on a multi-million dollar "deal," investors in real estate are being required to offer much larger equity positions, or down payments, to lenders than was the case early in the century.

These changing terms and conditions will be a centerpiece of the discussion below, as the financing of real estate investments is considered.

Investment in real estate often involves borrowing a portion of the money needed. Indeed, mortgage loans today comprise the largest single business demand on the nation's credit markets. To support this kind of credit, real estate offers tangible collateral. It has long life, a fixed location, a permanent record of title, and laws that fix methods of conveyance and the process for making claims against it. While some mortgage loans are for short terms, such as **construction loans** and warehouse lines of credit extended to mortgage companies, most are for terms of over ten years and are classified as long-term loans. It is this long-term nature of real estate financing that distinguishes it from other types of credit.

Patterns leading up to the Great Recession, however, revealed regular exceptions to this "long-term nature" of the real estate financing mentioned above. Loans with 25- or 30-year amortization schedules often had terms requiring the loans to be renegotiated, or paid off entirely, after the passage of only three or five years. Lenders were able to limit their risk and exposure to changing interest rates and economic conditions, and borrowers (investors) were granted very low cost financing for real estate investments. The problems arose when the "music stopped" and investors were left with no refinancing options, and loans that had come due.

For example, a group of investors might have bought a warehouse in 2004 for $10 million, financing 80 percent of the price with a five-year interest-only loan at 5 percent; the duty of the investors was simply to come up with the 5 percent or $400,000 (5 percent of the $8 million borrowed) each year. In 2009, with falling rents and increasing vacancies and a distressed lending market, the investors likely found the property's value had fallen to $6 million or $7 million and no new financing was available. Coupling this with the likelihood that perhaps one or more of the investors offered personal guarantees for the original $8 million financing, and the gravity of the picture is revealed. The lenders lose, as the interest-only loan cannot be paid off with new financing; the property is likely foreclosed upon. The borrowers/investors lose their original equity interest of $2 million.

The lender cannot cover its outstanding mortgage balance on the resale, and one or more of the investors may be called to account for the personal guarantee he offered on the original loan.

Some lending has been and remains available with long-term conditions, though equity or down payment requirements on new loans has increased significantly; down payments of 35 percent, or more, are becoming the rule rather than the exception. Lending for longer terms brings special risks, not always foreseeable and not always under the control of a lender. These include such uncertainties as future government fiscal and monetary policies, the probability of continued economic fluctuations, and the growth patterns of development projects facing increasing concern with environmental constraints. Even though such increased risks command higher interest rates, it has not proven adequate for many lenders. Partially because of these increased risks, a number of the historic sources for mortgage loans are withdrawing from this market.

In years past, most mortgage loans, especially residential mortgage loans, were made by savings institutions that hold deposit assets. As this source began to withdraw from mortgage lending in the late 1970s, it was gradually replaced with funds raised in the financial markets through the sale of mortgage-backed securities. Some standardization of residential loan practices and the advancement of computer technology made the shift in sourcing possible. Financing for commercial loans has been slower in making a transition to the new source because of the unique nature of each loan. But securities backed by pools of commercial loans are finding growing markets.

Differences have always existed between the residential mortgage market and the commercial loan market. Today, most residential loans are made by loan originators with the underlying intention of selling them to institutional investors such as Fannie Mae or Freddie Mac (considered below). Thus, they tend to follow more standardized procedures and conform to secondary market requirements. In contrast, many commercial loans are made by loan originators such as banks or insurance companies that intend to hold them in their own portfolios; terms of the loans are often not as long as was typically the case until the early 2000s. Whereas an institutional lender like GE Financial or General Motors Acceptance Corporation (GMAC exited bankruptcy along with GM in 2009) might have offered 20- or 30-year financing until 2004 or 2005, those sorts of terms are now the exception. GE Financial, if they offered a commercial loan, would now likely attach 3- or 5-year balloons to the mortgages, requiring refinancing or repricing of the interest rate after that shorter period.

THREE RISKS FACING THE REAL ESTATE LENDER

Real estate lenders face three separate risks:

1. The lender faces *default risk*, the risk that the borrower will default, leaving the lender with an asset requiring management and maintenance, and whose value may well be far less than any attaching mortgage balance.

2. The lender faces *interest rate risk*; having contracted to a set interest rate on a given loan, the lender has little recourse (except with special loan terms or the re-pricing of the interest rate on many commercial real estate loans).

3. The lender faces *reinvestment risk*. As the loan is paid off, the lender has no assurance that as profitable an investment as the mortgage itself even exists for the new incoming funds.

It is in the environment of these ever-existing and changing risks that the mortgage provider and real estate borrower operate.

To better understand the mortgage market, this chapter will examine briefly the two levels on which it functions: (1) the loan origination, or primary market, and (2) the investment, or secondary market. In addition, we review the cost of borrowed money, echoing the spirit of the 20,000 square foot office building investment at the beginning of this chapter, and the purposes an investor achieves, and risks faced, by using borrowed money.

PRIMARY MORTGAGE MARKET

The **primary mortgage market** is where loans are originated. It is the market where borrowers negotiate with lenders, discussing the cost of a loan in terms of the interest rate and discount that will be charged.

The rapid expansion of the secondary market that began in the early 1980s opened the door to many new participants in loan origination. Origination is no longer limited to those institutions with deposit assets or those who brokered loans for them. Loan originators today include home builders, real estate brokerage firms, financial services companies, investment bankers, and automobile credit companies, as well as mortgage companies and the institutional lenders. Originators can sell their loans to secondary market operators who convert large blocks of loans into mortgage-backed securities. These "operators," such as Lehman Brothers and Bear Stearns, suffered grave losses on the securities as a result of the failure of the underlying properties during the Great Recession. Some of them went bankrupt, and many are no longer participating in such security issues.

Several factors encouraged this shift. Because of previous problems with real estate loans, as with the Savings and Loan debacle in the late 1980s discussed below, government auditors discouraged further lending in this field. Perhaps a more important reason was the laws and regulations that were phased in to tighten controls on those institutions that hold federally-insured deposits. One was a risk-based capital requirement and the other was a risk-based premium for federal deposit insurance. Essentially, these rules provide a rating structure for the risk level of different kinds of loans. If a lender elects to make more risky loans (such as for commercial real estate), the capital requirement was increased and the cost of deposit insurance was higher. Some institutions were fully prepared to meet the increased costs while others were not. While new and even more restrictive formal regulations are still evolving at the beginning of the 2010s, lenders are already requiring much tighter lending terms on commercial real estate loans.

Within this dynamic environment, both residential and commercial borrowers are finding alternative sources for loans. Mortgage bankers and mortgage brokers are picking up new business as they often represent non-regulated sources. Large real estate brokerage firms often have subsidiaries capable of arranging for mortgage loans. Many lenders in the primary market are not subject to banking restrictions and deposit insurance regulators.

SECONDARY MORTGAGE MARKET

What has made mortgage money more available for a variety of loan origina-tors has been the expansion of the secondary market for these loans. At its beginning, the **secondary mortgage market** consisted of the Federal National Mortgage Association (FNMA or Fannie Mae), created by Congress in 1938 for the sole purpose of providing a market for loans insured by the Federal Housing Administration. After World War II, Fannie Mae's authority was expanded to include VA-guaranteed home mortgages.

Fannie Mae grew modestly and was partitioned in 1968, with a part becoming the Government National Mortgage Association (GNMA or Ginnie Mae), and the other part re-chartered as a private corporation holding close ties to the government, retaining the Fannie Mae name. Fannie Mae is now effectively a ward of the US government, though it still attempts to maintain a private-sector veneer. Direct backing of Fannie Mae, and Freddie Mac, by the federal government, reached $400 billion in late 2009, against a portfolio of loans and other assets of close to $1.7 trillion; many of the loans on Fannie and Freddie's balance sheet were non-performing, facing foreclosure, in arrears, or "under water." (A loan is under water if the home's value is less than the outstanding mortgage balance.) As a "private corporation," Fannie Mae was able to enter the conventional mortgage market and has since pro-vided funding for a large percent of the residential mortgage market, thus the breathtaking breadth and depth of its circumstances.

The Emergency Home Finance Act of 1970 created the Federal Home Loan Mortgage Corporation (FHLMC or Freddie Mac) and authorized it to create a secondary market for conventional mortgages. Parallel authority and limitations to deal in conventional mortgages were given to Fannie Mae. To alleviate credit concerns raised by acquisition of conventional mortgages (that lack federal backing), several eligibility restrictions and/or risk sharing requirements were imposed on the mortgages Fannie Mae could buy. Now, of course, the loans and the underlying securities based upon those loans do have federal backing, effectively, and the unraveling of the mortgage and credit crises will take a number of years.

The Secondary Mortgage Market Enhancement Act of 1984 (SMMEA) clarified and modified several of HUD's regulatory powers over Fannie Mae. It required HUD to respond within 45 days to any request for new program approval made by Fannie Mae under the Charter Act (with a 15-day exten-sion permitted) and authorized Fannie Mae to purchase and deal in subordi-nate lien mortgages.

The Financial Institutions Reform, Recovery, and Enforcement Act (FIR-REA) of 1989 made regulation of Fannie Mae and Freddie Mac consistent.

Until 1989, Freddie Mac was owned by the Federal Home Loan Bank System and its member thrifts and governed by the Federal Home Loan Bank Board (later reorganized into the Office of Thrift Supervision). FIRREA severed Freddie Mac's ties to the Federal Home Loan Bank System, created an 18-member board of directors to run Freddie Mac, and subjected it to HUD oversight. FIRREA created the Resolution Trust Corporation (RTC) to dispose of foreclosed real estate as the thrift industry failed in the late 1980's. (FIRREA and the RTC were introduced in Chapter 6.)

Following the "thrift crisis" of the late 1980s, the General Accounting Office and the Department of Treasury were instructed to conduct studies of Fannie Mae, Freddie Mac, and the Federal Home Loan Banks. These studies laid the foundation for comprehensive regulatory modernization for both Fannie Mae and Freddie Mac in 1992. The new regulations fell well short of anticipating the collapse of much of the residential real estate market during the Great Recession.

The Federal Housing Enterprises Financial Safety and Soundness Act (FHEFSSA) of 1992 modernized the regulatory oversight of Fannie Mae and Freddie Mac. It created the Office of Federal Housing Enterprise Oversight (OFHEO) as a new regulatory office within HUD with the responsibility to "ensure that Fannie Mae and Freddie Mac are adequately capitalized and operating safely." OFHEO did not achieve this primary objective, with the failures of Fannie and Freddie. Adjacent to the collapse of Fannie and Freddie and under the auspices of the Housing and Economic Recovery Act (HERA) of 2008, OFHEO and the Federal Housing Finance Board were combined to form the new Federal Housing Finance Agency.

HERA was passed to strengthen governmental oversight of Fannie Mae and Freddie Mac. It established the Federal Housing Finance Agency (FHFA), which replaced OFHEO and HUD as Fannie Mae's safety and soundness and mission regulator. Among other things, FHFA has broad authority to require Fannie Mae and Freddie Mac to hold capital above statutory minimum levels, regulate the size and content of Fannie Mae's portfolio, and approve new mortgage products. Since the meltdown of the banking and finance industries in 2007, 2008, and 2009, the rebuilding programs are "works in progress" with many uncertainties remaining. Remaining abreast of changes in these particular "moving targets" is highly recommended, for the lender and real estate investor alike.

EVALUATING THE COMMERCIAL LOAN

In some respects, evaluating a commercial loan is somewhat similar to evaluating a residential loan. Specifically, the lender is going to be concerned primarily with the source of the funds that will be used to make the loan payments. With a residential loan the lender will look at the income of the borrower because that is the primary source of the necessary funds. Therefore, the lender will evaluate the borrower's employment history and debt paying history, or credit score.

The funds used to pay the debt service on a commercial loan come from the property rather than the borrower. So the major focus of the commercial lender is to evaluate the property, both for its ability to generate sufficient income and also its adequacy as collateral for the loan. Likewise, the residential lender will be concerned with the value of the house and will require an appraisal.

Another similarity is that both residential and commercial lenders will be concerned with how much of the borrower's income or the property's income will be committed to debt service. In a residential loan assessment the lender will use ratios to determine if the borrower is committing too much of their income to the monthly payment. Typically the lender does not like to see more than about 28 percent or 29 percent of the borrower's income committed to the monthly obligation.

With a commercial loan the lender will likewise be concerned with the amount of the property's income that is being committed to debt service. The lender will calculate the **debt coverage ratio** (DCR) to be assured that there is not an excessive amount of the property's income being committed. The debt coverage ratio is the ratio of income to debt service, that is, how much does the income "cover" the debt service. Mathematically, the debt coverage ratio equals the net operating income or NOI divided by the debt service. The Heights Colony Apartments Case Study begins to portray the importance of mortgage financing to the real estate investor. That case follows:

CASE STUDY **10.1**

The Heights Colony Apartments

404 Heights Avenue. Anytown, U.S.A.

Unit Mix	No. of Units	Unit Type	Size	Mo. Rent Per Unit	Annual Rental Income
	24	A	700 sq. ft.	$780	$224,640
	24	B	750 sq. ft.	$850	$244,800
	20	C	820 sq. ft.	$900	$216,000
	20	D	880 sq. ft.	$970	$232,800
	12	E	950 sq. ft.	$1,090	$156,960
Totals	100		80,200 sq. ft.		$1,075,200

Pro Forma

Gross Scheduled Income	$1,075,200
Less Vacancy and Credit Loss (5%)	($53,760)
Miscellaneous Income	$26,000
Adjusted Gross Income	$1,047,440
Operating Expenses	
Fixed Expenses	$259,800
Variable Expenses	$180,800
Total Expenses	$440,600
Net Operating Income (NOI)	$606,840

Using the Debt Coverage Ratio Method

Unlike the ratios used in residential loan qualification, the debt coverage ratio is not based on any specific standards. The lender will look at the type of property, the experience of the developer, the risks involved, the strength and quality of the property's income, and other variables. Typically the ratio will vary between 1.2 and 1.4 for most properties. The formula for calculating the debt coverage ratio is DCR = NOI ÷ DS. In other words, the ratio equals the net operating income divided by the debt service. Refer to Example 10.1 to see how the debt coverage ratio is used to determine the maximum loan amount that the lender will provide for the Heights Colony Apartments.

In Example 10.1, a coverage ratio of 1.3 is used. A maximum loan amount of $5,847,000 is calculated. If a coverage ratio of 1.2 were used, a monthly payment of $42,142 is discovered (versus the $38,900 per month with a less generous DCR of 1.3). This equates to a lender now willing, with the lower DCR, to loan a maximum loan amount of $6,334,000. Compared to the lending maximum of $5,846,964 with the DCR of 1.3, this is almost one-half million dollars more on the same property. This illustrates the importance of using the most appropriate coverage ratio. The lender's experience, and the investor's risk tolerance, would dictate which coverage ratio to use. With a lower DCR comes a greater risk that the property will fall short of income expectations and be unable to cover its loan payments, leading to foreclosure or the necessity of investors to "feed" an underperforming property until such time that its income returns to "normal."

EXAMPLE 10.1

Using the Debt Coverage Ratio — The Heights Colony Apartments

Net Operating Income	$606,840
Debt Coverage Ratio (required by lender)	1.3
Allowable Debt Service = NOI ÷ DCR =	$466,800 ($38,900 per month)
Lender's required interest rate is 7%	

Maximum possible loan amount?

Using the TI BA II Plus calculator:

38,900 PMT (monthly payment)

7 ÷ 12 = I/Y (interest rate per month)

30 × 12 = N (number of months in 30 years)

CPT PV = $5,846,964

Based on the lender required interest rate, loan term, and debt coverage ratio requirement, the lender will lend $5,846,964 (rounded) on the Heights Colony Apartments.

Evaluating the Property

Most lenders will require an appraisal of the property that is to be pledged as collateral for the loan. For a property that is basically an income producing property, the appraiser will rely heavily on the income approach to establish the property's value. Considering the Heights Colony Apartments, the appraiser will develop a Pro Forma based on market data. Like many commercial loans, this loan request is for a property that is not in existence. The loan is required in order to build the project. Since there are no actual income and expense figures for the Heights Colony Apartments, the appraiser will use figures based on what other similar properties are incurring.

The appraiser will establish the gross scheduled rent from market information. Additionally, other sources of income, vacancy rate, and expense information will be developed. From this information the appraiser will determine the net operating income. This dollar amount is the factor that establishes the property's value. However, the value is not expressed as an annual income figure but as a capitalized value at a moment in time. So the appraiser uses a "capitalization rate" (**cap rate**) to covert the annual net operating income into a capitalized value. See Example 10.2 for the mathematics involved in determining value. Basically, and employed everywhere in the field of real estate investing, dividing a property's NOI by a suitable cap rate provides an estimate of value. In the early 2000s, cap rates of 6 percent or 7 percent were common; cap rates of 10 percent or more became the norm as the Great Recession unfolded.

EXAMPLE 10.2	Calculating Property Value—The Heights Colony Apartments

Net Operating Income	$606,840
Cap Rate	9%
Property Value = NOI ÷ Cap Rate =	
606,840 ÷ .09 =	$6,742,667 or $6,743,000 (rounded)

In the calculation used in Example 10.2 a cap rate of 9 percent was used. It is fairly obvious that this number is critical in establishing value. For example, if a cap rate of 10 percent were used, the final value of the property would be $6,068,400, a difference of $674,600. An inverse relationship exists between property values and cap rates; a higher cap rate leads to a lower estimate of value. So the selection of the proper cap rate is truly significant. There are numerous methods of developing a proper cap rate. Some of the important factors involved in the determination of the appropriate rate are: type of property, ambient interest rates, typical rates of return on similar investments, risk factors, stability and quality of the income produced by the property, and other considerations. Cap rates, or discount rates, are considered at length in Chapter 13.

Using the Loan to Value (LTV) Method

Once a value is established, the lender will then establish the loan amount for the project being considered. In previous times lenders would make loans based entirely upon the appraised value. So if a property appraised at $1,000,000 and the lender was willing to lend 80 percent of the value (80 percent LTV), they would loan $800,000. If the borrower was able to build the project for $800,000 then they would not have to inject any cash into the development.

Since the financial devastation of 2007, 2008, and 2009 lenders are requiring real equity in projects and lower LTVs. There is no standard but a 75 percent LTV is probably about the highest that can be arranged unless there are extenuating circumstances. A 60 percent to 65 percent LTV, or lower, is more common. Some real estate investments will attract no lending offers, whatsoever, unless the investors are of substantial net worth and offer personal guarantees for the borrowed funds. Considering the Heights Colony Apartments, see Example 10.3 for an example of the determination of an acceptable loan amount, using the LTV approach.

| **EXAMPLE 10.3** | **Using the Loan to Value Method—The Heights Colony Apartments** |

Assuming the Value Established in Figure 10.1 $6,742,000 (rounded)

The Lender Required LTV   70%

Maximum Loan Amount = Value × LTV = 6,742,000 × .07 = $4,719,400

Lender Criteria

There are no rigid standards for setting lender criteria. They vary from month to month, from lender to lender, and from property type to property type, so a borrower must determine the criteria that are currently being used by several different lenders before attempting to establish the feasibility of a proposed development. As an example, in mid-2009 the following criteria were fairly prevalent.

Debt coverage ratios were 1.2 to 1.4; LTVs were 60 percent to 75 percent; interest rates were typically 6 percent to 6½ percent by banks, 7 percent to 7½ percent for life insurance companies and sometimes LIBOR (London Interbank Offer Rate) + 1½ percent for short-term loans, repricing the interest rate monthly or quarterly. (LIBOR is an international equivalent of the Federal Funds Rate established by the Federal Reserve, and charged between banks for overnight loans.) It has been illustrated how loan amounts can vary dramatically with the criteria used. A project that may be feasible under certain assumptions may instantly become infeasible under different criteria. Far more demanding loan terms are expected by commercial real estate lenders in the years ahead.

EFFECT OF UNDERWRITING ON COMMERCIAL BORROWERS

How do federal mortgage pools affect an investor in commercial properties? First of all, much of the credit demand for residential mortgage money has shifted from savings deposits and insurance company reserves to the financial markets. The historic participation of institutional lenders in residential loans—savings associations, commercial banks, and life insurance companies—in mortgage lending for their own portfolios can be more focused on commercial loans. This is particularly true for smaller communities. Federal restrictions on lending, such as not allowing more than a certain percent of a depository institution's net capital to be loaned to any one borrower, have been modified for institutions with less than $100 million in assets.

Mortgage companies, both full service bankers and brokers, with their great expertise in knowing sources for long-term mortgage loans, have expanded their market share of commercial loans. Also, there is a growing effort by private lenders, such as large commercial banks, to pool blocks of commercial loans for the issuance of mortgage-backed securities.

WHY BORROW MONEY

For an investor, the purpose of borrowing money is singular—to increase the return, or yield. Like any venture, the result might not always be successful, but the intent is always the same—to make a profit. A **commercial loan** differs from a **residential loan** in several ways, but for the investor as well as the lender, one key difference is that the property being acquired is expected to repay the loan. (Commercial loans are being defined broadly here as loans that are not classified as residential.) So both the lender and the borrower must examine the property being pledged as collateral to assure themselves that the loan can be repaid in a timely manner. In contrast, **residential loans** look first to the borrower's personal income, unrelated to the property itself, for loan repayment; the commercial loan may not even hold the borrower personally liable, as with a **non-recourse loan**. So the effect of borrowed money must be measured in direct relation to the property's income and what the result is on the borrower-investor's yield.

Impact of Mortgage Loans on Investment Returns

There are basically two investment return considerations. Typically an investor will look at the return on an investment that is not financed and the return on an investment that is financed. If there is no financing, then the amount of money invested is the overall cost or purchase price. The return on total capital investment is frequently called the Overall Rate of Return (ROR). If there is financing, then the amount of money invested is the equity or down payment. This rate of return on a leveraged project is called the Return on Equity (ROE). This ROE is often called the cash-on-cash return or the equity dividend rate in real estate circles. No overriding regulatory authority dictates the naming of measures in real estate, as with the naming of financial statement accounts with publicly traded companies.

Considering the Heights Colony Apartments, refer to Example 10.4. Both ROR and ROE are determined. In most cases the project cannot be built without borrowed money. So the ROE would be the most important consideration. This return is based on a static view of the property at a certain point in time. It does not consider the time value of money, the potential profit from the ultimate sale of the property, the holding period, the net present value of the cash flows, and other features of the investment. In evaluating the desirability and profitability of a proposed investment, the internal rate of return (IRR) or the manager's rate of return (MRR) should be considered. These items are discussed in other chapters of this book.

Internal Rate of Return (IRR)

The IRR is equal to that return which will produce a net present value of zero when discounting all of the future cash flows. In Chapter 13 a discussion of the calculation of the IRR is given. The cash flows considered include the initial cash outlay, the cash flows during the holding period, and the reversion proceeds. The reversion proceeds are the net results of a sale at the end of the holding period.

Manager's Rate of Return (MRR)

This rate of return is similar to IRR with the exception that the discount rate is allowed to vary over the holding period. For example, if the holding period is determined to be five years, the IRR calculation assumes that the discount rate is the same for both the incoming cash flows and the investment opportunities that provide alternate options. This is allowed since returns on investment opportunities do not stay constant over a five year period. This calculation is much more sophisticated and like any projection it looses accuracy the further in the future the projections are made.

EXAMPLE 10.4	**The Heights Colony Apartments**	
	Total Capital Investment (TCI) (per appraisal)	$6,742,000
	Net Operating Income (NOI)	$606,840
	Overall Rate of Return (ROR) = NOI ÷ TCI = 606,840 ÷ 6,742,000	= .09 or 9% (this is also the cap rate)
	Loan Amount, with a 70% LTV (LA)	$4,719,400
	Net Operating Income	$606,840
	Debt Service (DS) is 12 monthly payments:	$376,780

To compute one payment, using the BA II Plus:

4,719,400	PV
12 × 30 =	N
7 ÷ 12 =	I/Y
CPT PMT =	$31,398.29

DS = 12 × $31,398.29 = $376,780 (rounding)

Net Cash Flow (NCF) = NOI − DS	$230,060
Equity (EQ) = TCI − LA	$2,022,600

Return on Equity (ROE) = NCF ÷ EQ
= 230,060 ÷ 2,022,600   .114 or 11.4%

Positive and Negative Leverage

It is important to evaluate how leverage affects the return on investment. If borrowing money reduces the return then it is said that there is negative leverage. In other words, if ROR is greater than ROE there is negative leverage. Borrowing money has lowered the rate of return of the project. Does this mean that it is inappropriate to borrow money? Absolutely not. More than likely the project would never get built without borrowed money. However, it may be an indicator that would limit the amount of borrowed money.

On the other hand, if ROE is greater than ROR, it would indicate positive leverage and would encourage the borrowing of as much money as possible. So it can be said that:

If ROE > ROR, there is positive leverage.
If ROR > ROE, there is negative leverage.

An important thing to keep in mind is that even when the cost of borrowing is less than the cap rate or overall ROR, borrowing can reduce cash flows and render the ROE less than the ROR. How is that possible? Well, loan payments include principal payoffs, and not just the interest. Thus, with the 7 percent loan in Example 10.4 above, the annual servicing cost of the loan is far more than 7 percent of the original loan amount of $4,719,400; the annual debt service is $376,780 or 7.98 percent of the LA. So were the investment to have had a cap rate or CR of between 7 and 7.98 percent, with a loan at 7 percent, the property would have had a higher rate of return on the money invested without a loan than with a loan. Positive and negative leverage are discussed in Chapter 14, as well.

PARTICIPATION BY MORTGAGE LENDERS

Another question that faces investors seeking mortgage loans is the position of the lender in regard to participation in the project. In earlier times, when interest rates were quite stable, long-term loans presented little concern for lenders. Since their earnings are based on the margin between cost of funds and what can be earned on the loan, when both elements were stable, the risk was minimal. But as interest rates became more volatile, this comfortable assurance disappeared. One way to reduce this risk is to sell the mortgage loan as described earlier in this chapter.

Another way to seek some risk protection is for the lender to participate in the mortgaged project. Still another way has been for lenders to forego such long-term loans altogether and undertake the risk of owning the property outright.

If the lender opts for participation, there are many ways to accomplish it, falling into two general categories: (1) income participation and (2) **equity participation,** as more fully described next.

Income Participation

The lender shares in the cash flow from the property for a limited period of time, usually the term of the mortgage loan. This type of participation takes the form of a percentage of the income from the property. This percentage may be based on gross rental receipts. For instance, gross rental income at time of loan origination amounts to $140,000 per month. The lender would be granted, say, 5 percent of all income over $140,000 and 10 percent of all income over $170,000.

The percentage could be based on net operating income, although this measure opens the door to disagreement over the proper deduction of operating expenses. The base for percentage calculation can vary: It may be either the before-tax or after-tax cash flow from the property. Lender participation in income could be on a per-lease basis, such as 20 percent of any increase over the initial rental structure as a required part of the mortgage repayment.

Equity Participation

If the participation is in the ownership of the property, the lender receives rights that may endure beyond the term of the loan and can represent a true equity share in the property. An equity participation may or may not require an additional investment by the lender on top of the mortgage loan. It is a method used by many large joint ventures between major lenders and property developers. An equity participation permits the lender to share in all the benefits that are derived from the property, including the deduction of depreciation, a portion of the increase in income that may be achieved, and any increases in the value of the property during the ownership term. Of course, there is a downside should losses be incurred.

FINANCING COSTS

While "the cost of borrowed money" is a standard definition of interest, the true cost encompasses many additional charges. It includes the **loan discount** and a number of fees. First, consider the three basic kinds of interest calculations.

Simple Interest

Interest paid only on the principal amount outstanding for a given period of time is **simple interest**. In mortgage lending, the percentage rate of interest is normally figured on an annual basis. For example, 9 percent per annum on a $1,000 loan means an interest charge of $90 per year. Sometimes the interest may be charged on a monthly basis. It is still simple interest, only a different time period is used for calculation.

Compound Interest

Interest paid on both the principal and earned interest added to the principal is **compound interest**. At periodic intervals, depending on the compounding period, earned interest is added to the principal balance and earns additional interest. For example, given the $1,000 above at 9 percent per year, monthly compounding raises the effective annual rate to 9.38 percent per year. This is illustrated with Example 10.5 below:

EXAMPLE 10.5	With the BA II Plus calculator, enter the following:

$1,000   PV

12   N (the number of months in a year, or the number of compounding periods)

9 ÷ 12   = .75 (the monthly interest rate)

CPT FV = –$1,093.38, the value of $1,000 in a year earning 9 percent compounded monthly.

The effective annual rate of interest is simply the $93.38 earned, divided by the $1,000 invested or 9.38 percent. Nine percent compound interest is greater than 9 percent simple interest. Compound interest favors the lender, simple interest the borrower.

Compounding is most often associated with the interest calculation applied to savings accounts. More recently, compounding is used in mortgage lending in certain kinds of graduated payment and adjustable rate mortgages, when the payment amount is insufficient to pay all of the interest due. In such a case, the unpaid interest is added to the principal, which compounds the interest cost to the borrower.

Add-On Interest

In the case of **add-on interest**, the interest cost of a loan for the full term of the loan is "added on" to the principal amount at origination of the loan. This method substantially increases the interest cost as interest continues to be paid on the full amount of the loan even though periodic payments are made that reduce the principal balance. It is a method more closely associated with installment loans as found in car and furniture financing. However, this method is sometimes used for short-term mortgage loans, junior mortgages, and seller-financed transactions.

The Truth-in-Lending Act (implemented by Regulation Z of the Federal Reserve Bank System) requires that lenders specify the cost of credit to the borrower. In Example 10.6, the annual rate of interest on a $5,000 loan with $172.22 payments over 36 months, amounts to 14.55 percent.

EXAMPLE 10.6	Consider a $5,000 loan at 8% for a term of 3 years:

Interest cost: $5,000 × 0.08 = $400 × 3 years = $1,200

Amount of note:

Principal due	$5,000.00
Interest due	$1,200.00
Face amount of note	$6,200.00

Monthly payment amount: $6,200 divided by 36 = $172.22

Application of an Interest Rate

How interest rates are applied is at the discretion of the lender. With most commercial loans, lenders consider interest as earned each day the loan is outstanding. But even this has a variation: What is sometimes called the "banker's rate" considers a day as 1/360th of the annual rate. The method used by federal agencies and others is a daily rate of 1/365th of the annual rate. On many mortgage loans, particularly residential loans, the interest is earned on a monthly basis, of one-twelfth of the annual rate. In this method, that portion of the monthly mortgage payment that applies to principal reduces the balance due for the next month's calculation. Interest may also be calculated on a quarterly, semiannual, or even an annual basis.

There is some variation in how interest is accounted for by the lender. In most mortgage loans, the interest is paid after the borrower has had use of the money. This means the monthly payment on the first of each month actually pays the interest for use of the money for the preceding month. It is sometimes called interest paid "in arrears." The other, less common, method is to require interest paid "in advance" of the use of money.

Loan Discount

An oft-misunderstood cost of borrowed money is the discount normally required at loan closing. The **discount** is a percentage of the loan amount. It is measured in "points" (one point is 1 percent of the loan amount). A discount is a cost of borrowed money and is tax deductible, as is interest. A discount can be defined as the difference between the face amount of a note and the price for which it is sold. It is a one-time charge, normally paid at time of loan closing. The discount may be paid in cash, or it can be deducted from the loan amount. In practical terms, the discount procedure allows subsequent holders of a note to adjust the return as may be needed to sell the note. This is necessary because the terms of an existing note are not subject to change once an agreement has been made.

The purpose of a discount is to increase the yield for a lender or a loan purchaser. To measure the yield, which is the same as return on an investment, the one-time charge must be converted to an annual percentage amount. Start with the question, "When is the discount earned?" Was the one-time charge earned the day the loan was closed? Was it earned that month, or that year? In one sense, it was earned the day the loan closed. But the loan will be outstanding for an unknown number of years. The industry uses several standards for the number of years a loan will be outstanding, but the net effect is easy to appreciate: If the payment is fixed, but the loaned amount is decreased with the discount charged, or the loaned amount is increased to allow for the discount, either way the lender is getting a higher payment for the same basic loan amount.

Other Loan Fees

Various fees may be charged by a lender for its services in processing a mortgage loan. Following are brief descriptions of charges that may be incurred.

Application Fee

A nonrefundable application fee is standard practice for all mortgage loans. The charge covers the cost of a credit report, a property appraisal, and the time spent reviewing the application itself. With commercial loans, the procedure varies with the applicant, the loan, and the lender. Most commonly, the lender imposes a nominal charge to help offset the cost of reviewing an application and to discourage frivolous and repeat applications. Commercial lenders also require applicants to furnish substantial supporting information for the application, including financial statements on the company and its principal owners. Real estate investment loan applications often also include such items as the leases for existing tenants, evidence of environmental compliance (discussed in Chapter 3), and such other documents—many with attaching professional fees—as may be required by a particular lender.

Origination Fee

An origination fee is a mortgage lender's charge for processing and closing a loan. Terminology differs a bit across the country and in some areas the fee is called a "brokerage fee" or a "finance fee." The fee is one to two points and is normally paid at closing. This can mean that if the loan does not close, the fee is not earned.

Mortgage companies customarily pay their loan representatives a percentage of the origination fee (up to 50 percent in some cases) as compensation for generating the loan package.

Commitment Fee

A commitment fee is a one-time charge made by a lender for a promise to fund a loan at a future time. A commitment for a permanent loan is a common requirement before a construction loan can be undertaken. Such a loan commitment normally takes the form of a letter from the lender to the borrower detailing the terms and conditions upon which the permanent loan will be made. By signing the letter agreement and paying the commitment fee, usually 1 to 2 percent of the loan amount, the borrower obtains a binding promise of funds.

Stand-By Commitment Fee

In mortgage lending, a stand-by commitment is a "back-up" promise to fund a loan if other sources fail. It is most commonly used by smaller home builders seeking construction financing. The stand-by is available, at a higher cost for the money, should the finished houses fail to sell within a specified number of months after completion. The "higher cost" could be a higher-than-market interest rate and a shorter-than-normal loan term. Its cost is two to four points of the commitment amount. In practice, builders do not really expect to use the stand-by, but purchase it to give assurance to the construction lender that its loan will be repaid.

Other Finance Charges

There are a number of ways for a lender to increase the yield from a loan. The nomenclature varies; some lenders are more imaginative than others!

Whatever it is called, the bottom line is that many of these fees are designed to increase the yield from a loan rather than as compensation for special services rendered.

- *Funding fee.* At the time a loan is funded, the lender may assess an additional fee as a further discount on the loan.
- *Renewal fee.* When a borrower asks to renew a mortgage note for an additional term, the lender may demand a renewal fee, usually one point. Renewal fees are common in construction lending and may be intended to increase a return from the loan. A six-month construction loan for a home builder is usually too short a time frame in which to build, sell, and close the transaction. Thus, a renewal fee may be expected.
- *Assumption fee.* When a new owner assumes an existing mortgage loan, the lender incurs some additional expense in reviewing and approving the assumption agreement. Hence, an additional fee is justified. The charge may be assessed as a percentage of the loan amount (in points), or as a flat dollar amount.
- *Warehouse fee.* Mortgage companies, without deposit assets to fund their loans, normally hold lines of credit with one or more commercial banks, called a "warehouse line of credit." When a loan is funded using the line of credit, the mortgage company delivers the mortgage to the bank as collateral where it remains "stored" with the bank until it can be sold to a secondary market investor. A warehouse line usually calls for interest at the bank's prime rate. In normal credit markets, the prime rate is less than long-term mortgage rates and the mortgage company can make a small profit while loans remain at the bank. When markets reverse, as they sometimes do, and the prime rate exceeds long-term rates, mortgage companies may assess a small charge, like a quarter point, as a special "warehouse fee" to offset the mortgage company's holding costs.

MORTGAGE LOAN AMORTIZATION

Amortization is the periodic repayment of the principal balance plus interest as it comes due. The literal meaning of amortization implies taking something to the end—to "death"—as with the payment of the entire balance of a mortgage, over time. How a loan is amortized is one way of classifying mortgage loans, as indicated below:

- *Straight mortgage loan.* The entire principal balance is due at maturity with only interest paid during the loan's term. This method is also called a "term loan," or an "interest only" loan.
- *Partially amortized loan.* Periodic payments are insufficient to repay the principal during its term, requiring a full payment of the remaining principal balance at maturity. The method is sometimes called a **balloon note**, as a large balance balloons at maturity. A common plan for such payments might be a loan that matures in ten years with payments calculated as if it were a 30-year term. With this plan, after ten years the balance due would amount to nearly 90 percent of the initial loan!

- *Fully amortized loan.* Periodic payments (usually monthly) include principal and interest computed (usually at a constant-level payment amount) so that the loan is fully paid at maturity. This is the standard for most residential loans.

Calculation of Amortized Payments

The repayment of a mortgage loan is normally calculated as a constant-level monthly payment for a specified number of years. The payment amount includes interest cost on the principal balance due each month plus a reduction of the principal itself. Since each payment reduces the principal balance, it necessarily reduces the interest cost for the next month. Thus, each successive payment comprises less interest cost with a larger amount applied to the reduction of principal. On a fully amortized loan, the payments over the term of the loan pay off the principal amount in full.

The monthly payments on a mortgage loan constitute an **annuity**. An annuity is any set of equally sized cash flows (payments) occurring at equally spaced intervals (monthly) for a fixed period of time (number of years). An annuity is defined as annual, or monthly, payments designed to deliver a specified principal amount, plus earned interest, in equal payment amounts over a given time period. It is the kind of payment offered by an insurance company to policyholders on certain kinds of life insurance policies. In the case of a mortgage loan, the mortgage amount becomes the present worth of future monthly payments. Put another way, if we consider the present worth of each future monthly payment, as discounted at the interest rate required by the mortgage loan, the sum of the discounted future payments is equal to the mortgage amount. While the "pure" mathematics of mortgage, or annuity, payments is not offered in this text, with payment calculations restricted to calculator applications as with the Texas Instruments BA II Plus, present worth calculations are explained in Chapter 13, "Discount Analysis."

Example 10.7 illustrates the periodic declination in the loan balance, the decreasing interest payments, and the increasing principal payments of a fixed-payment mortgage of $100,000 at 7 percent per year with monthly payments for 30 years.

EXAMPLE 10.7

$100,000	PV
12 × 30 =	N
7 ÷ 12 =	I/Y
CPT PMT =	−$665.30

The balance at the end of one year becomes:

2nd Amort, P1 = 1, P2 = 12, (for the first and last months of the first year)

BAL = 98,984
PRN = 1,016
INT = 6,968

[Adding the PRN (the principal) and the INT (interest) together for the first through twelfth periods (From P1 = 1 to P2 = 12), gives the first year's mortgage costs: 1,016 + 6,968 = 7,984. Dividing this total by 12 gives the monthly payment of 665.30.]

The balance at the end of year two becomes:

2nd Amort, P1 = 13, P2 = 24 (for the first and last months of the second year)
BAL = 97,895
PRN = 1,089
INT = 6,894

Here, the increase in the principal payments between the first and second years, from $1,016 in year one to $1,089 in year two, is observed. Likewise, declining interest payments are observed, from $6,968 in year one, to $6,894 in year two.

[Setting P1 = 1, and P2 = 360 provides the calculator user a view of the principal and interest payments over the entire term of the loan—$100,000 in Principal (or PRN) and $139,509 in Interest (INT)]

The accrued interest due on a loan is always paid first with the balance of the payment allocated to principal. Thus, the borrower begins to build equity, even though small, with the very first payment.

Payment Amount

Terminology differs between home loans and commercial loans in defining a monthly payment. In home loans, the payment amount is called the "mortgage payment" and includes principal and interest plus what the borrower must pay for annual taxes, insurance, and any assessments on the property. The tax, insurance, and assessment money is held in escrow for payment by the mortgage servicing agent when due. This relieves the borrower of concern for making timely payment and assures the lender of continued priority for its mortgage lien.

In commercial loans, the payment is normally limited to principal and interest and is called debt service. Taxes, insurance, and other property assessments are expected to be paid directly by the borrower as a part of the operating expenses for the property. In such cases, lenders may require proof of these important payments in the form of tax receipts and a copy (some lenders require the original) of the current insurance policy.

MORTGAGE REPAYMENT PLANS

How a mortgage loan is repaid directly affects an investor's cash flows. The type of mortgage used affects the overall cost of the loan itself, and thus the amount of the invested capital. So it is important to know the basics of mortgage loan terminology, what kinds of loans are available, and the normal procedures used in the industry.

As a part of the explanation of mortgage loans, two key words should be identified. Term means the length of time over which there remains an outstanding balance on the loan. Maturity is that point in time when the loan must be paid in full.

The fully amortized, constant-level payment loan that once completely dominated the industry began to give way to new designs in the mid-1970s, primarily in the field of residential loans. Two new repayment plans were introduced. One was a graduated payment design, initially encouraged by the FHA for home loans, and the other, an adjustable rate plan that allowed a lender to change the interest rate during the term of a loan without altering any of the other terms or conditions. Adjustable rate loans have been at the center of the credit crisis, with a great many residential and commercial loans "adjusting" to unaffordable levels and leading to the failure or foreclosure of both types of properties.

Further explanation of the three basic repayment plans follows.

Fixed-Rate Mortgage

In a fixed-rate loan, two basic characteristics do not change over the life of the loan: the interest rate and the repayment term. If, in addition, the payment amount itself is fixed, as is true for most loans of this type, the mortgage is called a "fixed-interest, constant-level payment" plan. It is the standard mortgage design used in long-term commercial and residential lending.

Adjustable-Rate Mortgage

An adjustable-rate mortgage is a long-term loan that allows a lender to adjust the interest rate at periodic intervals during the term of the loan without altering any other conditions. The purpose is to shift a portion of the loan risk—that of fluctuating interest rates—to the borrower. It was intended primarily for the benefit of savings associations, which customarily hold some of their loans in portfolio. Having a method of adjusting their income provides a better match between their fluctuating cost of funds and their loan income. For the borrower to accept the additional risk, the key inducement has been a lower initial interest rate, sometimes as much as 2 to 3 percentage points less than a fixed-rate loan.

A number of state and federal regulations control some features of adjustable-rate plans to protect home buyers. The Federal Reserve Bank has expanded its Truth-in-Lending rules, Regulation Z, to require certain disclosures that will allow the unwary consumer better information to make an informed decision in home financing. These rules do not apply to commercial borrowers who are considered business-wise and not in need of protection.

Prime Rate Loan

A common form of adjustable-rate mortgage found in commercial lending is based on the bank's own prime rate of interest which is not subject to as many regulations. It is important to recognize that a bank's prime rate is set by the bank itself, and can be changed at any interval of time. There is no standard except for a tendency to "follow the leader." Non-regulated lenders sometimes use the "New York prime rate," which is the rate usually published in financial newspapers. If a major bank changes its rate, many lesser banks tend to follow the same adjustment.

In this procedure, the bank's prime rate becomes the base rate with interest points added to match the risk level of the loan. Say the loan is offered at "prime plus two." This would mean whatever the bank's prime rate might be plus two additional percentage points. If the bank's prime at initiation of the loan is 8 percent, the loan's effective rate would be 10 percent (8 + 2 = 10). The prime rate may change any day (it is not subject to control), and when it does, so does the effective rate for the loan.

Construction Loans

Construction loans are short-term loans made for the purpose of providing the financing necessary to allow for the construction of a project. They are typically made by short-term lenders such as commercial banks. The payment of the loan is expected to be made from the proceeds of a permanent loan. Most often the construction lender will require that the borrower already have a commitment for the permanent or "take-out" loan. Since the collateral is not in place at the time of the loan request, the interest rate will typically be higher than the rate of the permanent loan. The rate differential is somewhat of a motivator for the borrower to close into the permanent financing as soon as possible. Many banks will charge two points or more over prime with interest to be paid monthly until the loan is paid off.

The funding of a construction loan will normally be scheduled in two week draws. The first draw will likely cover expenses already incurred, architect fees, engineering fees, permit fees, appraisal fees, and other upfront costs. At this point the collateral is the land. As construction progresses, an architect or other professional will inspect the progress and indicate the amount of work that has been completed. The borrower will then prepare a "draw request," the proceeds of which will be used to pay sub-contractors and suppliers. In some cases it may be agreed by the lender that the draw request will include enough funds to pay the interest on the amount of funds that have already been drawn. As construction progresses, the collateral will include the land and the completed improvements.

Mezzanine Loan

Mezzanine loans are often second mortgages, or unique lending agreements specially tailored for a piece of land with "unusual" features (like a new casino on the Gulf Coast) or special needs. Capital assets such as stock may also serve as collateral; "mezz" financing resides between (like a "mezzanine") the equity in a property and other lending, thus its name. If the company (usually a LLC) fails to make the payments, the mezzanine lender can seize the stock in a matter of a few weeks, as opposed to the many months it often takes to foreclose on the real estate beneath a mortgage. Mezzanine loans can also be made using the property as collateral. In either case, the holder is in a special lien position and therefore higher risk is involved. Higher risk always demands a higher yield so mezzanine financing will almost always be more costly than traditional first lien financing.

Mezzanine loans are typically fairly big. Most mezzanine lenders are unwilling to do all of the required paperwork for a loan of less than several million dollars. In addition, mezzanine lenders typically want big projects. If the property is not worth several million dollars, it may be hard to attract the interest of any mezzanine lenders.

There are three typical uses for a mezzanine loan. First, suppose the owner of a $10 million shopping center has a $5 million first mortgage from another lender. The owner wants to pull out some equity, but he cannot simply refinance the shopping center because the first mortgage has either a *lock-out clause* or a huge defeasance prepayment penalty. In this instance, he could probably obtain a $2.5 million mezzanine loan (or simply a second mortgage) to free up some cash.

Second, suppose an experienced office building investor wanted to buy a partially-vacant office building in a fine location. Once again, assume that the purchase price is $10 million (when the office building is still partially-vacant) and that the existing first mortgage is $5 million. The right mezzanine lender might be willing to lend $4 million. This loan would be 90 percent loan-to-value. But when the vacant space is rented, the property will increase to $12 million in value. Suddenly the mezzanine lender is back to 75 percent **loan-to-value** and his rationale is obvious. This kind of deal is called a *value-added* deal.

The third and final use of mezzanine loans is for new construction. Suppose a developer wanted to build a 400 room hotel across the street from Disneyland. Hotels may be temporarily out of favor, and a commercial construction lender might only be willing to make a loan of 60 percent LTV. If the total cost was $20 million, the developer would ordinarily have to come up with 40 percent of $20 million or $8 million. A $3 million mezzanine loan solves the developer's problem. The commercial construction lender would advance $12 million, the mezzanine lender would make a $3 million mezzanine loan, and the developer would "only" have to come up with $5 million.

MORTGAGE VARIATIONS

As the economy changes, mortgage lending has adopted some variations in how loans are offered to better accommodate the demand. A few of the innovations are explained next.

Shorter-Term Loans

The 30-year term for a mortgage loan has become so widely accepted that many have considered it an optimum time period. Enthusiasm for minimal down payments and monthly payments hit a peak a few years ago when government housing experts began pushing the 40-year mortgage term. The longer term saves very little in monthly payment amount and substantially increases the total interest cost. For example, in the payment chart shown in Example 10.8, the difference between a 30-year and a 40-year term payment amounts to $20.30 per month. The $1,028.63 payment is reduced to $1,008.33, and requires the payment for ten years longer!

What has been overlooked is the effect of reducing, rather than increasing, the term of the loan. The results in total savings on interest costs are spectacular.

What frightens many borrowers is the idea that shortening the term of a loan substantially increases the monthly payment. For instance, doesn't cutting a 30-year term loan to 15 years just about double the monthly payment? Not at all. Take a closer look at Example 10.8 and compare the monthly payment amounts on a $100,000 loan. The difference between payments on a 30-year and a 15-year loan amounts to $171.59, or an increase of 17 percent to cut the term in half.

The idea of paying more towards the reduction of principal and less to interest costs sometimes brings comments such as "Interest is tax-deductible and I would lose some of my write-off." But where is the advantage in paying a greater amount simply to be able to recover only 15 or 28 percent of the payment in a tax saving?

EXAMPLE 10.8

For a $100,000 loan at 12% interest, the following table compares repayment costs over the full term of the loan.

Term	Monthly Payment	Months Paid	Total Cost	Interest Cost
40-year	$1,008.33	480	$483,998	$383,998
30-year	$1,028.63	360	$370,307	$270,307
20-year	$1,101.12	240	$264,269	$164,269
15-year	$1,200.22	180	$216,040	$116,040
10-year	$1,434.81	120	$172,177	$72,177

Biweekly Payment Plan

Another way to reduce the total cost of interest by earlier repayment of a loan is to make biweekly, rather than monthly, payments. Some people are paid every other week and may prefer to make their mortgage payments at that interval. If the every other week payment amount is set at just half the monthly payment, the result is one additional monthly payment each year—26 biweekly payments instead of 12 monthly payments. Again, the result is a much quicker pay-off of the principal balance resulting from the extra month's payment each year.

A Negative View on Early Pay-off

In economic terms, consideration should be given to the opportunity cost of a faster loan pay-off. What this means is that the money given to accelerate loan repayment could be used for other investment that would earn a return.

Therefore, that opportunity for additional return is lost when the money is used to pay off an existing loan prematurely or at a faster pace than necessary. It is an offset to the amount of interest saved.

Shared-Equity Mortgage

A type of home mortgage that can be of interest to expansion of a business is the shared-equity mortgage. In this kind of transaction, two or more parties hold an ownership position in the property and dual liability for the mortgage. The purpose would be to assist someone in the acquisition of a property. An example could be an employer joining with an employee to buy a house in a remote, or a high-cost, area to assist in a job transfer. Normally, the employee is given an option to buy out the employer's portion within a limited number of years. Or, in case of a transfer, the employer could purchase the entire property at the appraised value.

Junior Mortgage

A mortgage is a pledge of property as security for a loan. There can be more than one mortgage claim against the same property as long as state laws or existing mortgage provisions do not prohibit it. Multiple mortgages present no real problems for a lender unless there is a default resulting in foreclosure. Then, under a foreclosure sale, the property may not produce enough money to pay off all the claims. This is especially the case with properties facing foreclosure during the Great Recession, as property values often do not cover even the first mortgage, much less junior mortgages or equity lines of credit. Whatever the proceeds are from such a sale, distribution is made to the claimants in accordance with the priority of their claims, not in a pro rata share as might be found in a bankruptcy action. Thus, whoever holds the highest priority of claim is more likely to be fully covered.

Since its priority of claim represents a greater risk for the lender, a junior mortgage loan commands a higher interest rate, and probably a shorter term. A common limitation on the size of a junior mortgage would be that the sum of any prior mortgages plus the junior mortgage cannot exceed 80 percent of the property value. However, not all regulated lenders are authorized to make real estate loans secured by other than first mortgages.

Wrap-Around Mortgage

A **wrap-around** is a junior mortgage since there must be an existing one for it to wrap around. A wrap mortgage is a new mortgage that includes in its amount the balance due on any existing mortgage or mortgages. It is sometimes used to facilitate seller-financed sales. The wrap acknowledges the existence of prior mortgages but declines to accept liability for them so as to avoid a dual liability. "Wraps" are uncommon in the 21st century, but enjoyed a period of popularity in the 1980s. As a brief example, an owner may have sold her property and held a 12 percent mortgage during the high rates of the early 1980s. Rather than pay off an existing and assumable 6 percent mortgage, she "wraps" the lower-rate mortgage with a higher rate one, this during a time when her buyer might otherwise have had to secure 15 percent or 16 percent financing. She actually helps to sell her property by offering seller-financing at

12 percent—the seller financing *is* the wrap-around mortgage! She is able to offer a still-competitive rate to the new buyer with the wrap, and make an effective interest rate profit on the difference between the wrap and the assumable existing mortgage. The seller receives payments on the wrap, in turn pays off the lower-interest rate assumable loan, and makes an effective profit on the difference by remaining culpable to the original lender on that lower rate loan. Terms of the existing 6 percent loan would still be dominant, but provided the new owner/buyer remains current with the new wraparound mortgage, everyone "wins." Except the holder of that assumable 6 percent loan!

SOME CONCLUDING REMARKS ON REAL ESTATE FINANCING

Real estate financing, and the use of real estate lending, to augment and lever returns to real estate investors is a centerpiece of the attractiveness of real estate investment. However, the nature of real estate lending is changing, with widespread foreclosures and failed residential and commercial property investments littering the US investment landscape; there was $160 billion in foreclosed or defaulting commercial real estate projects in the US at the end of 2009. The remarks above only begin to tell a still-evolving story, but the benefits—and risks—offered to the real estate investor with mortgage financing are broadly unchanged. The ensuing years will reveal more precisely the damage done to this sector by the Great Recession; the willingness of lenders to participate in real estate financing has changed, but the exact nature and permanency of that change is not yet certain.

The importance of real estate lending is intact, and will remain so. As with the lessons learned with the collapse of the thrift industry in the late 1980s, the early 2000s wrote another important chapter in the real estate financing "story."

KEY TERMS

add-on interest	conventional loan	mezzanine loans	residential loans
amortization	debt coverage ratio	mortgage loan	secondary mortgage
annuity	debt service	amortization	market
balloon note	discount	non-recourse loan	simple interest
cap rate (CR)	equity participation	origination fee	underwriting
commercial loan	foreclosure	primary mortgage	standards
compound interest	loan discount	market	wrap-around
construction loans	loan-to-value (LTV)	refinance	

DISCUSSION QUESTIONS

1. Discuss the function of and the participants in the primary mortgage market.

2. How does the secondary mortgage market affect commercial borrowers?

3. How does borrowing money increase the return on an equity investment in real estate?

4. Define the meaning of "coverage ratio" and how it is used.

5. What is the purpose of a discount charged on a mortgage loan?

6. How is the rate determined on a prime rate loan?

7. What are the following lender variables in your area?
   Debt coverage ratio, interest rate, and LTV

8. Discuss the advantages and disadvantages of a wrap-around mortgage.

9. What is the current status of Fannie Mae and Freddie Mac?

10. How might an investor in a typical real estate investment enhance her returns with mortgage financing?

11. What is the main risk facing a real estate investor from using mortgage financing to fund a "deal?"

12. What are the three main risks facing a real estate lender, whether lending on a commercial investment or a primary residence?

CHAPTER 11

Tools of Analysis

This chapter begins the focus on analysis procedures that will help an investor evaluate and compare investment opportunities. Up to this point the text has offered information on real property that is of general concern to an investor. Some has been background information on the nature of real property ownership and general constraints on its use. Several chapters have been devoted to a study of basic property taxes and federal income tax laws. An overview has been given of business organizations, the tax ramifications of each, and financing practices. The next step is to examine analysis procedures: How does one figure investment return and make reasonable comparisons between properties?

Real estate offers a variety of investments, and the returns derived are generally not precise in measurement. Unlike fixed-income investments, such as savings certificates or annuities, income from real estate can be more subject to fluctuating market conditions. Nevertheless, analysis is necessary in order to make basic comparisons. The next few chapters will explain the kinds of information available on real estate opportunities and explain some of the problems associated with the presentation of this information. The advantages of a standard analysis form will be illustrated as one way to make better comparisons among real property investments.

By definition, income property investments offer some kind of periodic income. Information on this income is usually found in a financial statement that can be a projection of what to expect (or hope for!), or it can be actual figures showing past experience. First, let's examine how financial information is offered. The three basic financial statements are: (1) the balance sheet, (2) the profit-and-loss statement, and (3) the operating statement. Examples and an explanation of each follow.

BALANCE SHEET

A **balance sheet** details the assets and liabilities of a person or business at a particular point in time. The difference between assets and liabilities is the **net worth,** or **equity.** A simplified balance sheet is illustrated in Example 11.1. The balance sheet is a history. It shows either the results of a business operation or an individual's financial progress. The important bottom line is the net worth. Take a second look at Example 11.1. Current assets and all liabilities are reasonably easy to verify and may be considered accurate for the purpose of a preliminary evaluation. The big question is the value of land and buildings. Are the figures in this statement the original cost of the land and buildings less depreciation, usually called book value?[1] Or are they appraised values? Or are they the owner's estimates of market value? A properly prepared statement is used to clarify the valuation, but many owners prefer to omit explanatory information. Serious investors would give little weight to an unexplained balance sheet value of property except as information that might help structure a deal.

EXAMPLE 11.1	Assets		Liabilities		
	Current assets		Current liabilities		
	Cash	$ 5,500	Accounts payable		$ 2,800
	Rents receivable	$ 3,100	Long-term debt		
			First mortgage	$300,000	
	Fixed assets		Less: Principal paid	$ 41,000	
	Land	$ 78,000	Balance due		$259,000
	Buildings	$385,000	Total liabilities		$261,800
	Less: Depreciation:	$ 91,000		Net Worth	
	Buildings (net)	$294,000	Partnership equity		$118,800
	Total assets	$380,600	Liabilities plus net worth		$380,600

---

[1] Book value is not necessarily the same as the IRS-defined "basis of value." Book value would consider the acquisition cost as the value of consideration paid for the property with no concern for the IRS distinctions based on method of acquisition.

A balance sheet is less important to an investor buying only the real property, in other words, one who is not buying the business that is operating the property. Even then, a balance sheet provides important information on outstanding debt and liabilities that could become liens against the property. A balance sheet should also offer the buyer some information on depreciation schedules.

PROFIT-AND-LOSS STATEMENT

Like the balance sheet, a profit-and-loss statement is closely related to the owner's confidential financial data and may be classified as proprietary information. The **profit-and-loss** or **income statement** lists the business income, all operating expenses, and other deductions including depreciation and mortgage interest, and allows for income tax liability. The profit-and-loss statement may or may not be available to a prospective buyer. The information it contains is not critical, unless the property acquisition is made through the purchase of an operating business or corporation. Example 11.2 is an example of a P & L statement in a simplified form as it might appear at the end of the tax year.

Profit-and-loss statements vary considerably in the amount of information given. Some offer detailed information. Others, like the one in Example 11.2, ignore detail and present only consolidated figures with greater detail provided in separate supporting statements. Since few standards prevail (except for publicly listed corporations), it is not uncommon to find an operating statement identified as a profit-and-loss statement. However identified, an operating statement is generally limited to those figures concerned with the business operation, not its financing or tax practices.

EXAMPLE 11.2	**Profit-and-Loss Statement**	
	Income from operations	$148,878
	Less: Expenses incurred	62,569
	Net operating income	$ 86,309
	Less: Interest expense	45,324
	Less: Depreciation allowed	36,531
	Income before taxes	$ 4,454
	Provision for income taxes	2,048
	Net Income	$ 2,406

OPERATING STATEMENT

The **operating statement** provides the kind of information that is most commonly delivered when real property is offered for sale. It is a record of all income less operating expenses, with the net operating income as the bottom line. This statement does not show depreciation, mortgage interest, or possible reserves for payment of income taxes. All three are important and will be discussed later, but none of the three are classified as operating expenses.

There are no true standards for presenting accounting information of any kind (except for publicly listed corporations), and this makes it more difficult to analyze the material. With an operating statement, the first problem is to understand the nomenclature used to identify income and expense items. The second is determining the source of the information presented. The third is making sure that no essential information has been omitted.

One way that serious investors overcome some of these problems is to develop a standardized statement form that can be used to transfer the information available on the property. If an item called for on the standardized statement form is blank after the transfer, some of the information may be missing. A standardized form is discussed and illustrated in Chapter 12, Figure 12.1.

In Example 11.3, the account terminology follows the pattern used by the National Association of Realtors, which has created a widely used standard within the industry. The statement is followed by a discussion of the various accounts.

The following item-by-item explanations cover the major accounts normally used in an operating statement. We begin at the first line.

Scheduled Gross Income

In a statement on income property, the first line usually represents the maximum income that the property can be expected to produce at full occupancy. It is variously called **scheduled gross income**, gross potential income, gross rent roll, total calculated income, or available gross income. Sometimes it even goes by the inadequate name of income. The first line may well show the actual income that has been received from the property. If so, there would be no line for vacancy and credit losses.

Vacancy and Credit Losses

If the statement shows no deduction for vacancy and credit losses, then either the first line represents actual income or it is misrepresented. The reason is that, except for very small rental properties, it is nearly impossible to realize a property's full potential gross income. There will almost always be a few premature vacancies, some rental income loss while units undergo renovation, and occasional failures to collect the proper rent. The most accurate figure to use for vacancy and credit losses would be, of course, the actual annual amount. But if the statement is an analysis, the vacancy and credit loss figures are often based on a percentage loss, usually between 5 and 10 percent of gross potential income. The flip side of the vacancy and credit loss figure is the occupancy rate. An average 92 percent occupancy rate would mean an 8 percent vacancy and credit loss.

EXAMPLE 11.3	Operating Statement		
	Scheduled gross income		$100,000
	Less: Vacancy and credit losses		7,000
	Gross operating income		$ 93,000
	Less: Operating expenses		
	Taxes	$ 6,500	
	Insurance	3,100	
	Utilities	6,900	
	Advertising	1,100	
	Management	5,000	
	Payroll, including taxes	14,000	
	Supplies	1,200	
	Services	1,100	
	Maintenance	1,900	
	Other	500	
	Total expenses		$ 41,300
	Net operating income		$ 51,700

Gross Operating Income

This is the actual income received during the period covered by the statement. The figure includes not only regular rental income, but also any miscellaneous income from services sold, parking fees, or utility charges. It is sometimes referred to as **effective gross income** or just effective income. As with many accounts in real estate, names of the accounts are often given by the preparer of the statement.

Operating Expenses

Accountants differentiate between fixed charges (taxes, insurance, etc.) and operating expenses. **Fixed expenses** remain stable regardless of occupancy, while **operating expenses**, such as utilities, will vary with occupancy. However, these differences are usually not noted in an income property operating statement. Operating expenses include all costs except mortgage loan interest (although some accountants do include interest). The reason interest should not be included as an operating expense is that it is a cost of financing. The purpose of the statement at this point is to learn how much income can be made from operating the property. Do not confuse operating expenses with the cost of financing. A property may operate at a reasonable operating profit, yet show a negative cash flow (loss) because it is overburdened with excessive financing costs.

Replacement Reserves

Expenses such as utilities, payroll, maintenance, supplies, advertising, and others are paid on a regular basis. However, there are numerous expenses that are not scheduled, not paid on a regular basis, but are significant because of the dollars involved. Some examples would be roof replacement, parking lot paving, HVAC replacement, and other capital expenses. In order to have the money available for an expense that may not occur until five or ten years in the future it is important to set aside some money every month to cover future expenses. For example, if it is anticipated that the roof will need to be replaced in ten years and it will cost $20,000 then at least $167 should be set aside for each of the 120 months prior to the needed repair.

Other Comments

Expense items in a financial statement can be factual and nevertheless fail to tell the full story. This problem mostly concerns the flexibility built into maintenance costs and replacement charges. If the property is new, maintenance costs can temporarily be held to a minimum, but restoration costs at a later date may be substantially higher. If the property contains such items as drapes, carpeting, and appliances, deterioration occurs almost daily. The cost of replacing them, however, may not crop up for three to five years. Good accounting procedure allows for these hidden expenses in a "replacement cost" account, thereby helping management to make informed decisions.

Tax laws require that assets such as drapes, carpeting, etc., with a useful life of more than one year be capitalized and depreciated with only a portion of their cost eligible for deduction from income each year. Since depreciation is not usually reported in an operating statement, some owners tend to overlook this cost when offering properties for sale.

While the depreciation deduction reduces tax liability, it is not an "out-of-pocket" expense. In fact, in many areas of the country, the building may increase in value rather than decline. The question of depreciation is examined in greater detail in Chapter 6. A reserve account for possible income tax liability is not normally found in an operating statement, as it is considered proprietary and not necessarily a cost of operating the property.

PRO FORMA STATEMENT

A **pro forma statement** is an estimate. It can be a balance sheet, a profit-and-loss statement, or an operating statement. It is a projection of future earnings and asset values. For the investor, "pro forma" should mean what may come to pass rather than what has already occurred. However, since the analysis for undertaking an investment is often based on future returns, the pro forma is an important tool. If prepared by a qualified professional, the pro forma statement can be invaluable in assessing future returns. Nevertheless, because it is a projection based on estimated results, the figures can be colored to present a distorted projection.

INCOME TAX STATEMENTS

The idea of keeping two sets of books hints of chicanery. Yet it is a common practice for both individuals and businesses, and it is not intended to deceive anyone. The reason it is common is that federal tax laws, designed to accomplish desirable social goals as well as provide tax revenues, have built up certain requirements that tend to distort the true value of an asset.

Here are a few examples. The tax distortion can be severe for an oil operator. The reserve value of a newly discovered well is not reported on a tax return until the production has been sold. Yet this operator undoubtedly sees a substantial increase in the asset value of the property as soon as the oil is discovered. And this asset would represent collateral value to a lending institution. Likewise, newborn calves are assets, but are not taxable income until they are sold. On the other hand, a banker dealing mainly in cash and fixed-value promissory notes has a minimal amount of asset distortion to reckon with. A real estate investor falls somewhere in between. The changing rules for calculating capital gains, the application of minimum taxes on tax-preference income, and the passive activity rules all have a bearing on how the real estate investor must keep records for tax purposes.

Providing a realistic statement on an operating property may require two sets of records—one for tax purposes, and the other for the property's owners and other interested parties. Footnotes can be used to adequately explain the major adjustments.

Does the prospective buyer of real property have a right to see the federal income tax statements that have been filed for the property? No. The seller has no legal obligation to provide this information because tax reports are considered confidential. However, the buyer may make the furnishing of tax reports a mandatory condition of the sale if it seems justified.

ACCOUNTING METHODS

The previous section identified the basic financial statements used in business accounting. It also explained some of the distortions that can occur in both balance sheets and operating statements. To effectively use a financial statement in analysis work, a real estate investor should understand that there are differences in: (1) methods of presenting financial information and (2) the people who prepare the statements. This section discusses the principal accounting methods found in the real estate field. The next section describes the general qualifications of people who prepare financial statements.

Cash Basis Accounting

Cash basis is the simplest method of keeping financial records and is used by most individuals and smaller businesses. Essentially, this **cash method** records income only when the cash is received and an expense when it is paid. Under this system, it is possible to shift income or an expense to a different tax period by delaying a charge or the payment of a bill. Thus, there can be some distortion unless adjustments are made at the close of an accounting period.

The 1986 Tax Reform Act prohibited the use of the cash method of accounting for corporations (other than S corporations), partnerships with corporate partners, and tax shelters if these entities have annual gross receipts over $5 million.

Accrual Basis Accounting

As business grows, the need for more accurate and timely records becomes essential. So most businesses eventually adopt the **accrual method** of keeping records. Under this system, income is recorded when it is earned (not when payment is received), and the obligation by the customer to pay for the service is listed as an account receivable. When payment is received, it reduces (debits) the account receivable account crediting cash. Likewise, an expense is recorded as an obligation when the debt is incurred (not when paid). The obligation is listed as an account payable item, which is offset when actual payment is made. With this procedure, the bookkeeping more accurately reflects the current status of the business operation.

PREPARATION OF STATEMENTS

Lacking standards, laws, or regulatory agency guidelines for the information it contains, a financial statement can be inaccurate to the point of misrepresentation. However, there are some limited restraints. The Securities and Exchange Commission (SEC) issues and enforces strict requirements for financial data presented to the general public when securities are offered for sale. Banking laws govern the information that a borrower can present to a regulated lending institution in an effort to secure a loan. False information or misrepresentation of facts to induce a loan can result in a felony offense. A third formal restraint is the antifraud and consumer protection laws.

But for the average real estate investor, the most important assurance of complete and accurate financial information is the reputation and integrity of the person or firm preparing the statements. The following sections outline the principal sources for the preparation of financial data in the real estate market.

Certified Public Accountants

The highest designation accorded a professional in the accounting field is that of **Certified Public Accountant** (CPA). It is a state-defined designation. Each state has its own requirements that may vary somewhat from each other. Basically, the standards call for certain minimum education, some experience qualifications, and passing an exhaustive examination on accounting procedures. Some states award a Public Accountant designation to those meeting lesser standards. All states require that a CPA pass its own licensing requirements before practicing within the state. Generally, a statement prepared and certified by a CPA can be relied upon for proper preparation and comprehensive information.

Audited Statement

In most states, only a CPA is permitted to prepare an **audit**. An audited statement is one in which the information offered has undergone certain verification procedures and carries the certification of the preparer. Verification includes a careful examination of all bank statements, individual verification of each account receivable, inspection and inventory of physical assets, and certification of all accounts payable.

Generally, neither laws nor regulations require the use of professional accountants in the preparation of financial statements unless the information is used in the sale of securities to the general public. However, lenders and large investors often require that financial information submitted to them for evaluation be prepared in audited form by Certified Public Accountants.

Statements Prepared without Audit

A statement prepared without audit is much less expensive than one prepared with full auditing procedures. "Without audit" generally means one prepared from the owner's records only. Verification procedures are reduced to a minimum, or eliminated. An unaudited statement prepared by an independent CPA (not an employee of the property owner) has the advantage of being prepared in accordance with recognized accounting procedures, but can easily pass on to the reader the same basic errors that the property owner might have made, albeit unintentionally.

Owner-Prepared Statements

Whether or not suspicion is justified, a financial statement prepared by a property owner is always suspect. Owners do not always possess sufficient accounting expertise to prepare an adequate statement. Besides, it is simply human nature for a buyer to question the seller's own information. An owner's statement is often used as a good starting point for discussion, with verification steps taken after a preliminary evaluation has been made and the buyer has developed some real interest in the property.

Sales Broker-Prepared Statements

A financial statement prepared by a broker trying to sell income property lacks credibility, unless the broker has a solid record of analysis expertise. Commercial brokers commonly use financial analysis sheets as a starting point in developing buyer interest. Some are comprehensive and accurate while others may mix fact with fantasy. Broker-prepared statements are commonly used as a screening device to select those properties that justify more detailed analysis.

PROBLEM AREAS IN FINANCIAL STATEMENTS

As there are no sets of generally accepted accounting principles, no Securities and Exchange Commission, and no Comptroller of the Currency lording over real estate reporting, prospective investors need to take great care in gathering and interpreting real estate investment data. Errors of *commission*, where misleading data on real estate is provided, are one less frequent problem with real estate "packages." Errors of *omission* are far more frequent, where material information that impacts the value of a property is not included in a report. The items below are among those often contributing to inaccurate portrayals of investment real estate values.

Time Span Covered

One can paint an excessively rosy financial picture by selecting the time span most favorable to the property—even if that period is reported with complete accuracy. An apartment property located in a winter resort area, for example, might show marvelous operating profits from November through April. The rest of the year might not look so great. Or if property has experienced a period of very poor operations, the time span reported might be selected before or after that period. The statement could thus be perfectly accurate for the specific period covered, but still hide the full picture. The obvious solution to this problem is to require continuous information for the past three to five years.

Management Costs

When a property is presented to a potential buyer, management costs might be dropped from the record. After all, the seller might say, the new owner will not employ the same management. Or the seller might rationalize that the new owner will personally run the operation, thus eliminating most management costs. To many it seems absurd, but real estate professionals know that many new investors fail to place any value on the time that they'll spend managing the property. And some financial statements fail to list management as a separate cost. Good management is crucial to successful operation and its cost should be recognized.

Tenant Improvements

Often overlooked by prospective real estate investors, and almost invariably not included in investment property pro formas by either sellers or brokers, are the expected costs of outfitting commercial space for a new tenant. Pro forma income statements will include lists of typical expected rental income and operating expenses, but will overlook the costs of "customizing" a unit for a favored tenant. As well, commercial tenants often expect 3–6 months, at a minimum, as a move-in "allowance." Prospective investors should contemplate the types of tenants they will be attracting, and the types of costly improvements those tenants might expect. Improvements of five to ten dollars a square foot are not uncommon for longer leases to nationally-known tenants.

Leasing Commissions

Investors typically do not make allowances for costly commercial leasing commissions suffered when commercial space, as with a warehouse or space in a strip-mall, is leased. For example, if a tenant is leasing a 2,000 square foot space at $10 a foot for five years, total rental income is $100,000 (5 × 2,000 × $10). If a 6 percent commission is expected to be paid (.06 × $100,000 = $6,000), then the prospective investors need to allow for this often-overlooked $6,000 expense.

Utility Costs

Utility costs need to be carefully examined, as these sometimes apply to an entire property, to individual units within a property, or even to adjacent properties. Time periods of utility consumption, special tenant needs for power or water, and prospects for continuing (or expanded) utility service in the property area should be considered. Water restrictions, brownouts, local "green" initiatives (sometimes restricting utility consumption) and other related issues need to be evaluated, as each could impact a property's value.

Use of National Averages

Occasionally a statement will represent the operations of a property—say, a motel—using cost figures developed from national averages for that particular type and size of property. These are an interesting study in what might be, but much less valuable in the examination of a specific property.

SUPPLEMENTAL INFORMATION

The information used to prepare any financial statement is derived from data maintained on daily operations. The information can be extensive or simplified, depending on the needs of the property management and its owners. As a guide to an investor, the following list of expense items and accounts will provide an introduction to the many factors that can be involved in a thorough analysis of an income property.

Certified Rent Schedule

This is a list of tenants and the rent paid by each, certified by a responsible official of the organization operating the property.

Inventory

The inventory is a list of all personal property that belongs to the business and is used in its operation. The owner's depreciated basis of value does not pass to a new owner, but such valuation can be helpful in determining the amount of the purchase price that should be allocated to each depreciable asset. The inventory list should be certified by the owner. It becomes a part of the sales transaction; in other words, the transaction is closed subject to delivery of all inventory items agreed upon at the time of closing. An inspection of the inventory is sometimes called for as a part of the closing procedures.

Accounts Receivable

Money owed to the seller may or may not be assigned to a new owner. Property sales are often handled as sales of the physical plant only and not of the going business. Accounts receivable are a part of the going business and are thus often retained by the seller. But if the business is sold as part of the property, receivables must be verified and adjusted to the closing date.

Accounts Payable

Like accounts receivable, bills owed by the seller may or may not be assumed by the new owner as part of the transaction. A new owner must be careful not to allow an unexpected demand for payment of an old or unknown bill to surface after a transaction has been closed. The most common procedure in a sale including inventory or supplies normally purchased on open accounts is to take whatever steps and file whatever notifications are required under the state's laws.

Cash Controls

Operating cash is rarely transferred to the buyer in a property sale. If it is passed on to the new owner, it would be prudent for the new owner to verify the amount at the time of closing the transaction.

Escrow Accounts

An operating property may have a liability in the form of tenants' deposits held for various purposes. The principal items held in escrow are:

- *Advance rentals.* Money paid for future rental when a lease is signed (usually a last month's rental, paid in advance) is a liability of the property and may fall to the new owner.
- *Security deposits.* Money held by a property owner as protection against loss of personal property loaned to a tenant is a liability that passes to the new property owner. A security deposit is commonly collected, for example, in exchange for keys to the leased unit. When the keys are returned, the security deposit is refunded.
- *Damage deposits.* Many landlords require a damage deposit as a part of a lease. This money is applied to repairs needed when the property is vacated. If there is no damage, it must be returned to the tenant. Damage deposits are assessed using a variety of factors, such as the amount of equipment in the rented unit, the type of business (commercial lease) that the tenant will carry on, or the number and kind of pets that the tenant will keep on the premises.

Insurance Policies

Existing hazard insurance and general liability policies may be transferred to the new owner and continued after closing a sale, or the new owner may take out new coverage. It is a matter of negotiation. If the decision is to continue the existing coverage, it should be examined to make sure the coverage is adequate and that the party insured is corrected to name the new owner. If new coverage is desired, the old policy may provide helpful guidance as to the proper coverage and disclose any special risks that need insurance protection.

Ad Valorem Taxes

Tax statements from previous years should be examined for proper assessment and tax rate. Because unpaid ad valorem taxes amount to a first lien on real property, the proper payment and prorating of this tax is an integral part of the closing procedures when property is transferred. Responsibility for proper handling usually rests with the closing agent and title company.

Sales Taxes

States and municipalities have widely varying rules for sales taxes. The tax may or may not apply to rental income. If the tax does apply to the investment property, the investor's prime concern should be: Has it been accurately reported and paid? If sales taxes are assessed against the property with the quality of a lien, they could become the new owner's obligation.

Utility Charges

The investor should verify, from recent bills, the number of meters, the number of buildings connected to each meter, and the rates charged. Notifying a utility company is usually sufficient to transfer billing to the new owner and provide a final cutoff for the seller. Failure to notify the utility of an ownership change can result in erroneous billings.

Lease Agreements

An operating property may itself be leasing property from others:

- *Furniture.* Apartment operators often rent out furnished units that use furniture leased from others. Large property owners often set up separate entities to acquire furniture and lease it directly to the tenants. Whatever the arrangement, the new owner must locate and list all furniture subject to separate leases, locate all lease agreements, and determine whether or not the seller carries a contingent liability for the furniture leased to tenants.
- *Equipment.* Certain equipment found with income property may be leased from others. Common examples are soft-drink machines and ice-makers. The investor must ask: Can the leases be transferred to me? If so, what are the stipulations?
- *Storage buildings.* Off-premise storage space may be leased, and it may be necessary to the continuing operation of an income property. A new owner is not necessarily responsible for an off-premise lease (unless a corporation is being acquired), but awareness of the property lease will help determine if continued use is essential.
- *Land leases.* The reference here is to property that's been added to the basic land area through a lease to improve or expand operations. Additional parking space, for example, is sometimes held under a lease agreement. Liability for the lease may not pass to the new owner, but the need to continue the lease must be examined.

Contracts Outstanding

Operating properties sometimes have agreements with suppliers and other vendors for continuing services. These include the following:

- *Advertising.* A contract with an advertising agency may be needed to handle publicity. Key radio and television spots may be reserved for timely presentation of advertising. Social networking efforts should be maintained or expanded.

- *Maintenance services.* Such services as pool cleaning and landscape maintenance may be handled by contract crews. These agreements are usually transferred with ease to a new owner, but doing so requires properly notifying the contractor(s).
- *Other services.* To avoid the overhead burden of a fixed payroll expense, property owners sometimes arrange for outside contractors to perform a number of other services. Laundry service is a good example, as is the servicing of heating and air conditioning equipment.

Salary and Wage Agreements

Investment property is rarely a wage-intensive operation. However, any operating property needs personnel. How much they are paid, when they are paid, and what extra benefits are provided is essential information for the smooth transition of ownership. The following obligations are all examples of remuneration to personnel:

- *Labor contracts.* Operating personnel may be working under a labor contract that provides either for union or nonunion representation. A new owner is not necessarily obligated to fulfill an existing labor contract, but an understanding must be reached with employees if the operation is to continue smoothly.
- *Health and accident insurance.* Many operating properties provide health insurance for their employees under group policies. Continuing these benefits is generally quite helpful in assuring the property's level of operation.
- *Workmen's compensation.* Laws passed in all states provide for fixed awards to employees in case of industrial accidents and dispense with proof of negligence and legal actions. There is usually a minimum number of employees required before participation in the state program becomes mandatory. For a new property owner, it is best to check the local requirements for proper compliance with the law.
- *Unemployment compensation.* In every state, some form of employment commission collects assessments from employers based on their records of stability with employment and disburses these funds to employees who lose their jobs. The rules vary among the states as to the amount of unemployment compensation that may be collected and the requirements for qualification. To insure the state funds during periods of sustained unemployment, the federal government also collects an unemployment tax from employers. This tax is not shared by the employees because the employer alone contributes to both the state and the federal governments.
- *Pension funds.* In general, only the larger companies can support a pension plan. They are seldom found with an average-sized investment property. Recent legislation designed to protect private pension fund participants has placed certain personal liability on fund administrators and discouraged their use.

STATEMENT ANALYSIS

A number of procedures are used to analyze and compare the information available from various financial statements. Some figures and ratios are more important for one kind of business than another. Analysis and comparison of the statements used primarily in real property investment are contained in the next chapter. The purpose of this section is to introduce practices used in other businesses, some of which are also basic to real estate.

One reason for examining other methods is that many investors in real property are successful operators in other lines of work. Analysis methods familiar to them may be applied, where possible, to real property analysis. Also, understanding other methods should provide some insight into the area of important financial ratios and what they mean.

Business analysts examine financial statements along five major lines as discussed below. These are: (1) liquidity, (2) leverage, (3) income/expense, (4) activity, and (5) profitability.

Liquidity

Liquidity is the ability to convert assets into cash. Is the financial condition of the property such that payment can be made on debts as they come due? This determination is made on the basis of the ratio between current assets and current liabilities. Two definitions of "current" are used. One considers all cash, accounts, and notes receivable due within one year as current. All liabilities due and payable within one year are likewise considered current. The other definition considers only cash on hand and liabilities now due as current. Using either time frame, the prudent analyst considers "2 to 1" a safe and adequate ratio—that is, $2 in current assets for each $1 of current liabilities.

Leverage and the Great Recession

Leverage is the debt-to-equity ratio. It is most commonly discussed in terms of a percentage of total invested capital. For example, if a business property has a total asset value of $1,000,000 with an indebtedness of $650,000, the debt ratio would be 65 percent ($650,000 divided by $1,000,000 equals 0.65). Or, conversely, the equity ratio would be 35 percent. Real estate investment has normally leaned more heavily on borrowed money than commercial enterprises. Debt ratios of 70 to 80 percent are not uncommon.

The over-use of debt in the years leading up to the Great Recession contributed to the failure of many real estate investments and the firms that loaned to real estate investors. As commercial and residential real estate exit the Great Recession, leverage ratios of less than 70 percent (and often 0 percent!), are becoming the norm. For the next decade at least, it seems, the aggressive use of debt in real estate will be the exception, and not the rule.

Income/Expense

Another financial statement ratio (which some analysts also classify as operating leverage) is the multiple of net income in relation to all fixed expenses. This ratio places special importance on fixed expenses, that is, those expenses, such as taxes and insurance, which must be paid in full whether or not a property is fully occupied. It is useful in determining a "break-even" point. The ratio may be expressed:

$$\frac{\text{Net Operating Income}}{\text{Fixed Expenses}} = \text{Multiplier}$$

The use of this ratio will show how low the income can fall before the property is unable to meet the fixed expenses. It is one determination of a break-even point. For this particular analysis, the break-even point would be when the multiplier equals 1.0—when the net operating income just equals the fixed expenses. The larger the multiplier, the stronger the operation. An example of this determination is shown in Example 11.4.

An operating expense ratio provides similar information. The operating expense ratio typically includes all fixed and variable operating expenses and compares them to effective gross income or gross operating income. In Example 11.4, that ratio would be total cash expenses ($18,785 plus $10,300) divided by $46,710 or around 62 percent. This seems high. Typical operating expense ratios for office and retail properties are closer to 30 or 35 percent.

EXAMPLE 11.4

Scheduled gross income	$49,350		
Less: Vacancy and credit loss	2,640		
Gross operating income			$46,710
Less: Expenses:			
Fixed expenses			
Taxes	$ 8,200		
Insurance	2,100		
Total fixed expenses		$10,300	
Operating expenses			
Utilities	$ 1,820		
Payroll	3,400		
Supplies	1,340		
Repairs	1,925		
Total operating expenses		8,485	
Total expenses		18,785	
Replacement reserves		2,745	
Total expenses and reserves			21,530
NET OPERATING INCOME			$25,180

Using the above figures in the income/expense formula:

$$\frac{25,180}{10,300} = 2.44 \text{ (multiplier)}$$

Activity

Activity tests reveal how effectively assets are being used. This ratio compares the gross operating income to total assets. To determine the ratio, divide the gross income from the property by the total asset value. Let's take an example of an apartment project worth $1 million producing gross annual income of $185,000:

$$\frac{185,000}{1,000,000} = 0.185 \text{ or } 18.5\% \text{ (activity ratio)}$$

The inverse of this measure (1/.185) is the Gross Income Multiplier (GIM), similar to the Gross Rent Multiplier (GRM) in Chapter 14. The GIM is often used as a thumbnail measure of the relative value of multi-unit residential properties. The GIM here is around 5.4, the inverse of .185.

Profitability

The success of an investment is determined by its profitability. For a real estate investment, a key element of profitability that does not appear in a normal operating statement is appreciation. However, if we consider that one of the purposes of an analysis is to provide a basis of comparison for similar investments, two additional ratios should be explored. These are profitability ratios that compare profit to the value of the investment. To accommodate appreciation, the value of the investment can be adjusted to current market value. One difficulty with this approach is that an increase in property value (**appreciation**) reduces the resulting ratios. An investor might use this ratio to help determine the need for an adjustment in rents. Two different ratios can be used for this analysis:

- *Return on capital invested.* The ratio of after-tax (net) profit to the current market value of the total investment.
- *Cash return.* The ratio of the cash flow before taxes (the net operating income reduced by the annual debt service) divided by the equity value. A similar ratio, the *equity dividend rate*, is estimated for prospective properties by dividing this same cash flow before taxes (estimated for the first year of a property's operations) by the expected down payment on the property.

AMORTIZATION TABLES AND LOAN CONSTANTS

Real estate professionals, including real estate investors, once depended upon the provision of amortization tables and loan constants, often by outside contractors, to aid in investment property analyses. These tables and constants were employed by the analysts to discover the attractiveness of differing loan terms, in differing operating environments; the loan constant is little more than the sum of annual payments on a mortgage, divided by the loan balance. Now, with hand-held calculators, investors can quickly and accurately amortize loans and discover property sensitivities to any operating or lending environment. The text and examples in Chapter 10 underscore the access that investors now have to a universe of new and expanded analytical tools, often as a function of little more than a $50 calculator!

KEY TERMS

accounts receivable	Certified Public	income statement	pro forma
accrual method	Accountant	liquidity	statement
appreciation	effective gross income	net worth	profit-and-loss
audit	equity	operating expenses	profitability
balance sheet	escrow accounts	operating	scheduled gross income
cash method	fixed expenses	statement	

DISCUSSION QUESTIONS

1. Describe each of the three principal financial statements—balance sheet, profit and loss statement, and operating statement.

2. What is a pro forma statement and how is it used?

3. What is the basis of accrual accounting?

4. Discuss the subject of liquidity in financial statement analysis.

5. What are some of the issues an investor ought to carefully consider when evaluating a piece of investment real estate, which issues are often unmentioned in real estate sales brochures?

6. Explain why it is important to include a replacement reserve expense item in an operating statement.

7. Explain the differences between fixed expenses and variable expenses.

8. Explain why it might be desirable to keep two sets of books.

9. List some expense items that may be based on contractual agreements.

10. Explain how "Net Worth" is calculated on the balance sheet.

CHAPTER 12

Comparison Screening

Chapter 11 emphasized financial statements—how they are prepared, what information they should contain, where the problem areas lie. It is important to know how such information is presented, since much of it is useful. However, the experienced real estate investor usually relies on an analysis prepared from the investor's own knowledge of property management and her own investigation of the property's operating figures.

How much an investor should spend on analysis depends on the intensity of interest in a property. The type of property, its location, and timing are all important investment analysis considerations, but these depend more on the investor's personal interests and personal financial considerations. Other chapters examine these considerations in more detail. Here, we consider solely the financial aspects of a preliminary property evaluation.

Since analysis costs time and money, the first step is to eliminate investment opportunities that are simply not worthwhile. This is usually accomplished through simplified initial screening procedures. For this purpose, most investors use general guidelines developed from years of experience—either their own or others'. Some guidelines are strictly personal methods of determining the most suitable investment properties. Other methods are so widely used that they are almost rules of thumb.

POPULAR GUIDELINES

Income Multipliers

One of the easiest and most common preliminary screening indicators for income property is the ratio between a property's annual **gross operating income (GOI)** and its price. This ratio—or multiplier—varies slightly with the location and age of the property. But, essentially, it denotes the fact that the value of an income property relates directly to the property's income.

The idea of income multipliers is intuitive; if a property is expected to earn an overall return of 10 percent on an investment of $1 million, the investor is demanding a **net operating income (NOI)** of $100,000, or a "multiplier" of ten. (Ten times $100,000 is $1 million.) This intuition is extended to the GOI; a smaller multiplier, of course, is indicated against GOI, which has not been reduced by expenses to get NOI! Examples of multipliers for various types of property are shown in Table 12.1.

To illustrate how the multiplier functions, consider an office building with a gross annual income of $485,000. Using the office building multipliers from the table, the following range of values would result:

$$\text{Low: } 5.25 \times 485,000 = 2,546,250$$
$$\text{High: } 8.7 \times 485,000 = 4,219,500$$
$$\text{Average: } 7.02 \times 485,000 = 3,404,700$$

Based on the multipliers alone, such a building would be valued at somewhere between $2,546,250 and $4,219,500. The purpose of a multiplier is not to pinpoint a value, but simply to determine whether a property is being offered at close to a reasonable price.

The list of multipliers in Table 12.1 was developed from market studies and appraisals of a substantial number of properties nationwide. However, a multiplier is of greatest value to an investor only when it has been calculated for properties in the investor's local area of interest, and at the time of investment. While location is typically held out as the most important contributor to value, timing is often *more* important. Any real estate investor with even limited experience could describe a "deal" where good timing made it "work," whereas the same cannot always be said of location. Good timing will save the worst location, but bad timing cannot help the very best location.

TABLE **12.1**

Gross Income Multipliers

Type of Property	Low	High	Average
Office buildings	5.25	8.7	7.02
Commercial buildings	4.0	9.0	7.1
Industrial buildings	8.33	10.07	9.47
Apartments	7.7	10.05	8.47

Source: Richard Ratacliff, Professor of Land Economics, University of Wisconsin.

In some areas of the country, the multiplier for a good apartment investment is as low as five to seven. Motel values are sometimes estimated at three to four times the gross annual room rental. (The motel estimate uses income from room rentals only, excluding restaurant, lounge, and other income.) Net income or NOI multipliers are sometimes used, as well, those multipliers typically restricted to non-residential properties and the gross income multipliers more frequently used with apartment buildings.

Cash on Cash

A common sense estimate of value strips away many of the variables and considers only the equity portion of an investment measured against the cash flow. The procedure provides what is variously called the **equity dividend rate** or **cash-on-cash return**.

This method determines (1) the amount of cash required to purchase the equity interest in a property (in other words, the difference between the sales price and the mortgage loan) and (2) the cash remaining from income after all expenses and debt service have been paid (the cash flow). The expenses for this method of valuation include all fixed and variable operating expenses, but no depreciation. Debt service includes both principal and interest. Potential income tax effects are ignored. Whatever cash remains—after expenses and all debt service are subtracted from income—is then compared with the cash required to purchase the equity.

For example, if the cash flow amounts to $40,000 and the equity interest costs $240,000, the multiplier number is 6 (240,000/40,000 = 6). In this measure of value, any number less than 10 is worth considering.

The same calculation in reverse is sometimes used to price a property for sale. For example, if the price is 10 times the cash flow plus assumption of the mortgage debt, a property with a $40,000 cash flow would price at $400,000 plus assumption of whatever mortgage debt is outstanding.

Per-Unit Value

Certain types of property—such as apartments and motels—lend themselves to using a "per-unit" value as a guide to the property's total value. While the size of the units in an apartment may vary considerably, investors commonly place a value on the property according to the number of units it contains. In evaluating a motel, they consider the number of rentable rooms. Two different methods are used:

1. *Market value.* By collecting recent sales data for the area, the prices paid for apartments can easily be converted to a price per unit. Appraisers routinely collect such data to guide their own evaluations. Under this approach to value, land costs are included in the per-unit price.

2. *Construction cost.* Any experienced builder of apartments or hotels can quote a reasonably accurate figure on construction cost per unit. Remember that the builder will not include the cost of land, sales costs, or start-up costs in this figure. The construction cost of a *new* building provides an upper-limit guide for an investor's preliminary evaluation.

The per-unit method of valuation is not so accurate as the square-foot method described below, but it can be quite helpful whenever detailed information or building plans are not immediately available.

Square-Foot Valuation

A value per square foot can be determined for any kind of building. An investor can determine this figure using either market values or construction costs. Office buildings, shopping centers, and warehouses are commonly evaluated by this method because none of these have standard rental units to measure. Many investors reduce all figures to a cost-per-square-foot basis during a preliminary evaluation. Both rental income and operating expenses are readily reduced to an amount per square foot of space to provide reasonably accurate information for comparisons. This square-foot method of valuation is a standard used by appraisers, the FHA, the VA, lenders, and investors. For example, income and expenses of $100,000 and $30,000 in a 10,000 square foot building comes to ten dollars and three dollars a square foot, respectively.

PROPERTY INCOME AND EXPENSE ANALYSIS

Once an investor has determined from preliminary (and relatively inexpensive) evaluation that additional investigation is justified, the next step would involve a more detailed financial study.

Without standards, financial information normally available is seldom in a format that lends itself to comparison. Unlike the Generally Accepted Accounting Principles or GAAP of accounting lore, no such Financial Accounting Standards Board exists for the privately owned real estate investment community. Therefore, the most effective procedure, after obtaining financial information from the best sources available, is to recast it onto a standardized form.

Given this lack of regulatory standards for financial reporting of real estate investment, owners and builders do not use a consistent format or nomenclature to present financial information. As a result, a potential investor can easily overlook important information. And without standards, there is little basis for any comparisons. For restructuring the financial data, an investor should select a comprehensive form, either a good one already on the market or one that the investor designs for her own purposes.

A suggested form—listing all major account headings for income and expenses, and using nomenclature recommended by the National Association of Realtors—is reproduced as Figure 12.1. The form suggested can be used for either a preliminary comparison of properties, or as a basis for studying operating problems.

For Comparison Purposes

To make a comparison with other similar investments, the standard format clarifies the income figures and operating costs by using the same account nomenclature. The not-so-obvious accounts that require special attention are management, replacement allowance, and repairs. For instance, should the free use of an apartment for the resident manager count as an operating cost,

FIGURE **12.1**

A Standard Form for Comparison Analysis

STANDARD ANALYSIS STATEMENT

Property _Skyline Apartments_ Date _6/1/2010_

Location _____ Price _$975,000_

Loan data:

Priority	Initial Amount	Rate	Term	Balance Due	Annual Payment
1st 2nd	560,000	8%	20 yr.	511,851	56,208.77

Account	Percent of GOI	
GROSS SCHEDULED RENTAL INCOME		188,200
Plus: Other Income		4,520
TOTAL GROSS INCOME	____	192,720
Less: Vacancy & Credit Losses	____	10,921
GROSS OPERATING INCOME	100	181,799
Less Operating Expenses		
Accounting & Legal	____	900
Advt'g., Licenses, & Permits		1,180
Property Insurance	3.67	6,670
Property Management	3.14	5,700
Payroll Resident Management	3.30	6,000
Other	4.82	8,762
Taxes—Work. Comp.		1,838
Personal Property Taxes	.80	1,450
Real Estate Taxes	4.35	7,900
Replacement Allowance	1.32	2,400
Repairs & Maintenance	3.56	6,470
Services Janitorial	____	
Lawn	____	1,260
Pool	____	2,430
Rubbish	____	2,720
Other	____	840
Supplies		
Utilities Electricity	4.62	8,400
Gas & Oil	2.33	4,230
Sewer & Water	.76	1,380
Telephone	____	290
Other	____	
Miscellaneous	____	
TOTAL OPERATING EXPENSES		70,820
NET OPERATING INCOME		110,979
Less: Total Annual Debt Service		56,209
CASH FLOW BEFORE TAXES		54,770
PROFITABILITY RATIO (NOI to total investment)		11.38%
CASH FLOW TO EQUITY RATIO		11.83%

or should it be a reduction in GOI as a part of the Vacancy & Credit Loss item? The answer is the analyst's choice as it makes no difference in the bottom line of NOI. But it becomes a critical item when a comparison of different properties is being made. So, whatever practices are selected, they must be consistently applied to each analysis.

Two other overlooked expenses are **leasing commissions** and **tenant improvements** with most non-residential properties. It is customary with most new commercial leases to pay a commission of between 3 and 10 percent of the base leasing period to a listing and/or "selling" broker. For example, if an owner of a warehouse leased a 100,000 square foot space for three dollars a foot for five years, he would expect to receive $3 \times 5 \times 100,000$ or $1.5 million in rent over the base period of the lease. If the tenant were brought to him by some national or regional real estate broker, as is commonly the case, he may be expected to pay a 5 percent commission (5 percent of $1.5 million is $75,000) upon occupancy of the property by this new tenant. As well, that new tenant may have, as a condition of the lease, $50,000 or more in expected improvements to the warehouse (such as an improved "dock" for loading or a new ventilation system). Such improvements and commissions are often overlooked, are not typically highlighted in investment property sales packages, and should be allowed for by prospective investors.

Always a key figure for comparison purposes is an operating property's profitability. The use of ratios simplifies this comparison. While there are a number of interesting ratios that might be applied, Figure 12.1 offers two important ones. These are the profitability ratio and a cash-flow-to-equity ratio.

Profitability Ratio

The **profitability ratio** compares the total investment in the property with the NOI. In this example (Figure 12.1), the total investment is considered to be the purchase price ($975,000) and the NOI is $110,979. The ratio is derived as follows:

$$\frac{110,979}{975,000} = .1138 \text{ or } 11.38\%$$

This profitability ratio, the NOI divided by the property's value from Figure 12.1, is also called the **cap rate** or **discount rate** in many real estate investment discussions.

Cash-Flow-to-Equity Ratio

The **cash-flow-to-equity ratio** narrows the measure to a comparison between the cash flow and the equity amount. This is also called the equity-dividend-rate or cash-on-cash return. Cash flow is identified here as the cash remaining after payment of debt service (both principal and interest) and before payment of income taxes, amounting to $54,770 in the Figure 12.1 example. The equity amount is the difference between the total investment ($975,000) and the balance due on the mortgage loan ($511,851), which amounts to

$463,149. The equity is simply the down payment plus other closing costs borne by the buyer. The cash-flow-to-equity ratio is calculated as:

$$\frac{54,770}{463,149} = .1183 \text{ or } 11.83\%$$

This cash-flow-to-equity ratio, or cash-on-cash return, is the **cash flow before taxes** from Figure 12.1 divided by the total down payment or equity.

There are other numbers that can be compared with ratios depending on the investor's special interests. The cash flow may be redefined as the cash remaining after payment of interest only (not including principal portion as identified above), or the preference may be to include an income tax payment as a reduction in the cash flow. Whatever election is made, it must be followed consistently to obtain accurate comparisons.

For Studying Operating Problems

The same standard analysis form suggested for comparison purposes may also be used to study existing operating problems. As a historical record of income and expense, the standard format ensures uniform handling of each item. When a substantial record of the previous year's operations is available, a good study can be made by comparing actual figures. For instance, if electricity cost two years ago was $10,945 and last year was $8,400, obviously some kind of an improvement has occurred. But has the improvement resulted from lower electrical rates, more efficient use of the facilities, or simply a drop in occupancy? The change in dollar amount of expenses is important but falls short of pinpointing the cause of a problem. It is the "Percent of GOI" column that gives a sound basis for more accurate comparisons.

Percent of GOI Column

The percent of GOI column (see the Standard Analysis Statement shown in Figure 12.1) is derived by calculating the ratio of an expense item against the GOI. It need only be calculated for those expenses that are important—an analyst's option. The percentage figure is most important in making cost comparisons. For instance, it helps answer the question posed in the previous section as to what caused the reduction in the cost of electricity. Theoretically, if the GOI declines, so should the expenses. If the reduction in cost of electricity shows up with no change in its percent of GOI, the reduction obviously would have resulted from a decline in occupancy, not from any improvement in efficiency.

If the investor has access to financial information on other similar properties, the percent of GOI column allows an easy comparison of their costs. For instance, a 200-unit apartment project would expect to have twice the cost of electricity as a similar but smaller 100-unit project. But the cost as a percent of GOI should be similar for the two properties. Professional property managers are often so familiar with their particular kind of property that they can simply scan a percentage column and point out the problem items that have excessive expenses. The dollar amounts themselves are important, but they are not as easy to compare as when they are reduced to a percentage figure. It is similar to the situation occurring with the reported financial statements of publicly traded companies; the statements have *some* meaning standing alone, but have far more meaning as various accounts in the income statements and balance sheets are used to generate ratios (liquidity and asset management ratios come to mind), and these ratios are contrasted with last year's ratios, and the ratios reported by other, similar, companies.

Several additional questions should be considered in regard to calculating the percentage figures. First, what figure should be used as a basis for the ratio? It is an option of the analyst as to whether or not the expense should be measured against the gross scheduled rental income, the GOI, or an income amount that eliminates other income. The use of GOI is favored because that is really what the property produces in total earned income each year, and expenses are paid from that cash flow. (And, as with some comments above, recall that this "GOI" is often referred to as effective gross income or gross effective income.)

Another question asks which accounts should be calculated as a percentage of GOI. Again, it is the analyst's option, but seldom are all accounts so measured. Selection of accounts is based on considerations such as which accounts are larger, which are more flexible, and which are most subject to management abuses. The answers vary with different properties. Two additional operating ratios, the breakeven and operating expense ratios, may highlight issues for the property that are important to both lender and investor.

Breakeven Ratio

The **breakeven ratio** reveals the percent of a property that must be leased to cover all cash outflows. It is equal to the sum of operating expenses and annual debt service divided by the property's **potential gross income** or "Total Gross Income" as in Figure 12.1:

$$\text{Breakeven Ratio} = \frac{(70,820 + 56,209)}{192,720} = .659 \text{ or about } 66\%$$

This ratio reveals that the property must be about two-thirds leased or collect 66 percent of its total potential gross income to cover all its cash operating and debt servicing costs. This measure is very important to the lender, who can survey nearby properties for typical occupancy levels and discover whether an expectation of the property being two-thirds rented—or one-third vacant—is realistic. Breakeven ratios may be over 80 percent for newer, preleased, and lower risk properties or as low as 50 percent for higher risk investments; the ratio depends on the risk-tolerance of the lender and investor and macroeconomic circumstances.

Operating Expense Ratio

The **operating expense ratio** reveals the portion of the GOI or effective gross income that is "consumed" by operating expenses. The ratio is equal to the operating expenses divided by the GOI. For the property in Figure 12.1:

$$\text{Operating Expense Ratio} = \frac{70,820}{181,799} = .390 \text{ or about } 39\%$$

Recalling that operating expenses typically include all out-of-pocket cash expenses except depreciation and debt service, this metric might suggest a property that is poorly managed if the ratio is too high. Conversely, it might show that either a lot of maintenance is being deferred with low expenses, or that a prospective investor should further investigate a suspiciously low operating expense ratio. Ratios of over 40 percent are typical for some office or residential properties, and lower than 20 percent for industrial properties or warehouses. This makes intuitive sense; the office property requiring landscaping, janitorial costs, water bills, and common-area electricity would be far more costly to "operate" than a warehouse requiring none of these.

Other Analysis Problems

When dealing with financial information, several other questions arise, such as: How much accounting detail is necessary? How should replacement allowances be treated? Which income and expense items require verification?

Accounting Detail

The accounting figures shown in the text illustrations are summations derived from more detailed information. How much detail is needed depends on the size of the operation and the management's concern for closely monitoring costs. In a small, closely held property operation, a well-maintained checkbook might be all that is needed. As the operation grows, or as the ownership becomes more distant from the day-to-day operation, greater detail is necessary for adequate control. All of the accounts identified in the Standard Analysis Statement (Figure 12.1) lend themselves to sub accounts with more detailed assignment of expenses. For example, the account "Advertising, Licenses, and Permits" has obvious components that might be important for management to monitor.

While detailed knowledge of an operation's costs is important, the need for this information must be balanced against the increased cost of keeping such records. The important question is: Can the detailed information be used to contain or reduce operating costs? The answer is a management's or owner's call. Detailed accounting information is not a requirement for income tax reports to the IRS. However, when the IRS undertakes a tax audit, it does demand verification of all figures submitted on a tax return.

Replacement Allowance

Certain rental properties contain substantial personal property that is consumed with their use. It is an operating cost often overlooked in financial statements. Foremost in this category of properties are apartments containing appliances, carpets, and drapes. Since these items are classified as capital assets and are normally depreciated over a cost-recovery period, the cost may be classed as "depreciation," which is not included in an operating statement.

Nevertheless, it is a cost of doing business and should be identified as such. It may be necessary to estimate the cost each year as replacements may not be necessary for three or four years. For this reason the item is listed in the statement as an "allowance" as it is not necessarily a cash expenditure every year. Some managers include this cost in the Repairs and Maintenance account, which recognizes the expense, but it is not as clearly identified as with a separate account.

Verification of Data

Information for the investor's standard analysis form should be verified wherever possible. An examination of bank statements, phone calls to utility companies and insurance agents, and discussions with the manager or management firm can clear up a number of questions.

The need to verify information at an early stage of interest in the property is not so great as in later acquisition steps. A property owner must authorize inquiries into his financial situation; most are reluctant to do so until a potential investor exhibits solid evidence of willingness to buy. An option agreement or earnest money contract to buy property can also be made subject to the purchaser's verification of certain financial data submitted by the seller.

Net Operating Income (NOI)

One of the most important figures in an operating statement is the NOI. In most such statements, it is the "bottom line." Yet its importance is often overlooked.

Referring again to Figure 12.1, NOI is that amount remaining from GOI after all operating expenses are paid. Note that in the expenses listed there is no deduction taken for interest or depreciation. Does this mean they are not important to an investor? Not at all. But it is also important to distinguish the operation of a property from its financing costs and its tax consequences that involve depreciation options. Determining whether or not a property is being operated successfully is the purpose of the NOI figure. Neither the debt burden of a property nor tax consequences for the owner are reflections of property operation. In another sense, if a property is losing money because of an overload of debt, firing the manager is not the answer!

NOI serves some other functions. It is the true measure of profitability on total capital invested (see Profitability Ratio, Figure 12.1). Also, lenders consider NOI as the amount of cash available to service debt payments. It is this figure that is used in the application of coverage ratios to measure acceptable loan payment amounts.

Income Growth and the Dividend Growth Model

As noted early in this text, and affirmed countless times by the real estate investor, real estate investments do not lend themselves easily to traditional financial or economic theory. However, *one traditional theory or model* does have applications in the real estate "world." This is the **dividend growth model**. Without investing pages of text into a description of this model, which is the minimum in traditional introductory finance texts, suffice it to say that the dividend growth model suggests that an investment's income is comprised of dividends and capital gains. This is also true of most real estate investments, where the investor is pursuing a dividend yield and a capital gains yield, as with a share of stock. The dividend is provided by the NOI (this reduced by costs of financing) and the capital gain by the appreciation of the real estate over time. The dividend growth model formally predicts that:

$$R = \frac{D1}{P0} + G \tag{1}$$

Where R is the overall required rate of return, D1 is the first year's "dividend" (or cash flow before taxes), P0 is the purchase price of the asset or the value of the equity investment (or gross purchase price of the real estate if no financing is used) and G is the expected growth rate in the dividend (or growth rate in the value of the property and/or its NOI).

To apply equation (1) in an actual real estate investment, suppose an investor buys a condominium in 2010 for $35,000 cash, and expects rental income of $6,000 per year ($500 per month), annual operating expenses of $2,500 and NOI of $3,500 ($6,000−$2,500). Assume the buyer paid cash and no financing was used. NOI is the property's effective "dividend." If the investor expects this dividend to grow at 5 percent per year, he also expects the property's value to increase 5 percent per year. Using equation (1), the return on the property is:

$$R = \frac{\$3,500}{\$35,000} + 5\% \text{ or } .10 + 5\% \text{ or } 15\%.$$

Two important remarks need to be made. First, the dividend yield (the NOI divided by the property's price or overall value) is exactly the same as the cap rate or discount rate mentioned above and further described in Chapter 13. Second, the overall expected or required return, "R," is greater than the cap rate, as this overall R includes the capital gains expectations. In other words, when an investor is said to "cap" a property's overall NOI of $3,500 at 10 percent to arrive at an estimate of value of $35,000 ($3,500/.10 = $35,000), he is not "limiting" himself to an expectation of only a 10 percent return. On the contrary, this cap rate is merely representative of the dividend yield he expects, the growth rate or capital gains is an addition to the investor's overall expected rate of return.

PROPERTY APPRAISALS

The **appraisal** is a well-known tool of professional real property analysts. It is designed to estimate value. An investor should be aware of the process used in determining an estimate because the process itself provides important information on the property and several approaches to its value. This section briefly explains (1) how an appraiser examines property and (2) the essential elements of the three basic approaches to value that are used in making final estimates of value.

An appraisal always estimates value as of a specific time. That time is usually the present but need not be. Retroactive appraisals are sometimes made, as in the case of settling an estate. Sometimes appraisals are made for some future date. At the beginning, therefore, an appraiser defines the time period that the evaluation covers.

Second, the appraiser must define the type of property holding that is being evaluated. Appraisals of real property are made for whole interests, partial interests, leasehold estates, mineral interests, air rights, frontage rights, and other types of ownership interests.

Third, the purpose of an appraisal must be clearly stated. A professional appraisal can reach only one final estimate of value for any one interest in a property. It never shows a buyer's price versus a seller's price. But the purpose of an appraisal can indicate which approach to value should be emphasized in reaching a final estimate. For example, if the appraisal is conducted to aid in settling an insurance claim for fire loss, the cost approach to value is the best way to establish replacement value. If the purpose is to determine land value of undeveloped land, the estimate must consider the lack of attributable income. If, on the other hand, undeveloped land is appraised for its value as an apartment site, a proportionate share of the apartment's projected income is attributed to the land, thus enhancing its estimated value. An appraisal of land in the process of condemnation to widen an existing highway may not reflect the property's frontage value. The reason is that value is based on the use of the land; the remaining land would retain the frontage value of the original property. As you can see, an appraisal's stated purpose does affect its final estimate.

Appraiser Qualification

Government inquiries into the reasons why many savings associations suffered financial losses in the late 1980s placed a part of the blame on faulty appraisals. To help correct the situation, Congress passed legislation in 1989 (Title XI of the Financial Institutions Reform, Recovery and Enforcement Act) requiring appraisers to meet federal guidelines for state certification. The teeth in the Act prohibits any federally insured depository institution from making a real property loan after December 31, 1992, without an appraisal made by a state certified appraiser. There are some dollar limitations on this requirement.

Since many mortgage loans are made by non-regulated lenders who are not required to use state certified appraisers, other qualification standards continue to be important. The appraisal industry offers professional qualification standards through several organizations composed of peer groups. For many years, these appraiser associations have set qualification standards and offer designations to their members who qualify for them. Indeed, the appraiser associations anticipated the need for federal guidelines and created their own Appraisal Foundation in 1987 to develop suitable standards. The federal law adopted many of their requirements. If an investor expects to borrow money to acquire a property, it is most important that the lender, or lenders, be contacted first for a lender list of approved appraisers. Otherwise, the appraisal may be rejected.

Home Values and Appraisals and the Financial Crisis

More recently, real estate appraisals have come under scrutiny with the financial crisis and the millions of foreclosures that began in 2007. Unlike inflated appraisals that checkered the real estate investment world in the 1980s, though, appraisals in the early 2000s seemed genuinely to have been driven by actual prices, especially among single family homes and condominiums. Appraisers, using the "market approach" discussed below, observed ever-increasing home values and reflected those in their appraisals. Home values by late 2007 began to decline, and in many markets—especially in Arizona, Nevada, California and South Florida—prices collapsed by early 2010, falling 50 percent or more in some localized markets. These declines resulted in home values falling well below outstanding mortgage balances, and the homeowners being **under water**; equity values in the homes were less than zero.

A home purchased in 2005 for $400,000, with an attaching conventional 80 percent mortgage of $320,000, might have fallen in value to less than $275,000. The homeowner was confronted with a situation where the home's debt was greater than its value, and clear incentives existed to "walk away," especially in markets where lenders had no recourse to pursue the debtor for assets other than the security on the mortgage, the home.

As the foreclosure "epidemic" unfolds, an inverse of patterns from the 1980s is revealed. Rather than making some appraisals at unsupportable higher values to encourage loan approvals, which occurred with the Savings and Loan crisis in the late 1980s, appraisers in some markets leading up to 2010 became "gun-shy." Anecdotal evidence suggested that some appraisers, to avoid the scrutiny and regulatory outcry of 20 years earlier, were actually providing very conservative estimates of home values. A home that might well have been worth $200,000, for example, might have been appraised at $185,000, limiting the likelihood of the new buyer getting financing (as the lender bases financing in large part on the appraiser's estimate of the loan's security's value) and also lowering the chances of the seller receiving an acceptable offer. Within this limiting environment many appraisals were made around that time.

Appraisal Approaches to Value

When evaluating a property, the professional appraiser relies on basic economic principles—supply-and-demand, conformity, highest and best use of the land, anticipation, and others. Estimates of value are made in accordance with three different approaches to value. These are (1) cost, (2) market, and (3) income. All three are explained below.

Cost Approach

The only approach to value suitable for any type of building is the cost approach. It calculates the cost of replacing a building at the time of appraisal, subtracts accumulated depreciation, and then adds the value of the land.

Replacement Cost

The cost of duplicating an existing structure at the time of appraisal is its replacement cost. Labor and material cost increases are fully included in this calculation. The computation may be made on a per-unit basis, as a contractor could do in preparing a construction bid. Or, if current cost figures are available for similar structures, a cost per square foot may be used.

Depreciation

Day-to-day deterioration of a building decreases its value and must be deducted from replacement cost for the purpose of this calculation. Depreciation can be found in three categories.

1. *Physical deterioration.* This category includes normal wear, rust, and rot that occur in building materials. This deterioration may be classified

as curable (as with a coat of paint) or incurable (not economically feasible to repair).

2. *Functional obsolescence.* Any loss of value in a building resulting from poor design, inadequate facilities, or outdated equipment is functional obsolescence. These factors, too, can be classified as curable or incurable, with proper adjustments made to the valuation. Curable items would include fuel oil heat, which could be replaced with electric. Incurable items might include 20-foot floor-to-ceiling clearance in a warehouse, within a market demanding 28-foot clearance, for new forklift or shelving systems.

3. *Economic (or external) obsolescence.* Any loss in a building's value resulting from factors outside the property is economic or external obsolescence. A new freeway's bypassing a service station, for example, lowers the station's value. Outside factors can also increase the value of a neighboring property. A new bridge across a stream may allow development of land that was previously inaccessible.

Land Value

The value of land is determined separately from the value of the buildings on it. Appraisers generally use the market value of the land, determined by studying recent sales of similar land in the vicinity. When conducting this study, an investor must remember that land can reflect an increase in value over the long term. But in the short term, as with periods in the later 1980s, early 1990s, and late 2000s, land values may fall.

Market Approach

Appraisal by the market approach concentrates on the sales prices of similar properties. Since no two properties are exactly alike, this approach compares the subject property with three to six similar, recently sold properties. The appraiser determines the plus or minus value factor of each major difference between the subject property and each similar property. For example, if a similar property had been sold two years earlier, it would be reasonable to assume that the subject property would reflect a change in value, either increase or decrease, because of the two-year time differential. A fireplace in the subject property would give it a plus factor in any comparison with a similar property lacking a fireplace. Comparisons are comprehensive, covering such points as location, size, physical condition, and amenities.

Remember that only actual sales prices reflect actual market values. Thus, the asking prices for similar properties are not an acceptable basis for comparison. Listing prices carry little information on value, until a sale takes place. The listing price is often just a "hoped-for" value of a seller who may not even price the property at a realistic value. However, the **relative spread** may carry additional information for the appraiser. For example, if a home listed at $400,000 sells for $396,000, the relative spread, or difference between the selling and listing price divided by the listing price, is only one percent ($400,000−$396,000 divided by $400,000). If, on the other hand, the $400,000 listing sold for $360,000, the relative spread was 10 percent.

The larger spread may suggest a deteriorating market, the narrower spread a healthy or growing market. Neither are forced or foreclosure sales comparable (unless, of course, you are appraising a property subject to forced sale). The willing buyer and willing seller standard of a free market sale is lacking in a forced sale. A sale by an estate or within a family can also give a distorted impression of a property's actual value in the free market.

Because sales prices can be influenced by financing deals, it is normal to consider how the price was determined. In order to more easily sell property, a builder or other seller might offer to "buy down" the monthly payment amount by paying part of the interest cost in advance to the lender. This payment of interest would be reflected in lowering the monthly payment amount for the buyer. By lowering the monthly payment amount in the early years, the seller can more easily qualify a buyer. A home may sell in this case, but at a distorted price.

Most lenders have since added a requirement that any "market value" used as a basis for property comparison be adjusted downward to reflect any excessive finance costs. Fannie Mae and Freddie Mac have revised their definitions of market value to "the most probable price that a property should bring."

The market approach to value is the one most commonly used to appraise residential property. The market for houses is large and continuing, so good comparisons are usually possible. The accuracy of the market approach, of course, always depends on the availability of sales figures for similar nearby properties.

Income Approach

The income approach estimates a property's value based on the income derived from it. The income considered is generally that obtained from the property's operations each year. The income approach is the most important analysis for a commercial property. For many investors, it is the only acceptable approach because it bases value strictly on the profitability of the property.

The first step in this approach is to calculate the property's NOI. This is the income remaining after payment of all operating expenses. The payment of debt service is not a consideration in the calculation of property value for this purpose. The way a property is financed can be critical for an investor; however, to include the cost of financing in an income approach to value can introduce a distortion. The successful operation of a property should not be confused with a possible overload of debt.

The second step in an income approach calculation is to select a rate of return or discount rate. (Discounting and discount rates are considered at greater length in Chapter 13.) This rate is not so much a mathematical calculation as it is a matter of individual judgment. An appraiser would most likely use a rate commensurate with current market rates adjusted to compensate for the risk involved with a particular property; a McDonald's building, of low risk, would have a much lower discount rate attaching to its appraisal than a vacant warehouse. As shall be confirmed below in Example 12.1, if the value of a property is its income divided by this discount rate, the higher rate results in a lower estimate of value. The third step in the calculation is to convert the annual NOI into a value for the property, dividing the NOI by the discount or cap rate.

| **EXAMPLE 12.1** | **Capitalization of Income to Estimate Property Value** |

Property A:

A 5,000 square foot concrete strip shopping center built in the 1960s has the following income and expense information:

Gross Potential Income (5,000 x $10 per foot)	$50,000
Vacancies and Bad Debts (10%)	(5,000)
Effective Gross Income	$45,000
Operating Expenses (insurance, repairs, etc)	(15,000)
NOI	$30,000

Capitalizing this NOI, at a discount rate of 12%, is accomplished with the following formula:

$$Value = NOI/Discount\ Rate = \$30,000/.12 = \$250,000\ \{V = I/R\}$$

Property B:

A 2,250 square foot Taco Bell built in 2000 has the following income and expense information:

Gross Potential Income (2,250 x $20 per foot)	$45,000
Vacancies and Bad Debts (0%)	0
Effective Gross Income	$45,000
Operating Expenses (taxes, insurance, etc)	(15,000)
NOI	$30,000

Capitalizing this NOI, at a discount rate of 8%, is accomplished with the following formula:

$$Value = NOI/Discount\ Rate = \$30,000/.08 = \$375,000\ \{V = I/R\}$$

Example 12.1 is noteworthy, as it highlights at least three issues: Size, age, and tenant quality all contribute directly to the discount or cap rate, and ultimately to the property's underlying value. Here, the larger property (Property A) has a greater Gross Potential Income, but the tenant mix suggests a higher vacancy rate and probability of unpaid rent or bad debts. The older strip shopping center is the riskier property; the likelihood of the NOI being achieved is far greater with the Taco Bell than with the older strip, even though the older strip may end up with a *higher* NOI! As well, that older strip shopping center, even though it generates the same NOI as the newer, smaller Property B, has a less stable NOI, and invites the appraiser to use a higher discount rate. Though the two properties have the same NOI, the Taco Bell building is far more valuable. With the selected discount rates that the appraiser likely observed on similar properties in the region, the Taco Bell is worth $375,000 versus the strip's value of $250,000.

Appraisal Conclusion

An appraiser uses all three approaches to value whenever practical. Some properties, however, do not provide sufficient data to allow all three methods. For example, a city hall appraised for insurance coverage would rely mostly on a cost approach to value. As a fairly unique kind of building, it would not have much in comparable sales for a market approach and no actual rentals to justify an income approach. Likewise, a major office building in a small city isn't usually amenable to market comparisons, and would lend itself almost solely to an income approach to estimating its value.

While some property owners and many lenders might desire a blend of all three appraisal methods—the cost, market or sales comparison, and income approaches—in coming to a final estimate of value, each method is actually well-suited for certain types of properties. The user of the appraisals should remember that the income approach would be best for a shopping center or office building, the market approach for single family homes, and the cost approach for unique properties like airports or hospitals. Using all three approaches for the same property generally produces three different estimates of value. The appraiser's job is to select the appraisal method most appropriate for a specific property, make an estimate of final value, and then provide reasoning that justifies this estimate.

FEASIBILITY REPORT

Both a feasibility report and an appraisal were mentioned in Chapter 1 as costs that could be incurred in a preliminary evaluation of investment property. The feasibility study can provide valuable information that is useful in comparing one investment property with another. By skillful use of market data, it attempts to determine the proposed investment's prospects for success.

Like an appraisal, a feasibility report uses background information to arrive at value estimates. A feasibility report, however, focuses more on market evaluation than on property evaluation. Feasibility reports are common with new residential developments and new commercial construction, where "in-place" tenants and rental income streams do not exist to support estimates of value. A feasibility study surveys the market area, charts population and business growth, analyzes present and future traffic patterns, and researches occupancy and income levels for comparable properties in the neighborhood.

Feasibility reports follow no standard pattern. The information presented varies, as does its sequence. However, the following outline represents a good and widely followed procedure.

1. *Conclusions.* Unlike an appraisal, conclusions are often presented first, since this is the purpose of a feasibility report.

2. *Property*. An adequate description of the property is presented.
3. *Market evaluation*. This is a detailed study of the market in the neighborhood, including any laws, regulations, and other restrictions that might affect future operations of the property.
4. *Environmental effect*. As environmental requirements continue to expand, separate reports are becoming standard practice for all large projects. A feasibility report may only detail the requirements, leaving it to other specialists to determine their impact.
5. *Income and expenses*. The profit potential of the project is studied in depth. One purpose is to determine the break-even point—for example with new building lots sold or square feet leased in a new shopping center—which is used along with the market study to show when positive cash flows can be expected.

PHYSICAL INSPECTION

Real property is tangible and should be inspected before an investment is undertaken. Many investors consider this so important that it is a part of the preliminary study. If an inspection is made in the early screening process, it may consist of only a drive-by, or, if appropriate, a fly-over of the property. Some of the important points that can be found in a simple inspection are as follows:

1. The general appearance of the property.
2. The nature of the surrounding area, neighboring buildings, and use of the land in that area.
3. The general traffic patterns in the vicinity of the subject property.
4. Land drainage around the property—a visit during or shortly after a rainstorm can be illuminating.

During such an inspection, questions should be noted that are not immediately important but call for additional study should the property be given serious consideration later. An example might be some nearby construction work, or a nearby stream or drainage channel, or perhaps a difficult traffic pattern that could be improved with street signs. If other information justifies further examination, a much closer physical inspection would be necessary.

KEY TERMS

appraisal	dividend growth model	leasing commissions and tenant improvements	operating expenses
breakeven ratio	equity dividend rate or cash-on-cash return	net operating income (NOI)	operating income
cap rate or discount rate	gross operating income (GOI)	operating expense ratio	potential gross income
cash flow before taxes			profitability ratio
cash-flow-to-equity ratio			relative spread
			under water

DISCUSSION QUESTIONS

1. Define an income multiplier.

2. What is the purpose of a standard analysis statement?

3. Describe the use of a percent of GOI column as found on a standard analysis statement.

4. Discuss the three basic appraisal approaches to value—cost, market, and income.

5. How does a feasibility report differ from an appraisal?

6. Which of the appraisal methods is most appropriate for a single-family home? An airport? An office building?

7. What factors might contribute to an appraiser selecting a low discount rate in an income appraisal? What might cause a higher discount rate to be used?

8. How are discount rates selected and used by the appraiser?

9. What is the impact of using a higher discount rate? A lower one?

10. Is a listing price a valid estimate of value? If not, why?

11. What is a relative spread, and what information does it provide the appraiser?

CHAPTER 13

Discount Analysis

The preliminary screening and analysis procedures outlined in Chapter 12 show the potential investor: (1) a few simple guidelines for evaluation, (2) the advantages of a standard form for financial analysis, and (3) an initial basis for comparing real estate properties. As shown in that chapter, the investor who uses net operating income (NOI) to determine value has a sound basis for investment analysis and comparison. That method reduces the many variables of investment to a single simple standard; NOI is divided by a percentage amount, and an estimate of the property's value is generated. The investor can use this estimate to determine a reasonable price for the property. This price or value can also be used for comparison with other possible property investments.

This income approach to estimating the value of real estate investments simply "capitalizes" the NOI. The NOI is divided by a selected discount or capitalization rate. Holding the NOI fixed at a given amount, a greater value is estimated with a lower discount rate (for a lower risk property like a national drug store chain), and a lower value results with the selection of a higher discount rate (as with a small strip center with a history of costly turnovers.) This is intuitive; if the value equals the NOI divided by this discount rate, an inverse relationship exists between the value and the discount rate—higher discount rates provide lower estimates of value. And, whatever discount rate is chosen, the analyst selecting the rate is merely recognizing the time value of money (TVOM), acknowledging that money received in the future has a certain value today—often far less than the sum of those future cash flows.

Real estate and many other investments produce income at periodic intervals over a lengthy time period. The idea behind the discount analysis approach is to determine what that future income is worth today—that is, to reduce each future receipt of income to its present value. Money expected in the future is not worth as much as money in hand today. This is what is meant by the TVOM.

RISK, RETURN, AND THE TIME VALUE OF MONEY

Risk

To appreciate risk, imagine a game, or choice of games:

- Game A, you win $100,000.
- Game B, you win $10,000,000 2 percent of the time, "winning" nothing 98 percent of the time.
- Which game do you play?

It is not as easy a choice as it may seem. Look at the expected values of the two games:

- Game A, you win $100,000. The probability (P) is 100 percent, so that is your expected value.
- With Game B, it is more complex:

$$\text{Expected value of Game B} = P(\text{winning}) \text{ Winnings} + P(\text{losing}) \text{ Zero,}$$
$$\text{or} \quad .02(\$10 \text{ million}) + .98(0) = \$200,000$$

And, $200,000 > $100,000, but do you play Game B? Likely not, as 98 percent of the time you go home with nothing. There is a one in fifty chance that your life will be changed, with the winnings of $10 million, but you can pass on that 2 percent chance by choosing the guaranteed $100,000 payout of Game A. Risk averse players choose Game A, with the lower expected value, but the far more certain payout.

A similar dynamic is at play with real estate, where a "player" or real estate investor requires compensation for assuming additional risk, and where that investor requires a higher return for investing in a riskier set of cash flows. The discount rate for the risk-taking investor will be higher, the rate for the low-risk investor lower; as noted above and in earlier chapters, the investor in an old strip center will demand a higher rate of return or discount rate, the investor in a building occupied by a national drug store chain a lower one. An expected cash flow with the old strip of $100,000 per year may be worth $1 million (using a discount rate of 10 percent), with such an expectation for a drug store chain being valued at perhaps $1.25 million, employing a discount rate of 8 percent. Example 13.1 illustrates this relationship.

EXAMPLE 13.1

Valuation with Risk-adjusted Discount Rates

Property Value = NOI ÷ Discount Rate; Discount Rate = NOI ÷ Value

For the Older Strip:

Value = $100,000 ÷ .10 = $1 million

For the National Drug Store:

Value = $100,000 ÷ .08 = $1.25 million

Analysts for major investors compare all available types of investment in an effort to determine the most effective placement of investment funds. Economists, analysts, consultants, and investment advisors employ a number of techniques to measure the anticipated yield from a proposed investment. No single procedure gives an absolute answer, particularly when the proposed investments are in real estate. However, discounted cash flow analysis and the *present value approach* have been accepted as theoretically correct methods. And, as the real estate field seldom presents conditions of certainty, varying discount rates are employed depending on the likelihood of the projected cash flows or NOI being achieved; that likelihood is higher with the drug store in Example 13.1, so the selected discount rate for the drug store is *lower*. With greater risk comes a higher rate.

Chapter 12 and the income approach to estimating value explained that capitalization is a means of determining property value as a direct function of income. Income-producing property is valued by its anticipated profit. Discount rates are "discovered" with the sale of comparable properties, those sales revealing the discount rate or rate of return *required* by an investor in a similar property. The investor cannot impose a higher discount rate on a property, and "force" a sale at a lower price to allow for that higher return; like the sale price, and directly related to it, the discount rate is agreed upon between buyer and seller, with the seller of course taking the lowest discount rate (and highest price) offered by a prospective buyer.

Changing Discount Rates and Risk Aversion Over Time

Obviously, as an investor's willingness to assume risk changes, so also do property values. If the investor in the strip in Example 13.1 demanded a return or discount rate of 20 percent in a difficult real estate market, the seller would either not sell or settle for a price of $500,000—or $100,000 ÷ .2—if no other buyers at lower discount rates came forward. Such has been the case with discount rates over the past few decades. In the high-inflation, high interest-rate environment of much of the 1980s, discount rates of 15 percent or more were not uncommon. With the go-go "bubble years" of the early 2000s, discount rates of *less than 4 percent* were observed with many property transactions in New York City.

Buyers at lower discount rates in 2005 or 2006 were regretting their property purchases within a few years, as escalating vacancies and falling rents and greater overall market risk aversion pushed those rates back toward 10 percent or more, cutting many property values in half, or worse. The experiences of buyers in the early 1990s are worth recalling, where discount rates in the low teens were common. As those discount or cap rates fell over the next 10 or 12 years, along with falling vacancies and rising rents, property values often tripled or quadrupled. Whether a similar buying opportunity is offered in the late 2000s is uncertain; only time will tell whether vacancies improve and discount rates fall following the Great Recession, rewarding those investors making distressed property purchases at the turn of the century's first decade. With typical discount rates moving from over 10 percent in 1990, to less than 6 percent by 2005, returning to 10 percent or more by 2010, clear evidence of the variability of risk aversion (and inflation, which is directly related to discount rates) is shown. This variability should be always kept in mind by the real estate investor and analyst.

Return

Among the most important jobs is the estimation of a property's prospective income, or NOI, along with the choice of an appropriate discount rate to divide into the income on the way to a valuation estimate. That NOI will change over time, subject to varying elements of macroeconomic and property-specific risk. It will also suffer from unexpected turnover among the tenants, and will fall due to recurring and often substantial repairs. Buildings often **go dark** for extended periods of time, just as they will sometimes be fully leased in a booming period of rising rents, as with the recent expansion from 2002–2006. It is in this environment that the appraiser or investor or independent analyst must winnow the property's expectations down to a single number to be capitalized by a single discount rate. Various analysts will employ prosaic or proprietary models to forecast future income. The analyst might forecast three economic environments, for example, with three separate attaching NOIs, and derive a single estimate of NOI by attaching probabilities to each economic outcome. Example 13.2 illustrates how one analyst might conduct such an endeavor. In that example, the bad and great economies each have a likelihood of 20 percent, the "average" economy a probability of 60 percent. Multiplying these probabilities by the NOIs for each environment yields a final NOI estimate of $56,000.

EXAMPLE 13.2 | **Estimating NOI for Differing Macroeconomic Environments**

Estimated NOI in a Bad Economy $20,000 with a probability of 20%

Estimated NOI in a Normal Economy $60,000 with a probability of 60%

Estimated NOI in a Great Economy $80,000 with a probability of 20%

Weighted Average Estimate of NOI $= .2(\$20,000) + .6(\$60,000) + .2(\$80,000)$

$$= \$56,000$$

This NOI of $56,000 is the return the analyst uses in estimating the overall property value, but that estimate has at least three flaws:

1. The NOI estimate is a fixed amount in the valuation model, even though it is known with near certainty that the amount will vary.
2. The NOI represents future cash flows, whose present value is uncertain.
3. The NOI estimate is treated as a perpetuity in the standard income valuation model, despite the likelihood that the property investment will be made for a fixed number of years, and not for the indefinite future.

In any valuation estimate, both the analyst and the investor recognize these flaws, and account for the resulting degree of uncertainty with their selection of discount rates: If the ownership period, variability of rental streams, or future selling or leasing environments are highly uncertain, a higher discount rate will be selected. The lower price resulting from a selection of a higher discount rate will compensate the investor with a higher expected return. With the greater certainty that attaches to a national tenant on a long-term lease, a lower discount rate results along with a higher property value.

Time Value of Money

In a practical sense, we all know that a dollar today is worth more than a dollar tomorrow. At a minimum, we could earn interest on a dollar today and it would be worth more than a dollar tomorrow. But, there is much more to the study of the TVOM than that. As managers of real estate assets or simply as homemakers, we need a manner to compare the value of different cash flows from different sources occurring years apart. It is with the analysis of the TVOM and its adjacent tools of future and present value analysis that we can begin this comparison and start to examine these contrasts. Comments in this chapter echo earlier references to the valuation of investment real estate; such efforts to estimate the value of real estate investments invariably base such estimates on the present values of expected future cash flows, and this chapter reviews the "basics" of the TVOM "universe."

Future Values

The **future value** of an investment is the current value grown at some predetermined interest rate for a set period of time. For example, $1,000 invested today at 3 percent for one year would be worth $1,030 in a year. Algebraically, in Example 13.3:

EXAMPLE 13.3   Future Value Calculation

$FV = PV(1 + i)^t$, where "$(1 + i)^t$" is the future value factor

FV = the future value

PV = the present value

"i" is the interest rate and

"t" is the number of periods

And, from the paragraph above

$FV = \$1,000(1 + .03)^1 = \$1,000(1.03) = \$1,030$

With the BA II Plus calculator

(see "Practical Applications with Your BA II Plus" in the supplements for this text)

For one period:	For two periods:
−1,000 PV	−1,000 PV
1 N	2 N
3 I/Y	3 I/Y
CPT FV = 1,030	CPT FV = 1,060.90

In Example 13.3, a second year's simple interest of $30 is earned, along with **compound interest** of $.90 (3 percent of $30). In the first year, the simple interest or $30 or 3 percent of $1,000 is earned; adding that to the initial "investment" of $1,000 gives the future value (FV) of $1,030. With the second year, the compound interest is earned upon the $30 interest received in the first year; the compound interest is the interest on the interest! Thus, the value at the end of two years of growth is the initial investment of $1,000, plus two years of simple interest of $30 plus a single year's compound interest of 90 cents; $1,000 + $30 + $30 + $.90 = $1,060.90, as with the calculator work above.

Compound interest is even better appreciated by extending the three percent annual accumulation out to 30 years; there, we see that the future value of the $1,000 growing at three percent is $2,427. [$FV = 1,000(1.03)^{30} = \$2,427.26$]. Replicating the entries in Example 13.3 with N = 30, the analyst sees that over that three-decade time frame, over $527 in compound interest is earned. With simple interest, the holder of the $1,000 "investment" would have earned only $30 per year each year for 30 years or $900. But, the future value of $2,427 reveals the extra "kick" from compounding; those 527 extra dollars are the interest earned on the interest over 30 years.

Present Values

The **present value** of an investment is its future value discounted back to the present at some selected discount rate. For single cash flows, the present value is the **inverse** of the future value. Example 13.4 is an extension of Example 13.3, and it reveals this inverse relationship:

EXAMPLE 13.4 Present Value Calculation

$PV = FV \div (1 + i)^t$, where "$(1 + i)^t$" is the future value factor and

FV = the future value

PV = the present value

"i" is the interest rate and

"t" is the number of periods

And, extending the example above for one period

$PV = \$1,030 \div (1 + .03)^1 = \$1,030/(1.03) = \$1,000$

With the BA II Plus calculator

(see "Practical Applications with Your BA II Plus" in the supplements for this text)

For one period:

1,030 FV

1 N

3 I/Y

CPT PV = −1,000

For two periods:

1,060.90 FV

2 N

3 I/Y

CPT PV = −1,000

The inverse relationship between the present and future values of single cash flows is readily apparent. The present value is multiplied by the future value factor "$(1 + i)^t$" to determine the future value, and the future value is *divided* by the same factor to discern the present value.

Present and Future Value Tables exist to aid the analyst in discovering present and future values in the absence of a business calculator. The table user would simply take the present or future value, and multiply or divide it by the relevant factor to determine the needed future or present amount. For example, $1,000 times the future value factor of 3 percent for one year would be $1,000 times 1.03 or $1,030. With the ubiquitous presence of calculators to facilitate these calculations, though, the use of the tables—popular with some teachers until late in the twentieth century—is now uncommon. Similar tables exist for calculating mortgage payments and mortgage balances over time, where mortgage values are divided by a mortgage constant to discover a mortgage payment; like other TVOM tables, they are now only rarely used. (The tables are available online and as a supplement to this text.)

Present and Future Values of Equally-Sized Cash Flows

An extended set of algebraic expressions is used to determine present and future values of equally sized recurring cash flows occurring for a fixed period of time. Such cash flows are known as annuities. One hundred dollars a month for ten years is an **annuity**. Monthly mortgage or car payments, whether for five or 30 years, are annuities. Varying rental payments are not.

A financial calculator generally has a wealth of annuity applications. Whether determining the accumulated value of a retirement account or discovering a mortgage payment—or ascertaining a mortgage balance after the passage of time or illustrating the principal and interest portions of a single or set of mortgage payments—the "mechanics" of multiple cash flow valuations are prosaic, and not far removed from the single cash flow applications that introduce this discussion. There is little need for the use of expansive algebraic expressions with mortgage calculations given the payment and amortization functions available with most financial calculators. Example 13.5 illustrates. In that example, the monthly payment and first and last year's interest are easily determined.

| **EXAMPLE 13.5** | **Mortgage Calculations** |

$200,000 mortgage, at 6% per year, with monthly payments for 30 years

   The Payment (Using a BA II Plus Calculator)

200,000 PV (the amount being borrowed)

30 × 12 = N (the number of months or payments in 30 years)

6 ÷ 12 = I/Y (the annual interest rate divided by 12 months per year)

CPT PMT = −1,199.10

   The First Year's Interest (Using the BA II Plus Calculator)

Compute the terms of the mortgage, leaving the payment in the display

CPT PMT = −1,199.10

2nd Amort, P1, 1, Enter, Down Arrow (↓)

P2, 12, Enter, Down Arrow (↓)

BAL = 197,544, Down Arrow (↓)

PRN = −2,456, Down Arrow (↓)

INT = −11,933

   The Last Year's Interest (Using the BA II Plus Calculator)

Following the work in B, above

INT = −11,933, Up Arrow (↑), four times (returning to P1)

P1, 349, Enter (the first month of the last year of a 30-year mortgage), ↓,

P2, 360, Enter (the last month of the last year of the mortgage), ↓,

BAL = 0, ↓,

PRN = −13,932, ↓,

INT = − 457

Example 13.5 illustrates the amortization of a mortgage. The payment is calculated in Panel A, the greater payment of interest in the first year of the mortgage in Panel B, and the greater payment of principal and payoff of the loan in Panel C. These mortgage measures may seem better suited for Chapter 10 and the consideration of real estate financing, but their inclusion here is by design. As with a rental property receiving interest payments monthly for 30 years, the borrower in this case pays over $431,000 (360 × $1,199.10) over time, but the present value of those cash payments, discounted at the lending rate of six percent, is exactly $200,000. As in Example 13.6, it can be seen that using the payment and the 6 percent interest rate "up front," the value of the mortgage can be backed out of the monthly cash flow entries:

EXAMPLE 13.6

Valuing an Annuity Stream, or Present Value of a Set of Monthly Mortgage Payments

$-1,199.10$ PMT

$30 \times 12 = $ N

$6 \div 12 = $ I/Y

CPT PV $= 199,999.83$ (or approximately $200,000)

The discounted present value of the mortgage payments is, appropriately, the amount borrowed or $200,000. (A couple check figures from Example 13.5 are also noteworthy—for example, the sum of PRN and INT for the first and last year of the mortgage in Panels B and C equals the sum of 12 monthly payments. PRN + INT equals 14,389, which also equals 12 times 1,199.10. It serves the analyst well to use these sorts of "double-checks" to back up and confirm any analysis, or to check the work of *other* analysts.).

The future value of these cash flows, as with the accumulation of a retirement account with monthly deposits, has little application in the real estate valuation realm, but would be accomplished with Example 13.6 by entering CPT FV instead of CPT PV with the last key strokes. The result? The future value of an accumulating retirement account earning one-half percent per month, with payments into the account of $1,199.10 each month, compounded monthly for 30 years? $1,204,514!

The Present Value of a Perpetuity

An annuity that has no end is a **perpetuity.** One hundred dollars a month forever is a perpetuity. Perpetuities have no future values, as they are forever increasing their values as the years go by. Perpetuities are perpetual! Their present values, however, are handled in precisely the same fashion as the basic income valuation model:

Value (Perpetuity) = Periodic Income ÷ Periodic Interest Rate

A $1000 per year income divided by an annual interest rate of 12 percent would provide a present value for this perpetuity of $1,000 ÷ .12 or $8,333. The $1,000 annual income is equal to 12 percent of the invested $8,333. Were discount rates to fall, the perpetuity would increase in value, with the reverse taking place were discount rates to rise: If the "market" suddenly required a 20 percent return on this investment, its value would become $1,000 ÷ .20 or $5,000. The inverse relationship between discount rates and asset values is again revealed. This perpetuity function is identical in purpose and application to the income valuation model where real estate value is estimated as the property's NOI divided by a selected discount or cap rate.

The Time Value of Money and Unequal Cash Flows

An investor in real estate will encounter varying cash flows from operations during the period of ownership, and a lump sum **reversion** at the end of the ownership period when the property is sold. The reversion is the amount of money available to the sellers of an investment property after the costs of sale and mortgage balances are subtracted from the gross sales price. These varying operating cash flows, and the hoped-for lump sum payout upon the property's sale, challenge the real estate analyst. To this point, property cash flows have been condensed into a single "convenient" estimate of the NOI, in which the estimate is then divided by a selected cap rate to estimate property value. But, in the "real world," how does an investor account for varying operating results and the liquidation of the property at the end of the holding period?

A Net Present Value Approach

A traditional approach to gauging the value of long-term investments, such as real estate, is the **net present value** or NPV criteria. With the NPV approach, an investor projects the cash flows from an investment, from beginning to end, and discounts all the cash flows back to the present. That value is then subtracted from the purchase price. If the difference is positive, the investor is "buying" the investment and its flows for less than their present value, and the investment makes sense. The NPV is positive. Though only infrequently employed in real estate analyses, Example 13.7 employs this tool in examining the desirability of an investment condo purchase. To simplify the example, it is an all-cash "deal."

EXAMPLE 13.7	**The Net Present Value or NPV Approach to Real Estate Analysis**

Condo Purchase Price	$40,000
Annual Cash Flows:	
Potential Gross Income (12 × $650) =	$7,800
Vacancy Allowance (.08 × $7,800) =	(624)
Effective Gross Income (EGI)	$7,176
Operating Expenses (30.28% of EGI)	(2,173)
Annual Net Operating Income (Cash Flow):	$5,003
Assumed sale in 3 years for a net sales price of:	$45,000

Net Present Value = Present Value of income and net sale − purchase price

With the TI BA II Plus:

Hit the CF key, then 2nd, CLR WORK, (follow these key strokes):

CFo, −40,000, Enter, ↓,

CO1, 5003, Enter, ↓,

FO1, 2, Enter, ↓,

CO2, $50,003, ↓,

FO2, 1, Enter, ↓,

CO3, NPV, I, 12, Enter, ↓, NPV, CPT, NPV = 4,046

IRR, CPT, IRR = 16.07

In Example 13.7, the investor pays $40,000 up front, and receives cash flows of $5,003 in years one and two, and $50,003 in year three (year three's cash flow plus the net sales proceeds). We are assuming the investor sells the condo in three years for $49,000 and pays $4,000 in commissions and other closing costs, netting $45,000. The question becomes: Is the sum of the present values of the three years' operating cash flows, plus the net sales price, worth $40,000 today? The undiscounted sum of those flows is $5,003 times three plus $45,000 or $60,009; is that enough of a "gain" from the $40,000 investment to make it worth it? Adopting a discount rate of 12 percent, and using the BA II Plus, the present value of the operating cash flows is $12,016, the present value of the net sales price is $32,030. The sum of those present values is $$44,046. The NPV is $44,046−$40,000 = $4,046. Using the calculator, and its NPV functions, as in Example 13.7, that same total is more easily derived; the NPV is $4,046, which is positive, and the "deal" is a good one. At lower discount rates, as with the income approach to property valuation, the deal gets even better. At higher discount rates, the NPV goes down, and at rates greater than the internal rate or return, the NPV is negative. For example, were the investor to require a return of 17 percent, the NPV would be a negative $849. To derive this, simply enter I = 17 after entering the cash flows in Example 13.7. (The supplement to this chapter on calculator applications may assist the reader.)

Though the NPV approach to investment valuation is uncommon in real estate circles, it provides an additional benchmark for the analyst or investor to use in considering varied real estate opportunities. The NPV approach basically betrays the profitability of a real estate investment beyond some minimum required rate of return (the discount rate of 12 percent chosen in Example 13.7). Where the internal rate of return of an investment exceeds that discount rate, the NPV is acceptable and is positive. The NPV approach is augmented by the internal rate of return metric considered below.

An Internal Rate of Return Approach

The **internal rate of return** (IRR) is the discount rate that forces the NPV to zero. While that definition may seem meaningful in traditional finance circles, it does not have a great deal of importance to the typical real estate investor! Problems 18–20 in the chapter supplement (included on the CD), for the BA II Plus, highlights this relationship. Similar to the selection and use of discount rates in this and prior chapters, the IRR is given *by* a property's expected or observed cash flows, not imposed upon them as with the NPV or income capitalization approaches. With the income or NPV approaches, a discount rate is selected, and the cash flows are discounted back to the present to provide an estimate of those flows' values. With the IRR method, the flows themselves, when contrasted with the purchase price for the property, betray the IRR. For example, if an investor buys an office building with an NOI of $50,000 for $500,000 cash, owns the property for five years and then sells it for $500,000, he gets an IRR of 10 percent. The IRR derives *from* the cash flows, and is not a percentage rate imposed from the outside *on* the cash flows to estimate a value. Example 13.7 illustrates: The condo's NOI and net sales price, contrasted against the purchase price, reveal the IRR of about 16 percent. Were the investor to analyze that property and use a discount rate of less than 16 percent, he would discover a positive NPV and would suggest a value of greater than the purchase price of $40,000. A rate higher than 16.07 percent would estimate a property value of less than $40,000, and a negative NPV. The bottom line? The IRR is a good "rear view mirror" approach to gauge property performance ex-post, or to contrast varying property investments *after the fact*. It is an awkward tool, as is the NPV approach, to use in advance of a property purchase—the simpler income valuation technique is generally preferred. It only follows that the better investment will have the higher IRR, but selecting those investments prudently with the income valuation models will provide the same desired outcome, the more accurate comparison of real estate investments.

SOME CONCLUDING REMARKS ON DISCOUNTING AND DISCOUNT RATES

It is in the realm of these present and future value calculations, NPV analyses, and IRR discoveries that the real estate analyst attempts to discern the best risk-adjusted choices. She tries to answer the question: "Given what we know about this property and the economy as a whole, do the purchase terms and cash flows make sense for the investor?" Or from the seller's point of view: "Given our projections, do the offered terms of sale make sense for our owner?" Either way, the buyer or seller is operating in a realm of uncertainty, and wishes to gather such information as is necessary to make a better decision. The tools considered in the last couple of chapters, and the preceding few pages, begin to describe the sorts of remedies that a real estate analyst offers a real estate buyer or seller.

Property selling prices in most jurisdictions (much of Texas being an exception) are public knowledge. Discount rates or expected IRRs on those properties are implied by the selling prices. Rental rates can be gathered by survey or from a number of real estate sources. Borrowing costs for investment properties are typically published or are readily available. Credit ratings of tenants, average costs of operation, and neighborhood data can be procured or estimated as well. Building-specific data will fill out the sort of information needed to provide a picture of a property's expected operations. But, as with any forecast, there are varying degrees of uncertainty attaching to any "prediction" about the future. Where the information is readily available, and forecasts can be made with some certainty, lower discount rates and higher values might be indicated; where tenancy or expenses are uncertain, or the economic environment is unfavorable, higher discount rates and lower values (and higher IRRs) will be the norm.

The "mission" of any investment analyst is to condense a set of predictions about future uncertain cash flows into a single current value. That is the simple objective of the income valuation model: to generate accurate predictions of a property's NOI, and to then select a suitable capitalization or discount rate to "boil down" that NOI forecast into a property value estimate. The process of mastering this protocol is as much an art as a science.

KEY TERMS

annuity	go dark	net present value	present value
compound interest	internal rate of return	perpetuity	reversion
future value	inverse		

DISCUSSION QUESTIONS

1. Explain what is meant by the "time value" of money.

2. What is the purpose of the discount calculation?

3. How is a capitalization rate determined?

4. Define an internal rate of return (IRR).

5. How could discount factors be used in marketing commercial property?

6. What is the relationship between the IRR and NPV calculations?

7. How does a change in risk, or risk perceptions, or risk aversion, impact discount rates?

8. What is meant by "compound" interest?

9. What is an annuity? A perpetuity?

10. How have discount rates varied, in general, since 1990?

CHAPTER 14

Computer-Aided Analysis

Many of the analysis tools used by investors, brokers, lenders, and other real estate practitioners are greatly enhanced by the use of computers. The current use of laptops and desktops is no longer a luxury but an absolute necessity in preparing a proper analysis of an investment opportunity.

Many software programs are currently available to help the investor and real estate practitioner in almost every phase of investment analysis. Many of these programs are reasonably priced and many can be downloaded from the Internet for free. An investor should examine the available programs and utilize those that fulfill his needs.

In this chapter several of the more common analytical tools used by investors will be examined to see how they can be easily adapted to computers by using spreadsheet software. One of the most commonly used spreadsheet programs is Microsoft Excel. It is very user-friendly; investors can set up their own unique programs to implement their own criteria when doing an investment analysis.

Three of the more useful tools of analysis will be examined in this chapter. The Excel analysis programs are included as part of this text and can be found on the CD in the book jacket. It is strongly suggested that the reader make copies of the spreadsheet programs and save the original. The integrity of the programs could be damaged if they are accidentally changed by the user. The analysis tools that we will examine are: (1) **Cash Flow Projections**,

(2) **Investment Analysis**, and (3) **Analysis of Offer to Purchase**. The three reports generated by the software program contained on the CD included with this book contain basically the same information displayed in different formats. As a result, all of the reports are generated in the same spreadsheet program. Hence, the basic information is entered only once. For convenience, the three reports are separated in "sheets" in the spreadsheet. The basic data that is used in these reports is provided by you, the analyst, in Sheet 1. The "Cash Flow Projections" report is contained in Sheet 2. The "Investment Analysis" report is contained in Sheet 3. The "Analysis of Offer to Purchase" report is contained in Sheet 4. Samples of these four sheets are shown in Tables 1 through 4 in this chapter.

CASH FLOW PROJECTIONS

Cash flows, or income dollars received, are the most important considerations in evaluating an investment. The best location in the world would be of little interest to an investor if there were no opportunity to generate income from the investment. There are basically two types of income to consider: (1) cash flows during the holding period of the investment and (2) cash generated when the property is sold at the end of the holding period.

If the holding period is one year, the investment analysis would be very simple and would not require a sophisticated computer analysis. However, this is seldom the case. Most investors plan on holding the property for a period of years and then selling at an optimum time. A sophisticated investment analysis can help the investor determine the optimum holding period. The cash flow projection shown in Table 14.1 shows the cash flows during the holding period, the cumulative cash flows, the discounted cash flows, the expected reversion proceeds, and the internal rates of return.

Holding Period

The cash flow study shown in Table 14.1, and contained on the CD included with this book, allows for a ten-year holding period. Generally, it is difficult to predict how long a property will be held at the time a purchase decision is being made. Because of the difficulty in predicting ambient interest rates, future markets for real estate, cap rates, and numerous other factors, most investors do not look at a ten-year projection. A five-year projection is much more common, so the spreadsheet is designed to be used for any holding period the analyst may choose. For example, if a four-year study is preferable, then the analyst may simply set the print area to show four years. The calculations are set to portray a study of any length between two and ten years.

TABLE **14.1**
Cash Flow Projections

		as of: 12/31/2010			
Property: City Lights Shopping Center					
Year End Date:	2011	2012	2013	2014	2015
INCOME AND EXPENSE ITEMS:					
Gross Scheduled Income	$ 1,240,000	$ 1,289,600	$ 1,341,184	$ 1,394,831	$ 1,450,625
Miscellaneous Income	$ 83,500	$ 86,840	$ 90,314	$ 93,926	$ 97,683
Gross Possible Income	$ 1,323,500	$ 1,376,440	$ 1,431,498	$ 1,488,758	$ 1,548,308
Less: Vacancy and Credit Loss	$ 62,000	$ 64,480	$ 67,059	$ 69,742	$ 72,531
Adjusted Gross Income	$ 1,261,500	$ 1,311,960	$ 1,364,438	$ 1,419,016	$ 1,475,777
Operating Expenses	$ 300,000	$ 312,000	$ 324,480	$ 337,459	$ 350,958
Miscellaneous Expenses	$ –	$ –	$ –	$ –	$ –
NET OPERATING INCOME:	$ 961,500	$ 999,960	$ 1,039,958	$ 1,081,557	$ 1,124,819
CASH FLOW ITEMS:					
Debt Service: Principal	$ 57,386	$ 62,598	$ 68,286	$ 74,493	$ 81,267
Debt Service: Interest	$ 700,916	$ 695,704	$ 690,016	$ 683,809	$ 677,035
Capital Expense & Refurb.	$ –	$ –	$ –	$ –	$ 500,000
Other Costs	$ –	$ –	$ –	$ –	$ –
NET CASH FLOW BEFORE TAX:	$ 203,198	$ 241,658	$ 281,656	$ 323,255	$ (133,483)
TAX RELATED ITEMS:					
Net Operating Income	$ 961,500	$ 999,960	$ 1,039,958	$ 1,081,557	$ 1,124,819
Depreciation	$ 261,538	$ 261,538	$ 261,538	$ 261,538	$ 261,538
Debt Service/Interest	$ 700,916	$ 695,704	$ 690,016	$ 683,809	$ 677,035
Taxable Income	$ (955)	$ 42,718	$ 88,404	$ 136,209	$ 186,245
Taxes Paid (+) or Saved (−)	$ (296)	$ 13,242	$ 27,405	$ 42,225	$ 57,736
NET CASH FLOW AFTER TAX:	$ 203,198	$ 228,415	$ 254,251	$ 281,030	$ (191,219)
CUMULATIVE CASH FLOW: (Before Tax)	$ (3,796,802)	$ (3,555,144)	$ (3,273,488)	$ (2,950,233)	$ (3,083,717)
CUMULATIVE CASH FLOW: (After Tax)	$ (3,796,802)	$ (3,568,387)	$ (3,314,136)	$ (3,033,106)	$ (3,224,325)

TABLE **14.1**
(Continued)

	as of: 12/31/2010				
Property: City Lights Shopping Center					
Year End Date:	2011	2012	2013	2014	2015
REVERSION PROCEEDS:	$ 3,457,386	$ 3,975,984	$ 4,518,510	$ 5,086,213	$ 5,680,418
CASH FLOW AFTER SALE:	$ 3,660,584	$ 4,217,642	$ 4,800,166	$ 5,409,468	$ 5,546,935
CUMULATIVE CASH FLOW: (Including Sale/Before Tax)	$ (339,416)	$ 420,840	$ 1,245,022	$ 2,135,980	$ 2,596,701
CUMULATIVE CASH FLOW: (Including Sale/After Tax)	$ (339,416)	$ 301,456	$ 892,215	$ 1,529,618	$ 1,855,750
DISCOUNTED CASH FLOWS: (Including Reversion)	$ 3,453,381	$ 3,753,686	$ 4,030,312	$ 4,284,805	$ 4,144,992
INTERNAL RATE OF RETURN:		−6.2%	3.1%	6.1%	5.4%
INCOME AND EXPENSE ITEMS:					
Gross Scheduled Income	$ 1,508,650	$ 1,568,996	$ 1,631,755	$ 1,697,026	$ 1,764,907
Miscellaneous Income	$ 101,591	$ 105,654	$ 109,880	$ 114,276	$ 118,847
Gross Possible Income	$ 1,610,240	$ 1,674,650	$ 1,741,636	$ 1,811,301	$ 1,883,753
Less: Vacancy and Credit Loss	$ 75,432	$ 78,450	$ 81,588	$ 84,851	$ 88,245
Adjusted Gross Income	$ 1,534,808	$ 1,596,200	$ 1,660,048	$ 1,726,450	$ 1,795,508
Operating Expenses	$ 364,996	$ 379,596	$ 394,780	$ 410,571	$ 426,994
Miscellaneous Expenses	$ –	$ –	$ –	$ –	$ –
NET OPERATING INCOME:	$ 1,169,812	$ 1,216,604	$ 1,265,268	$ 1,315,879	$ 1,368,514
CASH FLOW ITEMS:					
Debt Service: Principal	$ 88,659	$ 96,726	$ 105,530	$ 115,140	$ 125,628
Debt Service: Interest	$ 669,643	$ 661,576	$ 652,772	$ 643,162	$ 632,674
Capital Expense & Refurb.	$ –	$ –	$ –	$ –	$ –
Other Costs	$ –	$ –	$ –	$ –	$ –
NET CASH FLOW BEFORE TAX:	$ 411,510	$ 458,302	$ 506,966	$ 557,577	$ 610,212

TABLE **14.1**
(Continued)

		as of: 12/31/2010			
Property: City Lights Shopping Center					
Year End Date:	2011	2012	2013	2014	2015
TAX RELATED ITEMS:					
Net Operating Income	$ 1,169,812	$ 1,216,604	$ 1,265,268	$ 1,315,879	$ 1,368,514
Depreciation	$ 311,538	$ 311,538	$ 311,538	$ 311,538	$ 311,538
Debt Service/Interest	$ 669,643	$ 661,576	$ 652,772	$ 643,162	$ 632,674
Taxable Income	$ 188,630	$ 243,490	$ 300,958	$ 361,178	$ 424,302
Taxes Paid (+) or Saved (−)	$ 58,475	$ 75,482	$ 93,297	$ 111,965	$ 131,534
NET CASH FLOW AFTER TAX:	$ 353,034	$ 382,820	$ 413,669	$ 445,612	$ 478,679
CUMULATIVE CASH FLOW: (Before Tax)	$ (2,672,207)	$ (2,213,905)	$ (1,706,939)	$ (1,149,362)	$ (539,150)
CUMULATIVE CASH FLOW: (After Tax)	$ (2,871,291)	$ (2,488,471)	$ (2,074,801)	$ (1,629,190)	$ (1,150,511)
REVERSION PROCEEDS:	$ 6,302,532	$ 6,954,052	$ 7,636,568	$ 8,351,772	$ 9,101,468
CASH FLOW AFTER SALE:	$ 6,714,041	$ 7,412,354	$ 8,143,534	$ 8,909,349	$ 9,711,680
CUMULATIVE CASH FLOW: (Including Sale/Before Tax)	$ 3,630,325	$ 4,740,147	$ 5,929,629	$ 7,202,411	$ 8,562,318
CUMULATIVE CASH FLOW: (Including Sale/After Tax)	$ 2,594,300	$ 3,386,067	$ 4,233,466	$ 5,139,033	$ 6,105,438
DISCOUNTED CASH FLOWS: (Including Reversion)	$ 4,733,134	$ 4,929,639	$ 5,109,354	$ 5,273,430	$ 5,422,951
INTERNAL RATE OF RETURN:	6.5%	7.2%	7.6%	7.8%	8.0%

Entering Data for the Analysis

The data for the study is entered on Sheet 1 of the spreadsheet program. Table 14.2 shows the layout of Sheet 1 where the data is entered. The information to be provided for each study is highlighted both on the spreadsheet and in Table 14.2. Excel calculates all of the non-highlighted data. However,

TABLE **14.2**
Cash Flow and Investment Analysis—*Data Entry*

Date of Report:	12/31/2010				
Property Being Analyzed: City Lights Shopping Center					
First Year End Date:	2011	2012	2013	2014	2015
INCOME AND EXPENSE ITEMS:					
Gross Scheduled Income	$ 9.92 $ 1,240,000	$ 1,289,600	$ 1,341,184	$ 1,394,831	$ 1,450,625
Increase in Gross Scheduled Income	4%	4%	4%	4%	4%
Miscellaneous Income	$ 83,500	$ 86,840	$ 90,314	$ 93,926	$ 97,683
Increase in Miscellaneous Income	4%	4%	4%	4%	4%
Vacancy and Credit Loss	$ 62,000	$ 64,480	$ 67,059	$ 69,742	$ 72,531
Percent Vacancy & Credit Loss	5%	5%	5%	5%	5%
Operating Expenses	$ 300,000	$ 312,000	$ 324,480	$ 337,459	$ 350,958
Increase in Operating Expenses	4%	4%	4%	4%	4%
Miscellaneous Expenses		0	0	0	0
Increase in Miscellaneous Expenses	4%	4%	4%	4%	4%
Capital Expense & Refurbishment					$ 500,000
Useful Life for Depreciation					10
Other Costs					
PURCHASE PRICE:	$ 12,000,000				
FIRST MORTGAGE:	$ 6,455,000				
Interest Rate	8.50%				
Term	30				
SECOND MORTGAGE:	$ 1,545,000				
Interest Rate	10%				
Term	30				
EQUITY: (Price-Mortgages)	$ 4,000,000				

NUMBER OF SQUARE FEET:	125,000				
DEPRECIABLE BASE:	85%	$ 10,200,000			
USEFUL LIFE (27.5 OR 39 YRS):	39.0				
INCOME TAX RATE FOR CASH FLOWS:	31%				
INCOME TAX RATE FOR CAPITAL GAIN:	28%				
DISCOUNT RATE:	6%	6%	6%	6%	6%
MONTHLY MORTGAGE PAYMENT:					
(FIRST)	$ 49,633				
ANNUAL		$ 595,600			
MONTHLY MORTGAGE PAYMENT:					
(SECOND)	$ 13,558				
ANNUAL		$ 162,702			
DEBT COVERAGE RATIO:	1.20	CAP RATE:	8.01%		
DESIRED RETURN ON EQUITY:	10%				
COST OF SALE:	5%	CONSTANT	10.30% (for refinancing)		

there are provisions for overriding the calculated numbers and inserting numbers as desired by the analyst.

For example, the vacancy rate is kept constant throughout the study. Whatever rate is used for year one is automatically used for each subsequent year. Many investment opportunities may show a high vacancy rate today, but the prospective buyer may be anticipating the injection of capital to facilitate leasing the property. Such a buyer may show a 20 percent vacancy the first year, a 10 percent vacancy the second year, and 5 percent thereafter. Since it is anticipated that the user will be making numerous changes in the spreadsheet, it is essential that at least one copy be retained unchanged so that there will always be a backup. It would be appropriate to make at least three copies immediately so that there will always be a copy to refer to. No part of the spreadsheet is protected in order to give users maximum flexibility in tailoring their studies.

Most of the data entry fields shown in Table 14.2 are self-explanatory. However, there are some features that need clarification.

Date of Report

This field will automatically show today's date. If another date is preferred, it must be entered as "data." This can be done by starting the entry with a space or with an apostrophe. For example, if the study was to show the last day of the year, it should be entered as "December 31, 2010" or, "12-31-10."

Gross Scheduled Income

When this number is entered, the rent per square foot is calculated in the field between the title and the first year income figure. The second year income is calculated by increasing the first year's figure by the percentage factor immediately below the income figure.

Vacancy and Credit Loss

This field is calculated as a percent of "Gross Scheduled Income" and does not need to be entered if a percentage is provided. However, it can be overridden if desired.

Capital Expense & Refurbishment

This field is used for any projected cash injections into the project. In this analysis, these capital expenses are subsequently depreciated using the useful life indicated in the row below the Capital Expenses & Refurbishment entry. These expenses are deducted from the cash flows and are depreciated for purposes of calculating income taxes.

Other Costs

This field is handled in the same manner as Capital Expenses & Refurbishment; however, these costs are not depreciated and are not considered as expenses in calculating income taxes.

Equity

This field is calculated by subtracting the First and Second Mortgages from the Purchase Price.

Depreciable Base

This figure is calculated by multiplying the percentage shown on this line by the purchase price. The analyst can change the percentage or the depreciable base may be entered as a dollar amount. This basically establishes the percent of the purchase price that is attributable to the building and improvements.

Discount Rate

This rate is used in calculating the discounted cash flows. Each cash flow is discounted by this percentage each year.

Cap Rate

This figure is calculated by dividing the Net Operating Income by the Purchase Price. It is then used to calculate the subsequent sales price at the end of the holding period. It is difficult to determine the actual sales price at the end of the expected holding period. However, the assumption is made that a subsequent purchaser will buy the property at the same cap rate that it is being purchased for today.

Cost of Sale

This is the percent of the subsequent sales price that will be deducted from the reversion proceeds. It should cover commissions, title policy, legal fees, and other closing expenses.

Displaying the Results

Sheet 2 of the spreadsheet (Table 14.1) displays the elements of the cash flow projections. All of the information and calculations contained in this sheet are derived from the data that were entered or calculated in Sheet 1 (Table 14.2). This spreadsheet is not protected since many analysts will want to tailor these studies to their particular needs. For that reason, it is again emphasized that several back-up copies should be maintained.

In analyzing the results of the study it is important to recognize one key assumption. All of the cash flows are considered to arrive at the end of the year. In a more sophisticated analysis a monthly pro forma would be more appropriate. However, in this study a cash flow item such as Capital Expense & Refurbishment is assumed to occur at the end of the year in which it is recorded. Referring to Table 14.2, in the year 2015 a capital expenditure of $500,000 is indicated. In the following year a depreciation deduction on this ten-year life asset is indicated. The depreciation deduction is also shown over the useful life of this deduction.

As with Sheet 1 most of the information is self-explanatory. However, additional clarification may be appropriate for some of the items. For example:

Capital Expense & Refurbishment

This category is for items that are deductible from cash flow since they represent out-of-pocket costs. However, they are not considered to be operating expense items and therefore are not deductible for tax purposes. Since they are capital expenses, they are depreciable in subsequent years. *Note:* It is essential that a number be inserted in the next line, which is titled: "Useful Life for Depreciation," found on Sheet 1 (Table 14.2).

Other Costs

This category of out-of-pocket costs is handled the same way as Capital Expense & Refurbishment except that there is no subsequent depreciation expense deduction. This category is not considered in any tax calculation.

Net Cash Flow Before Tax

This figure considers all income and expenses associated with the project. It is possibly the most significant number to be used because it indicates the cash flows that can be anticipated during the holding period. After tax flow is quite significant, however, it is difficult to establish the effects of taxes since there are so many variables having to do with the owner's tax circumstances.

Cumulative Cash Flow (Before Tax)

This category considers the net cash flows shown above and also considers the initial cash outlay (equity). It does not, however, consider reversion proceeds.

Cumulative Cash Flows (After Tax)

This category considers the net cash flows after tax as well as the initial cash outlay in the form of equity dollars.

Reversion Proceeds

This category represents the net dollars received after selling the property. It is difficult to determine what a property will sell for several years from now. So, the assumption is made that the subsequent purchasers will purchase the property at the same cap rate that the present purchasers are willing to accept. The sales price, then, is calculated by dividing the future net operating income (in the year of the sale) by the cap rate calculated at the time of purchase. From that figure, the mortgage balances and the cost of sales are deducted. The cost of sale is a percent of the sales price that is specified on Sheet 1.

Cash Flow After Sale

This category considers cash flows from rental income and sale of the property minus the original investment (equity).

Cumulative Cash Flow (Including Sale/Before Tax)

The dollar figure shown in any year would represent the sum of all previous years' pretax cash flows plus the reversion proceeds in that year.

Cumulative Cash Flow (Including Sale/After Tax)

These figures show the cumulative cash flows after tax as well as the proceeds from a sale in the same year. The gain from the sale is calculated in the manner described in Chapter 6, "Property Taxes and Income Taxes." That gain is then multiplied times the Income Tax Rate for Capital Gain as entered in Sheet 1 (Table 14.2) of this spreadsheet program.

Consider Table 14.1. The calculation for cumulative cash flow including the sale after the fifth year would be as follows:

Cumulative cash flow (After tax)		$ (3,224,325)
Plus reversion proceeds		5,680,418
Less tax on reversion proceeds:		
Sale price of asset: $1,124,819/0.0801	$14,042,685	
Less cost of sale: $14,042,684 × 0.05	$ 702,134	
Realized selling price		$13,340,550
Initial basis of value (purchase price)	$12,000,000	
Plus: Capital Expense	$ 500,000	
	$12,500,000	
Less: Depreciation (Cumulative)	$(1,307,690)	
Adjusted basis of value		$11,192,310
Capital gain		$ 2,148,240
Capital gain tax (at 28%)		$ 601,507
Cumulative Cash Flow (Including Sale/ After Tax)		
for year 2015		$ 1,855,750

Discounted Cash Flows

These figures are the Cash Flow After Sale figures discounted by the discount rate shown in the input area. The first year rate is automatically replicated for the life of the study; however, the analyst may enter a different rate each year in the input data area on Sheet 1.

It would be relatively simple for the analyst to add rows of figures that would represent discounted cash flows or Reversion Proceeds, Net Operating Income, Net Cash Flow Before Tax, or Net Cash Flow After Tax. Simply insert a row in the spreadsheet, and then enter the address of the first entry in the row of figures to be discounted and divide by (1+Discount Rate). This entry should be replicated over the next nine entries in the row.

Internal Rate of Return (IRR)

This all-important indicator is described in Chapter 13, "Discount Analysis." The cash flows used in the calculation of internal rate of return are figures for which it would be relatively simple to set up a new row to perform such a calculation. The pretax figures are considered more appropriate for a generic study since tax consequences are very specific to the investment entity purchasing the property. As an example of the data used in the calculation, the cash flows used to determine the IRR in the fourth year in Table 14.1 are as follows:

Down Payment	Year1 NCF	Year2 NCF	Year3 NCF	Year4 NCF	Reversion Proceeds
($4,000,000)	$203,198	$241,658	$281,656	$323,255	$5,086,213

The cash flows produce an IRR of 12.09%

EXAMPLE 14.1   Using the Texas Instruments BA-II Plus, the following key entries can confirm the IRR calculations in Excel. Strike the CF (cash flow) key, and clear the CF entries by striking 2nd, CLR WRK. Enter the first cash flow (CF0) by entering – 4,000,000 (the down payment). Striking the down arrow key brings up CO1; enter 203,198 for the first cash flow, hitting the down arrow (bringing up the cash flow frequency or F01), and enter 1 for the first cash flow's frequency. Follow this with CO2, CO3 and CO4 (241,658, 281,656, and 323,255 plus 5,086,213 for the fourth cash flow), each with a frequency of 1. That last cash flow, the fourth cash flow, is the sum of the property's operating proceeds, and the reversion or sale at the end of year 4: 5,409,468. Having entered these five cash flows (the down payment and four positive cash flows), hit the IRR key, then CPT, and you should see 12.093 displayed. This is the internal rate of return.

The first year IRR is not shown because a sale in the first year will always produce a zero or negative cash flow. Since the flows are considered to be received at the end of the year, the sales price will be no higher than the original purchase price.

The use of the IRR is very appropriate in doing a sensitivity analysis. The analyst may vary any array of input items and examine their effect on the internal rate of return of the investment. This is conveniently done by selecting New Window from the Window menu in Excel. Using this feature, the analyst may look at the input area and the cash flow projections at the same time. Any variable may be tweaked and the results observed. For example, the study shown in Table 14.1 can be examined to determine the effect of injecting capital in the first year and raising the rents accordingly.

Using the example of the fourth year study shown above, the analyst may examine the effect of spending $500,000 to make improvements in the first year. As a result of these improvements, rents can be raised by 8 percent the first four years and a fairly stable 4 percent thereafter. The IRR in the fourth year now becomes 14.6 percent instead of 12.09 percent. Since this represents an increase in the return to the investor, the possibility of investing additional capital and vigorously raising rents should be considered.

Practical Application

One huge advantage of the use of computers is the ability to do sensitivity analysis. In other words the analyst can do many "what ifs" in a short time period. Consider the Heights Colony Apartments that were introduced in Chapter 10. The information is given again here as Case Study 14.1 and can

CASE STUDY **14.1**

The Heights Colony Apartments

404 Heights Avenue. Anytown, U.S.A.

Unit mix	No. of Units	Unit Type	Size	Mo.Rent Per Unit	Annual Rental Income
	24	A	700 sq. ft.	$ 780	$ 224,640
	24	B	750 sq. ft.	$ 850	$ 244,800
	20	C	820 sq. ft.	$ 900	$ 216,000
	20	D	880 sq. ft.	$ 970	$ 232,800
	12	E	950 sq. ft.	$ 1,090	$ 156,960
Totals	100		80,200 sq. ft.		$ 1,075,200

Pro Forma

Gross Scheduled Income		$ 1,075,200
Less Vacancy and Credit Loss (5%)		(53,760)
Miscellaneous Income		26,000
Adjusted Gross Income		$ 1,047,440
Operating Expenses		
Fixed Expenses	$ 259,800	
Variable Expenses	$ 180,800	
Total Expenses		$ 440,600
Net Operating Income (NOI)		$ 606,840

be used to familiarize the reader with the software found on the CD in the back of this book. To experience the ease of use of the software it would be appropriate to insert the data from the Case Study into the input area of the spreadsheet software and then analyze the three reports.

Exhibit 14.1 shows the resulting "Suggested Offering Price" based on several assumptions. The study shows the results when several interest rates are assumed as well as several desired rates of return on equity (ROE). If the interest rate is set at 8 percent and the ROE is set at 10 percent then a suggested offering price of $6,751,468 would result. If the investors would settle for an 8 percent return on equity and an interest rate of 7.25 percent were achievable then an offering price of $7,438,853 would result. The difference between these two prices is $687,385, a fairly significant number.

Obviously many other variables can be "tweaked" to produce numerous other studies. At the end of this chapter there are several discussion questions that are designed to familiarize the reader with the capabilities of the software included herein. Virtually all of the data entered into the study can be adjusted based on current conditions and comparable area information. The quality of the results as always is a function of the accuracy of the input data and the knowledge and experience of the analyst.

EXHIBIT 14.1

Interest Rate	Assumptions: Constant (K)	ROE	Suggested Offering Price
8.00%	8.81%	10.0%	$ 6,751,468
8.00%	8.81%	9.0%	$ 6,863,846
8.00%	8.81%	8.0%	$ 7,004,318
7.75%	8.60%	10.0%	$ 6,891,633
7.75%	8.60%	9.0%	$ 7,004,010
7.75%	8.60%	8.0%	$ 7,144,483
7.50%	8.39%	10.0%	$ 7,038,814
7.50%	8.39%	9.0%	$ 7,151,191
7.50%	8.39%	8.0%	$ 7,291,664
7.25%	8.19%	10.0%	$ 7,186,003
7.25%	8.19%	9.0%	$ 7,298,381
7.25%	8.19%	8.0%	$ 7,438,853

INVESTMENT ANALYSIS

Cash flow is not the only indicator that an investor will consider before purchasing a property. There are numerous other features that need to be evaluated. Table 14.3 shows an additional spreadsheet study that may prove useful in evaluating a prospective purchase. All of the information portrayed in this "Investment Analysis" is derived from the input data portion on Sheet 1. In essence, this study is provided at no extra expense or effort.

The analyst will typically look at all indicators when making a go/no go decision on the purchase of the property. No single indicator is necessarily a "deal killer." Many properties are purchased even when showing negative cash flows. The investor may see great opportunities to turn the property around by injecting capital and vigorously raising rents. So this list of indicators should be evaluated in its summary effect, not just as individual items.

While most of the information is self-explanatory, a brief description of the data may be beneficial. The top portion is the typical pro forma for the City Lights Shopping Center. The middle portion contains information pertinent to the prospective purchase of the Center. The bottom portion breaks out some

TABLE **14.3**
Investment Analysis

			12/31/2010	
PROJECT NAME: CITY LIGHTS SHOPPING CENTER				
Gross Scheduled Income				$ 1,240,000
Other Income				$ 83,500
Vacancy & Credit Loss				$ 62,000
Adjusted Gross Income				$ 1,261,500
Operating Expenses				$ 300,000
Net Operating Income				$ 961,500
Debt Service	First		$ 595,600	
	Second		$ 162,702	$ 758,302
Net Cash Flow				$ 203,198
Price				$ 12,000,000
Loan(s)			$ 6,455,000	
			$ 1,545,000	$ 8,000,000
No. of Sq. Ft.			125,000	
Loan Constant (for refinancing)			10.30%	
Debt Coverage Ratio			1.20	
Desired Return			10%	
Equity				$ 4,000,000
Net Operating Income				$ 961,500
Net Cash Flow				$ 203,198
Price per Sq. Ft.				$ 96.00
Gross Rent Multiplier				9.68
Constant (on existing loans)				9.5%
Return on Equity				5.1%
Overall Return				8.0%
Expenses per Sq. Ft.				$ 2.40
Income Going to Debt Service				60.1%
Income Going to Expenses				23.8%
Rental Rate (per sq. ft.)				$ 9.92
Positive or Negative Leverage				NEG
New Loan Amount (to be refinanced)				$ 7,779,126
New Equity				$ 1,602,500
Suggested Offering Price				$ 9,381,626

of the more significant indicators such as return on equity and return on overall investment. A brief examination of some of the indicators follows.

Gross Rent Multiplier (GRM)

This is an indicator sometimes used in comparing the subject property to comparable properties. It is calculated by dividing the gross scheduled income into the purchase price. Because it uses gross income, it can be misleading. If the gross rent is high, but, because of high expenses and debt service, the net cash flow is small or negative, then the GRM has little or no significance. Indicators such as return on equity and others that use net incomes are much more meaningful. However, as an indicator of comparative value, GRM may be useful. For example, seven comparable shopping centers have sold recently, showing an average GRM of 11.5. The fact that City Lights shows a multiplier of 9.68 is an indicator that it may be a potentially good investment. So armed with this bit of positive information, the analyst would investigate further.

Constant (on existing loans)

This number is calculated by dividing the current debt services (combined) by the existing mortgage balances. This figure is somewhat misleading since the true mortgage constant is a function of the debt service and the original loan balance. However, it does indicate what percent of the debt is being paid as debt service. This may be handy for use in determining whether to refinance or keep the existing financing. The constant is larger for shorter-maturity loans; more principal is being repaid each year.

Return on Equity (ROE)

This indicator is determined by dividing the net cash flow by the equity required. This is sometimes referred to as the "bottom line" or the "net spendable." This ratio, or one quite similar, is sometimes called the equity dividend rate (EDR) or cash-on-cash return. Capital appreciation is not captured by the year-to-year EDR or ROE. It is a significant indicator because it basically tells investors what return on investment they can expect. A return of 5.1 percent as shown for City Lights does not seem to be impressive, but many other factors need to be considered. Cash flow is just one of the features an investor looks for. For example, a five-year cash flow analysis as shown in Table 14.1 may show that after a holding period the property may be sold at a significant profit. During the holding period, there may be significant tax advantages. Likewise, there may be an excellent opportunity for cash preservation. Or, additionally, there may be an opportunity for "value gain." This advantage, almost unique to real estate, is described in Chapter 1.

A very high ROE may excite the analyst initially; however, by itself it may not be the only factor to consider. Obviously, the ambient real estate market may be very significant to the continuing ability to generate a high return. There may be a very large amount of deferred maintenance, hence the high return. The current owners may have pocketed all of the cash flow and not maintained the property adequately. Many other factors must be considered along with ROE.

Overall Return or Capitalization Rate (Cap Rate)

This number is calculated by dividing the net operating income by the total purchase price of the property. For an investor, this may not be as significant as ROE. However, for an appraiser, this factor may be the most significant because it indicates the property's ability to generate income without considering the burden that has been imposed on the property in the form of mortgages.

The amount of financing is not indigenous to the property but a feature that is added later based on the needs of the owner. The EDR or ROE are typically greater than the overall return or cap rate, if debt is used in the purchase. However, debt entails risk. If no debt is used in a property purchase, the ROE or EDR and cap rate are equal. Extending Case Study 14.1, the property has an NOI of $606,840. With a cap rate of 10 percent, a value of $6,068,400 is implied. Absent any debt financing, the down payment or equity becomes the purchase price of $6,068,400, and the overall return is the EDR of 10% ($606,840/$6,068,400).

Income Going to Debt Service

This figure essentially indicates how much of the gross scheduled income is used to make the mortgage payments. It is primarily a comparison indicator. For example, 60 percent is a large percent of income to commit to debt service. It may indicate that the purchaser should look at the possibility of refinancing. By itself it is not greatly significant but simply a feature that the investor should analyze.

Income Going to Expenses

Similarly, this figure indicates how much of the gross scheduled income is used to cover expenses. It is primarily a comparison indicator. This measure is the same as the operating expense ratio, and is the percentage of collected income or adjusted gross income (or effective gross income, depending upon the account names chosen by the preparer of the statements) that is paid out in operating expenses. Figures of around 30 percent or 35 percent are typical for strip shopping centers. By itself, it is not greatly significant but simply a feature that the investor should analyze.

Rental Rate (per sq. ft.)

This number is determined by dividing the gross scheduled income by the total number of square feet in the building and gives an indication of the rental rates as compared to other similar projects. It should be analyzed by evaluating market rates for comparable buildings.

Positive or Negative Leverage

If the overall rate of return or cap rate is greater than the mortgage "constant" (the cost of borrowing money), borrowing more money will produce higher returns on equity. This is called positive leverage. In other words, leverage works for you. However, if the cost of borrowing money (the "constant") is greater than the overall return, borrowing more money will decrease the return on equity. This is called negative leverage.

TABLE **14.4**

Analysis of Offer to Purchase

12/31/2010

CITY LIGHTS SHOPPING CENTER

Asking Price			$ 12,000,000
Loan Amount	First	$ 6,455,000	
	Second	$ 1,545,000	$ 8,000,000
Equity Required			$ 4,000,000
Gross Scheduled Income			$ 1,240,000
Other Income			$ 83,500
Less Vacancy and Credit Loss			$ 62,000
Adjusted Gross Income			$ 1,261,500
Operating Expenses			$ 300,000
Net Operating Income			$ 961,500
Debt Service	First	$ 595,600	
	Second	$ 162,702	
Net Cash Flow			$ 203,198
Return on Equity			5.1%
Return on Cash			8.0%
Gross Rent Multiplier			9.68
Expenses per sq. ft.	No. of Sq. Ft.=	$ 125,000	2.40
Rents per sq. ft.	Monthly $ 0.83	Annual $	9.92

Recommended Offer

Desired Return on Equity			10%
Available Financing Constant (K)			10.30%
Debt Coverage Ratio			1.20
Available Financing	Based on NOI of	$ 961,500	$ 7,779,126
New Debt Service			$ 801,250
New Net Cash Flow			$ 160,250
New Equity			$ 1,602,500
Suggested Offering Price			$ 9,381,626

New Loan Amount, New Equity, and Suggested Offering Price

When deciding how much money can be borrowed to finance the purchase of the subject property, the buyer must know the lender's debt coverage ratio and the current loan constant for this type of investment property. Recall the loan constant is little more than the annual debt service (12 monthly payments of principal and interest) divided by the amount borrowed. Loan constants are not commonly used anymore, given the power of even the simplest hand-held calculators to accurately portray real estate investment performance.

With that information, the New Loan Amount is calculated. From this, debt service is calculated and subtracted from the property's net operating income, thus giving a new net cash flow. From this, given the desired return on equity, or EDR or cash-on-cash return, the amount of equity can be determined. Thus, adding the new loan and the new equity, the optimum or "suggested offering price" can be determined.

ANALYSIS OF OFFER TO PURCHASE

As with the Investment Analysis, the Analysis of Offer to Purchase (Table 14.4) is provided automatically using the information in the input area known as Sheet 1. This report is simply a restatement of the data in the previous reports and is found in Sheet 4 of the Excel spreadsheet. The Suggested Offering Price is developed in the manner described in the previous section.

Since all of the information is extracted from Sheet 1, the input area, it is strongly recommended that the analyst not change any of the cells containing numbers. However, the format and data contained in this report can be modified to suit the needs of the analyst.

KEY TERMS

analysis of offer to purchase

cash flow projections

cumulative cash flows

depreciable base

gross rent multiplier

holding period

internal rate of return (IRR)

investment analysis

positive or negative leverage

return on equity

DISCUSSION QUESTIONS

1. Given the information shown in Table 14.3, explain what is meant by "negative leverage." How is this determined? Since there is negative leverage, discuss the reasons for using borrowed funds in making this investment.

2. Using Table 14.3 as a source of information on a given property, list at least five items that would induce an investor to purchase this shopping center. Also, list at least five items that may be potential concerns to an investor.

3. The cash flow projections described in Table 14.1 show the current and projected features of a shopping center that is being

evaluated for potential investment. Discuss the five most important features that you would focus on and explain why you feel they are important.

4. Given the information in Table 14.1 and the fact that you as an investor wanted a 20 percent internal rate of return when you sell the property in four years, what items would you change and by how much to obtain this result? How realistic are these changes? Please justify each recommendation.

5. Using the information provided in Table 14.4 and assuming an 11 percent desired return on your equity, a debt

coverage ratio of 1.25, and a mortgage constant of 10.35, what should you offer for this property?

6. Using the Heights Colony Apartments information, and assuming a purchase price of $7,500,000, a down payment of 25 percent and an interest rate of 7.5 percent, what would be the cumulative cash flow (including the sale, before tax)?

7. Using the same information as in question 6, what would be the cumulative cash flow (including the sale, before tax) if you could purchase the project for $7,000,000?

8. Contact lenders in your area and determine the interest rates, debt coverage ratios, and LTVs that they are currently using for small apartment projects. Apply those to the Heights Colony Apartments and determine the optimum offering price.

9. The Great Recession has changed much of the real estate lending landscape. Speak with some local lenders and real estate professionals. What are some of the changes in real estate lending in your area for both homebuyers and real estate investors in the period from 2007 to late 2009?

CHAPTER 15

Managing Real Property Risk

An investor can acquire an interest in real estate several different ways. The investment can be a beneficial interest in a real estate trust. It can be as an inactive participant in a real estate syndicate or as a member of an LLC. Or the investment can be as an active owner. Whatever the investment method may be, risk management and evaluation is important.

From an income-producing standpoint, as well as for income tax purposes, there are several different categories of real property investment. Following are the principal distinctions:

1. *Income property* produces a return from leases spanning a month or longer, such as an apartment or office building. The IRS also identifies this kind of investment as trade or business property to separate it from investment property.
2. *Investment property* is the same as income property except that the investor retains minimal management responsibility and is subject to special tax limitations.
3. *Inventory property* derives its income from a sale or exchange, such as with vacant land or building lots or condominiums.
4. *Business-type real estate* produces income from the day-to-day sale of services, such as a restaurant, or day-to-day rental, such as a hotel. In both cases, specialized management produces income from a business operation separate from the rental of space alone.

The distinction between income property, investment property, and inventory property is concerned with tax law, as earlier described in the text.

The taxation of real estate income varies with changes in the tax law; the susceptibility of real estate returns to changing perceptions of risk is constant.

This chapter examines income property from the standpoint of risk management and some common concerns affecting all properties. These are principally leasing methods and the general operation of properties. This is followed by an evaluation of raw land, its risk as an investment, and its development for further construction purposes. The next chapter reviews major questions involved with the operation and marketing of the principal classes of income property and business-type property. First, a look at the special risks involved with assessing the reliability of an income stream.

RISK ASSOCIATED WITH INCOME STREAM

As previously discussed in this book, investment analysis of any kind is a study of risk. As an investment's risk increases, so must its expected return. When an investment is expected to yield a return from a continuing income stream, the character of that income must be carefully considered. Four traits of the income stream must be examined in terms of risk: (1) quantity, (2) quality, (3) durability, and (4) regulatory concerns (which are discussed in the next section).

Quantity

The more income a property produces, obviously, the more the property is worth. A property that produces $50,000 per year in net income is generally worth five times as much as a property that produces $10,000 in annual income. This is the most obvious component of risk, and by far the most amenable to comparison. The difficult aspect of measuring the quantity of income comes in determining the probability of its continued attainment. Is the expected income a realistic projection? Does the income figure include any noncash returns that would create a distorted comparison with another property's income? And is the quantity of income being compared with that of another property produced over a like period of time?

Quality

The quality of income refers primarily to the nature of the source of that income. A rental property consisting of rooms and small apartments that cater to transients is almost certainly worth less to an investor than a small, well-leased industrial warehouse—*even if the properties produce the same quantity of net income*. The *quality* of the two income streams makes the difference. The assurance represented by the well-leased industrial warehouse tips the balance, when compared with the uncertainties of a transient clientele. Yet present income and future projections may indicate an identical return for the same amount of investment. The quality of the income indicates the reliability of that income. Higher quality income is of lower risk, and has greater value!

Durability

Two main factors constitute the durability of income. One is the term of the assured income, and the other is the useful life of the property. A property with 15 years left on its lease has a more durable income than one with only three years to run. This is not to say that there are not potential advantages in a lease expiration—indeed, expiration can permit a new lease on better terms. But these possibilities must be weighed in light of the quantity and quality of the expected income.

The expected useful life of a property is always a limiting factor for the investor, especially when the analysis concerns an older property. As a property grows older, the costs of maintenance and repairs can absorb more and more of its expected income. Durability of income indicates the expected life of that income.

REGULATORY RISKS FOR LAND OWNERS

Two other areas of concern affect a land owner. They add additional risks and possible liabilities that must be evaluated. One is the effect of environmental protection rules and laws while the other is the removal of barriers to the disabled. Environmental concerns pose the potential for restrictions on the use of land. The various laws concerned with protection of the environment are examined in Chapter 3.

Concern for disabled people is addressed by the Americans with Disabilities Act, which is discussed next.

Americans with Disabilities Act

The Americans with Disabilities Act became law in July 1990. The Act attempts to remove barriers to disabled individuals in such areas as employment, transportation, and access to public facilities. While real estate investors should be aware of the broad nature of this Act, only that section of the Act addressing public accommodations is considered in this text.

Scope of the Act for Public Accommodations

The Act identifies "commercial facilities" as those intended for nonresidential use and whose operations will affect commerce. Specifically excluded from the Act are facilities covered or expressly exempted from coverage under the Fair Housing Act of 1968.

Public accommodations operated by private entities are covered by this Act if they affect commerce. Many accommodations are included in the list:

Hotels and motels.

Restaurants and bars.

Theaters, concert halls, and stadiums.

Grocery stores, clothing stores, hardware or shopping centers. Banks, laundromats, beauty shops and other service facilities. Terminals or depots.

Museums, libraries, or galleries.

Amusement parks, zoos, and other places of recreation.

Schools, nurseries, and other places of education.

Day care centers, senior citizen centers, and homeless shelters.

Gymnasiums, bowling alleys, or golf courses.

Discrimination Prohibited by Public Accommodations

No individual can be discriminated against on the basis of disability in the full and equal enjoyment of the goods, services, facilities, privileges, advantages, or accommodations of any place of public accommodation by any person who owns, leases, or operates a place of public accommodation. Providing unequal or separate facilities for disabled people is prohibited.

Specific Prohibitions Public accommodations covered by the Act must make reasonable modifications in policies, practices, or procedures where necessary to accommodate persons with disabilities. No person with disabilities may be excluded or denied services because of the absence of auxiliary aids unless taking such steps would fundamentally alter the nature of the good or service being offered or would result in an undue burden on the owner. Architectural and communication barriers to the disabled members of the public must be removed where such removal is readily achievable. If removal of such a barrier is not readily achievable, accommodations must be made available through alternative methods if such methods are readily achievable.

Practical Effect of the Act

While court rulings have had, and will continue to have, a substantial impact on the law, some of the issues have been made fairly clear. Following are some of the more obvious changes that need to be made in how buildings are structured:

- *Access.* Ramps and wide doorways are needed to better accommodate those using wheelchairs. New buildings for public usage will have wider hallways for this purpose.
- *Facilities.* Those with restricted reach need to be accommodated with lowered facilities: light switches and elevator buttons should be within easy reach, water fountains should either be lowered or provided with access to sanitary drinking cups. For other disabled persons, identification numbers, such as elevator floor numbers, should also be displayed in braille, and bathroom facilities need to be equipped with suitable hand bars.
- *Safety Equipment.* Fire and smoke alarm systems must function with both sound and flashing light warning signals.

Businesses are allowed special expense deductions for costs incurred in equipping a building for the handicapped.

LEASES

The types of leasehold estates have already been discussed in Chapter 4. That chapter examined the limited rights of ownership conveyed with a lease and gave a general outline of the laws that apply to leases. This section considers the types of lease and rental payment provisions most commonly used with income property. Based on how rentals are paid, leases for commercial properties fall into three categories (with combinations of these possible). These are term leases, net leases, and percentage leases.

Term Lease

The **term lease** is also called a gross lease or a flat sum lease. In legal terminology, it is a less-than-freehold estate in which the property is leased for a definite, fixed period of time and is identified as a tenancy for years. In most states, such a lease must be in writing if it extends beyond one year. Unless a statute, or an agreement, states otherwise, the tenancy is considered to be personal property and passes to the tenant's heirs upon death.

The services provided for tenants by the landlord vary with the lease conditions but commonly include the exterior maintenance of the building and parking lots, furnishing of all or a part of the utilities, trash disposal, and payment of all taxes and insurance for the building (but not its contents). These services have shown erratic cost increases and have popularized the use of general escalation clauses in all kinds of leases.

Escalation Clause

A clause in the rental agreement permitting an adjustment of rental payments, either up or down, to cover certain specified contingencies is an **escalation clause**. There are few limits to the types of cost items that may be included under escalation clauses. Landlords are wary of long-term commitments to furnish space and services to tenants because future costs are not determinable. As a result, the term lease often allows for annual adjustments in rent to compensate for increases in taxes, insurance, utilities, maintenance, and management. To provide a measure of protection for the tenant, the escalation provision usually requires the landlord to produce (1) some form of documentation of increases in operating costs and (2) details on how these costs are being allocated to each tenant. This allocation can be done on a basis of the square footage under lease or as a percentage of the space occupied in the building.

Further protection for the tenant facing an escalation clause would be a cap—a limitation on the amount of increase that can be charged in any one year. If there is an advantage for a tenant leasing under an escalation clause, it stems from permitting a lower initial rental rate. Otherwise, the landlord would have to estimate future costs and base the rent on speculative cost increases.

Service Agreement

Another method of handling the future possibility of fluctuating costs in a term lease is to separate the lease of space from the cost of specialized services. A separate agreement, or an addendum to the lease, can allow contract services such as maintenance of heating/air conditioning units, groundskeeping, and cleaning to be shared by the tenants in a fair and reasonable manner.

Net Lease

A **net lease** is one in which the tenant not only pays rent for the occupancy, but also pays for maintenance and operating expenses of the premises. This kind of lease is favored by investors who want a steady income without handling the problems associated with management and maintenance. Buildings offered for lease in this manner include free-standing facilities used by drug or grocery store chains, oil company service stations, and fast-food franchises.

While there is a broad range of such leases, the tenant is generally responsible for expenses relating to the premises as if the tenant were the owner. These expenses include such costs as real estate taxes; special assessments; insurance premiums; all maintenance charges, including labor and materials; cost of compliance with governmental health and safety regulations; payment of claims for personal injury or property damage; and even costs of structural, interior, roof, and other repairs.

With risk minimized, the rental charged is figured as a fair return on the invested capital only. The landlord retains such tax benefits as are available to real estate investment. However, a lease for longer than 30 years is subject to an IRS interpretation as ownership for the tenant. If so construed, the lease payments are treated as mortgage payments, and the tax benefits of ownership are passed to the tenant for the purpose of calculating tax liabilities.

There is some variation among real estate professionals in the way they use the word "net" when discussing such a lease. One interpretation is that the single word "net" means that the tenant pays all operating expenses *except* property taxes and insurance. The term "net, net" means the tenant pays all expenses *and* the insurance but not the property taxes. "Net, net, net"—or "triple net"—means what has been described above as a net lease, that is, the tenant pays all costs, including taxes and insurance. For example, a 1,200 square foot store in a 12,000 square foot strip might be responsible for 10 percent of the property taxes, landscaping, and insurance. For retail centers, these so-called **pass-throughs** average between $2.50 and $6.50 per square foot, depending on the property's age and location.

Escalation clauses are generally included in those net leases that require the landlord to pay for either taxes or insurance. Otherwise, the lease is written to provide a fixed return for the investor over the term of the lease.

Percentage Lease

A lease that bases the rental on a percentage of the monthly or annual gross sales made on the premises is a **percentage lease**. It is the most common lease form for stores and shopping centers. Rental payments are based on gross sales figures, not on any computation of profit. The use of sales figures to determine rental charges is most common for stores where products are sold, rather than where services are rendered (which occurs most often in office buildings). Sales figures can be easily verified through a lease clause that

(1) permits the landlord to audit the tenant's records or (2) requires periodic submittal of a certified copy of the tenant's sales tax reports.

There are three ways that rental can be computed in a percentage lease:

1. Straight percentage of gross sales.
2. Minimum base rental plus a percentage of gross sales.
3. Minimum base rental or a percentage of gross sales, whichever is larger.

For example, a store paying 4 percent of sales that has $1 million in sales will pay $40,000 in annual rent. To give some protection to the tenant, sometimes a ceiling, or cap, is included in the percentage rental. However, a minimum base rental is desirable because it provides the landlord with the protection of an assured income to cover mortgage payments and operating costs. Without a minimum, it is possible for a tenant to achieve a volume of sales on high margin merchandise that gives an adequate profit but does not provide the landlord with sufficient rental income to cover the costs of leasing the space.

An escalation clause appears in most percentage leases, but it is usually more flexible than a term lease's escalation clause. After all, under a percentage lease any increase in sales prices due to inflation (or any other cause) should result in an increased rental payment. Most commonly, the escalation provision adds to the minimum rent requirement all or part of any increases in taxes, insurance, or other agreed upon expenses. The escalation clause may permit the tenant to recapture an increase in the minimum rent caused by an escalation clause when the percentage rent exceeds certain specified levels.

Percentage leases give the shopping center owner a good incentive to cooperate with the tenants in advertising and promoting the center. Careful tenant selection and judicious placement of the stores within the center can achieve maximum benefit from shopping traffic; greater sales can thus be realized.

Rental Percentages

Several real estate organizations such as The Institute of Real Estate Management and the International Council of Shopping Centers publish percentage lease tables that can be used as general guidelines for lease negotiation. Some examples of percentage ranges as applied to various classes of merchants are shown in Table 15.1.

Lease Covenants

The **covenants** in a lease agreement specify what each party to the lease must, or must not, do with the premises. Lease conditions determine who pays for what. Following is a point-by-point consideration of the relevant expense allocations.

Taxes

Except under a net lease with special terms, property taxes are paid by the owner. Some leases call for an escalation in the rental structure if taxes increase. The exact responsibility for payment should be spelled out in each lease, including (1) whether the tenant pays all, some, or none of the base year's taxes; (2) when taxes are paid; and (3) how taxes are paid. If the

TABLE **15.1**

Examples of Lease Percentage Ranges

Business	Percent	Business	Percent
Auto supplies	3–5	Gift shops	7–10
Barber & beauty shops	7–10	Groceries (large)	1–2
Books & stationery	5–7	Hardware stores	4–6
Bowling lanes	8–9	Motion picture theaters	10–11
Cocktail lounge	8	Office supplies	4–6
Convenience store	4–6	Parking lot/attendant	40–60
Department stores	2–4	Restaurant & fast foods	5–7
Discount houses	1–2	Shoe stores	5–6
Drug stores	2–6	Sporting goods	5–7
Furniture	5–8	Toy stores	4–5
Gas stations (cents per gallon)	1½–8	Women's dress shops	6–7

tenant's operations create an increase in the tax assessment, this should also be anticipated by the lease. (Any taxes due on the tenant's property could become a claim against the landlord if protection is not provided.)

Insurance

The landlord usually pays for hazard insurance for the premises. A tenant does have the right to know how the leasehold interest is being protected against loss, and may require the landlord to provide a copy of the insurance policy. If the cost of insurance increases, the increase may be prorated to the tenant in accordance with an escalation clause. If the activities of the tenant create an increased risk for the property, the resulting increase in insurance cost may be passed on to the tenant.

Other types of coverage must be considered in lease agreements. The landlord may require that the tenant maintain liability insurance with a protective clause in favor of the landlord. If plate glass is a part of the premises, a separate insurance policy may be required (it can be the responsibility of either the landlord or the tenant). Any other special risk of exposure that must be covered should be spelled out in the lease agreement.

Maintenance

Under the normal division of costs between a landlord and tenant in rental property, the landlord pays for exterior maintenance and the tenant pays for interior maintenance. But the line between exterior and interior is not always easy to define; it needs to be defined in the lease. Such things as electric-eye-operated doors, exterior lighting for the special use of the tenant, trash and garbage areas, and exterior protective screens or walls used only by the tenant are all subject to dispute if maintenance requirements are not clearly detailed in the lease.

Parking

The lease agreement should detail the tenant's rights to parking facilities, both for employees and for the tenant's customers. Furthermore, the lease should allocate the costs of lighting and upkeep for the parking area (in whatever shares may be agreed upon by the parties). Additional charges on a per-car basis are sometimes written in lease agreements, especially for office buildings. Or employees may be offered parking privileges in exchange for a pay reduction, the amount depending on the accessibility of the space. At large shopping centers, the common practice is to set aside a specific area—away from major customer traffic patterns—which is reserved for employee parking.

Improvements and Trade Fixtures

A lease should specify who pays for improvements and who pays for trade fixtures. Normally, improvements are made by the landlord and added to the rental price. Improvements remain the property of the landlord. Trade fixtures usually belong to the tenant, are paid for by the tenant, and may be removed by the tenant at the termination of the lease. "Improvements" might include new walls or bathrooms; trade fixtures the pizza ovens in a new pizza joint. Trade fixtures installed by the landlord may become a part of the leased premises as a sales inducement for the tenant. If so, the landlord's ownership should be clearly determined in advance. Structural changes in the building may be agreed upon, but are generally not a part of the tenant's leasehold rights.

Terms, Payments, and Conditions

The term of the lease should be clearly stated, as should the date or time that rental payments become due. Different payment deadlines may apply to a base rent and to a percentage (or gallonage, in the case of a service station), so as to allow time for computation or verification. If the lease permits any adjustments in rental payments (such as the recapture of tax and insurance payments against a percentage over base rent), when these adjustments are allowed should be clarified in the lease. And it should specify the time that any escalation payments become due.

Many other conditions that limit leasehold rights may be included in the lease. The lease may or may not be assignable. If it is assignable, what are the continuing obligations of the original tenant? The lease should say. Limitations are usually placed on how the property may be used as a protection to other tenants and to the landlord's continuing property value. Furthermore, the right to sublet all or part of the leasehold interest may or may not be granted under the original lease.

OPERATION AND INCOME PROPERTIES

All types of income property have substantial similarity in basic areas of operation. These include management of the premises and proper handling of tenants plus control of the utilities and other services.

Management

All income properties require management—some more, some less. An operating property is a form of business that requires the collection of rents, the keeping of records, and the protection and maintenance of the property itself. The investor must either hire outside management or be willing to spend time handling the management responsibilities. These responsibilities are (1) maintenance of the premises, which includes both repairs and capital improvements; (2) securing, screening, and locating tenants in the most effective way; (3) collecting rents in a timely manner; (4) supervising all operating personnel; and (5) controlling the use of the premises by tenants and their customers.

Maintaining the Premises

Income properties are usually maintained, at least in part, by the landlord or owner. Even though tenants may be responsible for maintaining interior walls and some of the heating or air conditioning equipment, the landlord should specify minimum maintenance standards. Various levels of maintenance are required, depending on the type of property and the conditions of the lease. Because of this flexibility, maintenance duties should be detailed in the lease agreement, for example, how often the tenant can require exterior painting, and so on.

As for capital improvements, such as the replacement of an air conditioning unit or the addition of a new sales area, the management should have written guidelines in the lease in order to make a fair allocation of costs to the tenants. An addition to the premises of one tenant may conflict with the premises of another, so the rights of the tenants need to be settled in advance.

Securing and Screening Tenants

Securing occupancy of a building may be done through leasing agents or through the owner's advertising and sales representation. The quality of tenants is always a major problem for the landlord and can easily determine an operation's success or failure. Management must seek the kind of tenants that fit the use intended for the building, that is, the type of work and services they perform should be compatible, and the customer groups they serve must be similar. An office building catering to the medical profession is not a suitable location for a nightclub. A shopping center with predominantly low prices and discount stores is not attractive to an exclusive dress shop.

Tenants of all types must be screened for financial responsibility. Major companies are often the preferred risk, of course. But in fact most tenants are small—as well as new to the area when the initial lease is consummated—and they should be investigated for their previous records of operations and creditworthiness. Evicting an undesirable tenant can be expensive and is better avoided by careful advance screening.

Both tenant and landlord have an interest in where an office, shop, or storage facility is located within a building complex. The choice of location can be based on (1) the flow of customer traffic (most important for a shopping center), (2) the availability of required utilities, or (3) the ease of access to transportation or to the handling of materials. Naturally, the choice of locations is more flexible in a new building than in an existing building, and immediate optimum use of the space is easier to accomplish. With an existing property that has tenants, it may be desirable to reject even a highly qualified prospective tenant if locating that tenant in the only space available could jeopardize future operations and leasing.

Collecting Rents

A most important chore of management is to make sure rentals are paid in accordance with the lease requirements. Delinquent rent should be investigated as there may be a mitigating circumstance and payment can be reinstated in a timely fashion. An additional charge for late payment is not uncommon. Eviction of a tenant unable to pay the normal rental in a timely manner can be costly but is necessary when conditions warrant such action.

Supervising Operating Personnel

Property owners often try to avoid becoming burdened with personnel problems—payroll records, personal issues, the complex set of equal employment and labor relations laws, and the need for constant supervision. Larger income properties can afford to employ highly competent, professional managers to handle personnel responsibilities. Medium-sized and smaller operations may prefer to use contract management companies, which are growing rapidly all over the country and provide much-needed expertise. Smaller property owners may simply serve as their own managers, aided by one or two maintenance and service employees.

Using service contractors is another growing method of avoiding the problems of directly employing people. Many services can be furnished by contractors, including janitorial service, maintenance of heating and air conditioning equipment, periodic and minor plumbing repairs, painting, and window washing. Many larger cities have contracting companies that provide all-inclusive services for operating properties.

Controlling the Use of the Premises

One of the most difficult management responsibilities is that of controlling how the premises are used after leases have been signed. A loosely drawn lease may leave a tenant free to operate a shop or office any way she sees fit. A leasehold does grant the rights of possession and use, but the landlord retains the right to protect the property against loss of value that may result from misuse. Limits on use may be spelled out in the lease, based on customary use, or negotiated between the building management and the tenant. Careful advance planning is the best procedure to prevent conflicts in this area. Unfortunately, even careful planning is not fail-safe—businesses change, and sometimes their products or services are changed by market requirements. When things do change, the interpretation and settlement of conflicting situations becomes a management responsibility. For example, a tenant restaurant that replaces its piano bar with pornographic entertainment can diminish the value of the property for other tenants—and create different problems for the management. But pornography has proven difficult to define, even by the courts. So management must walk a thin line in dealing with the change. Consider one more example: The introduction of a new chemical process or electronic testing procedure—which may later prove hazardous to occupants, customers, or the building itself—is always of concern to an alert management.

The tenants' customers are even more difficult to control, and sometimes necessitate security agreements in the lease. This is especially true for large shopping centers, which can become hangouts for undesirable characters. This problem must also be considered as the landlord examines prospective tenants and the types of automobile and pedestrian traffic they are likely to attract to the premises.

Utilities and Other Services

The furnishing of utilities and various other services to the tenant are still very much an accepted part of the covenants found in an income property lease. But increasingly, they are excluded from the obligations of the landlord. Landlords once paid for almost all utilities, arguing that utilities could be furnished to tenants most cheaply through the use of a single master meter. Today that practice has given way to separate meters for each tenant, or to a strict allocation to each tenant of the month-to-month costs. Rapidly rising utility costs are, of course, the reason.

Landlords are also attempting to shed their obligations for as many non-utility services as possible.

Utilities

Included in the category of utilities are electricity, natural gas, water, and sewer facilities. The trend among landlords is to pass on these expenses to their tenants.

Electricity   This cost is most easily separated from the landlord's responsibility through the use of a separate meter, very much like telephone service is separated. Commercial properties have long used separate meters to allow each tenant to pay electric charges. Apartment owners once tried to use a single meter, furnishing electricity to tenants as a part of the services provided under their basic rental payment. But, newer apartment houses are including separate meters for each apartment, and older units are converting to separate meters where possible. When conversion is not practical in much older buildings, landlords usually allocate the single-meter costs so that each tenant pays a proportionate part of the total cost. Common area electricity consumption (for hallways, parking lots and other common areas) is shared according to the lease agreement.

Natural Gas   Gas is not always a necessity for apartments and office buildings. But when gas is used, it is generally handled the same way as electricity, that is, separate meters for new buildings and allocation of cost increases for older buildings with single meters. Industrial and commercial use of natural gas is almost always measured through separate meters, since it is more often a processing component than a landlord-provided service.

Water Potable water is far more precious today than it was only a few years ago. Yet even now many lease agreements for apartments, office buildings, or smaller commercial buildings do not call for separate metering of water. Rental increases in term leases and escalation clauses in commercial leases generally have been sufficient protection for the landlord to justify continuing this service as part of the leasehold rights. Larger commercial properties and industrial buildings are more easily adapted to separate water metering, and they usually do provide this separation.

Sewer Sewage disposal is usually provided (and charged for) by the same entity that furnishes water, often a municipally owned utility plant. Sewage services are generally more costly than water fees, and are billed along with the water, based upon water consumption.

Other Building Services

The kinds of services provided for tenants vary substantially and are often negotiated at the time a lease is drawn up. Following is a brief review of the services most commonly found in the leasing of income properties.

Janitorial Service Sweeping, cleaning, and polishing public areas are services provided in shopping centers, apartments, and office buildings. In addition, office buildings often provide the same service for tenants' office space. Older lease forms usually included this kind of maintenance as a part of the building services covered by the basic rental fee. Now some landlords are assessing these costs as a separate monthly maintenance charge that is determined by the costs incurred. Office buildings that provide cleaning services for the tenants' offices include this cost in escalation clauses.

Building Maintenance Service Painting and plumbing, electrical, and other building repairs are normally the responsibility of the landlord. Lease provisions define the tenant's area of responsibility (usually interior maintenance) and the landlord's. As maintenance costs increase, the landlord may want to include repairs in the escalation clause, thereby permitting an increase in rent to cover the added costs. The need for repairs is unpredictable—unlike cleaning services—so they are not as easily translated into a monthly service charge. However, some leases allow for an all-inclusive service charge that includes repairs as they become necessary.

Heating and Air Conditioning With some forms of income property—such as warehouses, shopping centers, and other commercial buildings—it has long been possible for the landlord to require that the tenant furnish, install, and maintain the heating and air conditioning equipment. The tenant's responsibility for maintenance expense includes the potential of lost sales (as would occur if a store's air conditioning failed for an extended period of high summertime temperatures). Normally the rental structure in these cases reflects the landlord's lower investment. In an office building with multiple occupancy, heating and air conditioning are considered part of the services offered to the tenant. The general practice is to include maintenance of this equipment in escalation clauses, allowing for annual increases.

Trash Disposal   This is an optional service that may be assigned to either the landlord or the tenant, depending on the terms of the lease. The disposition of trash has become an increasingly difficult problem—suitable dumping grounds are becoming scarcer and farther removed from the source of the trash. However, there has been some recognition of the salvage value in trash, and a few companies have devised their own procedures for separating usable materials from waste. Recycling of paper, plastics, glass, and many metals has become the norm. For instance, office buildings that contain large accounting operations—and, thus, large quantities of good quality waste paper—may recover marketable materials through a simple sorting of the trash. While trash disposal is still commonly seen as an expensive nuisance, environmental concerns are growing. What some have found is that reducing pollution can also be profitable.

Security Systems   Alarmed by criminal activity, businesses have sought better methods to protect their investments. This is another service that may be the responsibility of either the tenant or the landlord. In practice, only larger office buildings consider a moderate form of security to be the landlord's responsibility; even then, the landlord accepts no liability.

Shopping centers usually provide for security through a merchants' association where each contributes a portion of the cost of maintaining guards and a security system. Owners of small buildings with a single tenant or a small number of tenants have considered security wholly the responsibility of the tenant(s) and often do not refer to the subject in leases. However, security is a matter of growing concern, and one that should be defined in all lease covenants.

While landlords have preferred a hands-off approach to security, a property owner is well-advised to cooperate with the tenant in furnishing property protection. Meeting requirements of the Americans with Disabilities Act mandates certain security measures in all public accommodations. Fire warning systems can reduce both insurance premiums and the potential for loss. Smoke detection units are mandated for residential rental property in many states. Sonic monitors detect sound and movement under the scanning unit in or on the premises. Electric eyes and laser-beam-type instruments can detect break-ins, and possibly prevent or reduce property damage from vandalism or robbery. Centrally located monitors have reduced the costs of surveillance to the point where even small companies (and many homeowners) find the service attractive.

LAND AS AN INVESTMENT

As an investment, raw land entails some special risks. Such land may be held for appreciation and resale to others for their use and development. Or the land may be developed into lots for sale to home builders or industrial parks for commercial developments. Land held for resale to others is deemed inventory property by the IRS.

Inventory Property

"Property held for inventory" is a term used by the IRS to distinguish undeveloped land or other property held for appreciation and future sale. The risk associated with this kind of property is very difficult to measure because the property lacks an existing income stream that can be evaluated. Its value depends on a successful sale at some point in the future. Because of this problem, many analysts prefer to classify such acquisitions as speculation, rather than investment. Regardless of the terminology, there are some guidelines that are helpful even though they do not lend themselves to straightforward statistical analysis.

Chapter 1 identifies the types of return that may be realized from real estate as (1) income, (2) appreciation, and (3) value gain. The tax shelter offered by real estate was also mentioned. It is appreciation (the passive form of increase in investment value) and value gain (the active input of expertise by the owner or management, resulting in an increase in property value) that provide the guidelines for examinations of inventory-type property.

Land Selection

Population growth patterns and the restrictions on land use directly affect future land value. Care must be taken in the selection of a tract of undeveloped land to be held for appreciation to ensure that it lies in the general path of population growth, that potential zoning problems will not grossly inhibit future use, and that utility systems and transportation patterns will support future use. The key word is "use"—basic land value is increased in direct relation to its growth in usefulness. It is the change in the land's usage capability that causes value to increase (or decrease).

Financing Land Acquisition

Loans to finance the acquisition of undeveloped land are not generally favored by lenders. Heavy investment by savings associations in land suitable for development was one of the major causes of their failure in the 1980s. And the commercial landscape was cluttered with failed sub-divisions following the Great Recession.

Nevertheless, if an investor can borrow money to acquire the land, the leverage achieved can enhance a return. Example 15.1, which shows the value of leverage in land acquisition intended for resale, helps explain the attraction. In Example 15.1, two scenarios are considered, one with and one without financing. The financial risk, and reward, is clear. In the all-cash example in Panel A, the investor pays $50,000 for the property, suffers annual property tax and insurance expenses of $1,600 per acre, and sells the property in three years for $80,000, paying a 6 percent commission against the sale price. The cash flows are described in the example. The internal rate of return (IRR) on this investment? Using the BA II Plus, though any financial calculator will suffice, an IRR of 11.8 percent is observed. With the use of financing in Panel B, an IRR of 18.3 percent is seen. That return is achieved with a 20 percent down payment of $10,000 per acre, the same tax and insurance costs as with the cash deal ($1,600 per acre per year) and $3,600 in interest per year to fund the $40,000 borrowed at 9 percent per year. The mortgage is paid off at the sale, and the same sales commission is paid as with the cash deal. The risk in this environment arises if the land does not sell as planned, or sells at a lower price. After three years, the investor has invested an additional $10,800 ($3,600 in interest for each of three years) in each acre of land. Ignoring the commission, he needs $20,800 to break even. The additional risk of the leveraged purchase is readily apparent; to achieve that higher IRR of 18.3 percent, the investor must expose himself to the greater risk that comes with borrowing. Given this risk, some speculative land investors or developers expect returns of 30 percent or more per year, with values doubling every three years or less, on this sort of investment. That would make this example one that the typical investor might reject.

EXAMPLE 15.1   *Consider a tract costing $50,000 per acre.*

Assume that after three years the land can be sold for $80,000 per acre, with the costs and cash flows as indicated below, first in Panel A with no financing and second in Panel B with 80 percent financing.

Panel A: All Cash Deal

$50,000 purchase price

$1600 per year in property taxes and insurance

$4,800 (6% of $80,000) sales commission upon sale in three years

$80,000 selling price in three years, price reduced by costs of sale (commission)

IRR using the BA II Plus

CF0 = −50,000 (the property purchase)

CO1 = −1,600 (annual property tax and insurance payment)

FO1 = 2 (accounting for two years of property tax and insurance payments after purchase)

CO2 = 73,600 ($80,000 price minus a $4,800 commission and minus $1,600 in taxes and insurance)

FO2 = 1 (accounting for the single net cash flow of $73,600 at the end of year three)

IRR, CPT, *IRR = 11.8%*

Panel B: Using 80% financing

$10,000 down payment per acre (20% of $50,000)

$1,600 per year in property taxes and insurance

$3,600 per year (9% of $40,000) in interest

$4,800 (6% of $80,000) sales commission upon sale in three years

$80,000 selling price in three years, price reduced by costs of sale (commission), the last year's interest, taxes and insurance and the mortgage payoff

IRR using the BA II Plus

CF0 = −$10,000 (the down payment of 20% of $50,000)

CO1 = −$5,200 (the annual costs of $1,600 in taxes and insurance and $3,600 in interest)

FO2 = 2 (accounting for two years of property tax and insurance and interest payments)

CO2 = 30,000 ($80,000 price minus $1,600 in taxes and insurance, a $4,800 commission, $3,600 in interest and a $40,000 loan payoff)

FO2 = 1 (accounting for the single net cash flow of $30,000 at the end of year three)

IRR, CPT, *IRR = 18.3%*

Timing

Timing is the key to success in holding land for profitable resale. The longer land is held, the greater the holding costs. Appreciation does not increase land values at a steady rate. Rather, increases come in spurts as potential use changes. Over a period of years, a tract of land may proceed through a whole litany of potential uses. It may first be suitable for single family residences, then for higher-density housing, then for light commercial use, then for a high-traffic shopping center or office building, and finally for high-rise structures. With each change in potential use, the land value jumps upward. So the basic question is: At what point can a specific piece of land be sold with a maximum differential between its cost (plus holding charges) and its selling price? The answer depends on the local situation. Astute landowners try to project the length of time until the next change in usage may occur, then decide if the costs of holding will be justified by the resulting increase in value.

Holding Land

There is no requirement that a land investor stand idly by and wait for the land to increase in value. On the contrary, many dealers in land find it advantageous to make some use of the land during the holding period. There are a number of ways for the landowner to recover at least some income from the property to help pay the taxes. The problem is to find a use for the land that neither encumbers it with a long-term lease commitment, nor alters the land itself in a way that could discourage a higher use later on.

Following are some suggestions for interim land use, which have general application in all regions. Note, however, that what is practical for a particular tract of land depends on its location and nearby population density.

1. Recreational facilities, such as playing fields for rent, or small race tracks are not uncommon.
2. Parking lots are a standard holding procedure for high-value downtown land.
3. Carnivals, fairs, outdoor concerts, and other special shows may rent land for short-term periods.

4. Mobile home parks in some areas have been used as a good way to ware-house land. Utilities can be designed for higher land use at a later time.
5. Golf courses have been used by some large developers to hold land for later development.
6. Farming partnerships for crop production, with season-to-season leases, are common.
7. Timber can be harvested from forested tracts.
8. Sod or turf production for replanting can be developed on land that is not intended for further use as farm land.

It is the local demand for usable land that best determines what interim use, if any, is most practical. In some cases, the temporary use has developed sufficient profit to justify continuing its operation. There is always the possibility that the higher use for the property may not materialize, and the interim use may be the only viable alternative. So, even if the landowner must make a sacrifice to accommodate an interim use, it is a good hedge against the future if the cost is not too great.

LAND DEVELOPMENT

Land may be acquired for holding; it also may be acquired for development. For the purpose of this discussion, development includes building streets and installing utility systems to service houses or commercial buildings that may be constructed at a separate time. Land development is an integral part of the design and construction work involved in most large apartment complexes and other commercial projects. Smaller builders, however, both residential and commercial, depend on developers to do the land planning, construct the service facilities, and then sell the finished lots to them.

Financing land development is an easier procedure than financing the acquisition of raw land. Restrictions have been placed on insured depository institutions on the loan-to-value ratio of land loans. These restrictions became particularly onerous, requiring developers to come up with 40 or 50 percent down payments, in the years leading up to 2010. Down payments of 25 percent or less were common only a few years earlier.

Among developers, LLCs are the favored ownership form, where clear descriptions of the risks and duties of the individual investors can be provided. These LLCs largely replace the joint ventures and real estate syndicates of yore, though for some large-scale developments where lenders desire some sort of equity interest, the joint ventures or syndicates may still be used. The LLC, though, is becoming more and more common.

Mortgage Clauses

A land development loan is usually made with a mortgage lien in favor of the lender covering the entire tract of land. Two covenants that have special application to a development loan are normally included. These are the plan used for development and the requirements for partial release of completed lots.

The Development Plan

In some cases, the lender specifies the order in which the mortgaged property can be developed. The purpose is to assure the continuing value of the entire tract during the development period. The plan must be agreeable to the borrower-developer and is generally a logical procedure to encourage a complete development.

The Release Clause and Bridge Financing

The initial mortgage on the entire development tract must provide a mechanism to permit the sale of lots to others as they are developed. This is most commonly accomplished by requiring a minimum payment of cash to the lender for each lot released, according to the terms of the **release clause**.

For example, a 20-acre property in north Florida was sold in the 1980s, and the seller got a mortgage for 75 percent of the purchase price of around $200,000. The mortage was for just under $150,000. As each one acre portion of the property was sold, the developer of the property who bought it had to pay off close to $15,000 to get the lot "released" from the master mortgage. The math makes intuitive sense: by the time the developer sold half the lots (each representing one-twentieth of the total), he had paid off the entire $150,000. Each lot was "released" so the individual lot purchaser could get a mortgage to buy the lot. Much of the purchase price flowed through the developer to the mortgage holder on the entire property, but some was "left behind" for the developer, he waiting until the sale of the last ten lots for his big payoff!

Bridge financing allows land developers to use borrowed funds to build homes, providing temporary mortgage financing until the home is complete and permanent financing can be arranged, typically by the home's purchaser. Similar financing is available to the lot-buyer, who borrows funds to build a home on her new lot, with monies being periodically released to the builder during construction. When the home is complete, and a certificate of occupancy is provided by local inspectors, *permanent* mortgage financing replaces the "bridge."

Lots

The above discussion of finished lots applies to land that is developed for the purpose of constructing buildings. But, not all lots offered for sale are suitable for building. In some states—primarily Florida, Arizona, and California—developers have acquired large tracts of land in relatively remote areas and divided them into lots of from one to ten acres each. These lots are then offered for sale through mass advertising programs, with small down payments and the balance in monthly payments over five to ten years. Many of these tracts are years away from practical development and have disappointed many buyers.

To prevent misrepresentation and outright fraud in this type of land sale, Congress created the Office of Interstate Land Sales Registration (OILSR) in 1968 to operate under the Department of Housing and Urban Development (HUD). The OILSR has since established specific rules and requirements under which land developers may offer their lots for sale. Severe penalties can be assessed against developers for failure to comply with the requirements. Essentially, the requirements call for full disclosure of information regarding the landownership, tax rates, proximity to schools, available utilities, and plans for future development.

Government regulations of this type are not directed toward the prudent investor, who examines in detail all aspects of a property and inspects the property before signing a contract to buy. The purpose of these regulations is to help protect the general public from unscrupulous promoters.

SOME CONCLUDING REMARKS ON MANAGING REAL ESTATE RISK

Whether purchasing a tract of rural land for later development, or buying an oft-vacant strip shopping center as an income-generating investment, any real estate investor faces varying levels of risk. Where that risk is greater, as noted regularly throughout this text, the value of the cash flows generated by the investment is lower. The greater risk attracts a higher discount rate, and whatever the size of a project's expected future cash flows, the present value of those flows is reduced with that higher discount or cap rate.

Managing the risk of properties already purchased, as with special attention to tenant selection and an owner's overall care for a property, should be a key objective of any owner. Where a property is properly cared for, attention is paid to the day-to-day operating details, and the owner does her best to address the small issues before they become cumbersome (as with something as simple as litter in a parking lot); the perceived risk of that property might be reduced relative to its peers. And, where risk is reduced for a given set of expected cash flows, the property's value is enhanced. It is towards managing the risk, and enhancing property value, that the real estate investor should direct her attention continuously. This is one of the principal manners with which the investor might create value over time.

The ubiquitous "flipper" may have been in the headlines in the early 2000s, making a profit through property purchases and sales over a period of only weeks. Those investors learned the limits of their trading "programs" by 2006 or 2007. It is with the longer haul, however, that attractive returns can be generated, based on something other than luck.

KEY TERMS

bridge financing	escalation clause	pass-throughs	release clause
covenants	net lease	percentage lease	term lease

DISCUSSION QUESTIONS

1. Discuss risk associated with an income stream.

2. List three important requirements of the Americans with Disabilities Act.

3. How can a term lease incorporate protection for the landlord against fluctuations in costs?

4. What responsibilities are normally handled by the management of an income property?

5. List three interim uses of undeveloped land while holding it for further development later.

6. What are some of the ways, overall, that a property manager might reduce the risk of a property's income streams?

7. Describe the risks attached to using leverage in land development.

8. What is a release clause and how does it facilitate land development?

CHAPTER 16

Marketing Investment Property

Independent of the particular economic environment in which a real estate investor is operating, certain issues confront him as he decides how best to "sell" his property and optimize his real estate investment income; a cornerstone of this optimization is the manner with which the real estate is marketed. In whatever kind of property an investor is interested, there is a need to study the market for its product. In this sense, the "product" of income property is rent: apartment rentals, office rentals, or store rentals. Successful investment is that which can market its product. If the product or services offered by the property are not marketable, the property itself suffers the same fate. Each kind of property is analyzed from a slightly different approach to the marketing question. For instance, an apartment developer studies local area occupancy rates and competing rental rates; for office buildings, the focus is more on potential business growth and the ability of the area to absorb additional space; and for shopping centers, the analysis is based on population in the area, traffic patterns, and income levels.

This chapter examines the special problems associated with major classes of investment property. These include (1) apartments, (2) office buildings, (3) retail store centers, (4) warehouse buildings, (5) special purpose buildings, and (6) business properties.

_____

APARTMENTS

Of the major types of income property investment, an apartment building offers a transient—and sometimes unstable—form of rental. Leases are often on a month-to-month basis, and termination by the tenant is seldom difficult. The continued high occupancy rate of an apartment is more dependent on its competitive location, management, and operating policies than are income properties offering long-term business leases. The unique problems associated with apartment properties can be summarized under the following headings:

1. Location.
2. The **building amenities**.
3. **Optimum mix** of apartment units.
4. Rules and regulations.
5. Furnished versus unfurnished apartments.
6. Nondiscrimination requirements.

Location

An apartment is, of course, a residence. Tenants expect a reasonable proximity to schools, shopping facilities, churches, and recreational areas. In addition, the apartment dweller wants easy access to transportation (freeways, buses, or trains) and to places of employment. Some successful apartment operators consider location the most important factor in maintaining a good occupancy rate. Others consider a good location of equal importance to sound management and an attractive building.

The Building and Its Amenities

An attractive, well-maintained building is obviously more desirable than a rundown property. As it competes with other apartments in the same area, the physical condition of the buildings and amenities (pool, tennis courts, clubhouse, and so on) govern an apartment's rental value. Higher rentals can generally be sustained by the apartment that offers better physical facilities, so long as the overall charges are reasonably competitive for the neighborhood.

Optimum Mix of Apartment Units

An essential element of continued good occupancy is the ability to offer the types of units that meet local market requirements. In larger cities, where apartment dwellers are a growing segment of total housing, the older "shotgun" approach to variations in the units offered has given way to careful research designed to determine precisely what the market requires. In smaller cities, it is common to mix the number of one-, two-, and three-bedroom apartments in an arbitrary manner that should offer something for everyone. In areas of increasing competition among apartment owners, the effort is directed along the guidelines furnished by market analysis. For example, in an area catering to young couples and singles, the demand may be for one-bedroom or studio-type units. Where the market is dominated by older couples and retirees, the best occupancy can be achieved in one- and two-bedroom units that emphasize ground-floor units and few stairs. There is a growing apartment market for larger families seeking less maintenance work when both husband and wife work at outside jobs. Or the family may want to live in an apartment while saving the money to purchase a home. Three- and even four-bedroom units are needed to accommodate these larger families.

When an investor uses apartment occupancy rates as a guide for additional construction, it should be noted that a distortion can occur during periods of high occupancy (generally in excess of 95 percent). Under these conditions, tenants may be living in larger, or smaller, units than they desire, until more suitable accommodations become available.

Rules and Regulations

One of the most difficult problems facing apartment management is establishing and enforcing equitable rules. People object to being told that their particular lifestyle is disturbing to a neighbor. Yet rules are very important and are primarily for the benefit of all tenants.

All rules should be clearly explained to the prospective tenants before a rental agreement is concluded. Tenants have a right to know what is expected. Besides that, an understanding of the rules and the reasons for them is the first step toward good enforcement. The rules should cover how and when the public areas (such as a pool) may be used, the hours during which noise levels are restricted, the proper disposition of trash and garbage, the parking requirements, any limitations on improvements or decorating within the rented unit, restrictions applicable to pets, and any limits on the activities of children. The apartment owner should keep in mind that a major cause of moveouts is incompatibility with a neighbor. Rules can help avoid potential conflicts.

Furnished Versus Unfurnished Apartments

A choice facing all apartment owners is whether to offer furnished or unfurnished units. Three factors are involved in making this decision: (1) a market requirement, (2) stable occupancy, and (3) additional income.

A Requirement of the Particular Market

In some neighborhoods, essentially the only way an apartment may be rented is to offer it furnished. If a survey of the market shows generally that furnished apartments are well-rented while unfurnished units are standing vacant, the apartment owner has little choice but to furnish.

To Stabilize Occupancy

Again, the market in the area controls whether or not a furnished apartment prolongs average tenancy. Generally, tenants with their own furniture will remain longer than those without. With a furnished apartment, tenants tend to judge the unit by the quality of the furniture, rather than by the quality of the unit itself; an exchange of furniture can thus provide a reason for continued occupancy. Another consideration in the furniture question is that unfurnished apartments can require more decorating because of possible damage to walls and doors as the tenants' furniture is moved in and out. Also, the unfurnished apartment presents a bare look to a prospective tenant, which may make it more difficult to rent.

Many tenants see the question of furnished or unfurnished units as a minor consideration in the length of occupancy. More important concerns for them are such items as compatibility with neighbors and their personal situations such as their progressing income levels.

In order to maximize occupancy and revenues, it may be necessary to adopt an advertising program. Exhibit 16.1 lists numerous items that could be considered in developing a program. The extent of the program will depend on the size, age, rental structure, and other features of the subject property.

EXHIBIT 16.1   **Apartment Project Advertising Strategy—The Bonita Apartments**

- Type of property: luxury, mid-rise apartments located in midtown
- Demand: business professionals, students, people looking for downtown living *(target audience)*
- Focus on amenities: swimming pool, health club, laundry room, activities room, concierge service, valet parking, all underground parking for tenants
- Focus on location: downtown location, theater district, medical center, inner loop, restaurants, entertainment, sporting events
- Display ads that feature amenities and focus on the central location of this mid-rise apartment
    - *Apartment Guide, Apartment Finder, The Daily News, The Central City Press*
- Press releases—focusing on the new development in midtown
    - *The Daily News, Uptown Magazine, Paper City, Envy*
- Internet sites and a home page with information about the property, such as photos, floor plans, and online application
- Television ads that feature the new project
- Signs that show availability and features
- Billboards near the property's location.

Other techniques to help ensure optimum occupancy:

- Free rent on valid leases (for example, one month free on a twelve month lease) or other types of promotions
- Referral fees for new tenants
- Relocation services such as corporate discounts
- Student discounts for local university students who attend full-time
- Working with local realtors
- Hiring a leasing agent who remains on the premises to show units
- Promotional coupons, for example, bring in the advertisement and receive first month's rent or no deposit
- Open house

For Additional Income

The rental of furniture to apartment dwellers is a big business in most major cities. Many apartment owners rent furniture as a sideline business. Larger operators can buy furniture at wholesale, then offer it for rent at the capitalized value of the retail price. Furniture is generally rented at a price that will pay for the furniture in about one-half of its useful life. And, there is often a residual value in the repair and resale of the used furniture. The return on the investment in furniture can prove to be greater than the return on the real property.

Nondiscrimination Requirements

Apartment leasing is, of course, subject to the nondiscrimination requirements of the Civil Rights Act of 1968 and subsequent additions to it. The Act requires the sale and leasing of all housing to be handled without concern for race, color, religion, sex, or national origin of the purchaser or lessee. An amendment to the Act that became effective in 1989 expands the protective provisions to handicapped persons and to people with children under the age of 18, called "**familial status.**"

Handicapped

An individual is defined as being handicapped if he or she has a physical or mental impairment, including AIDS or the HIV virus. Exceptions to the handicapped provision include those addicted to a controlled substance and those whose tenancy imposes a direct threat to the health, safety, and property of others. However, there are few guidelines as to how to make these determinations. Under the Fair Housing Law, a tenant may make reasonable modifications to the premises (at the handicapped person's expense) and must restore the unit to its original use upon termination of occupancy.

Familial Status

The definition of familial status is one or more individuals under the age of 18 domiciled with a parent or another person having legal custody of the individual(s). The effect of this protective provision is that apartment projects must not restrict occupancy by families with children except as may be necessary to comply with local health and safety limitations on the number of persons per room. Available facilities must be adapted for children. There are exceptions to the rule, primarily for housing devoted to the elderly.

Screening of Tenants

One of the many important advantages that come from experience in apartment management is the ability to screen prospective tenants in a fair and reasonable manner. The problem of screening has become more difficult because of the need to be nondiscriminatory. The landlord's desire to obtain immediate full occupancy must be tempered by the longer-range goal of maintaining that occupancy. Noise, objectionable use of the premises, and a tendency to vandalism are all qualities that can be detrimental to an apartment owner, who has an implied obligation to maintain a reasonable living standard for all tenants. One first-time apartment owner recently bemoaned the fact that he never realized a tenant would consider the living room carpet a suitable place to change the oil in his motorcycle!

Most sellers of apartment properties are unwilling to provide detailed information concerning their property until a prospective buyer has indicated a strong interest in the possible purchase. Typically, information similar to that shown in Exhibit 16.2 is provided in order to stimulate sufficient interest to generate an offer to purchase. In some cases an option agreement is entered into giving the prospective buyer the right to access much more detailed information. The option agreement will be subject to the seller providing detailed information about the property and the buyer's approval of that information. Using information given in this chapter and in Chapter 5, the section on the commercial earnest money contract, it would be beneficial to develop a checklist of all of the information that a prospective buyer should request from the seller.

EXHIBIT 16.2   Apartment Property

The Heights Apartments
303 East Street
Any town, Any state

Investment Summary:

Purchase Price:	$1,400,000
First Lien Balance:	$529,450
Original Loan:	$650,000 30 years, 8.5%
Building Size:	16,376 sq. ft. (591 sq. ft. common area)
Lot Size:	27,500 sq. ft.
Lot Frontage:	125 ft.
Lot Depth:	220 ft.
Year Built:	1986
Total Number of Units:	25

Unit Mix:

24	1/1 bd/bth	625 sq. ft.	Rent: $450–540 /mo
1	2/1 bd/bth	785 sq. ft.	Rent: $540 /mo

Operating Data:

Gross Scheduled Income:	$158,895
Vacancy and Credit Loss:	5%
Operating Expenses:	$32,930
Debt Service:	$59,995

OFFICE BUILDINGS

The investor in an office building may acquire property that is preleased (prior to construction) or already existing under lease. Or, the building may be built or purchased with the expectation of leasing it to others; that is, for speculative leasing. (Owner-occupied office buildings are not considered in this text because they are a limited form of investment and are more relevant to a business analysis than to analysis of an income property investment.)

Preleased Buildings

Preleasing is generally restricted to single-tenant office buildings (built to a tenant's requirements), the ground-floor space in high-rise office buildings, and larger users of upstairs space. A prelease arrangement offers substantial advantages for both the landlord and the tenant. The landlord can use the leases for the **preleased building** to support applications for financing, and the assurance of one or more major tenants helps to lease the balance of the space. An important reason for the success of several major office building developers is their ability to prelease a large portion of a new building to a major company, and then name the building after that company. The business operations of the major tenant attract supporting supply and service businesses to the same location.

For tenants, a major advantage of preleasing is the opportunity for planning of their own floor space, creating the optimum layout for their individual operations.

Speculative Office Space

Those who build office space for speculative leasing must have some assurance that a market will exist for that space. While this point has been sometimes overlooked in the enthusiasm of a rising market or by investors seeking tax advantages, sensitivity to the market seems to be regaining its importance. The best first step is a market analysis, prepared by a person or firm with adequate experience in the office leasing field. The necessary information can be listed as follows:

1. Amount of competing vacant space in the area.
2. Quality of competing buildings (an opinion).
3. Current rental and escalation requirements.
4. Vacancies and reasons for them.
5. Record of space absorption rate in the area.
6. That portion of the market the builder may expect to capture.

From this information, a realistic projection of rental income may be made for the **speculative space**. Of particular importance in the market analysis is the absorption rate. How fast other space is leasing is a better indication of market depth than the current occupancy rate. It is also important to remember that rental rates depend more on the market for office space in the local area than on the construction costs incurred. Therefore, a market analysis must precede the final construction budget. The maximum investment in the office building should be based on the projected income.

Location

One service provided by a modern office building to its tenants is access to supporting service industries. Attorneys favor locations near courthouses or major clients. Doctors locate near hospitals or other medical facilities. Hotels locate near good transportation systems in active business areas. All of these advantages—and many more—still occur in the downtown areas of most major cities. However, for a variety of reasons, downtown areas have suffered setbacks for a number of years. New freeway patterns and the growth of suburban areas and regional shopping centers have brought a trend away from downtown areas. There are now four prime areas for office buildings:

1. Downtown areas of cities.
2. Regional shopping centers. These are not always ideal locations, but can be good if a full complement of supplemental services (banks, restaurants, apartments) are available to tenants. An office building is best located on the periphery of a shopping center, with easy access for nonshoppers.
3. Airport locations. Passengers and freight traffic generated by major air terminals have brought a need for supporting office space to service airlines and their customers.
4. Along freeways or heavily traveled thoroughfares. Urban freeways have sprouted rows of new office buildings catering to the easy access provided by freeways (although congestion in some growth areas is negating this ease of access). The majority of office workers depend on cars for transportation, and many favor office locations away from overcrowded downtown sites.

Parking

The automobile created the need for freeways. With freeways came more growth to outlying areas, to the detriment of downtown growth. The problem with downtown areas has not only been **accessibility**, it has been the availability of parking. Most downtown areas, locked into high-cost land-use patterns, have not managed to keep pace with the growth in demand for parking space—and loss of occupancy for office buildings has been the result. Most building codes for new buildings now require a certain minimum amount of parking space based on the square feet of rentable office space. But the cost of parking has not been cheap, which has further encouraged development in lower-cost outlying areas.

Most outlying office buildings and those in shopping centers offer free parking for tenants and customers. Buildings along freeways closer to the downtown area and those in the downtown area itself usually make an additional charge for parking space to both tenants and their customers or clients.

Use of Available Space

Office buildings are most commonly leased on a "per-square-foot" basis. However, there are two methods of calculating the square footage being leased. One is the net leasable area, which comprises the amount of square footage within the actual perimeter of the office space being leased. The other is a calculation of the gross leasable area, which allocates to each space actually rented a proportionate share of the corridors, wash rooms, elevator space, and maintenance areas. This latter method is also called the "New York Plan." The normal ratio between net and gross leasable areas holds that 80 percent of the total area is usable for tenant's offices with 20 percent allotted to corridors and service areas.

Newer office buildings are installing additional wiring to better handle the increased use of high-tech gear and more communication equipment. Some older buildings are undergoing retrofitting but are not always structured to handle the additional load.

Service features in office buildings—a top-floor restaurant, health club, lounges, meeting rooms, and the like—are plus factors in leasing space. But they can be costly to maintain and may justify additional rent. Some major office buildings offer a subsidy payment for a good restaurant operator to provide quality service for the tenants.

Leasing Conditions

Office space is leased to major tenants for as long as 25 years. Smaller tenants often lease for five- to ten-year terms. Seldom does a term last less than three years. Too short a term does not allow time to amortize the cost of standard tenant improvement allowances. Lease extension options can cause the landlord problems as the uncertainty they create can complicate future leasing plans; therefore, they should be avoided if possible. Sometimes a major tenant requires an option as part of the lease agreement, but the agreement should give some protection of future rent.

Expansion options are also troublesome as they may conflict with future leasing plans. Some tenants who anticipate expansion are willing to pay a premium to hold adjoining space for future growth. However, it is proper to advise any tenant occupying space that is under option to another tenant that there is a commitment outstanding for that space.

Escalation clauses are especially important for the landlord. More than other forms of income property, office buildings have a special vulnerability to rising costs because they customarily furnish all utilities, heating and air conditioning, and janitorial services for the tenant as part of the lease agreement.

Lease agreements should include a covenant covering rules and regulations for the tenants' proper use of the building. These rules are for the benefit of all tenants, and the building management must enforce them. When the office building is part of a larger shopping center or other multi-building complex, rules may be drawn up and enforced by a tenants' association or a merchants' association.

Tenants

Experienced management is needed to screen prospective tenants and assign to each the most suitable space in an office building. The local market is controlling, but there are a few general guidelines.

It is difficult to mix medical and general office tenants. General office tenants usually object both to the overloading of elevators and passageways by handicapped persons and to the odors common in medical facilities. Professional people, such as lawyers and accountants, prefer that a certain prestige be associated with their location. They do not favor unorthodox neighbors, such as discos and nightclubs.

Businesses that attract large numbers of the general public can create parking problems and congestion within a building if they are not located for easy access. Companies that take multifloor occupancy and require frequent elevator travel between upper floors should be located so as to cause minimum delays for the other tenants.

Referring to the information given in Exhibit 16.3, compile a list of additional items that a prospective buyer would need in order to make a decision

---

EXHIBIT 16.3   **Office Property**

9900 Richmond Office Building

Property:	9900 Richmond Ave. at Briar Drive
	Any town, Any state
	Four-story steel structure/brick & glass façade with pre-cast concrete parking facility.
Building Size:	95,000 sq. ft. gross construction area
	92,750 sq. ft. net rentable area
Land:	110,000 sq. ft.
Sales Price:	$20,000,000
Financing:	20% down; balance at 8.75% over 30 years

Pro Forma

Income:

Gross scheduled income		$1,750,000
Parking income		61,000
Gross possible income		$1,811,000
Vacancy and Credit Loss (5%):		($90,550)
Gross Effective Income:		$1,720,450
Expenses:		
Utilities	$132,800	
Janitorial	64,000	
Maintenance & repair	32,000	
Administrative	91,200	
Other payroll cost	7,000	
Insurance	18,000	
Contract services	48,000	
Taxes	128,000	
Total Expenses:		($ 521,000)
Net Operating Income:		$1,199,450

whether to buy or not. Typically, a seller of income properties will reveal only very basic information until a prospective buyer indicates a sincere interest in the property. In many cases the buyer must make an offer to purchase subject to review of additional information. This can be done with an option or a purchase contract. Much of the items of information can be found in the chapter of this book that describes a typical commercial real estate contract. It is fairly obvious that much more information concerning the physical features of the property will have to be provided. Likewise, a great deal of financial data will have to be forthcoming.

RETAIL STORE CENTERS

The market analysis for a successful shopping center must look to the market that is reasonably available for the goods and services offered by the merchant tenants. The question here is not limited to finding tenants as with an apartment or office building analysis. The question is: Will the tenants have a market for their wares?

Market analysts know statistical buying patterns—how much various kinds of people spend on food, on clothes, on eating out, on entertainment, and on many other things they buy. What is needed are figures on the population in the market area, their income levels, the area's growth pattern, plus freeway and street patterns. With these figures, an estimate can be made of the potential sales volume for each class of store, which in turn determines the gross sales that may be achieved by future tenants.

The following discussion considers how the trade area is determined, the nature of its population, and its income and spending patterns.

Trade Area

Trade areas are not determined by drawing a circle around an existing or proposed location and then counting the people within that boundary. A careful examination must be made of the forces that can direct people to the specific location in question. These forces may be identified as **traffic patterns,** proximity of other competitive facilities, and limiting geographical features.

Traffic Patterns

Regional shopping center locations are a creation of the freeway system; to a lesser degree, all other shopping centers also develop from traffic patterns. The ease with which a shopper can enter a store or service facility has long controlled both store location and land value. (Note the growth of smaller communities whose service stations and fast-food stores are concentrated on the right-hand side of the entering highway.) To assess the trade area available for a particular location, it is first necessary to examine all streets, highways, and freeways that carry traffic to or through the subject location. Then study the areas that access routes lead from.

What is the land use of the areas along the access routes? If one of the major highways leads from a large steel-fabricating plant employing mostly male workers who live on the other side of town, the market potential from that area would most likely be minimal. If another boulevard leads directly from undeveloped land that has been purchased by a developer and destined for home builders, the market potential is good, but not immediate. If a major highway leads from several small communities with limited shopping facilities, that population could be considered market potential. If the subject location sits along a thoroughfare that simply connects several densely populated areas or business districts, the high volume of passing traffic is a probable market plus. Of course, a major resource for any shopping center is an established and growing series of residential subdivisions surrounding the proposed location. However, proximity of a good subdivision is of no benefit to the shopping center if there is limited access between them. Streams, political boundaries, even some right-of-way easements can separate entire subdivisions, encouraging traffic patterns to develop in unexpected directions.

City planning commissions and highway departments develop master plans for street and freeway construction. These are important guides to future population trends and are public information. Zoning restrictions for surrounding areas should be charted to provide an indication of how growth patterns might develop. Undeveloped land within a short drive of the subject location can be a big plus. A major shopping center itself encourages development of more houses in the immediate area.

Competing Facilities

The trade area for a shopping center is restricted by existing competition. Furthermore, the nature of that competition is a factor in determining the types of goods and services that may be offered for sale. People will travel greater distances to purchase major hard goods than they will to purchase necessities, conveniences, and services. A nearby major regional shopping center usually restricts a new development to a neighborhood convenience center type of outlet. The important considerations are to (1) weigh the market that is served by existing facilities, and (2) define the subject location's trade area outside the competitive sphere. A new center always has an initial impact from curiosity seekers, but the trade flow soon returns to that of greatest convenience for shoppers. Attracting traffic from a competing facility is always possible through promotions and special inducements for shoppers. But there is no monopoly on sales promotion ideas, and the traffic can flow both ways. The prudent analyst bases market size on proven statistical values, rather than on transient promotional techniques.

Limiting Geographical Features

The concern for geographical limitations is not for obvious features like a shoreline or a mountain range; it is for the lesser features such as an unbridged stream. Population trends often follow the line of lowest-cost development, and this can mean avoiding expensive stream crossings, rough terrain, and areas of potential hazard such as flooding or sliding land. These limitations are, of course, reflected in street and highway patterns. However, it may be an area that a shopping center analyst should consider as a means of increasing the trade area. That is, would an offsite improvement, such as a bridge or connective street, justify the cost? Most communities welcome private support in the construction of new streets or bridges; if a new trade area can be opened, the cost may be justified.

While the above commentary holds true in many areas, recent technological advances in heavy road equipment have opened up much more "rough terrain" for development. A good example is the growth of housing along the frontal range of the Rocky Mountains. The city of Denver, Colorado, is witnessing development that may someday see housing extended from Colorado Springs to Casper, Wyoming. Houses can be built by successfully intruding into mountain ranges with beautiful views—and, unfortunately, such homes are more subject to loss in forest fires.

Population of the Market

Once the limits of a trade area have been defined, it is easy to determine the population within that area. The U.S. Population Census statistics (taken every decade), combined with local area planning commission figures, provide a good starting point. The number of electric power meters and water taps gives a solid indication of the number of families in a given area. Furthermore, the rate of increase or decrease is determinable from the number of new meters installed during a given period, less the number removed. The population of each neighborhood or subdivision in the trade area should be calculated, along with the estimated growth trend for each.

Income and Spending Patterns

Every decade, the U.S. Census Bureau produces a set of figures on average income levels for each census district. Private market research organizations are constantly attempting to determine income levels in local neighborhoods. These figures are estimates at best, but they do provide a basis for analyzing the purchasing power of a given market or trade area.

How income is spent varies with the trade area in question. There are obvious differences in the buying practices between rural communities and manufacturing centers, between commercial areas and service industry areas, between older people and younger ones, between upper-income and lower-income families, between two areas dominated by different ethnic groups, and so on. The Bureau of Labor Statistics (an arm of the U.S. Department of Labor) produces statistics on living costs in different regions of the country, which provides a guide to how much is spent for basic necessities. Local research is needed to reveal the complete patterns of local spending.

The gross income of the entire trade area can be allocated among all the major categories of purchase. For example, food may take 12 percent of the income from a trade area; apparel, general merchandise, and appliances, 8 percent; drugs 3 percent, and so on down the list of goods and services that are offered by the subject shopping center. The total buying power of the trade area in each category must be reduced to the amount that can be reasonably attained by the subject center. Of the total amount represented by food purchases (12 percent of the gross income of the area), perhaps the subject center can attract only 55 percent. For general merchandise sold through department stores, competition could be greater—the subject location's market share could drop to, say, 40 percent of the trade area's total spending for this category.

With the market share calculated in dollar amounts for each category of goods and services, the shopping center investor can more readily compute the expected rentals from percentage leases. Furthermore, a carefully calculated market share for each category indicates the potential sales volume for each prospective tenant—an important sales tool to give a merchant considering leasing a new or additional outlet.

As with office properties and apartment properties, sellers are typically unwilling to divulge detailed information regarding a property until there is a strong interest on the part of a prospective purchaser. As an exercise, refer to the information given in Exhibit 16.4 and make a list of the additional information that would be requested by a prospective buyer in an earnest money contract.

EXHIBIT 16.4   Retail Property

North Oaks Shopping Center
Any town, Any state

Land Area: 8.76 acres

Location: Property is in the rapidly growing northwest quadrant of Any town and is in the highly accepted Round Rock School District. Daily traffic count exceeds 65,000 cars at the intersection fronting the property.

Leasable Area: 95,000 sq. ft., center completed in 1996

Major Tenants:

	% Rent	Sq. Ft.	Rent ($)
Grocery Store	1	24,000	480,000
Drug Store	1.5	9,500	285,000
Variety Store	1.5	17,000	459,000
Video Store	1.5	15,000	405,000
Office Supply	1.5	11,650	314,400
Savings & Loan		6,000	180,000
Cleaners	3	4,500	135,000
Liquor Store	4	4,500	135,000
Lease Space		2,850	85,500

Sales Price and Terms: $25,000,000   20% down, balance at 8.5%, 30 years

Pro Forma

Income:

Gross Scheduled Income	$2,478,900
Percentage Rents	50,000

	CAM Charges		47,500
	Gross Possible Income		$2,576,400
	Less Vacancy (3%)		($77,292)
	Gross Effective Income		$2,499,108
Expenses:	Insurance	$ 38,000	
	Ad Valorem Taxes	175,000	
	Repairs and Maintenance	78,000	
	Utilities	43,000	
	Management Fee (3%)	85,500	
	Other	23,500	
	Total Expenses		($443,000)
Net Operating Income:			$2,056,108

Shopping Center Leases

Chapter 15 discussed the subject of leases and rents for all income properties, but emphasized stores and shopping centers. The reason for this emphasis is that preleasing and quality of the lease are more important for shopping centers than for almost any other kind of real property investment. The financing of a shopping center is uniquely dependent on its leasing program and its overall success is heavily dependent on the quality of tenants and the lease conditions. The lease restrictions peculiar to shopping center operations are considered next.

Exclusive Sales Covenants

All merchants love exclusive sales agreements. But for the shopping center owner/investor, these agreements can be potential pitfalls. A major tenant, such as a supermarket or department store, may demand to be the only supermarket or department store in the shopping center. The owner may have to make this concession, but it can present problems downstream for two reasons: (1) the center may expand so that additional stores are needed to satisfy demand, and (2) the type of merchandise sold within a store tends to change as trade practices shift to meet competition. Motor oil is not a customary item in a grocery store, yet many supermarkets sell it. The variations in service and food offered under the name of "restaurant" are almost unlimited. Any covenant limiting the freedom of the tenant to offer specific products or services must be clearly worded as conflicts can easily occur.

Lease Tie-Ins

A lease that is tied to the continued occupancy of another merchant creates a potential loss of two tenants. A smaller merchant may count on the heavy traffic generated by a large department store outlet; this smaller tenant will have a so-called **lease tie-in** granting her exit rights if the larger tenant departs. If the larger store develops internal problems unrelated to the center and withdraws to be replaced by another store, the smaller merchant under a tie-in would have the right to cancel its lease, compounding the center's problems.

Below-Cost Leases

In order to attract a major tenant to a new center, the owner is sometimes tempted to offer an initial less-than-cost lease arrangement with the expectation of recovering the cost from smaller tenants attracted by the major tenant. Major tenants are fully aware of their drawing power in the market, and they use it as an effective negotiating point. (The merchandising power of an organization such as Wal-Mart is such that it seldom leases space anymore, choosing instead to buy land within or next to a center to construct its own building.) However, any agreement by a shopping center owner to grant less-than-cost rental rates results in an extra burden for the rest of the tenants. The competitive disadvantage to other tenants may preclude their successful operation—and shorten the economic life of the entire project.

Parking

Because shoppers most often drive their own cars, shopping centers require more parking space than other forms of property investment, except for, possibly, entertainment or sports centers. A rule-of-thumb for a center is that for every square foot of rentable shop space, there must be three square feet of parking area. The requirement varies a bit with the type of stores—supermarkets have the greatest parking requirements; service facilities the least.

Employees' parking is most always designated to a more remote area so as not to interfere with customers' more close-in parking. The gradual increase in the number of smaller cars has changed parking lot design a bit. Architects once assigned about 320 square feet to each car space, but today some have reduced this to 280 square feet.

Management

In addition to the management requirements common to all forms of income property, shopping center owners must cooperate with tenants to promote the center. Almost all percentage leases in shopping centers automatically make the landlord a partner in the success of the tenant. Some managements participate passively, granting advertising allowances and special concessions for the tenants' promotional activities. Others take the lead in organizing and directing an almost continuous flow of advertising and promotional programs. The larger centers often provide entertainment or interesting displays in the public mall areas and feature the center's attractions in mass-advertising programs.

The most common method of cooperation between landlord and tenants is some form of merchants' association. A requirement to join and contribute dues or assessments can be a part of lease requirements. In this manner, decisions on sales promotions are shared by all of those who can benefit from them.

WAREHOUSE BUILDINGS

For many years warehouses have increased in numbers, in the ways they can be used, and in popularity as a real estate investment. Warehouses are no longer limited to just another form of industrial property but now can be found as service centers and even retail outlets. Mini-warehouses have multiplied as storage facilities. Investor interest stems from several advantages: warehouses can be built on lower-cost land in outlying areas, they require minimal maintenance, and they require less management than the people-oriented operations of apartments and office buildings. The following sections consider the three major classes of warehouses: (1) industrial-type storage warehouses, (2) office warehouses, and (3) mini-warehouses.

Industrial-Type Storage Warehouses

Merchants and manufacturers have traditionally used warehouses for seasonal storage of goods and have often preferred to rent warehouse space rather than build their own. If the amount of storage space needed varies from year to year or the time needed for seasonal volume is limited, renting is probably more economical. Warehouse space in larger cities may be available for special purpose usage. A refrigerated warehouse may be available to store such goods as candy. Some warehouses offer the services of local delivery of the goods held in storage. In this way, they serve as a distribution point for a manufacturer. However, the separate business of distribution is not considered in this text.

Investment in an industrial warehouse built for lease to others is examined next as to accessibility, construction features, and management.

Accessibility

A warehouse does not require obvious visibility to the general public. It can be located on a back street or other out-of-the-way area, as long as large trucks can maneuver into a loading position. The availability of railroad siding promotes the usefulness of an industrial warehouse by providing an excellent interchange point between rail and truck transportation, but this is not mandatory. Dockside warehouses and the storage facilities at municipally owned airports are sometimes available for private investment.

Construction Features

Industrial warehouses can be built with floors either at ground level or at truckloading height, although the latter is much preferred. Warehouse floors must sustain heavy loads and should be constructed with at least six-inch reinforced concrete.

Ceilings must accommodate high racking of stored goods and should be at least 14 feet high. Ceiling panels are very seldom used in a warehouse, so the height is the clearance beneath the roof supports. Warehouses are usually heated but are not always air-conditioned and should be insulated.

The roof and walls should be as close to fireproof as practical, and in most areas the installation of a fire protection sprinkler system is an economical step as it can reduce the cost of fire insurance. In selecting a warehouse site, an investor must not only check the street widths and patterns, but also research the water lines to make sure they will support a fire protection system. Adequate fire protection can reduce the insurance cost for both the building and its contents and may allow a slightly higher rental structure.

Industrial warehouses require little office space. Sometimes a movable shed-like structure inside the building—used for record keeping and security controls, and sometimes heated or air-conditioned—will suffice.

Management

From the investor's point of view, an industrial warehouse leased to a stable tenant requires very little management. The building is constructed for minimal maintenance, the tenant requires few services, and the management consists mostly of keeping adequate accounting records of the lease operation.

Office Warehouse

The expanding requirements of service industries, manufacturing plants in high technology industries, and industrial supply outfits with storage requirements have spawned a fairly new type of service center. Such space can be used for light manufacturing, repair services, the sale of industrial supplies, or the contract storage of business records.

The most common construction is a long, single-story building, divided by common walls into suitable leasable units. The individual units are normally about 85 percent warehouse space and 15 percent office facility. Limited parking for employees and customers is usually available in front of the units while truck-loading accommodations are at the rear entryways.

Construction Features

The buildings generally combine features available for small offices with substantial warehouse space to the rear. The warehouse space is typically heated but not always air-conditioned. The floors are not designed for heavy loads. Walls may be concrete block, brick, or tilt-wall concrete. Roofs are usually nonbearing and lightweight, with 12- to 14-foot clearance. Modules used in construction vary from 1,500 to 3,000 square feet and can be leased singly or in multiples.

Office areas are generally well finished with tile floors or carpeting. Heating and air-conditioning units are furnished, but their operation is normally a responsibility of the tenant. The office space may be used for administrative work, clerical activity, or as a sales outlet with display racks and sales counters.

The exterior appearance is usually similar to that found in an office park or modern industrial park, with modest landscaping and paved parking areas. Access need not be from highly visible freeways or thoroughfares, but many are so located because of the possibility for leasing space as sales outlets.

Rental Rates and Management

Office warehouses are leased for rates that are generally higher than for industrial warehouses because of an office warehouse's more accessible—and thus costlier—land. They offer a combination of office and warehouse space at somewhere between the separate cost of each.

While office warehouse space is usually offered for multitenant occupancy, the management requirement does not approach the level required for either an office building or an apartment. Very few services are furnished to tenants. Interior maintenance, utilities, heating, and air-conditioning are usually all responsibilities of the tenant. The management may have the chore of maintaining the exterior walls and roof plus trash disposal. Parking lot and landscape maintenance also fall to the management.

Mini-warehouses

Another fairly recent development in warehousing is the mini-warehouse. The demand for such space comes from the increasing number of apartment dwellers and others who have limited storage and a growing amount of personal goods. Older apartment houses often furnish a small enclosure of space, usually in the basement, for the tenant to store out-of-season or surplus possessions. Modern apartments have done away with this feature, partly because of safety requirements, but the need for such space remains. Thus, long rows of mini-warehouses have been built in most major cities.

Construction Features

Mini-warehouses are usually rows of single-story buildings with common walls separating the individual units, which range from small 50-square-foot units to units of more than 450 square feet. They are constructed of fireproof block or brick, each with a single large door to the front. There may, or may not, be a paved floor. Utilities may be limited to a single light bulb, with no heating or air-conditioning.

Rental Structure

The big attraction for an investor is the relatively high return from this low-cost form of investment. Further, the mini-warehouse requires little management other than policing the area. Costs and rents vary considerably, but one good rule of thumb has it that the construction cost is about one-half that for an apartment, while the rental rate per square foot is about the same as an apartment. Usage is usually limited to the storage of goods—no personal use may be made of the facilities as a place to work or to offer anything for sale. (Where such rules have not been enforced, there have been cases of individual tenants converting mini-warehouse space into living quarters.)

Location

Because the mini-warehouse caters to the general public, it is best located in an area that is easily accessible and generally visible from main thoroughfares. Since most customers come from apartments, a good location is always near several apartment complexes.

Other Applications

The concept of the mini-warehouse has much wider application than just storage space for apartment dwellers. It is said that the idea originated with an owner of enclosed boat stalls near a country lake. More and more, the owner found that his tenants were using the boat stalls not just for boats and marine equipment, but for surplus furniture, clothes, and other personal equipment. The next step was to build boat stalls in the city! After all, the need was obvious. Many sports require special equipment that can be stored in protected cubicles when not in use during the off-season. In some areas of the country, small tracts of land can be rented by city folks for home gardening and their special equipment is more easily stored than hauled back and forth. Families with vacation cabins in remote areas need protected space to secure furniture and other personal goods while they are away from their cabins. The mini-warehouse story is a classic example of the free enterprise system at work—find a need, then try to be the first to satisfy it.

SPECIAL PURPOSE BUILDINGS

In a sense, all buildings are "special purpose," as their design restricts their uses to specific operations. However, in the jargon of real estate, special purpose has a more precise meaning. It is that category of building that offers a specific kind of service and is more difficult to convert to any other usage. Examples of special purpose buildings include bowling alleys, service stations, recreational structures, theaters, and automobile dealerships. Because of the close relationship between these buildings and their services, they are often owned by the business operators, rather than by property investors. But many are built for lease to professional business operators and can offer excellent investment opportunities.

Financing

As an investment property, special purpose buildings are seldom built without a lease in hand. Lenders are unlikely to advance money unless the usage is clearly known in advance. The preleasing of a special purpose building might be undertaken by a major distributor or a franchise operation. Many service stations are owned by individuals who have preleased the facility to a major oil company, which in turn subleases the premises to a qualified service station operator. A good lease from any major company is an attractive form of collateral for most lenders. Some companies, in an effort to expand their outlets, may offer to lease an acceptable tract of land from an owner and then add a partial guarantee to support a loan to build a suitable building.

Some categories of special purpose buildings find financing support from product distributors. Such is the case with bowling lanes, other recreational facilities, some theaters, and automobile dealerships. The tie, of course, is an assured outlet for the manufacturer or distributor of that product. Without such help, it is difficult to induce a lender to risk money for a building that is limited in its usage.

On a larger scale, most major hotels are classified in the special purpose category. Principal hotel operators such as Hilton, Hyatt, Sheraton, and Marriott build a few of their properties, but many are investor-owned. The hotel operator undertakes a management or a lease agreement with the hotel owner and grants the use of a valuable trade name. In this kind of transaction, the operator offers little or no financial support to the investor-owner. Hotel investments are made by a few wealthy individuals, some large insurance companies, pension funds, and labor union trust funds, usually after a long-term management contract has been arranged with an operator.

BUSINESS PROPERTIES

This section focuses on an interpretation of a "business property" as one that comprises a business operation using land and buildings to create income. Professional real estate brokers have long been aware that a transaction involving such real property as a motel, hotel, restaurant, or specialized recreational facility requires as much knowledge of the business operation as of the real estate involved. Brokers who trade in businesses sometimes list this type of property for sale as a business venture. But the disposition of a business property that involves real estate is a specialized field requiring brokers to be qualified both in real property transactions and in the management and operation of the business concerned.

While the concepts developed in this section center on a business operation, they have application in other areas of real estate investment. The thrust of this review is an evaluation of income and its effect on property value. The difference between business property and income property is that business property income is derived from services rendered that are not always directly related to the property. For example, a motel restaurant's success depends more on the quality of the food and service than on the quality of the building.

Projected Earnings Potential

The value of a business property is based on the future returns that may be realized over the remaining useful economic life of the property. The basis is approximately the same as for any income property except that business property income derives from the sale of goods and services (in addition to property rentals) that add substantially to the overall value of the property. The following factors are considered in estimating potential income:

1. The types of services offered. For a motel, consider the number and size of rooms, plus the public facilities offered. For a restaurant, consider the kind of food offered. For a recreational facility, consider the activities that are provided.
2. The style of services offered, such as luxury, standard commercial, or minimum utility.
3. The proposed price of the services.
4. The **available market**. How much demand is there for the services offered? Is there competition in the local area? Are there seasonal swings in activity? What is the statistical record for the proposed type of business in the local area? Are there any special events, sports activities, fiestas, cultural events, or other activities that stimulate the market?
5. Normal operating ratios and cost ratios for similar businesses in the area.

An estimate of potential earnings can be developed from the information assembled under these five headings. The statement of operations would contain the same basic information outlined in Chapter 11 for financial statements. The expenses of operation are deducted from the projected gross income, leaving the net operating income as a basis for property evaluation.

In the evaluation of business property income, the results from each department of activity (such as room rentals, restaurant sales, lounge and bar sales) should be assembled separately, as each involves separate projections. Multiple projections can be made for each department to reflect the highest and lowest estimates of business activity. This procedure is known as a sensitivity analysis.

Relation Between Market Value and Earnings

To some degree, the market value of real estate used as a business operation is more sensitive to the business's earnings record than is an income property to its longer-term rentals. A well-managed motel in a prime location that produces high profits will reflect a value for the property substantially in excess of the cost of building it. While management is important to the operation of all income properties, it assumes dominant proportion when a complex business must be operated to produce an income from the property. One reason for a business property's greater sensitivity to its earnings record is the greater variety of income and expense components that affect the success of the entire operation.

There is no real difference in the ratio of market value to earnings for business real estate and income property. Both ultimately must reflect the capitalized value of the earnings, which can be either the past record of earnings or the projected figures. And, the capitalization rate to be used is equally dependent on what the investor considers a fair return on his or her equity investment under prevailing market conditions. However, the market for business-type property is not so broad-based as that for other income property, primarily because of the need for specialized management skills. As a result, the purchaser of a business property adds a premium for expertise and, thus, may demand a slightly larger return on the equity investment. This would, of course, result in a slightly lower price for a business property than for an income property with identical after-tax income.

CONCLUSION

This book has covered a lot of ground, all of it pertinent to an investment in real estate. Unfortunately, the field is so complex that the coverage of many subjects has been limited to an explanation or a suggestion that certain problems do exist. An example is the important subject of income taxation, which affects all investments, but is subject to frequent changes and needs up-to-the-minute information.

The Great Recession, as with comments in many of this text's chapters, has likewise changed the "rules of the game" when it comes to real estate, but the playing field itself is largely unmodified. The prudent real estate investor is still faced with a sometimes complex, but often prosaic, choice between varying investments in general and among real estate investments in particular. The real estate investment community periodically comes under pressure to respond to new investor or regulatory demands. Such was the case with the Great Depression, with the explosive growth in the U.S. after World War II and again near the turn of the 21st century. It is incumbent upon the investor to stay apprised of the changing contours of the real estate "game," and to tailor his behavior and decision-making accordingly.

It is not the purpose of this book to recommend one form of investment over another, but to point out the risks and the rewards that can be realized from different forms of property investment. In the final analysis, only an individual investor can decide whether or not the risk is acceptable. More than the actual property is involved—the investor must consider personal goals; the area best suited to those goals; the type of property that she best understands; income and tax positions and the outcome of various investments; and, yes, even such factors as the investor's age and health.

Knowledge is successful investment's first essential ingredient. Use it well!

KEY TERMS

accessibility	familial status	preleased building	trade areas
available market	lease tie-in	speculative space	traffic patterns
building amenities	optimum mix		

DISCUSSION QUESTIONS

1. Discuss marketing problems faced by an apartment developer.

2. What is meant by building an office building on speculation?

3. List the advantages of preleasing space in a shopping center project.

4. How are warehouse properties used today?

5. How can business property used to operate a business, such as a restaurant, be evaluated?

6. Compare the evaluation and marketing of business real estate with the evaluation and marketing of income property.

7. Explain the concept of special purpose buildings, giving examples of how the financing support is set up.

8. List some of the requirements for management of business properties.

9. Compare the pitfalls of "exclusive sales contracts" and explain why one may be hesitant about them.

10. Explain why an owner would accept a "less-than-cost" lease agreement with a major tenant.

GLOSSARY

A

Accessibility The ease with which people and transportation vehicles can gain ingress to, and egress from, a given property.

Accounts Receivable Monies to be received in the future. May or may not be assigned to a buyer when a property is purchased.

Accrual Method Income is recorded when it is earned, not when it is received and an expense is recorded when it is incurred, not when it is paid.

Acquisition Debt For tax purposes, debt incurred in acquiring, constructing, or substantially improving any qualified residence (principal residence plus one other) and which is secured by that residence.

Active Income Income earned by one's labor, compensated for in salary, wages, commissions, fees, or bonuses.

Ad Valorem Latin, against, or to, the value, as with an ad valorem (or property) tax.

Add-on Interest A method of computing interest for installment loans, whereby the amount of simple interest that would be due at maturity on the full amount of the loan is added on to the principal at the inception of the loan. The total is then divided by the number of installments in order to determine each payment amount.

Adjustable Rate Mortgage A mortgage note that allows a lender to adjust the interest rate at periodic intervals. The rate change is most commonly tied to the movement of a regulator-approved index, such as the yield of government bonds.

Adjusted Basis The purchase price, plus capital improvements, less depreciation, of a capital asset.

Adjusted Basis (Installment Sales) The value of a property sold increased by capital expenditures made and decreased by depreciation taken during the period of ownership.

Adjusted Basis (Section 1031 Exchanges) The purchase price of a replacement property reduced by the capital gain (not the capital gains tax) deferred in a 1031 exchange.

Adjusted Basis of the Home The original purchase price of the home increased by capital improvements and other allowable costs, and reduced by uninsured capital losses, other allowable deductions, and depreciation to the extent the home was used as a part-time rental or parts of it as an office.

Advance Rentals Rent paid in advance of the due date which must be accounted for when payment is received.

Alienation Police power giving the authority to protect health, safety, and general welfare of citizens.

Allocation The apportionment with a property purchase of amounts to depreciable (buildings, etc.) and non-depreciable (land) assets.

American Jobs Creation Act of 2004 (AJCA) Legislation providing broad federal tax reductions, while also limiting the use of Section 1031 to permanently avoid taxation on the sale of appreciated real estate investments; AJCA reduced piggybacking by investors from Section 1031 to the marital exclusions of capital gains taxation upon the sale of their primary residence.

American Recovery and Reinvestment Act of 2009 (ARRA) Federal government initiative, in concert with the stimulus package and FED monetary responses, to temper the economic impact of the recession which began in late 2007.

Amortization (Mortgage Loan Amortization) The systematic and continuous payment of an obligation through installments until such time as that debt has been paid off in full.

Analysis of Offer to Purchase: Protocol employed by a prospective investor (or seller) in determining the suitability of an offer to buy (or sell) at a certain dollar amount.

Annuity A set of equally sized cash flows occurring periodically for a fixed period of time, as with mortgage payments.

Applicable Federal Rates (AFR) Short-term (three years or less), mid-term (three to nine years) and long-term (more than nine years) interest rates published monthly by the IRS to determine gift and income tax consequences of below-market loans.

Appraisal An estimate or opinion of value.

Appreciation A passive increase in investment value resulting from scarcity and price inflation.

Asbestos Fire-retarding fiber found naturally in the environment, but leading to lung damage with commercial uses in its friable form.

Assets Something of value.

Assignment The transfer of rights and interests in a contract or lease.

Audit The examination of accounting records and the supporting evidence by a Certified Public Accountant to determine the adequacy and accuracy of the information.

Automatic Rights that are not recorded in the state that recognizes them.

Available Market The statistical record for the proposed type of business in the immediate area.

B

Balance Sheet A record of asset, liability, and equity account values for an individual or institution at a particular point in time.

Balloon Note A promissory note that is only partially amortized over the term of the loan leaving a principal balance due at maturity.

Breakeven Ratio A property's operating expenses plus debt service divided by its scheduled gross income or potential gross income.

Bridge Financing Temporary mortgage financing arranged for the period of construction, such bridge replaced with permanent financing upon the completion of construction.

Brownfield Contaminated lands that are granted some exemptions from normal Environmental Protection Agency (EPA) clean-up standards.

Building Amenities Features of a property that make it more attractive to prospective tenants.

Building Codes Codes intended to protect the public against low quality, and possibly dangerous, construction practices.

Business Use of the Home A portion of a residence can be used for business purposes and therefore be eligible for certain tax deductions not normally allowed for a residence.

C

Cap Rate (CR) A property's net operating income divided by its value. (CR = NOI/Value; Value = NOI/CR)

Cap Rate (Discount Rate) An investor's or appraiser's required rate of return on income-producing real estate. Net operating income is divided by this rate to provide an estimate of the real estate's value.

Capital Gain The gain on the sale of a property that is subject to taxation.

Capital Gain Income The difference between the selling price and adjusted basis of a capital asset.

Capital Improvement A property expense that expands the size or extends the life of a building.

Carbon Monoxide An odorless, colorless gas produced by the combustion of fuels such as natural gas, oil, and propane in devices such as furnaces, water heaters, and stoves.

Carrying Charges Costs that are part of operating expenses or for development and resale.

Cash Flow (Cash Flow before Taxes) Net operating income reduced by debt service and other non-operating cash expenses.

Cash Flow Projections A set of predicted cash inflows and outflows, typically tied to operating income and expenses, capital costs, and costs of debt; such cash flows depend upon a set of assumptions about the macroeconomic environment and factors specific to a given investment.

Cash Method An accounting method that recognizes income and expenses as received, or paid, respectively.

Cash-Flow-to-Equity Ratio (Cash-on-Cash Return, Equity Dividend Rate) Cash flow or cash flow before taxes divided by the total equity investment (down payment plus buyer's closing costs) in a property.

CERCLA The Comprehensive Environmental Response, Compensation and Liability Act of 1980.

Certified Public Accountant (CPA) A license granted by the various states to one who has met the requirements of experience, knowledge, and professional standards for accounting work.

Collateral Property or other assets pledged as security for a debt.

Commercial Land Land that is suitable for non-residential development.

Commercial Loan Loan secured by a non-residential asset.

Common Stock The evidence of an ownership interest in a corporation that carries the right to a share of the earnings, usually distributed in the form of a dividend.

Community Property A property in which spouses are treated as equal partners; each owning a one-half interest.

Compound Interest Interest earnings on interest already earned.

Condemnation The process of taking private property for public use, or the eviction of occupants from a property that does not meet some community standard.

Consideration Something of observable material value, generally cash, that is exchanged for some other tangible or intangible asset, as with the consideration exchanged for a piece of real estate or a set of leasehold rights.

Construction Loan Short term loan made for the purpose of providing the financing necessary to allow for construction of the project.

Conventional Loan A mortgage loan not directly underwritten by a government agency, generally subject to more demanding underwriting standards.

Corporation A form of business created under state chartering laws as an artificial person with limited rights and powers to transact business of a designated nature.

Cost Approach Appraisal method estimating a property's value as the sum of the market value of the land plus any improvements, with the improvements' values reduced by the accumulated costs of wear and tear and aging.

Cost Recovery Period The number of years over which to recover the depreciable portion of an investment property's purchase price or capital improvements.

Covenants Lease terms or promises by the tenant or landlord which specify the duties and responsibilities for both, during the term of the lease.

Credit-tenant A tenant recognized regionally or nationally whose credit standing is such that a lease signed by this tenant can be used ubiquitously as collateral on most construction, rehabilitation, or development loans.

Crossover Easement The unencumbered access to all of the retail buildings in a shopping center.

Cumulative Cash Flows The sum of all cash flows to date.

Curtesy In some states benefits held by a husband in his deceased wife's property that are similar to dower rights. Curtesy rights are not so clear as dower rights and may be defeated by a wife in her will.

D

Debt Coverage Ratio Net operating income divided by annual debt service. This measure reveals how much the net operating income "covers" the debt service.

Debt Service Monthly mortgage payment, often annualized as 12 of these payments in pro forma estimates of an investment property's expected annual cash flows.

Deed Restriction A common method of privately limiting the right to use land.

Default Risk Likelihood that the principal or interest on a loan or other financial obligation will not be paid by the borrower or issuer.

Defer To delay or postpone, not eliminate, as with a tax liability in a Section 1031 exchange.

Delivery The final act of the grantor signifying an intention that the deed shall currently take effect.

Demised Premises Typically described as a specific number of square feet in a specified location in the building.

Depreciable Base The value of the building that is being depreciated.

Depreciation (Cost Recovery) That portion of an investment's value that may be deducted against taxable income in a given operating period.

Devisee A person other than an heir, to whom a grantor conveys property by will.

Discounted Cash Flow A future expected inflow of cash reduced by some selected percentage, recognizing the greater value of a dollar today over a dollar tomorrow. Cash flows from income properties that have been discounted based on the time value of money.

Disposition The right to sell or mortgage property, including the right to determine the duration of the ownership term.

Dividend Growth Model Algebraic expression describing investment returns as the sum of a dividend yield and a capital gains yield.

Dower right An estate owned by a wife.

E

Easement An implied or formal right of an individual or entity (as with a neighbor using a foot path or a public utility accessing power lines) to the use of another's land.

Economic or External Obsolescence Characteristics impacting a piece of real estate's value, such as neighborhood deterioration or a repositioned highway, that are outside the control of the property's owner.

Economic Recovery Tax Act of 1981 (ERTA) Tax law that established generous depreciation schedules for real estate investments.

Effective Gross Income Often referred to as gross effective income, gross income, or gross operating income. This is the income an investment property is expected to produce (or has produced), reduced by allowances for vacancies and bad debts.

Electromagnetic Forces Disturbance at the atomic level of electrically charged particles, enhanced on or near electrical transmission lines or electrical devices.

Eligible Basis The lesser of the percentage of units in a low-income project that are leased to qualifying tenants or the percentage of square feet leased to such tenants, times the qualifying costs of construction or rehabilitation.

Eminent Domain The right of the government to take private property for public use.

Endangered Species Act An Act passed in 1973 that prohibits the "taking" of endangered species as listed by the federal government.

Environmental Impact Statement A special predevelopment study of the effects that a new project would have on the surrounding land, air, and water.

Equity The value of a property in excess of all indebtedness.

Equity Dividend Rate or Cash-on-Cash Return An estimate of value that strips away many variables and considers only the equity portion of an investment measured against the cash flow for that investment.

Equity Participation A loan wherein the lender participates in the cash flow from the pledged project.

Escalation Clause A lease provision to cover certain specified contingencies, such as costly escalations in property taxes for which the tenant has assumed responsibility at the lease signing.

Escrow Accounts An account where monies are held for future distribution.

Escrow Agent Neutral third party that holds funds, such as in a Section 1031 exchange, outside the direct control of the actual owner of those funds.

Estate The degree or quality of interest that a person has in land, the nature of the right, its duration, and its relation to the several rights of others.

Estate in Severalty An estate owned by one person or entity; sole ownership.

Estoppel Letter A letter outlining specific current conditions attaching to a financial relationship, such as one stating that the tenant is in agreement and compliance with all terms of an existing lease.

Exclusion That portion of a capital gain that is not subject to taxation, such as with the exclusion from taxation of portions of the gains on the sale of a primary residence.

F

Familial status One or more individuals under the age of 18 domiciled with a parent or another person having legal custody of the individual(s).

Feasibility Report Document describing the likeliest economic outcomes of an investment in real estate, typically prepared for lenders and investors to describe the profitability of new real estate development. A formal study designed to determine the odds of success or failure of an income property.

Fee Simple Absolute The highest and most extensive estate in common law. It is inheritable and not limited to a particular class of heirs. Termination of an estate held in fee simple absolute can be accomplished only if the owner dies without a will and without heirs.

Fee Tail A form of estate controlled by the grantor after his death through restrictions on the class of potential transferees.

FIRREA (1989) Financial Institution Reform, Recovery, and Enforcement Act.

Fixed Expenses A property's expenses that remain stable regardless of occupancy.

Foreclosure The act of a mortgagee to protect its rights against a mortgagor, by repossessing the real estate recorded as collateral for the mortgage. Specific rules and regulations for the act vary by state and with federal decree.

Freehold Estate The right of title to land for an uncertain duration but at least for the life of the owner.

Functional Obsolescence Features of a piece of real estate, such as ceiling heights or building configuration, that reduce the property's value and generally cannot be "cured."

Future Interests Rights to real property that allow possession at some future time.

Future Value The amount to which a current dollar amount will grow at some predetermined interest rate.

G

General Public Individuals outside any social organization or common employer.

Go Dark Real estate term for a commercial space that has become vacant.

Gross Income Often referred to as effective gross income, gross effective income, or gross operating income. This is the income an investment property is expected to produce (or has produced), reduced by allowances for vacancies and bad debts.

Government Influences Government subsidy and assistance programs that effectively direct how land is used.

Great Recession That period of time between 2007 and 2009 that was marked by the most pronounced contraction in U.S. economic activity, by a number of traditional measures, since the late 1930's.

Gross Operating Income Often referred to as effective gross income, gross effective income, or simply gross income. This is the income an investment property is expected to produce (or has produced), reduced by allowances for vacancies and bad debts.

Gross Profit Percentage (Selling price – adjusted basis)/selling price.

Gross Rent Multiplier The value or selling price of a property divided by its potential (scheduled) gross income.

H

Heir One who has the right to inherit property under statute of descent and distribution.

Hold Harmless An agreement between parties to a contract, such as a lease, where the actions of one cannot be used against the other in a legal proceeding.

Holding Period The period of time an investor is expecting to hold, or has held, a property.

Home Equity Debt Debt other than acquisition indebtedness secured by the home, to the extent that the aggregate amount of debt does not exceed the fair market value of the home reduced by the acquisition indebtedness.

Homestead Protection (Exemption) Afforded homeowners in many jurisdictions, where the property in question is the primary residence. Allowances include protection against bankruptcy or other creditor judgments and reduced property taxes.

I

Income Approach Appraisal method estimating property value as the property's net operating income divided by a selected cap rate or discount rate.

Innocent Landowner Defense A defense that may be maintained provided the landowner made an appropriate inquiry into the previous ownership and uses of the property prior to acquisition.

Installment Sale (Income) Property sale where at least one payment is received in the year after the sale. Installment sale income is cash representing a portion of the selling price received after the year of sale.

Interest Rate (Inflation) Risk Likelihood that interest rates or inflation will rise, lowering the value of an interest-bearing bond, security, or certificate.

Internal Rate of Return (IRR) Informally, the average annual profitability of an investment, or, formally, the discount rate that forces the net present value to zero.

Investment Analysis A broad review of the projected risks and returns attaching to a long term deployment of capital resources.

Inverse A given value divided into one, as with the inverse of five being one-fifth.

Investment Interest Costs of financing directly attributable to the acquisition and ownership of an investment property, which interest is deductible in most cases only up to the property's net income.

Involuntary Exchange (Involuntary Conversion) When a property owner loses her property to fire, eminent domain actions, condemnation, or other expropriation beyond the owner's control, trading any proceeds for a replacement property, deferring tax on the appreciated property's effective "sale" to an insurer or government body.

J

Joint Tenancy A form of property co-ownership that features the right of survivorship.

Joint Venture An association of companies and/or individuals organized for the purpose of undertaking a specific project.

Joint-Stock Company A form of business ownership permitted in some states, which is a general partnership with some of the features of a corporation.

Junior Mortgage A mortgage of lower lien priority than that of another, as with a home's second mortgage or a home equity line of credit.

L

Land Trust A form of ownership permitted in a few states that allows a landowner to convey title and the full power of managemnet to a trustee and to designate a beneficiary.

Lead Controlled or banned in gasoline, paint, and plumbing, due to its impacts upon childhood development and human health.

Lease Tie-ins A lease that is tied to the continued occupancy of another merchant in the same shopping center, such as with a grocery-store anchored strip shopping center.

Leasehold Estate The right of a tenant to possession and use of land (but not necessarily the power of disposition) for a specified period of time.

Leasing Commissions Fee paid to real estate brokers for delivering commercial tenants to an investment property. The fee is typically a percentage of the base period of the lease, generally three to five years. Follow-on commissions may be due for later renewals by the same tenant.

Leverage (Positive or Negative) If borrowing produces a higher return on invested equity, there is positive leverage. If it lowers equity returns, there is negative leverage.

Leveraged Purchase Property purchase using debt financing.

Life Estate The ownership of land with duration limited to the life of the party holding the land, or the life of some other person.

Like-Kind Property Capital assets held to produce income, as with investment real estate.

Limited Liability Company (LLC) A form of business created to afford all investors (people, institutions, etc.) the opportunity to avail themselves of the pass-through features of an S corporation, the liability protection of a C-corporation, and the simplicity of a partnership, in a single business form. Like a Sub-S, the LLC allows all income and expenses to "pass through" directly to the LLC's members, to be taxed at the individual, and not the company, level.

Limited Partnership A partnership consisting of one or more general partners who are liable for obligations and responsible for the management, and one or more special partners who contribute cash and are not liable for debts or liabilities beyond the cash contributed.

Liquid An asset that can be converted into cash.

Liquidity The ability to convert assets into cash.

Living Patterns People's styles of living that influence growth patterns.

Loan Discount A charge by the lender allowing for a discount on the interest rate.

Loan-to-Value (LTV) A proposed or existing mortgage loan divided by a property's value or selling price.

Long-Term Lease A lease for a long period, which frequently allows the leasehold interest to be sold.

M

Market Approach Appraisal method estimating property value as a function of the selling prices of similar properties.

Mezzanine Loan Basically a second or subordinate lien, tailored to a set of unique borrowing needs, typically arranged with an institutional or corporate real estate developer/borrower.

Mill(age) One one-thousandth. Metric with which property taxes are assessed.

Mitigation (Banking) The legal process of allowing and compensating for wetlands destruction with the wetlands being replaced by "new" wetlands creation or the purchase of new wetlands from a "bank."

Mortgage Loan Amortization From the Latin, "a mort" or to death, representing the ultimate exhaustion of the balance on a mortgage with the periodic payment of the principal and interest on the loan.

N

Negative Amortization Where the balance due on a loan increases over time, with interest payments during the period less than the effective interest costs on the loan, the difference added to the loan balance.

Net Lease (Triple-net Lease) A lease where the tenant not only pays rent for the occupancy, but also pays for maintenance and operating expenses of the premises. A triple net lease designates one where the tenant may be responsible for virtually all of a property's operating costs, as with many long term warehouse leases.

Net Operating Income (NOI) Total cash income of a property reduced by its operating expenses.

Net Present Value (NPV) The present value of an investment's future cash flows minus the cost of "buying" those cash flows, as with the present value of all the future cash flows of a given piece of real estate, minus some assumed current price.

Net Sales Price (Realized Selling Price) Gross sales price reduced by the costs of sale.

Net Worth Or owner's equity, in the absence of preferred stock or other security "hybrids," is the difference between total assets and total liabilities.

Non-freehold Estate The right of title to land for a specified duration, a lease for a term of years.

Non-recourse Loan Loan for which the property alone is held as security, and no recourse against the borrowers' other assets exists for the lender. Exceptions to this limited lender recourse exist in cases of environmental degradation to the property after the loan is closed, or in cases of fraud by the borrower.

Non-transient A lease of at least six months.

O

Operating Expense Ratio A property's operating expenses divided by its gross operating income or effective gross income.

Operating Expenses Recurring costs, excluding depreciation and amortization and debt service, encountered in the normal course of business. With real estate, these typically include management, insurance, property taxes, repairs and utilities. In real estate operating statements, depreciation—a noncash expense—is generally excluded.

Operating Income Often referred to as effective gross income, gross effective income, or gross operating income. This is the income an investment property is expected to produce (or has produced), reduced by allowances for vacancies and bad debts.

Operating Statement A record of all income less operating expenses, with the net operating income as the bottom line.

Optimum Mix The ability to offer the types of units that meet local market requirements.

Option Pre-arranged purchase or loan terms, exercisable according to the terms of the agreement by the holder of the option.

Origination Fee A common mortgage closing cost based on the size of the loan, and expressed as a percentage of the loan, as with a "one percent origination fee."

P

Partnership An association of two or more persons to carry on a business as co-owners.

Part-Time for Rental Purposes A dwelling unit that is used part-time as a rental unit and part-time as a primary residence.

Passive Activity Income Earnings derived from any activity involving a trade or business in which the taxpayer does not materially participate.

Pass-throughs (Lease Provisions) Property costs, like insurance and taxes and common area maintenance, that are passed through to tenants typically based upon their relative occupancy of a building. A tenant occupying 20 percent of the square footage in an office building would generally be responsible for 20 percent of these overall costs.

Pass-throughs (Subchapter S and LLC Provisions) Income and losses of S corporations and limited liability companies are taxed at the individual shareholder or member's level, based upon the individual's (or member's) relative ownership; a 10 percent owner declares 10 percent of the income or loss.

Percentage Lease Common lease form for stores and shopping centers. Rental payments are based on gross sales figures, not on any computation of profit.

Perpetuity An annuity with no end, as with a monthly stipend that goes on forever.

Phase Assessment A pre-purchase assessment defined within the Superfund Act, also called an "environmental due diligence assessment." Phase I, II, and III assessments exist depending upon the exposure of the property to environmental damage, or existing or unmitigated damage.

Polychlorinated Biphenyls (PCB) A chemical, linked to a number of illnesses, used prior to 1979 as paint thickeners, insulators, in plastics, and in other commercial applications.

Polychloroethylene (PCE) A dry cleaning or industrial cleaning agent found to be associated with liver and kidney damage. Associated with soil and ground water contaminations nationwide.

Portfolio Income Essentially passive income, with some exceptions and exclusions to prevent taxpayers from reducing taxable unearned income with passive income losses.

Potential Gross Income The maximum possible rental receipts of an investment property, unreduced by allowances for vacancies or bad debts, over some operating period, typically a year.

Positive or Negative Leverage If borrowing produces a higher rate of return then there is positive leverage. Likewise, if borrowing produces a lower rate of return then there is negative leverage.

Potentially Responsible Party Under CERCLA, those parties who are potentially responsible for clean-up of environmentally contaminated sites.

Preferred Stock A class of stock issues by a corporation that is eligible to receive dividends and a pay-off in priority over any class of the corporation's common stock.

Preleased Buildings Buildings that are leased before they are built.

Present Interest The ownership of real property now.

Present Value The amount that a single or set of future cash flows is worth in current dollars.

Primary Mortgage Market The market where the borrower actually receives the loan for a real estate purchase, as with a homebuyer getting a purchase loan from the local bank.

Primary Residence (Principal Residence) Single location claimed by a taxpayer as the taxpayer's home. Such location in the eyes of states with income taxes is not chosen by the taxpayer, but is the one where the taxpayer actually lives for the majority of the year.

Pro Forma A projection of future earnings and asset values.

Profit and Loss or Income Statement Lists the business income, all operating expenses, and other deductions including depreciation and mortgage interest, and allows for income tax liability.

Profitability The ratio of after-tax profit to the current market value of the total investment or the ratio of cash returned to the current market value of the equity.

Profitability Ratio NOI of a property divided by the property's price or value. This ratio is conceptually equal to the cap rate or discount rate.

Purchase Money Mortgage Seller financing of real estate, where the seller holds a loan, with the real estate sold being the collateral for the loan.

Q

Qualifying Tenants Individuals or families meeting the set-aside requirements for low-income housing.

Quit Claim Deed (Quitclaim Deed) A deed of conveyance that operates as a release of whatever interest the grantor has in the property.

R

Raw Land Any land lacking the facilities needed to support building construction.

Real Estate Land and the improvements attached thereto.

Real Estate Investment Trust (REIT) Legal entity holding ownership of investment real estate on behalf of many dispersed shareholders, who pay taxes on the real estate's income at the individual taxpayer level only. Ownership, control, and dividend distributions subject to SEC and Treasury Department dictate.

Realized Selling Price The total consideration less selling expenses and fixing-up expenses.

Refinance Paying off an existing loan with the proceeds of a new loan.

Rehabilitation (Substantial) Repair or refurbishment of a qualifying structure. Substantial rehab is an amount at least equal to the adjusted basis of the property or $5,000, whichever is larger.

Relative Spread Selling price minus the listing price, such difference then divided by the selling price. In some analyses, the relative spread can also be defined as the listing price minus the selling price, divided by either the listing or selling price.

Release Clause Mortgage provision that allows the mortgagor to sell portions of a large tract of land, and have those portions "released" from the mortgage for some over-weighted payment or consideration.

Relief of Debt Terms that release a borrower or guarantor of debt from the duties of a borrower or a guarantor, such release being treated as an effective receipt of cash for computation of capital gains tax liability.

Remainder An ownership interest (estate) in land that cannot take effect or be enjoyed until after another estate has been terminated.

Remainderman Individual owning a future interest in a property, subject to the termination of the ownership interest of another.

Residential Loan Loan secured by a residence.

Resolution Trust Corporation of 1989 (RTC) Resolution Trust Corporation, created by FIRREA to dispose of the assets, primarily real estate and defaulted mortgages, belonging to failed thrifts in the late 80's and early 90's.

Return on Equity (Investment) That rate of return based on the equity (total funds) invested.

Reversion (Reversion Proceeds) The gross sale price of a piece of real estate, minus the costs of sale and any outstanding mortgage(s).

Reversions Rights to future interests in a property that are presently in the possession of another.

Right of Survivorship A feature of joint tenancy whereby the surviving joint tenants automatically acquire all the rights, title, and interests of the deceased joint tenant.

S

S Corporation A corporation that, for tax purposes, can qualify and elect to be treated similar to a partnership, with income and expenses "passing through" to shareholders as a function of their relative ownership. A person owning 20 percent of a Sub-S would carry 20 percent of its income or losses to her personal tax return.

Scheduled Gross Income The highest possible income a property could earn if fully leased. Often referred to as potential gross income.

Secondary Mortgage Market A market where previously originated mortgages are sold to investors, as with the local bank "reselling" a loan to Fannie Mae, who then resells the loan in whole or in part in the mortgage-backed security markets.

Selling Price Gross selling price before reductions due to costs of sale.

Separate Property Property owned by a married person in his or her own right during the marriage.

Set-aside Requirements The 20-50 rules states that at least 20 percent of a low-income development is occupied by families earning less than 50 percent of the local area's HUD-determined median family income; the 40-60 rule holds that at least 40 percent of the low-income project must be occupied by families earning less than 60 percent of the HUD-determined median family income. One standard or the other must be met for a property to qualify for low-income credits.

Sewer and Drinking Water Services Services generally, but not always, provided by local municipalities or small area providers.

Simple Interest Interest earnings on only the original invested amount, and not on any accumulated interest.

Sole Proprietorship A business operated by a single owner.

Speculative Space Portions of a building that are not leased prior to construction of the building.

Subdivision A large tract of land divided into a number of smaller parcels.

Syndicate An association of individuals or companies, usually in the form of a limited partnership or LLC, organized to carry out a particular business activity.

T

Tangible Land can be seen and touched; it has a specific form and size, and it cannot be lost or misplaced.

Tax Assessment Local government established real estate value (typically an approximation of but often less than market value) against which property taxes are determined.

Tax Credit Direct reduction in a federal tax bill, as opposed to a simple reduction in taxable income, as with a "tax deduction."

Tax Reform Act of 1986 Tax act passed to replace the 1981 Economic Recovery Tax Act, establishing new and less generous depreciation schedules for real estate investments.

Tenancy at Will A leasehold estate that lasts as long as landlord and tenant wish it to last.

Tenant Improvements Property repair and refit costs to prepare a vacant space for a new commercial tenant. Such costs might include new wiring or plumbing for a large industrial tenant, or new grease traps for a restaurant.

Tenants in Common Two or more persons holding undivided interests in land, each with a separate right of disposition and without the right of survivorship; interests need not be equal.

Term Lease (Gross Lease) A less-than-freehold estate in which the property is leased for a definite, fixed period of time and is identified as a tenancy for years.

Time-Sharing Ownership The holding of rights to the exclusive use of real estate for a designated period of time.

Title Exceptions Title matters that may have to be cleared up prior to the closing of a transaction.

Trade Areas The area around a retail facility from which prospective customers originate.

Traffic Patterns Frequency and direction of human or vehicular movement on or near a given piece of real estate.

Trust Assets under the control of a trustee for the benefit of a designated beneficiary.

Trustee Administrator of a trust.

U

Under Water Condition where the market value of a mortgaged property is less than the outstanding mortgage balance.

Underwriting Standards With respect to mortgage borrowing, a set of rules and conditions (such as minimal household income relative to a mortgage payment, or minimum credit score) with which the mortgage broker and borrower must comply.

Undivided interest Ownership by two or more persons that gives each the right to use the entire property.

V

Value Gain The ability of an owner or manager of real property to rehabilitate, upgrade, expand, or even reorient a property to increase the property's value.

Variance An exception from zoning rules to allow a specific use, outside the zoning regulations, on a given property.

W

Wetlands Protection Defense of land meeting the wetlands designation, under the 1987 Clean Water Act.

Words of Conveyance Words like "I hereby grant and convey."

Work Letter Sets out the work that needs to be done to the leased premises, and designates who pays for it, before occupancy.

Wrap-Around A secondary or subordinate loan which basically wraps around an existing assumable loan. These loans were common in the 1980s, but are far rarer now, with most investment real estate loans "due on sale," preventing the seller from "wrapping" an existing assumable loan.

Z

Zero Lot Line A "border" between homes (patio homes or townhouses) or commercial properties that consists of a shared wall.

Zoning Laws The utilization of a municipality's police power to protect the health, safety, and general welfare of its citizens through the direction of land uses and development.

INDEX